Earth vs. the
Sci-Fi Filmmakers

Other Interview Books by Tom Weaver and from McFarland

Attack of the Monster Movie Makers: Interviews with 20 Genre Giants (2014)

They Fought in the Creature Features: Interviews with 23 Classic Horror, Science Fiction and Serial Stars (2014)

I Was a Monster Movie Maker: Conversations with 22 SF and Horror Filmmakers (2011)

Science Fiction Confidential: Interviews with 23 Monster Stars and Filmmakers (2010)

I Talked with a Zombie: Interviews with 23 Veterans of Horror and Sci-Fi Films and Television (2009)

Eye on Science Fiction: 20 Interviews with Classic SF and Horror Filmmakers (2007)

Science Fiction and Fantasy Film Flashbacks: Conversations with 24 Actors, Writers, Producers and Directors from the Golden Age (2004)

Return of the B Science Fiction and Horror Heroes: The Mutant Melding of Two Volumes of Classic Interviews (2000)
(A combined edition of the two earlier Weaver titles *Interviews with B Science Fiction and Horror Movie Makers* and *Science Fiction Stars and Horror Heroes*)

Other McFarland Books by Tom Weaver

Poverty Row HORRORS! Monogram, PRC and Republic Horror Films of the Forties (1993)

John Carradine: The Films (1999)

By Tom Weaver with Michael Brunas and John Brunas

Universal Horrors: The Studio's Classic Films, 1931–1946 (McFarland, 1990)

By Tom Weaver, David Schecter and Steve Kronenberg

The Creature Chronicles: Exploring the Black Lagoon Trilogy (McFarland, 2014)

Earth vs. the Sci-Fi Filmmakers

20 Interviews

TOM WEAVER

McFarland & Company, Inc., Publishers
Jefferson, North Carolina

The present work is a reprint of the illustrated casebound edition of Earth vs. the Sci-Fi Filmmakers: 20 Interviews, *first published in 2005 by McFarland.*

Library of Congress Cataloguing-in-Publication Data

Weaver, Tom, 1958–
Earth vs. the sci-fi filmmakers : 20 interviews / Tom Weaver.
     p.   cm.
Includes index.

ISBN 978-0-7864-9572-6 (softcover : acid free paper) ♾
ISBN 978-0-7864-8217-7 (ebook)

1. Science fiction films—United States—History and criticism.
2. Motion picture producers and directors—United States—Interviews.
I. Title: Earth versus the science-fiction filmmakers.   II. Weaver, Tom, 1958–
   PN1995.9.S26E27 2014   791.43'615—dc22   2005003515

British Library cataloguing data are available

© 2005 Tom Weaver. All rights reserved

No part of this book may be reproduced or transmitted in any form or by any means, electronic or mechanical, including photocopying or recording, or by any information storage and retrieval system, without permission in writing from the publisher.

On the covers: Front and back images of the Venusian invader from the 1956 film *It Conquered the World* (permission granted by Academy Pictures Corporation, © Susan Nicholson Hofheinz). *Cover design by Marty Baumann (www.bmonster.com).*

Printed in the United States of America

McFarland & Company, Inc., Publishers
Box 611, Jefferson, North Carolina 28640
www.mcfarlandpub.com

Dedicated to the memory of
Acquanetta
Merian C. Cooper
Nelson Gidding
Alex Gordon
Suzanne Kaaren
Anna Lee
Janet Leigh
Bri Murphy
Dan O'Herlihy
Jack Pollexfen
Lyn Thomas
Katherine Victor
Irvin S. Yeaworth, Jr.

Acknowledgments

Mega-thanks to Bob Burns for the loan of many incredible photos—and also for providing one of the "interviews" in this book by excavating out of his archives an audio tape of a Q&A session with *King Kong*'s Merian C. Cooper at a private party in 1964. Similarly super-sized appreciation to the Astounding B Monster himself, Marty Baumann, who brilliantly designed this book's covers. Check out Mr. B.'s website www.bmonster.com for other examples of his amazing design work—not to mention the coolest genre-related news, reviews and interviews on the web.

Sincere thanks also go to Eric Aijala, John Antosiewicz, Buddy Barnett (*Cult Movies*), Rudy Behlmer, Ted Bohus (*Chiller Theatre*), Mike and John Brunas, the incomparable gang at the Classic Horror Film Board (David Colton, Larry Sutliff, Gary Prange, Kerry Gammill et al.), Jim Clatterbaugh (*Monsters from the Vault*), Kevin Clement (*Chiller Theatre*), John Cocchi, Glenn Damato, Joe Dante, Jack Dukesbery, Mike Fitzgerald, Fred Frederic, Mike Gingold (*Fangoria*), Richard Gordon, Susan Hart, Jack Hill, Jeff and Joe Indusi, Paul Jensen, the late Ed Kemmer, Richard Kiel, Bob King (*Classic Images*), the Lincoln Center Performing Arts Library staff (Louis Paul, Christine Karatnytsky, Dan Patri, Christopher Frith), the Little Prince, Tim and Donna Lucas (*Video Watchdog*), Dave McDonnell (*Starlog*), Scott MacQueen, Boyd Magers (*Western Clippings*), Jeffrey Martin, Mark Martucci, Paula Mathieu, Burr Middleton, Barry Murphy (amazing proofreading skills!), Ray Nielsen, Erin Ray Pascaretti, the Photofest gang, Oconee and Jeannie Provost, Fred Rappaport, Ann Robinson, "Rufus," Mary Runser, Dan Scapperotti, Rich Scrivani, Rob Shofner, Denny and Bob Skotak, Tony Timpone (*Fangoria*), Gregory Von Berblinger and Lucy Chase Williams.

Abridged versions of some of the interviews featured in this book originally appeared in the following 'zines:

GENE BARRY: "World Warrior," *Starlog* #315, October 2003
GARY CLARKE: "I, Too, Was a Teenage Werewolf," *Starlog* #311, June 2003
GARY CONWAY: "The Original 'Monster Kid,'" *Chiller Theatre* #19, 2003
MERIAN C. COOPER: "Queryin' Merian," *Monsters from the Vault* #18, Summer 2004
ROBERT DIX: "In His Father's Footsteps: An Interview with Robert Dix," *Classic Images* #338, August 2003

DONNIE DUNAGAN: "'Here's to a Son of the House of Frankenstein!'—The Donnie Dunagan Interview," *Video Watchdog* #112, October 2004
ALEX GORDON: "The Day His World Began," *Fangoria* #229, January 2004
PETER GRAVES: "The Man Who Saved the Earth," *Starlog* #329, December 2004
GARY GRAY: "God on the Radio," *Classic Images* #348, June 2004
ARCH HALL, JR.: "B-Movie Hall of Fame," *Fangoria* #237, October 2004, and "Sadists and Scoundrels," *Fangoria* #238, November 2004
STEPHEN KANDEL: "*Wax* Kandel," *Chiller Theatre* #21, 2004
CAROLYN KEARNEY: "Horror Heyday: Actress Carolyn Kearney on *The Thing That Couldn't Die* and Other Horrific Highlights," *Cult Movies* #39, 2003
KEN KOLB: "Sailing with Sinbad," *Starlog* #312, July 2003
ROBERT L. LIPPERT, JR.: "Lon on the Loose!," *The Phantom of the Movies' VideoScope* #52, Fall 2004
JAN MERLIN: "*Adrian Messenger* ... Unmasked!," *Video Watchdog* #105, March 2004
MARY MITCHEL: "Panic Time," *Starlog* #310, May 2003
ELLIOTT REID: "Of Fun, Films & Flubber," *Starlog* #316, November 2003
BURT TOPPER: "Stranglers in the Night," *Chiller Theatre* #21, 2004

Contents

Acknowledgments vii
Preface 1

Gene Barry 3
Gary Clarke 13
Gary Conway 31
Merian C. Cooper 45
Robert Dix 61
Donnie Dunagan 86
Alex Gordon on *Day the World Ended* 114
Peter Graves 133
Gary Gray on *The Next Voice You Hear...* 149
Arch Hall, Jr. 161
Stephen Kandel on *Chamber of Horrors* 212
Carolyn Kearney 223
Ken Kolb 238
Robert L. Lippert, Jr., on Lon Chaney, Jr. 260
Jan Merlin on *The List of Adrian Messenger* 271
Mary Mitchel 292
Elliott Reid 313
Stanley Rubin on *The Whip Hand* 335
Frankie Thomas on *Tom Corbett, Space Cadet* 344
Burt Topper on *The Strangler* 367

Index 379

Preface

It was 1988 and I was about 50 interviews into (what I laughingly call) my "career" when friends started saying to me, "You're going to run out of people to interview soon, you *know* that, right?" Others shared with me their opinion that in another few years, almost nobody would give a hoot about old black-and-white movies any more and it would start to get tough for me to get my articles and interviews into print.

The late '80s were when the gloom-and-doomers began sounding the death knell and now here it is 2005 and the end is not yet in sight, I'm pleased to say. In fact, on a personal (and self-aggrandizing) note, I had a very satisfying moment in 2004 when three of the people who had been on my "Must Interview!" list right from Day One—Arch Hall, Jr., Peter Graves and Donnie Dunagan—fell into my web almost simultaneously; in October 2004, my interviews with all three were on newsstands at the same time, in *Fangoria*, *Starlog* and *Video Watchdog* magazines, respectively.

The Hall, Graves and Dunagan conversations have also come together between the covers of this new compilation, my tenth book of interviews for McFarland and my eleventh overall. These past ... how I hate to do the math ... 25 years of locating and chatting with the oldtime Hollywood pros have been a wonderful adventure; ditto the experience of getting some of them to film festivals and autograph shows, to participate on the DVDs of their old movies, etc. These people's genre movies and/or TV series were a very big part of my childhood, and to be able to interact with them now is, in a word, fabulous. So, as always, a great big thank-you to them, and also to all of my "civilian" friends who have helped make these interview books possible.

Gene Barry

> *The War of the Worlds was the all-time great kick-off for science fiction-type movies.*

Call it the Mother of All Battles: The combined military might of every nation on Earth taking on the war machines of Martian invaders in *The War of the Worlds*.

When English science fiction novelist H.G. Wells' most famous novel debuted in the dwindling days of the nineteenth century, the defenses that Man was able to deploy against his interplanetary opponents were still comparatively crude. But the subsequent half-century of real-life industrialization and scientific advances leading up to the first film version of Wells' tale were reflected in that 1953 Paramount picture. Heading the cast, as well as the hi-tech team of Earth scientists desperate to turn back the tide of Martian incursion: new-to-Hollywood film star Gene Barry.

Born in his grandmother's 116th Street (Harlem) apartment, the eldest son of a manufacturing jeweler who later lost his business and home in the Depression, Gene Barry (real name: Eugene Klass) began his show biz career singing on the radio and appearing as a band vocalist. Changing his name to Gene Barry (a half-a-steal from acting world legend John Barrymore), he made his 1942 Broadway bow in the long-running *Rosalinda* and racked up other credits on the Great White Way, then made the move to Hollywood. Enemy agents abducted nuclear physicist Barry's young son in an attempt to wrest H-bomb secrets from Barry in the gripping *The Atomic City* (1952), his movie debut.

One of the top-grossers of 1953, producer George Pal's *The War of the Worlds* was another impressive early credit on Barry's acting résumé, which also includes the TV hits *Bat Masterson*, *Burke's Law* and *The Name of the Game*. In addition to his workaholic list of big- and small-screen credits, TV's dapper Best Dresser has also continued to make nightclub and cabaret appearances, and (in the '80s) added the Broadway musical *La Cage aux Folles* to his list of smash successes.

Growing up in tough times—do you think that contributed to the work ethic that you obviously have?

No, I don't think so. I think that actors are so motivated because once you finish a job, it's over, you need *another* one. You're *always*, "What's the next thing I'm gonna do?" What's the next job, what's the next movie, what's the next television show, what's the next play? It's *always* like that, because they're limited runs. As a result, you have to keeping looking ahead, looking towards the next job.

I can understand that attitude for the average actor, obviously, but once an actor gets very financially comfortable, which I'm willing to bet you did, do they still have that drive?

I am comfortable, yes, but I don't think an actor *ever* loses the drive for that next great role. It's like an artist painting pictures.

Did you really get Barry from John Barrymore?

I had to come up with a name fast [*laughs*]! And there was John Barrymore and Elaine Barrie—Elaine Barrie was his girlfriend at the time. She spelled it with an –ie and he spelled *his* name Barry-more. So I said, "Hey. Gene Barry. That's a good name for me." My name was Eugene but I was always called Gene, there was the first half, and I took the last name Barry. Gosh, that was back in the '30s!

Did you grow up a movie buff?

Yeah, I went to all of the movies as a kid—all of the old pictures, the Gary Cooper pictures, the Clark Gable movies, even Fredric March movies. I loved movies.

What were your favorite types of movies as a kid?

I think dramas. 'Cause I was essentially an actor. I didn't want to be a *cowboy* or anything, I wanted to be a dramatic actor.

When did you first go out to Hollywood?

I was playing in Louisville, Kentucky—there was a big series of musicals I was doing there. My wife Betty was with me, and I had an old car, an old Frazer. I finished the engagement and I asked Betty, "Shall we drive out to California? We're halfway there!" And she said, "Okay. Let's go!" Michael, our first child—our only child born at the time—we put him in the back seat and we strapped him in and we drove on. Six days later, we arrived in California! We arrived, we checked into a motel, I visited a couple of friends, and I made a call to the agent who worked [in California] in conjunction with my New York agent. He said, "Let's meet," and we did, and in the next three weeks he took me around to various studios and I was offered contracts by three or four studios. I took the one at Paramount. Just like that. In a matter of three weeks, I was under contract to Paramount.

And you had come out there with no prospects.

Not really. I was just going to look [Hollywood] over and figure out if we were going to stay there for a while or go back to New York. In New York, I earned a living in the theater. I was signed by Paramount, I got this contract, and stayed with

Signed to a Paramount contract after just three weeks in Hollywood, Gene Barry was joined by Ann Robinson in producer George Pal's *The War of the Worlds*.

them for two years. My first big movie was *The War of the Worlds*, I played the lead in that. I played in six movies at Paramount.

At the time, they had a group of young actors they called the Golden Circle—were you part of that?
   No, no, no. I was making fairly important money. Those Golden Circle kids were making $125 a week. I was a New York actor, Paramount respected me differently.

According to my sources, you made $1000 a week at Paramount.
   And more than that in the second year.

That had to be nice after all those years in New York, where money probably got short from time to time—am I right about that?
   Well, sure. But I had this beautiful, wonderful apartment on the corner of 56th Street and Seventh Avenue, up on the fifteenth floor. The mistake I later made was getting rid of it—coming back to New York and closing it down. It would have been a great place for us in all these later years that we went back and forth to New York. It was right across the street from the stage door of Carnegie Hall, the southeast corner of 56th and Seventh.

As you acted in your first movie, Paramount's The Atomic City, *were you thinking to yourself, "This is for me," or did you miss the stage at all?*

"Aliens R Us" in these wacky studio gag shots of Ann Robinson and Barry.

More behind-the-scenes hijinks for *War of the Worlds*' **still photographer. (Photofest)**

What does an actor want? An actor wants success, and he wants to play roles. And if movies were going to make me a bigger star, then that's what I wanted. The fact is, when I went into TV, I didn't even *want* to go into TV.

After Paramount?
After Paramount, yeah. I didn't want to go into TV.

Because in those days, TV was a big step down for a movie actor.
Well, I don't know if it was a *big* step down—I made a lot of money when I went into it! Well, we'll get to that…

What were your feelings when you were offered War of the Worlds*?*
I was excited. George Pal, that was his big, big movie. *The War of the Worlds* was the all-time great kick-off for science fiction-type movies. As I remember, George Pal was okay, he was fine [to work with]. I had no problems, and he had no problems with me. Ann Robinson was in that with me, and the director was Byron Haskin.

What do you remember about him, and the way he worked?

Not much! I was just enthralled by what was happening to my life. Here I was in a movie of this size, when I had just arrived recently out here. I think Ann Robinson and I both felt the same way.

There's a behind-the-scenes "gag shot" of you and Ann reading H.G. Wells' War of the Worlds. *Did you ever read the book?*

Oh, sure. I think I read it before, earlier in my life, and then I read it again [for the movie].

The Wells book—obviously—is set in the nineteenth century, when it was written. Was it a good idea for Paramount to move the story into the 1950s?

Actually, I think it was. It was a very successful movie. It was a great thing for me to get into and I *got* it and … budda-boom.

Approximately how long did it take to shoot?

I think about five, six weeks or so. We even had to do some exterior shots in the desert [the scenes of Barry and Ann Robinson with tanks] and that sort of thing.

Ann Robinson says she was a little scared out there in the desert with all the tanks roaring past.

[*Laughs*] Oh, *was* she? It was part of being an actor, you do what you have to do. Ann and I got along very well. Maybe I shouldn't say this, but I was hopeful that she would have a better career than she had. She didn't go on to the level that I expected her to. Does *she* feel that way?

She's had a couple husbands and a couple sons and such a nice life that I don't think she has any regrets at all.

Really? That's great, I'm delighted to know that. I didn't know what happened to her, actually; I don't even know that we've been in touch more than just a few times during these many years. She has sons, you say? They must be grown men by now. *I've got* two *grown men, and a grown daughter.*

And you must be a grandfather by now.

Oh, I've been a grandfather for 27 years [*laughs*]! My grandson is in our business, in a sense; he works for a major company.

How did you feel about War of the Worlds, *and your performance, when you first saw it?*

An actor becomes very hypercritical about himself. He really does. You don't like everything you do. There are scenes you *like*, and then you say, "Oh, *why* did I do *that*?"—that sort of thing. And you say, "I wish the director had let me do it over" and other [self-recriminations] like that. That happens with every actor.

Your mom and dad—did they live to see you become a movie star?

In the end, it is God's humblest creations that decide *The War of the Worlds*. (Photofest)

Yup. Yup, they did. And my father didn't want me to be an actor, he wanted me to be an artist. I had an art ability, and he said, "You don't wanna be an *actor*. I'll send you to the best art school in New York!" He couldn't afford it, but he said so! I said, "No, I want to be an actor," and that's what I did, I just went out after acting. I got my first important role on Broadway for Max Reinhardt, the famous German director—I did a major role in a musical called *Rosalinda*. Reinhardt was the director and it was produced by the New Opera Company, and we ran for two years [1942–44]. I was in my very early twenties.

And your father's offer to send you to art school—that was before Rosalinda*?*
 Yeah, that was before. Then I worked with Mae West [in producer Michael Todd's *Catherine Was Great*], I did a major role with Mae West in a Broadway play. Then I did one for Jule Styne—it was Jule Styne and Sammy Cahn's first musical. A failure [*laughs*]!

Why did you leave Paramount after making those six pictures there?
 Why? It just happened. I don't know … the contract ended, and times were bad, I guess. Or maybe they didn't think that highly of me [*laughs*], I don't know. Who

the hell knows? Actors go as long as they can [at a studio] and then you go elsewhere. I've been at many different studios, I've had a *pretty* good career…

Many past articles on your career call you a "song and dance man" at heart.
   Because I did a musical that was for Mike Todd, you see—that's where *that* came from. I was always able to move well and I was always able to sing. I also toured the world as a singer, as a *nightclub* singer. I played London, I played Italy, France, South America, and I think I even played in the Orient, in Hong Kong.

I believe the first time you sang in a movie was in Paramount's Red Garters *[1954].*
   I forget. If you say so, then I did!

Were you more comfortable singing in Red Garters *or fighting Martians in* War of the Worlds?
   Oh, Jesus, it was another role!

Was science fiction appealing to you at all as an actor?
   Not necessarily, no.

The move into TV—you said you were going to tell me about that.
   An agent that I had at the time, Herb Tobias was his name, said, "They want you to do a TV series…." What was the name of it? What was my first TV series?

Bat Masterson?
   Bat Masterson. I said, "I don't want to go in television. I mean, if I go into television, it's gonna be the end of my movie career." And it just about worked out that way. I had a fine television career—but I had a lousy *movie* career [*laughs*]! It's the truth. In those days, it was a negative stamp, making the move into TV. But I became successful in television. *Bat Masterson* was known internationally, really and truly … but I've forgotten about it. You mention these titles and they come back to me, all of these things that I did but I no longer think of. What I'm trying to say is, you don't sit and think of all of the things you did in the past. [An interviewer] brings things up, as *you* have, and then I suddenly remember them.

I think you might be surprised how many of the actors I talk to do live in the past!
   They do, huh?

After Bat Masterson *went off the air, you said it was "a monster" and that it nearly did you in and that you'd never do another TV series. Then you did a bunch more! What made you change your mind?*
   I couldn't get a good movie. Working in TV did exactly what I thought it would do, it screwed me out of my movie career.

Over the years I've read in a couple different places that you were working on your autobiography.
   I didn't write it. I started to, and I didn't.

Barry says he would find it "thrilling" to be on board for a cameo in the 2005 *War of the Worlds* remake.

If you weren't an actor, what would you be?
 What *would* I be...? [*Pause*] You know, I would probably have been an artist. I have talents as a painter and in drawing, things like that, which I haven't continued with. But here at home I go back into the room where I keep my artwork and stuff, I look at it and I ask myself, "Why didn't I continue with this?" Really. Some of it is very good.

They're talking about making another War of the Worlds. *Do you think it should be brought up-to-the-minute, like yours was?*
 I think they *should* bring it up to now, yes. Absolutely. We didn't play it as 1800s, we were in the 1950s. And this new one should also be current, you could bring so many more aspects to it—think of all the things we've got today. It could be fantastic. Who's going to do it, do you know?

Supposedly Tom Cruise.
 Tom Cruise? If they need an old man in it, tell 'em to come to *me*!

If you were offered a cameo, or any part at all—
 Of course I would take it. It would be thrilling.

Gary Clarke

> *I don't want to sound jaded about [these monster movies],
> 'cause I'm not. They were great fun, and they were
> major steps in my career.*

It was a stroke of exploitation movie genius: *I Was a Teenage Werewolf* with Michael Landon and *I Was a Teenage Frankenstein* with Gary Conway were big box office hits for AIP in 1957, so a two-in-one follow-up was devised for release the following year: *How to Make a Monster*, about an embittered AIP makeup man (Robert H. Harris) who changes the unwitting young actors playing Teenage Werewolf and Teenage Frankenstein in the company's newest production into his instruments of murder. Conway repeated his Teenage Frankenstein role but Michael Landon, unhappy with the ribbing he got from his peers for playing a varsity-jacketed lycanthrope, balked. Enter Gary Clarke, a beginning film actor as close to 30 as he was to being a teenager, but possessed of a boyish look and a facial similarity to Landon that made him an ideal choice for the new production.

The Mexican-French Clarke (real name: Clarke F. L'Amoreaux) followed up that same year with yet another offbeat genre role (a young convict shanghaied into space aboard a *Missile to the Moon*) before TV stardom came his way: Regular roles on *Michael Shayne* with Richard Denning, *Hondo* with Ralph Taeger and, most memorably, the "adult Western" *The Virginian* with Lee J. Cobb and James Drury. Amidst all these on-camera assignments, he was also forced to do some acting *behind*-the-scenes, playing an East Coast dork in production meetings with the creators of TV's *Get Smart* in an attempt to conceal his true identity and get some writing gigs on the popular spy spoof series!

Gary Clarke, teenage werewolf/space traveler/Western star/make-believe dork, shares some of his believe-it-or-not experiences...

How early did you get interested in acting?

I actually remember the *minute* that I got interested. I was in, oh, the ninth grade, something like that, and I lived in East L.A., which was predominantly a Chicano neighborhood. *I'm* half–Mexican, half–French. We had a habit, the guys in the neighborhood, we played football right there in the street. And one of the guys we played with, *his* folks owned a little mom-and-pop grocery store where they had these *incredible* Hostess chocolate cupcakes—*not* the kind with the filling, this was before that. We'd play, and then we'd go into the store and get some of these two-for-a-nickel cupcakes and some milk and we'd go across the street and sit on the lawn and just start talking about stuff. I began telling them jokes, and making up stories about school, and I had them in stitches. The one guy, the kid whose parents owned the store, said [*in a Chicano accent*], "You can make money doing that! You could make money making people laugh like that!" There was a ring of truth in it. I got into drama class, and just went from there. So early high school, I think, is when I was interested. That was the moment.

How did you break into the business?
Oh, that was funny. I was in the high school play, and the girl who was playing opposite me had a single mom. The mom brought a guest with her the opening night of the play, a gentleman by the name of Doc Bishop. Doc Bishop was a talent scout from 20th Century–Fox—he was the guy who discovered Shirley Temple. After the play, he came up and he said, "When I see plays like this, I keep score of people who attract my attention more often than not. You were by far the one I watched the most. I would like to have you come out to 20th Century–Fox and let's talk." So I did, I went out. I was just about 17. He took me around and I met everybody, and then he said, "Look, I want to put you under contract, but you're 17. Let's wait 'til you're 18. Now, don't do anything stupid, like get married." Okay. So the first thing I did was get married! I got married and, I dunno, several months later I called him and he answered the phone and I said, "Mr. Bishop? This is Clarke L'Amoreaux." He said, "Oh, hi, Clarke! I understand that you got married. Is that true?" I said, "Uh … yes, sir, but—" And he hung up. That was it. Never talked to me again! So I kind of gave it up for a while. Pretty soon I had three kids, three boys—two were born in one year, one in February and one in December. In three years, I had three boys.

At that point, I decided that I wanted to get back into [acting], I kinda missed it. I was working in a machine shop, I was delivering 900 newspapers a day, I had different kinds of jobs. So, I called my old high school drama teacher, who was very supportive, and I said, "Miss Hoffman, I think I'm ready to get back in the business. I think the business *needs* me now, so I'll give it a break." (Just kidding!) "How 'bout the Pasadena Playhouse?" She said, "Well, I know the director of the Pasadena Playhouse, let me see what I can do." So the following night, it was eight o'clock and I was asleep because I had to get up at one and deliver papers. The phone rang and it was … I've forgotten her name, let's call her Madame La Zonga. She was very proper, and had a kind of Russian accent. She said, "My good friend Aura Hoffman called me and said that you should come and read. We are reading for *Berrrnarrrdine*, we want you to come and read tomorrow night, seven o'clock." And I in my stupor said [*groggy, half-awake, voice cracking*], "…*Who* ish thish?" She went through it all again and this time I got it and I told her I'd be there. So I showed up at the Pasadena Playhouse the next night, at *eight* o'clock. Because … hey … it's *me*, y'know? They're lucky I'm *here*.

Are you kidding again, or were you cocky like that in those early days?

Yeah, definitely cocky, 'cause I had been *it* in high school. I was gonna "dazzle 'em with my footwork." But I didn't realize—big fish, little pond! Anyway, I saw the door with the right number and I opened it, and there were some people in there. And I said [*brashly*], "Is this where the auditions are?" They stopped and looked at me, and the director said [*coldly*], "Ummm … yes … and you've just interrupted a reading. Take a seat, and we'll be with you."

I closed the door and I went in and I sat down, and I listened to these people read. And my thoughts were, "Hey … these guys are *good*. Some of 'em *might* even be … better than *me*!" It came my turn, and I got up to read, and it was like I had never read before. I couldn't focus on the script, everything was kind of black around the edges, and I was going like [*talks gibberish in a cracking voice*]—I even started reading the stage directions [*laughs*]. The director said, "Clarke, Clarke. Hold on a second. Look, everybody gets nervous, I don't want you to worry about it. Here's what we're gonna do: I'm gonna have Fred here take you in the next room, run through the lines with you. Just get comfortable, and then come back and read." I said [*voice cracking again*], "Yes, sir, thank you very much, okay, yes, sir…" So Fred took me in the next room and he worked with me for about ten minutes and then he told me, "You're doing okay now. Come back in when you're ready," and he left. And I *was* feeling better now. I was really gonna impress 'em, so I memorized like three pages of dialogue. I was in there for maybe another 10 or 15 minutes at the most. Okay, now I felt like I was ready and I exited my room, opened the door to *their* room … and everyone was gone. I was the only one at nine o'clock, nine-thirty at night at the Pasadena Playhouse! Walking in there, I was figuring on dazzling 'em with my footwork, and instead I'd tripped all over myself. They left me—I don't know if they forgot or they did it on purpose, but … it was a lesson never to be forgotten!

The next night they were having an audition at a little

Gary Clarke (pictured here with *How to Make a Monster* girlfriend Heather Ames) knew he wanted to be an actor right from the days of making classmates laugh in grade school.

theater group in San Gabriel. They were doing a melodrama, *Leonora's Lost Love*—I'll never forget it. It was one of those things where it was run by a clique of people, four or five people, and when they picked the shows, *they* got the plum roles, and then they cast for the rest. It was one of those kinds of little groups where they say [*very chipper*], "Okay, and is there anybody *new* here tonight?" I raised my hand. "And what is *your* name?" "My name is Clarke L'Amoreaux." "Yay, Clarke! Let's hear it for Clarke!" [*Clarke applauds*] So everybody read, but there were only these little parts to read for. As they were reading, I loved the part of the villain. The mustache-twirling, "heh-heh-heh, my fair maiden!" villain. So I said when they called me, "I'd like to read for the part of the villain." "Well, that part is already taken."

But the guy who *had* the part said [*condescendingly*], "Oh, ho ho ho, that's okay. Let him read, we can see how he does!" So I read, and I must have done an incredible job, because I *got* the part on the spot. The guy who was the villain was given the part of the hero and the guy who was going to play the hero was given the lead in the olio section and so on! So I started there, doing all kinds of little theater work. I later ended up in Glendale, and I must have done 50 shows over there. An agent came in and saw me, put me under contract—strange guy. Byron Griffith. The first time he called me over to his house, he wanted me to do a scene with somebody, so we could take it to the studios. (The studios then were having agents bring in new clients who would do a scene for several of the casting people. That was a way to check out the talent.) So I went to his house, and the little girl that he had there for me to read with was Connie Stevens. We did a scene from a play that I had done at Glendale Center Theater, and then we started going around.

At that time, I was working in a machine shop. I got a call one day from Byron, who said, "Gary, they're doing a teenage movie, and I think I can get you a part as a member of the good gang. Can you get down here right away?" I said [*breathless*], "Yeah!," and I hung up and I went to my boss Mr. Grimley—somehow I'm remembering all these names! I went to Mr. Grimley and I said, "I'm really sick. I feel like I've got … uh … diarrhea … and … uh … pernicious anemia. I don't know what it is…" He said, "All right, go home, go home, go on." So I went home and I changed and I drove from San Gabriel to Hollywood and read for the part, and I got in as a member of the good gang. I went back to work the next day and my agent called me again and he said, "Gary, they have just lost the lead in the movie. Can you get down here?" Yes! So I had a relapse [*laughs*] and went home and changed and went down, and I read every day for five days. I didn't go back to work, I just kept calling in sick.

This is Dragstrip Riot *[1958] you're talking about.*

That's right. And the director was a … was an *idiot*, pardon my French. They kept saying, "Gary's the hero, he should have blonde hair." My hair was kinda brownish. Blonde hair, huh? Well, my mother worked in a beauty shop, so at three o'clock in the morning, one of the girls at the shop bleached my hair platinum blonde. I went back down and they were thrilled. I got the job not because I was the best actor, I think I got it because I was so willing to do *any*thing—I was there every day and

I bleached my hair, I made friends with the people and so on. We had a three-week S.A.G. contract, and I got in S.A.G. through that movie. Probably one of the worst movies ever made in America. If not, then the second worst. Connie Stevens was in it, Fay Wray, Steve Ihnat, Yvonne Lime. We were under contract for three weeks and we shot for three weeks and we were nowhere near done. So the producer O'Dale Ireland said, "Listen, if you guys help me out, you'll all be stars. This thing is really coming together." Well, we must have shot for six *months*, stealing things where we could. We didn't get paid after the three weeks—just promises of how great this picture was gonna make us. And it was non-union, so if the union caught us, we were in trouble. *And*, as fate would have it, I *did* get caught—I was the only one who got caught. I was pulled up in front of a committee, there must have been 25 people on it, all of whom were these famous faces that I had seen on the screen most of my life. I was sitting in this chair in the middle of the room, kinda like an inquisition I felt, and all these people came in: "Oh, wow, there's so-and-so," "Woo, there's what's-his-name," "Gee, I saw *him* just a week ago!" They were smiling and laughing and talking to each other, and they all sat down. They didn't get stern, but they realized there was something to *do* here. They started talking to me about the history of the Guild—one guy in particular did most of the talking. He told me where the Guild had come from and what they had accomplished over the years, how they used to have box lunches that were old and now we've got warm food on the sets when we're on location. Very eloquent—I was impressed. The guy that did all the talking was Ronald Reagan. And everybody came up to me afterwards and shook hands and put an arm around me! It was *wonderful*, just great.

The "idiot" director of Dragstrip Riot *who you mentioned—that'd be David Bradley?*

I did not like the man. I think he lasted a week, and then we had another director come in. Somebody who didn't last long enough for me to remember his name! And then O'Dale Ireland, the producer, started directing, which was really funny 'cause he wasn't a director! Mostly we kinda directed our*selves*. Dale knew how to raise a few bucks, but he didn't know very much about film. But he was great fun. He and Steve Ihnat and I, after the film, roomed together for a while, and that's a whole 'nother story!

How did you get the part of the Teenage Werewolf in How to Make a Monster*?*

Here's my thinking on how I got *How to Make a Monster*: They had just finished *I Was a Teenage Werewolf* and *I Was a Teenage Frankenstein*, and Michael Landon, the Werewolf in *Teenage Werewolf*, wasn't available, or didn't *want* to do another monster thing. And there was a physical similarity between Landon and me. I remember in the mid-60s we were both on a TV telethon, there were maybe 10 or 15 of us TV personalities on there, and at one point they had us all line up. I was on one end in my *Virginian* wardrobe and Michael was on the other side in his *Bonanza* wardrobe. And when I saw a picture of us, we looked like bookends. So I got the part probably because Michael wasn't available and because the producer Herman Cohen saw me in *Dragstrip Riot* or something, and he said, "Oh. *This* guy could do it."

Do you recall if you had to audition for it?

I did. I don't remember ever getting anything I didn't have to audition for.

Had you ever seen Teenage Werewolf?

Yeah, I had seen it. I was a movie maven at the time and I went to them all the time. That was my business, so … how better to see what was goin' on?

Teenage Werewolf *was a big moneymaker. Did you see playing the Werewolf role in a follow-up as a good opportunity?*

Oh, sure. I also saw it as a good way to *eat* [*laughs*]. That was a primary motivation, I think, at the time!

Herman Cohen—what memories of him?

Herman was great. He treated me well, he was generous and I liked working with the man. It was a fun experience. There's a scene where the guy who is taking over the studio [Eddie Marr] is in a studio screening room viewing rushes. The weird makeup man [Robert H. Harris] puts that magic stuff on my face and turns me into a werewolf, I sneak into the screening room and I throttle this studio executive and bite his neck and sever the jugular vein and … disembowel him [*laughs*], whatever they had me do. The actor says to me, "Take it easy, will ya? I just got a new suit," and I say okay. Well, then Herman comes up to me and says [*in a soft voice*], "This is that guy's last day of work here. I want this to be a *good shot!*" So when the director calls *action*, I throw this guy all over the place! We do a couple of takes, because Herman keeps saying, "Okay, let's do it again. Gary, gimme a little *more*, will ya?" [*Laughs*] I kept saying to the guy, "Sorry…!"

You also drool all over him during the attack scene. Did you do that in every take?

Yes! He must have had a quart of drool on him. They gave me some fizzy stuff that makes you look like you're foaming at the mouth. It wasn't supposed to stain his suit.... I don't know if it *did* or not.

You talk about Herman Cohen as if he was directing. What was Herbert L. Strock doing?

Oh, they were good friends, Herb and Herman worked hand in hand. Any time Herman would throw in something like that, it was okay. There were some times when I recall Herb saying, "Herman … I'd rather do it *this* way," and Herman would say [*casually*], "Okay"—just like that. I think they were both agreed upon the idea of me … *mutilating* this poor guy in the screening room [*laughs*]!

Was Herman on the set a lot?

I don't know if it would be excessive, but he was there, his presence was felt.

Was it always you as the Werewolf?

Do you mean, "Was there a stunt double?" No. And as far as I know, Gary Conway played *his* monster in every scene.

Studio executive Eddie Marr regrets his no-more-monsters edict (and wearing his new suit) when Teenage Werewolf Clarke strikes.

If they had arranged for a stuntman to play the Werewolf, would you have been disappointed? Did you want *to play the Werewolf?*

I would have preferred playing the Werewolf. Always, even when I was on *The Virginian*, I always wanted to do my stunts. The only thing I couldn't do on *The Virginian* was drop a horse. Maybe I could have *learned*, but they thought it was too dangerous, "You could break a leg" and [objections] like that. But I did my fights and all the riding.

Was it makeup or a mask on you as the Teenage Werewolf?

Makeup. The hands were gloves, and they had a hair thing, a helmet-like [wig] for the top of my head. But the hair on the face was glued on every day, along with the makeup. The fangs they just slipped in.

What recollections of the other people in the cast?

Robert H. Harris was fun, he was good. Also supportive: "What do you think about *this*?," "Do you think *this* would work?"—we'd have conversations like that. Definitely a professional. Paul Brinegar, who played Harris' assistant, was the same. Brinegar was a bit of a joker. "If you're gonna do it, you might as well have fun," I think, was his credo.

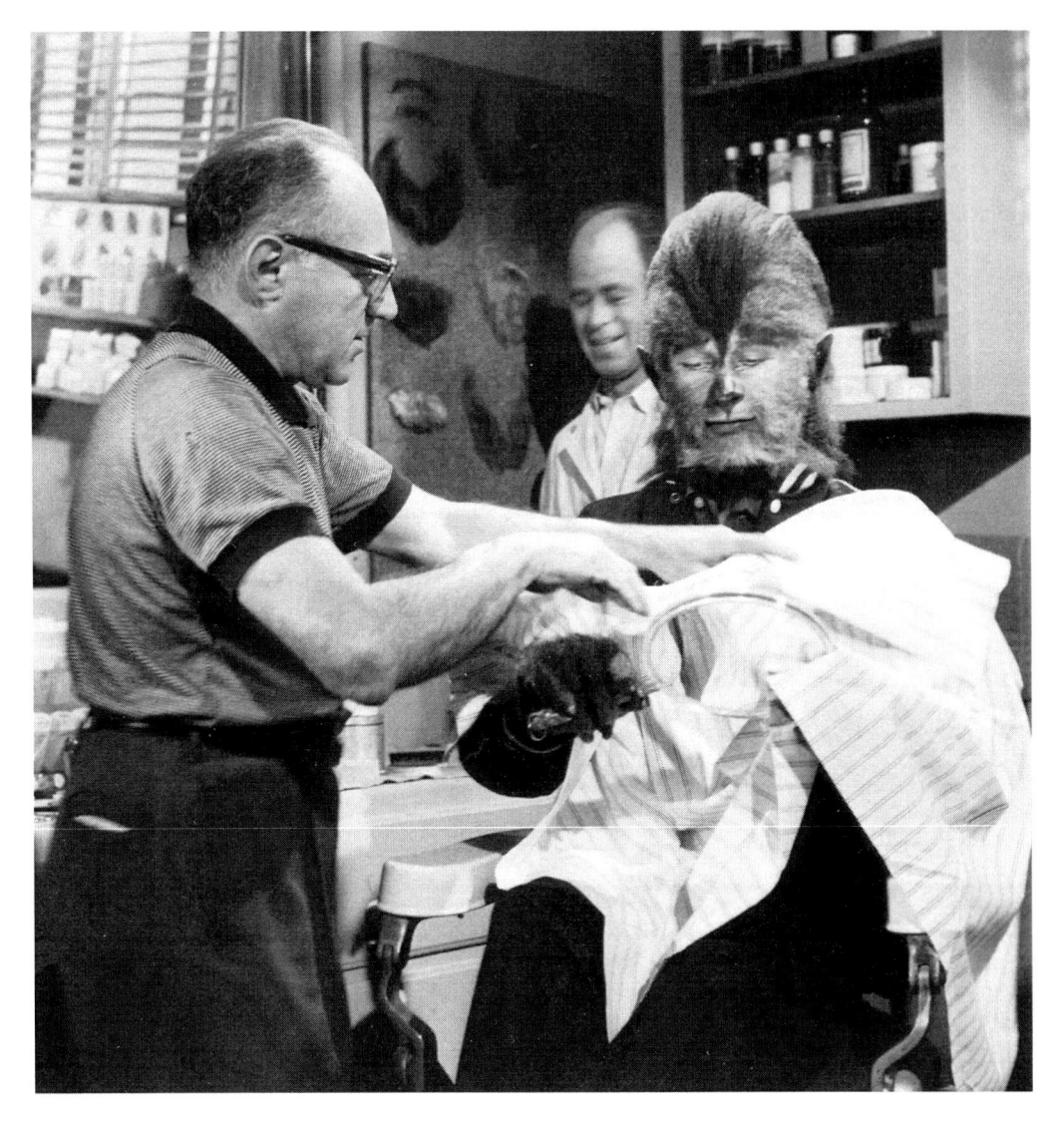

Clarke admires the work of Philip Scheer, the makeup man (the *real* one), in a behind-the-scenes *How to Make a Monster* moment.

And, closer to your age, Gary Conway?
    I didn't work very much with him, mostly just at the end. We got along fine. It was pretty cut-and-dried: Gary was there, and when he wasn't there, he was gone [*laughs*]. He had muscles, I remember that—he really worked out a lot. And he was pretty serious about his work. We laughed *some*, but he was serious, almost nervous about his work. But did, I think, a very credible job. Also, remember the scene where two girls from the high school newspaper come into the makeup room to interview Gary Conway? One of them, the brunette, was Jackie Ebeier, and in real life she was the girlfriend of my best friend Steve Ihnat, who is no longer with us. That was fun, having Jackie in the movie, and Steve got to come on the set.

Clarke, grappling here with Teenage Frankenstein Gary Conway, says he would have resisted any offer to replace him with a stuntman in *How to Make a Monster*'s action interludes.

You were in a lot of pictures with him early on.

We did *Dragstrip Riot* ... one called *Date Bait* [1960] ... *Strike Me Deadly* [1963] ... *Passion Street, U.S.A.* [1964]—yes, we *were* in a few together! And we were roommates for a long time. My best friend.

According to Herbert Strock, the fire at the end of How to Make a Monster *was accidentally started prematurely and so the scene had to be filmed in a big hurry.*

I don't remember anything like that. I remember the fire and a lot of stuff burning and thinking, "Hey, this is pretty good!" In comparison to the stuff I did on *Dragstrip Riot*, *How to Make a Monster* was a piece of cake.

Dragstrip Riot *is a picture I've never seen.*

[*Laughs*] Ohhhh! I'm sorry to hear your life is so empty!

What did you do in Dragstrip Riot *that you say* How to Make a Monster *was a breeze compared to it?*

It was an incredible experience, it was fun to do, because we learned so much. For one thing, we rode our own motorcycles. I mean, I didn't *own* one—they brought in a motorcycle wrangler who had like five or six motorcycles. And there's one scene where I'm in my Corvette and these five guys are chasing me. Except one of the guys got hurt, so they only had *four* guys. So they locked down the camera.... I drive by in the Corvette ... they shut off the camera.... I put on a biker's outfit, jump on a motorcycle and I join the four guys who are chasing *me*. So there's one scene where I'm chasing myself!

After one day's shooting, Steve Ihnat and I want to take the bikes home. We're riding Triumphs. We're coming along one of those roads that run from the Valley to the beach, and we're doing about 50. I'm behind him and we're heading into this tunnel, and suddenly his bike starts shaking. I'm watching him, I'm maybe 20 yards behind him. He can't stop it, it keeps shaking worse and worse and worse, and he loses it and he slides for I don't *know* how far. He gets up, and it looks like he's okay. But he's scraped *all* of the skin off his knee, down to his bone. And also off of his knuckles. He had a big gold ring that saved part of his knuckles. They took him to the hospital ... scraped the knee injury out with a heavy brush ... pulled the skin together like you would pull together a paper sack ... tied it up ... and the next day, he was back shooting! There's a scene toward the end of the picture where he has to get up from behind a bush, and you can see him hobbling out with one leg very stiff. We did all of our own stunts, so *How to Make a Monster* was a piece of cake.

Did you think the fact that the final reel of How to Make a Monster *was in color was a good idea?*

Yeah, that was cute.

Michael Landon did, according to Herman Cohen, refuse to do How to Make a Monster. *Once your career got a little further along, would you have turned down a second Teenage Werewolf movie the way he did?*

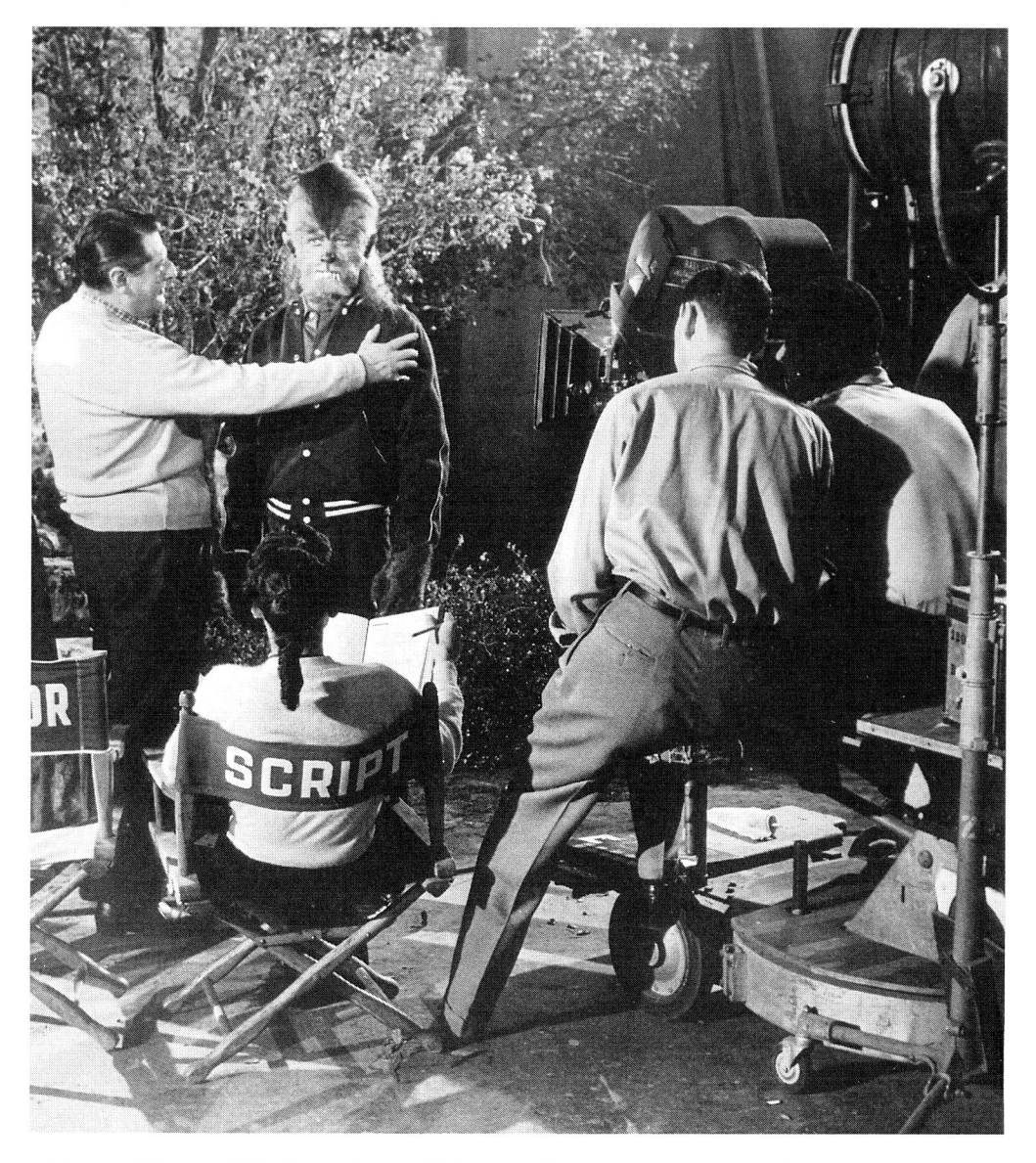

Teenage Werewolf Clarke on the set of *How to Make a Monster*'s movie-within-a-movie *Werewolf Meets Frankenstein*.

Depends on how hungry I was. Well, if I had already been offered *Michael Shayne*, I don't think I would have done [another Teenage Werewolf movie], only because it probably wouldn't have fit in with what the studio would have wanted.

How did you feel about it the first time you saw it?

It was a monster movie. I wasn't gonna be nominated for anything. But it was fun. A little different from *Dragstrip Riot*. The first time I saw *Dragstrip Riot*, I wanted to just get under my seat. The first reaction was laughing at my first line.

[Laughs] *That's not good!*
And then it went downhill from there!

Your wife at the time, was she an actress?
I wasn't married at that time. I was already married and divorced. I was divorced before I ever got into the motion picture business.

Missile to the Moon—*how did that happen to come your way?*
That film was great fun to do and I wouldn't have missed it for the world ... but I look at it now and I say, "What a wonderful plot! Two convicts—a bad convict and a good convict [Tommy Cook and Clarke]—are escaping, and they just happen to climb into this spaceship. Then the builder of the spaceship, along with a couple of his friends, get on board and take off, unaware that these two convicts are hiding on board trying to catch their breath. Then they land on the Moon, which just happens to be inhabited by all the Miss Universe contestants from that year." What a plot! But [*laughs*], I didn't care about the plot—I got to work with all the Miss Universe contestants! It was fun, it was great. My girlfriend in it, the Moon maiden who falls in love with me, was Leslie Parrish. She was wonderful, a good actress. So we had fun on that film. But there was overacting and all that stuff.

Were the Miss Universe girls friendly? Did you have a nice time working with them?
Yeah, they were friendly. Most of them had never done anything [acting-wise] before. But they were conscientious and they did the best job they could. It *was* what it *was*, it was a very inexpensive film, made to make money, and, thankfully, the people who worked on it had a good time. There was no prima donna stuff, everybody was friendly with everybody, and they too realized that they probably would not be nominated [*laughs*]!

The older actors like Richard Travis and Michael Whalen—any particular memories of them?
They were the old pros. They just *did* it. I'm sure we, the younger actors, had our remarks [about these older actors], because, y'know, we were the *new* generation coming up, and these guys had their style and we had *our* style. A couple of years ago, I ran into that script again and I saw that I had made all of these actor's [notations] in the margins, "What is he thinking before he says this?" Ask somebody in the audience and they'd say, "Who *cares*? Let's get back to the *broads*!"

Tommy Cook was fun—and a great tennis guy, he loves tennis. He had his own ideas about how he wanted to do it—even though he was my age, the guy had been around a long time [Cook had been a child actor], so he was a pro of a different sort. But I got along with him, and he actually taught me some stuff—"Remember this angle," "Try this," "Do this." K.T. Stevens [the evil leader of the Moon maidens] was funny, and she loved joking about her part. She just played it to the hilt. I didn't spend that much time with her, but the scenes that we were in were fun. There were a couple of times when she didn't look the way she thought she should look—there might have been something a little askew with her hair, or her wardrobe,

Robert H. Harris chides Clarke's wolf for doin' what comes naturally.

or her makeup, and she just wanted to be damn sure that it was the way she wanted it. She wasn't *bad* about it, she was just firm. Again, no prima donna stuff.

Special effects have come a long way since you shot your fight scene with the giant spider!
It was hard not to laugh. Here comes that thing, obviously on strings and wires—everybody knew it, and everybody knew the *audience* was gonna know it. It reminded me of that picture Bela Lugosi did, *Bride of the Monster* [1956], where in the scene where he fights the octopus, he has to wrap the tentacles of the thing around himself. Our spider scene was kind of like that. So it was fun to laugh at. The whole thing, with the rock men and the spider and all that stuff, was hysterical.

Missile to the Moon *includes scenes of the space-suited Earthmen on the Moon surface—shot in Red Rock Canyon—but I just know, looking at all the purposely opaque helmet visors, that they must all be doubles.*
I think they shot that second unit stuff before they started [shooting the film with actors]—the second unit went out into the desert and shot some scenes of these guys fighting the rock men. Tommy Cook was the other escaped convict, and I was

taller than Tommy. But in the second unit stuff, the guy with my voice was the shorter of the two [*laughs*]. So somebody goofed!

The Moon kingdom sets—did you think they looked okay, or did you find them just as laughable as everything else?

I don't want to sound jaded about [these movies], 'cause I'm not. They were great fun, and they were major steps in *my* career. The Moon sets, when they exploded (or *im*ploded, or whatever they did), were okay for the time. For what they spent, I think they did a good job.

In 1958, when you made your monster pictures, where were you living?

In Hollywood. Steve Ihnat and I had a couple of apartments that we lived in. One was a big house with no furniture. A two-story house with two chairs, a card table and a couple of pads for beds. When we weren't working, we were out looking for jobs. We did construction, we did delivery stuff, we did ... whatever.

Even though you were co-starring in these occasional movies, you still had to do all that in-between stuff?

Oh, yeah! You'd get paid [for starring in a low-budget movie], but it wasn't much, it was three, three and a quarter a week or something like that. That would last a while. But those jobs were few and far between at the time.

If The Virginian *and some of your other, better credits had never come along, if you had simply continued getting parts in movies like* Missile to the Moon *and these other exploitation things, how long would you have stuck with the acting?*

I probably *would* have stuck with it, because in the interim I would do stuff on stage. I *love* stage work. So it wasn't just [those movies]—doing movies like that was just how we made our money. I at that time had aspirations of really making something of myself, and it always seemed to keep moving in that direction. Then writing came into it, and that was a major, major step for me. When I started writing, it was like comin' home.

You wrote a number of episodes of Get Smart.

I wrote about eight of 'em, I think. And I invented the character Hymie the Robot. (Dick Gautier says I rejuvenated his career!) I got that job in a very strange way: After *The Virginian*, I started writing—'cause I had time [*laughs*]. I was having lunch with Bill Kiley, the head of NBC publicity, with whom I had become very friendly, and he was telling me about this NBC series about a bumbling spy [*Get Smart*]. I said, "Gee, I have an idea. Can I show it to you?" He said yeah, and I said I'd bring it in in a couple days. I went home and wrote it and brought it back to him, and he said, "This is perfect. This is right up their alley."

I gave it to my agent and I told him what my friend from NBC said, but I also told him, "Don't tell 'em Gary Clarke wrote it." I said that because, when I had been working on *Hondo*, I had an idea for a *Hondo* segment and I wrote a script and I handed it to the producer [Andrew J. Fenady]. He looked at it and handed it back

More green cheese? Clarke, Leslie Parrish, Richard Travis, producer Marc Frederic et al. at the *Missile to the Moon* wrap party. (Notice equally cheesy Moon backdrop.) (Photograph courtesy Fred Frederic.)

and said, "Gary, you're an actor. You act. Let the writers write." That stuck with me: "Hey ... actors aren't supposed to write. Producers don't want to mess around with actors' ideas." So I had my agent present the first script to the *Get Smart* people as having been written by Clarke F. L'Amoreaux—my real name. And, because they weren't reading any unsolicited material, he *lied* about me: "This is a new guy right out of New York. If you don't read this now, you're gonna miss out on something. Do yourself a favor, it's a half-hour show, just *read* it." And they *did* read it, and they said they wanted to see me.

"See you"—that's bad.

That's right, I *was* concerned that as soon as they saw me, they would say, "Oh! You're an actor. Never mind. Forget it." So I dressed up as dorky as possible. I parted my hair in the middle. I got some fake glasses. My pants were too short. And I talked like [*talking in a dorky voice*], "Gee, I'm glad you liked it!" That's how I went in to meet the *Get Smart* people, who were Mel Brooks and Buck Henry and Leonard Stern. And I *continued* as Clarke F. L'Amoreaux, visiting the *Get Smart* people with every new script. I wrote three shows like that, and after the third one I said, "That's enough of that. I'm tired of it. If they don't like my work, they can fire me. But they gotta know who I am." So I went into Mel Brooks' office, and he and Buck Henry were there. I said, "Do you guys have a minute?" "Yeah, Clarke, come on in." I said, "I should have told you this a long time ago, but I was worried ... maybe because what I would tell you would mean that you wouldn't hire me as a writer. But we've got three shows under our belts now and I ... I just ... I..." "What is it? What is it, Clarke?" "Well, I'm really Gary Clarke. I'm an actor. I was on *The Virginian*." And Buck Henry said, "Yeah. We know." [*Laughs*] "*What*??" "Yeah, we know." "Well, why didn't you *say* something?" "We wanted to see how long you'd carry it on." They laughed, I laughed. So they were great. Working with those guys—wow! That was something.

How did you happen to come up with the idea for Hymie the Robot?

I had been messing around with a story, a very dramatic one, about a guy who puts an ad in the paper for a wife. This woman comes in, very skeptical, and the guy tells her he wants her as his wife for show purposes and that's all. In name only. No futzing around. She doesn't believe it, but she agrees to do it for a year. Every night she locks her door ... but then she begins to *like* the guy. And by the time her contract's up a year later, she's head over heels in love with him and wants to marry him and wants to have his children. He says, "No, we have a contract"—he's very cool about it. Finally she says, "Well, you're gonna *have* to stay married to me, because ... I'm gonna have your baby." And he says, "I don't *think* so," and he opens his chest and there's all this circuitry and stuff. It was just an idea that I had that kinda "stuck," and then when I was told about *Get Smart*, I thought it'd fit. It was as simple as that.

TV was better to you than the movies were. Did you enjoy being on weekly series?

Oh, yes. I noticed that I started *breathing*, and that was a big difference—"Hey, I've held my breath for three years!" I loved having the opportunity to go in every week and try something new. And I was always doing that.

Do you recall playing a small part in an episode ["The Weird Tailor"] of the Boris Karloff TV series Thriller?

Oh, yeah! That was fun. I remember working on that opening scene where I arrive home drunk. Steve Ihnat helped me with that, trying to decide, rather than just walking in, *how* I would walk in and what I would do. We came up with the character Pan, seeing if coming in like Pan [the Greek deity] would work. I think there was a little statue of Pan in that big fancy hallway. But the best part of that whole thing was meeting Boris Karloff. What a sweetheart. Wonderful man.

On The Virginian, *you had a chance to work week after week with Lee J. Cobb, a real "actor's actor."*

So professional! I'm working with him on *The Virginian* for, oh, I don't know, a couple of months and, *man*, just to be able to work with this guy...! It gets so that when I'm around him, I'm tongue-tied. So after a few months, I decide that I should have a little conversation with him—I was still tongue-tied, and *maybe* there was *some*thing he would say that would help. So we're riding out to location, Jim Drury's in the front seat, Doug McClure is in the middle in the back seat, Lee is on the right and I'm on the left, and Jim and Doug know that I want to talk to Lee about something. So we get to the location, they get out, the driver gets out and I'm there with Lee, who's just lit up his ever-present cigar. He's just kind of relaxing, staring straight ahead. I said, "Lee, this ... uh ... I don't mean to ... I just thought ... thought *maybe* you might be able to shed a little light ... but maybe this has happened to you before but I ... uh ... uh ... uh.... I've noticed that when I, I, I'm around you that I'm tongue-tied. I just ... you know, I just admire your work as an actor and here we've been working for months and I find that I'm around you and I can't *talk*. And I just thought maybe there would be something that you could ... [*nervous laugh*] ... that you could *say* that would help ... would help..."

Gary and Jerrene Clarke (joined by little Ava and Natalie Clarke) in a recent pose.

He takes a long draw on the cigar ... lets the smoke curl out ... doesn't say anything. I wait for what seemed like two days and he doesn't say anything. I say, "Look, I don't want to intrude on your morning, Lee, but this is just something that has been kind of *eating* at me," and I stammer it all out a second time. Another draw on the cigar. More smoke curling out. Doesn't even look my way. And I'm watching him. I say, "Well, obviously this isn't a good time to talk. And you can go to Hell and kiss my butt for all I care!" I get out of the car, slam the door. I'm pissed off. And, ironically, virtually all my scenes are with Lee [*laughs*]!

So we're doing these scenes, and for me they're going well because I don't *give* a damn. I'm thinking, "Hey, Lee. Hey, big shot. Who *gives* a damn?" We're doing the scenes, and the director Virgil Vogel comes up to me at one point and he says, "I don't know what you're doin', Gary, but keep it up, it's *great*." The second-to-last scene of the day, or something like that, Lee's in his chair and he's again smoking his cigar and I'm pacing back and forth waiting for the cameras to get set up. Back and forth like a pacing lion. And I glance over at him a couple times and I catch this little glint in his eyes, this little gleam. It hit me like a ton of bricks—like the butt of a pistol on my forehead. I look at him and I say, "You son of a bitch—you did that on purpose. *You did it on purpose!*" And he laughs ... stands up ... picks me up ... hugs me ... and that was *it*. Imagine Lee J. Cobb going that far to help a fellow actor get past a little block! 'Cause, I mean, it took guts to do what he did—he didn't know how violent I was, or *could* have been. (Well, I *wasn't*, and he probably knew that.) So after that, I just *adored* the man.

You moved to Phoenix in 1987 and yet you continue to work in movies and TV.

And I've just been hired by the church I go to, North Phoenix Baptist Church, to write 13 60-second radio spots and 26 half-hour radio shows. They're getting ready to do some TV spots that I may be writing too—they want to promote the church. The 60-second radio spots are an opportunity to use my nine-year-old daughter Ava—named her after Ava Gardner, of course. She and I [began working together] when we did our version of "Who's on First?" for about a thousand people at the church. It used to be, "Here's Gary Clarke and his daughter!" *Now* it's, "Here's Ava Clarke and ... what's-his-name." [*Laughs*] She's great, so I'm using her on the radio spots. So, yes, there's still stuff here to do, and I would still love to do something on stage. And—I will. It's in my blood. It ain't ever goin' *any*where.

Gary Conway

A glorified bouncer was what I had been, and [starring in AIP movies] was a better job than that!

The expression "Monster Kids" has recently been coined to describe the legions of Baby Boomers who, as tykes and later teenagers, grew up on black-and-white monster fare on TV's *Shock Theater* and in the drive-ins and hardtops of the late 1950s and early '60s. But only one "kid" actor ever got to *play* a monster in a Hollywood movie of that era: Gary Conway, who at 19 starred as the "I" in producer Herman Cohen's lurid *I Was a Teenage Frankenstein* (1957). Assembled by Dr. Frankenstein (Whit Bissell) out of the body parts of dead teenagers, Conway's lonely, lovesick—but lethal—Frankenstein has become an iconic AIP movie monster with his crude putty face, bulging eye, fright wig and tight T-shirt. The movie itself, however, came nowhere near the quality of the one that inspired it, Cohen's earlier *I Was a Teenage Werewolf*, and Conway explains why in this recent interview.

Boston-born Conway (real name: Gareth Carmody) moved with his parents to Los Angeles while still a child and, years later, was majoring in art at UCLA when B-movie opportunities came knocking. Hair dyed blonde, he film-debuted in 1957 as a young warrior in Roger Corman's *The Saga of the Viking Women and Their Voyage to the Waters of the Great Sea Serpent*, a role which he feels led to his casting as Teenage Frankenstein. Serious about his art studies, he wasn't certain he wanted to be known for these movies (creating a screen name for this reason), although he knew that acting was an improvement on his current jobs, which included bouncer at local wrestling events.

After reprising the Teenage Frankenstein role in Cohen's *How to Make a Monster* (1958), Conway became active on TV, eventually co-starring in the detective series *Burke's Law* and top-lining the Irwin Allen sci-fi adventure *Land of the Giants*. He has written and produced action films of the 1970s–'80s, began a new sideline career as a painter, established the vineyard and winery Carmody McKnight (www.carmodymcknight.com) and authored a book on that experience (1995's *Art of the Vineyard*). With his wife, former Miss America Marian McKnight, he has also co-produced several independent motion pictures, including their most recent, *Woman's Story* (2004).

[No opening question.]

I always wanted to be an artist, but as a teenager the idea of making a living as an artist was something that I wasn't sure I could do. At that age, 16, 17, 18, it was really vague in my mind. I had so many things I *wanted* to be, from a writer to an artist to ... *every*thing. Being an actor crept in there, but it seemed a little bit distant to me at that point.

Did you act in school?

Yeah. In fact, I have to tell you something: I had a few times in my life where I sort of shone through as an actor, especially in Mount Vernon Junior High School in Los Angeles. They had an acting class by a man named Kerrian—I still remember him well. He was a marvelous teacher and *every*body in the school tried to get into that class. It was rather a legendary class in that school. When they did the plays, it was a big deal, because he had made so much out of that department. Well, of course, I tried *out* for it like everybody else, and I made the class, and then I starred in all the main plays. I found that I had a penchant for acting. When I got on the stage, I felt at home there.

I didn't quite follow it in high school, because in high school I really got into my painting. A little bit into athletics, and a *lot* into the painting. Really, I became a very fine artist, very young. I was given a scholarship—actually, I was given *three* scholarships, believe it or not. I got one to the Otis Art Institute of Los Angeles, one to Chouinard and one to Art Center. I took the one in Otis. To this day, I paint.

When I was in UCLA, I was cast in a play, *Volpone*, by the head of the theater department. Just about that time, too, I was cast in a film by Roger Corman [*Saga of the Viking Women*].

How did that happen?

I think a casting agent suggested me—they wanted somebody who was pretty buff. This casting agent had seen me around the UCLA campus, and he told me, "They're doing this film and perhaps you'd be good for it. Why don't you go see about it?" I went and they cast me.

Gareth Carmody adopted a *nom de screen* (Gary Conway) because he wasn't sure he wanted a lasting link to movies on the level of *I Was a Teenage Frankenstein* and *How to Make a Monster*.

Did you have to bleach your hair yourself to play that part?

No, they bleached it for me. Mainly we shot around Hollywood. There's actually a canyon in Hollywood, Bronson Canyon, and that's where we shot the cave scenes. We did some ocean stuff at, I think, Malibu. They got a boat out there and we were able to do the water action there. Then we went on a stage. Abby Dalton carried on from that to do a lot of interesting things. Betsy Jones-Moreland, I remember her well. She was a very nice person and we became really good friends. Susan Cabot was so beautiful, I remember, so strikingly beautiful. Beautiful and interesting. She stands out in my mind.

Brad Jackson—it was the strangest thing. He was an interesting looking guy, but he was so *odd*, there was something really "off" on him. I don't think he could have done much after that because he was almost ... zombie-like in this thing. I could tell there was a screw loose, even though I was young and naïve and hadn't come across that many "characters."

You had two fight scenes in the picture. Did you get any training beforehand, or did you just go in there and start mixing it up?

At that age, you can get with it pretty quickly. I later studied karate and other things, but at *that* point I was just a pretty good athlete and I was able to handle stuff like that. When we were out in Malibu and they had those big wooden boats, this image comes back to me: I remember I was almost *solely* pushing that thing out and pulling it in. I was *the one*, almost, to keep the whole thing afloat [*laughs*]. I was pretty strong, and young enough that I didn't have to worry about twisting my back, or whatever. Nowadays if I tried to do that, I'd have too many problems, the small of the back and the shoulder and all of that would prevent me.

So, no injuries for you at all on that movie? You were probably one of the few who didn't get hurt!

No, no injuries. That was a time in my life when I was ... you know ... bulletproof [*laughs*]!

Abby Dalton's sister had a role in the movie 'til she fell off a horse, and they instantly replaced her.

People did fall off horses. But I was tough. Let me tell ya, I was really tough then.

Do you have any recollection how much money you made doing Viking Women*?*

It was probably under $200 a week.

With Roger Corman, I'm sure *it was!*

I'm jumping ahead now, but I remember that later on, when I got a contract to Warner Bros., which was a big deal at that point, I was paid $250 a week. The first show I did there was *Hawaiian Eye*, and Bob Conrad took me aside and asked, "How much you getting?" I was a little embarrassed, I said, "Around 250 a week." He said, "*What*?!" And, he confessed at that point, that was his second year there at

Warners, and he and the whole cast *together* doing *Hawaiian Eye* were getting a thousand dollars a week.

Each?

No, all four of them, together! And that was the number one show in the country at the time. Can you imagine that?

So, coming in the door there at Warners, you were probably making as much as any of 'em.

That's right. That's why they got real pissed-off. In those days, at the start of [major-studio-produced] TV series, you really only did a series if you were under contract, and they already had you working at a set rate in your contract.

What did you think of Corman, your first movie director?

He was a very laid-back director and he didn't really *say* much, as I recall. He was just, "Move the camera here," "Move the camera there," "Do this," "Do that." We didn't deal with the guy very much, and I remember that being … odd.

Were you enjoying the experience?

For me, it was *such* an exciting experience. I'd never done a film. so everything about it was interesting. To me, most of these people were really professionals, and I was an amateur, of course. So I looked up to *every*body.

Were you having enough fun that you thought to yourself, "I could happily do some more of these"?

I had *great* fun, and I said, "Well, this is a *lot* better than the things I've been doing to make a living." I think it was right on its heels that these other opportunities [the Teenage monster movies] came up. And without me really thinking much about it, I sorta made a decision, "Well, I suppose I could at least do this and muddle through."

When did the name change to "Gary Conway" come in?

I was an art student, somewhat of a serious art student at that point. It occurred to me that maybe someday I would be teaching in a school, maybe I'd even be teaching at UCLA—I felt I wanted to do *some*thing rather seriously, and I would have to deal with the professors. When I did *I Was a Teenage Frankenstein*, the casting person or the producer, I can't remember who, but *some*body said, "Now, this name Gareth Carmody…?"—they made *some* kind of comment like that. And along *with* that, I was thinking, "You know, I probably will be uncomfortable to have a movie out called *Teenage Frankenstein*, and I'm trying to be a serious art student." I was still living with my parents, believe it or not.

Well, sure you would be, you were only like 19.

I remember discussing it with my dad, the idea of changing my name. By the way, you have to remember, in those days *every*body changed their names when they became an actor, it was almost automatic. I don't know why! You could have a *great* name, and they'd want to change it. I thought the AIP films were kind of off-brand, and so I didn't think I wanted to be known for them.

According to Herman Cohen, your parents were schoolteachers—
Right.

Cohen told me that your parents came to the set of Teenage Frankenstein, *he sat down with them and, in the discussion that day, your name was changed. He actually remembered being part of that decision-making process.*

That's very interesting ... that *could* very possibly be. Making that decision was not something I did right away, I *did* discuss it with my parents, I remember that very well because, after all, they gave me my name to begin with. My father was a poet and he didn't give me the name Gareth very casually—he loved that name, that was the name he thought a lot about. Although by *that* point [1957], everybody called me Gary, including my mother. The "Gareth" had sort of slipped away. So I didn't change the name Gary. The Conway was appropriate because it was still a family name. So in a way, it was sort of rescuing my family name, one that would have disappeared. And I still use the name Carmody now, especially when I paint, by the way. I actually am signing lots of works and graphics as Gary Carmody Conway, so now I have *both* sides [of the family represented]. It was complicated when I changed my name, I didn't realize all of the ramifications later in life.

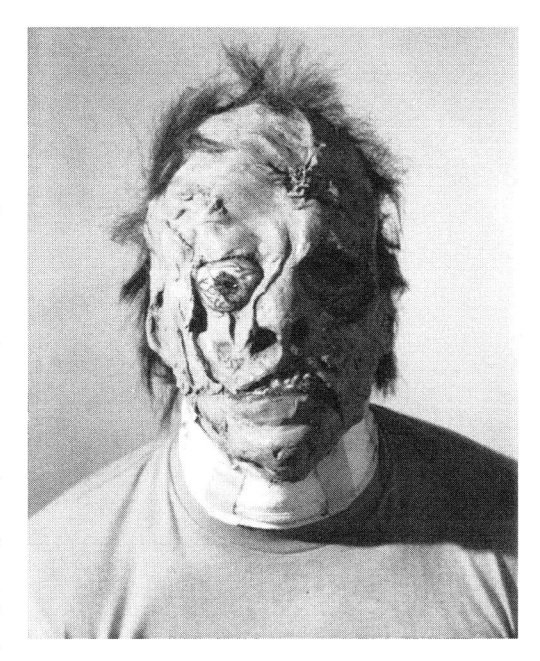

For perhaps all the wrong reasons, Philip Scheer's Teenage Frankenstein mask has become one of the most recognizable 1950s monster faces. (Photograph courtesy Academy Pictures.)

Teenage Frankenstein *was shot in October 1957. Were you still going to school then?*
Oh, yeah.

So you had to take a week or two off from school to make the movie, obviously.
Yeah, that's right, I think I did. I must have worked around my classes. It's funny that you bring that up, because I don't have a good memory of how I engineered the skipping of the classes. But I don't remember it being a big problem.

You got the part through an audition, or a whatever...?
I remember it being almost a *fait accompli*. I have a feeling that Herman Cohen must have seen rushes or something on that *Viking* film, and I think it was already a done deal by the time I went in there.

Boys' night out: Conway and Whit Bissell (in hat) are joined in a behind-the-scenes shot by producer Herman Cohen (left) and director Herbert L. Strock (with glasses). (Photograph courtesy Academy Pictures.)

Herb Strock, the director of Teenage Frankenstein, *told me, "I always thought Herman liked boys, and thus enjoyed casting males in films. Herman really seemed to enjoy asking males to strip down to their skivvies in auditions." Any comment on that?*

I don't remember the casting process, I think I just got the part. Now, later on, once I *got* the role, I remember he took me out for dinner, which I think is what people should *do*, just talk about the script and so on. I remember he drove me in his car. That was really the only time I ever had a, let's say, close encounter with him in any way. He was a totally cool guy as far as I concerned. He was fine. I remember this, though: I don't know whether he was bragging or *what* he was doing, but I remember him telling me, "You know, I'm the youngest member of the Producers Guild." At that time, he seemed like an older guy, so the concept of being the youngest guy in the Producers Guild was one that didn't overly impress me. But I suppose today, if I heard somebody say that, I would probably do a little doubletake.

At that moment in time, what Herman was doing was real independent filmmaking. You have to give these people a lot of credit, to have done what they did.

You said you weren't sure you wanted your real name on Teenage Frankenstein. *Well, on* Teenage Werewolf, *Herman must have felt the same way, a little embarrassed, because he used a pseudonym on the screenplay credit.*

Now *that's* interesting. Even *he* didn't want to be a part of it, eh? [*Laughs*] It's ridiculous, but only 'til recently, I was always a little bit ... I don't want to say "embarrassed," but...

Embarrassed about being in Teenage Frankenstein*?*
Yeah, or being in those offbeat films. But, as odd as they were, they have stood the test of time. That's one of the things that's interesting in life: The things that one thinks are so inane become the cult classics. They take on a certain aura, while the films that people back then thought were so wonderful ... later on, they're *not* that wonderful [*laughs*]. The films that never took themselves seriously take on a better glow, because they never were meant to *be* serious. There's a kind of truth in that.

The monster mask and makeup—how much of an ordeal was that?
It took a long time, that makeup. They put that mask on me, and then added stuff. I'd spend a long time in the chair, yeah, and I do remember that being a bit of an ordeal. It was a basic mask, so they didn't have to start from scratch every day. Then, once I got that mask on, the makeup man did what he had to do.

Was it hot? Could you see and hear?
It was all of the things you'd suspect: It was hot, it was uncomfortable, you would sweat under it. And when you have a mask on, you don't quite see the same way, your orientation isn't perfect. But, considering the role, a lot of that would not weigh against my interpretation of the part.

Was Herman Cohen on the set much?
I don't have any particular memories, nothing stands out, that he was there or not there or what. I don't remember him being around much, I think he was the kind of guy who didn't really intrude. I don't ever remember him coming up and saying, "Gary, why don't you do it *this* way?" He seemed to leave well enough alone, I guess, and let Strock just do his thing.

After *Teenage Frankenstein* and *How to Make a Monster*, my path and Herman Cohen's path never crossed again, and I think it would have been interesting if they had. So many, many times now, when I look back, I wish I had done certain things. Well, *that* [never again seeing Cohen] is a minor one. But I did *Burke's Law*, and *Burke's Law* was magical—every star of the '50s and '40s was on that show, and all the way back to Gloria Swanson. There was such an opportunity there to have dealt with those people more intimately. And even later on, I did a pilot for Link and Levinson, who had been writers on *Burke's Law*. They were doing a show that, as I think about it, was a predecessor to *Murder, She Wrote*. It had Bette Davis playing a detective and Doug McClure as her sidekick. I was also in it—I wasn't going to be in the series, but I had a big part in that pilot. What I recall about Bette Davis was that she had her trailer inside the sound stage, and for whatever reasons we just became very good friends. She had me in the trailer and I was always talking with her and sharing with her, and she actually was very open in many ways. I should

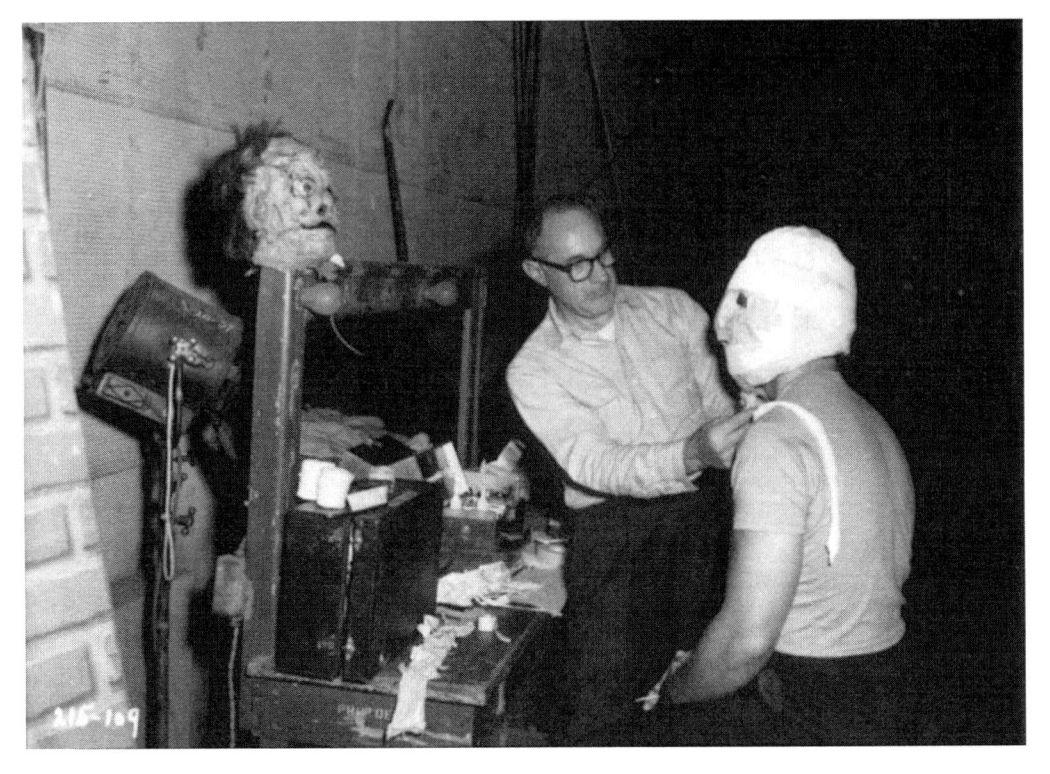

Behind-the-scenes on *Teenage Frankenstein* with Conway and makeup artist Philip Scheer. (Photograph courtesy Academy Pictures.)

have taken it a lot more seriously at the time. I guess you figure these people are gonna be around forever, or you'll be back, or whatever, but these are actually fleeting moments, and you don't recapture them that quickly. Often they *don't* come back. And to have had more contact with her or have maybe written something down at the time, would have been meaningful. I don't know *how* many calls I've had from people writing biographies on these stars, and sometimes I'm embarrassed to admit that I didn't get to know them that well. Well, I guess, as an actor, when you're young, you're just so damned self-centered, everything is about *you* at that point, and all of these other people are in your peripheral vision. So anyway, getting back to those Teenage Frankenstein films, that was the same thing: In recent years, while Herman Cohen was still around, I suppose it would have been interesting had we gone out for a drink and said, "Hey, remember the time…"

You would have enjoyed it, I think. He was a nice guy right to the end.

But we never did. That's what happens. Actually, your interview here is great because you're sharing *with* me a lot of things that I had no knowledge of. It's filling in some gaps.

You said in an earlier interview that you had a memory of Herman Cohen taking charge on the last scene of Teenage Frankenstein *directing-wise.*

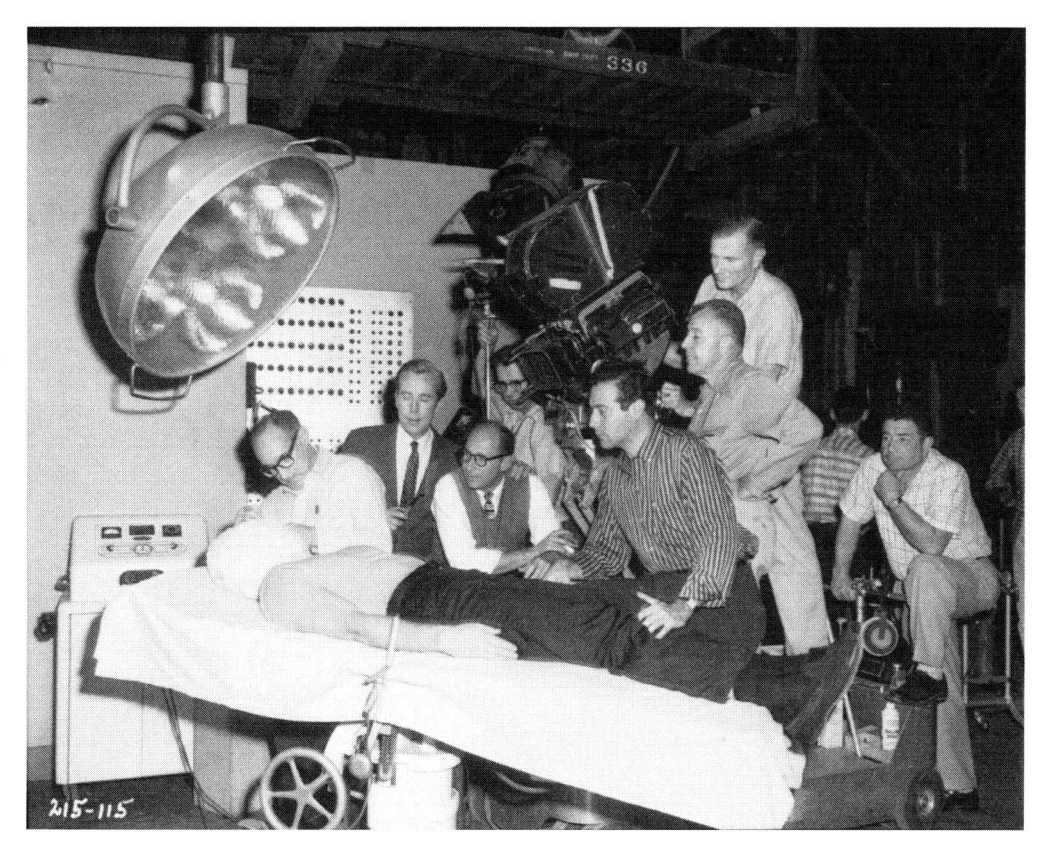

Conway (on table) gets some professional attention from makeup man Scheer as co-star Whit Bissell, director Herbert L. Strock, producer Herman Cohen et al. stand by. (Photograph courtesy Academy Pictures.)

Yes, and the film went to color for that last scene. I've never forgotten something that came out of his mouth that day, he said, "We'll put the last scene in color so when audiences leave, they'll think the whole *film* was in color."

That's brilliant!

Isn't that brilliant? That's always stayed with me because ... you know ... he just might have been right. This is what indie filmmaking's all about: inventiveness. Those were the early days for that.

Did you get much direction from Strock, or was he another Corman?

I think, frankly, in all of those situations, the director became (as they became in television) the traffic cop. Every director I ever worked with, essentially, was a traffic cop, having some knowledge of camera and just being sure that the lines were somewhat said. Later on, I conceived of what directing *should* be, which is much more a filmic interpretation of things—and *none* of that was in any place that I ever remembered seeing!

But certainly I don't remember anything *unpleasant* in my dealings with directors, and I suppose that's a very good thing. Because the director can ruin your life [*laughs*]—really, he can! Because you're very vulnerable, you're there at that moment, all eyes are upon you, and if he makes your life miserable, I don't think you'd ever forget that. Strock was pretty cool and competent and just did his thing. After all, what did he have to work with? He had only so-many days. You know what?, it wasn't even a matter of "days," it was *hours* [*laughs*]! And the budget—we don't even want to *know* about that! But for some crazy reason, *I Was a Teenage Werewolf* and *I Was a Teenage Frankenstein* have stayed on for*ever*, haven't they? Can *you* figure it out? What is the deal there?

I consider myself the most sophisticated film viewer/filmmaker/so on and so forth. *But*—those films, if they're on TV, I will *watch* them. Maybe it's the naïveté, but there's something ... something *wonderful* about them. You know, I *think* what it is, looking back, is that they were not full of themselves. When you think you're not doing anything so great, is often when some of the things you do become more interesting. As I started to say a minute ago, I think a lot of the major films the studios were then doing were just too impressed with themselves, "We're doing beautiful drama" and "This stuff will live on forever." Well, actually, when you go back and look at a lot of those movies, the acting is *really* bad, it's over the top, the filmmaking is very, very static, and the music never stops in the background, it's real schmaltzy. They really have nothing much to offer, looking back at them; really, most of them are ordinary. But somehow, *these* little odd guys [the cheapies] have their own quirkiness and character...

Their own little personalities.

You're right. And they stand out. The bigger studios *did* learn their lesson at one point, they realized, "You know, the films we oughta be making are these teenage movies and these other kinds of films!" They tried to do it, but of course with their budgets too big, and the honesty kinda leaves. By the way, when I look back at black-and-white films, *that* really is where some great photography comes in. I'm not saying *those* films, the Teenage Frankenstein films, had great photography [*laughs*], but the films that were done by some of the [bigger] studios—the film noirs, for instance. Black-and-white stands up a lot better than color in terms of creativity.

I often find the photography more artistic in a black-and-white movie than in a color.

Oh, sure. The lighting and so on. The black-and-white has a way of sort of simplifying the visual. There are a lot of reasons why black-and-white is interesting and lasting.

Do you remember shooting the scene in Teenage Frankenstein *where your head is in a birdcage on a table?*

I must have been under the table. Scenes like that are what makes these films so endearing [*laughs*]! Whatever had to be done, *we* had to do it—there were no computers at work here. If they wanted your head in a birdcage, man, you better be under the table and the birdcage had to be on your head. The computer wasn't gonna save you on that one!

The star of Teenage Frankenstein, *Whit Bissell?*

Just a nice, nice guy. And I remember his *skin*—isn't that odd? I remember him having very, very nice skin, very beautiful skin. *Why* that sticks in my mind, I have no idea!

Where did you see the picture for the first time?

Look, in those days, with those low-budget pictures, there was no such thing as having the "studio screening," the studio party, a premiere—I don't remember any of that. The films just got thrown out there. When *Teenage Frankenstein* came out, I believe I saw it at [AIP president] Jim Nicholson's house.

Your parents' reaction to these pictures?

Now that I'm a parent and *beyond*, I can understand how they probably were getting a big kick out of the whole thing. But I don't remember them making a great deal out of it.

When *I Was a Teenage Frankenstein* came out, it was an instant hit. One image I have is of me driving to Westwood, to UCLA and, I think it was at the Crest Theater, I see this long line, which was unusual… "What the *hell* is that long line?" I look up at the marquee and it says **I WAS A TEENAGE FRANKENSTEIN**… and I thought, "Oh, God…" It actually made me glad I changed my name. I mean, when I'm talking about it now, today, none of it makes any sense. It was my teenage mind at work.

What kinds of movies—if any—did you like back then?

The European films, Italian films, Soviet films were sorta hitting. Once I had this first sorta introduction to *avant garde* motion pictures, I considered *that* more the art form of motion pictures than Hollywood, which was basically making dramas at that point. Those [Hollywood dramas] were like the second rung. Then in this *third* rung were teenage movies and monster movies and sci-fi movies and all of them. Little did we all know that, all these many years later, that's all Hollywood *cares* about any more. *They* make all the sci-fi stuff, they make all the teenage stuff and all the teenage horror movies, and the little indies like myself—*we* go now and make the dramas! It's a topsy-turvy world. But, really, at that point, it was peculiar being in a teenage movie, especially something calling itself *I Was a Teenage Frankenstein*. In my mind, by its very name it relegated you to a third-class creative status, or third-class artist, or third-class *whatever*. Fortunately, it was not a porno film [*laughs*]—I guess that would have been the *fourth* rung down! A glorified bouncer was what I had been, and [starring in AIP movies] was a better job than that!

A bouncer at wrestling events.

Yes, in downtown L.A. The *official* job title you had was "usher," but it basically ended up being a bouncer at the wrestling matches *and* … even worse … the roller derbies. They all drank beer, all the guys in the audience, and everybody wanted to fight each other, and you had to part the sides constantly.

Groups of people wanted to fight other groups of people.

Oh, God, yes! What a job! You get there, you think you are going to be an usher, it's an afternoon job, you're barely getting paid, and you end up risking your life every afternoon [*laughs*]!

According to Herman Cohen, Michael Landon got kidded by his peers a lot about Teenage Werewolf, *and that's why he refused* How to Make a Monster. *Did you have to endure any kidding at all?*

You know, I think I did, but it was nothing that really bothered me. Remember, I had changed my name—that was the whole point, so I wouldn't *get* that. I remember when I was approached about doing *How to Make a Monster*, I really didn't want to do that, I thought, "I already did this *one* thing, and I'm gonna have to live with *that*..." Then they said, "Well, Michael Landon is going to be in it"—right to the very last minute, I was hearing that Michael Landon was gonna be in that film. By the way, I saw *Teenage Werewolf*, I thought that was a pretty good film.

It's a much better film than Teenage Frankenstein, *I think.*

The werewolf movies have always seemed better than Frankenstein movies, when you get right down to it. I think it has nothing to do with the particular people playing the Werewolf and Frankenstein or anything else, it's just that the werewolf is just *far* more captivating and eerie. Even as a kid, the werewolf movies were the ones that really got to me. I remember the Frankenstein movies never really scared me that much. I think, going back to Shelley, the Frankenstein films made a better social statement. And the lab scenes in every Frankenstein movie were memorable. Frankenstein movies, and there've been just a slew of them, are always interesting, that central character is always compelling, but in terms of having mystery and mood and so on, the werewolf is way out in front, the werewolf is better. And I definitely think *Teenage Werewolf* was a better film than *Teenage Frankenstein*. When I was at a recent convention, I was looking at an original poster for *Teenage Werewolf*, and that's a great little poster.

Yeah, even the poster is better than Teenage Frankenstein's *poster!*

Absolutely! The Werewolf character is more interesting, more captivating. I mean, Frankenstein is not a captivating character. He's a monster, he doesn't look good...

And, in a lot of Frankenstein movies, that's about it!

That's right. And the change from the nice-looking guy into the werewolf, with the hair and everything, is a unique visual moment in *any* film. To this day, everything that [monster moviemakers] have done, and they've done endless special effects, really hearkens back to that image, the image of that face turning into that monster. But the Frankenstein is static, you don't have that gimmick. When the Werewolf changes, it's an arresting moment in film—visually, very few moments compare to that. So that's what I think it was, I just think that the werewolf character's a more interesting character.

In *How to Make a Monster*'s closing reel (shot in color), mad makeup man Robert H. Harris stalks Garys Clarke and Conway in his burning museum.

I probably shouldn't tell you this but Boris Karloff, in a 1958 interview, talked about the low level that Frankenstein movies had sunk to—and he used Teenage Frankenstein *as an example!*

[*Laughs*] I don't blame him! But now, as time passes, they're *all* in the same "genre"!

The thing that surprises me about How to Make a Monster *is how little you're in that movie. Did school conflict?*

It may have. You're right, I'm in it very little. I think that's just the way it was in the script—which I think was written with Michael Landon in mind.

Were you still going to school in April 1958 when you did How to Make a Monster*?*

Yeah, I was. I think it was right after that that I went into the Army—that was very close on its heels. Incidentally, a funny thing struck me the other day: If somebody were to make *Teenage Frankenstein* today, it would be a *big* hit, a hundred million dollar movie. Wouldn't it be?

If it was made right, I think it would *stand an excellent chance.*

I think so. It would be fabulous. But, again, you have to look at those scripts and those films with a different eye, you have to look at them like you're looking at a comic book. The problem with some of those films, they're so simplistic. And we don't even want to begin looking at the holes in the script!

Yeah, we haven't got that much time!

You'd need a *lifetime*! But if all of those holes were filled in, then they probably wouldn't have their weird little charm. And they *are* captivating. *How to Make a Monster*, again, is a great title.

The fire scene in How to Make a Monster—*any memory?*

Vaguely. I don't have too many memories of that film. I remember showin' up, I remember being with Gary Clarke [the new Teenage Werewolf]. I don't think we were together that much, maybe once or twice. I'll tell you what I remember about it: that he wasn't Michael Landon. I thought Michael Landon was just really right for the part, and Gary Clarke did not strike me [as just right]. Nothing against Gary Clarke, 'cause I think he was an interesting guy, he was a good actor, he seemed to be real enough. But he just didn't look like Michael Landon, and I really associated Michael Landon with that part. So that was disconcerting to me, *not* having Michael playing it. At that point, Gary Clarke couldn't complain that way about *me*, because I had already been the Frankenstein [*laughs*].

And the two wacky makeup men, Robert H. Harris and Paul Brinegar?

Brinegar ended up being Wishbone on *Rawhide*. He became quite a fixture, didn't he? I remember him being a quirky guy. And Robert H. Harris was one of the consummate character actors.

What are you concentrating on today?

I am more focussed on my work than ever before in my life. I completed a film recently, *Woman's Story*, which I wrote and directed. I've written a lot of screenplays over the years, *Over the Top* [1987] and the *American Ninja* series and others. I became a sought-after writer. And I produced a few things. But with *Woman's Story* I decided to write and direct, and I'm proud of it. I have to tell you, I think it's a beautiful film. It's a different film than what Hollywood's making, and I think it's visually compelling and a film of substance.

I'm also involved in the distribution of the film, 'cause Hollywood again is making *Teenage Frankenstein*s—they're not interested in the dramas. And *I'm* not interested in making *Teenage Frankenstein* as a director. So, it's funny, I'm at the other side of the river at this point.

Merian C. Cooper

(From the Bob Burns Archive)

King Kong's a pretty interesting picture for me...

On Saturday night, November 28, 1964, in the projection room of the Hollywood Boulevard mansion of cinephile Bob Forbes, approximately 40 of Forbes' friends gathered for one of their regular 16mm screenings, this time a showing of *King Kong*. What made the occasion unique was that the guest of honor that evening was Merian C. Cooper, who co-wrote, co-produced and co-directed the 1933 fantasy-adventure classic.

Following a lengthy introduction made by Forbes, Cooper talked about *Kong* and a few of his other movies; after *Kong* was screened, he took questions from the audience, including some from his friend Frank Nugent, the *New York Times* movie critic turned Hollywood screenwriter (who died at age 57 less than six weeks later). Also in attendance were Cooper's wife, former actress Dorothy Jordan, and a worn armature of Mighty Joe Young (borrowed from RKO) that arrived in a wooden box marked KONG and was passed off as the King Kong armature.

Sci-fi/horror/fantasy film archivist Bob Burns, who attended the event, was given a copy of an audio recording of the night's festivities; this is the first time that a transcript of this presentation has appeared in print. Some of the factual errors made by Cooper and Forbes (the extent of Cooper's involvement with Western Airlines, the exact number of Max Steiner's Academy Award nominations, etc.) have *not* been corrected; keep in mind that these are people speaking informally, off the tops of their heads, in a party atmosphere. Cooper died in April 1973 at age 79.

—Tom Weaver

Bob Forbes: Tonight we have as our guest General Merian C. Cooper [*applause*], and also his film, and it really is literally *his film*, *King Kong*. And I must tell you something about General Cooper ... about some of his experiences. ...He is really a man who has led four lives in one. Those four lives are as a military leader; an explorer and author; a pioneer in commercial aviation; and as a motion picture producer and entrepreneur. We'll start in order and just take them as they appear in the list. As a military figure, he was the founder and organizer of the Kosciusko squadron—

Cooper: [*corrects the pronunciation of Kosciusko*]

Forbes: All right, thank you. I thought I messed that one up [*laughs*]!

Cooper: Everybody does!

Forbes: Everybody does? All right, then I *did*. The general was the founder and organizer of the Kosciusko Squadron in Poland after World War I, and there he was a fighter ace, an air ace. During the Second World War, General Cooper was chief of staff of the China Air Task Force, the famous Flying Tigers. In 1942 he was chief of staff of the Allied Air Forces in the Southwest Pacific … later chief of staff of the Fifth Air Forces in New Guinea. And now he's a brigadier general in the United States Air Force, retired.

Now, as an explorer and author, General Cooper traveled through the Orient, Africa and Persia, and the experiences from *these* travels, he wrote the books *Grass, The Sea Gypsy* and *Things Men Die For*. Now, it was during one of his adventurous travels that he met [his longtime colleague] Ernest Schoedsack, which eventually led him to Hollywood and the motion picture business.

As a man of business, Life Number Three, he turned his aviation knowledge to work for him by organizing Pan American World Airways *and* Western Airlines, which was then called the Western Air Express. After this … if *this* isn't enough [*laughs*]—he decided, "Well, I might as well go and try something else," and … he decided to enter the motion picture business. Actually, it was from the success of one of his exploring motion picture journeys that brought him to the motion picture business. …He is the recipient of the Academy of Motion Picture Arts and Sciences' special award for his innovations in the motion picture industry. And the award reads, and he showed it to me himself and it's actually there … I even went and checked it, and it's there [*laughs*]. "To Merian C. Cooper, for six times changing the course of the motion picture industry." And this means that six times General Cooper has been able to innovate something which has made all other people copy him, and these six times … if I'm not correct, I'm sure you'll correct me, General? [The six times were] *Grass* [1925], one of the first documentary films, setting a new technique which we know today as documentary film work. *The Four Feathers* [1929], the first use of actuality footage with Hollywood scenes … in other words, films shot in actuality situations, intercut with scenes from Hollywood studios. *King Kong*, our feature tonight, the first science fiction motion picture.

Cooper: If you can call it such! [*Laughs*] I know that's what they said.

Forbes: Well, I'm sure we'll get some comments from you on that. *Flying Down to Rio* [1933] … set a *tradition* in musicals, and certainly started one of the most interesting motion picture careers, Fred Astaire and Ginger Rogers.

MERIAN C. COOPER

Beauty and the Boss: *King Kong* star Fay Wray and producer-director Merian C. Cooper.

Cooper: The first *dance* scene, not the first musical.

Forbes: ...*La Cucaracha* [1934], the first [live action motion picture produced in its entirety in] three-color process, which was the forerunner of modern color photography. And, the last of the six, if *that* isn't enough, *This Is Cinerama* [1952], the founding of Cinerama, *with* Lowell Thomas. Now, outside of *this* [*laughs*], when General Cooper finished doing *this*, he said, "Well, I better get busy and do some more," so these are some of the pictures that he produced while he was head of production at RKO, or [a producer] at RKO: *Little Women* [1933], *The Lost Patrol* [1934], *The Last Days of Pompeii* [1935] ... these are films out of the '30s and I think you've seen them ... I know *I* have. Now, General Cooper then went into association with John Ford and produced pictures such as *The Fugitive* [1947], *Fort Apache* [1948], *3 Godfathers, She Wore a Yellow Ribbon, Mighty Joe Young* [1949], *Rio Grande* [1950], *The Quiet Man* [1952], *The Sun Shines Bright* [1953]. And co-produced, with Lowell Thomas of course, *This Is Cinerama* and *The Best of Cinerama* [1963], and produced on his own *The Searchers* [1956].

All right, now, the fifth life, or the fifth side of General Cooper is about ready to bud on the scene, and that is that he is now producing in association with the CBS Television Network, [a series] called *The Boilermakers*, and he told me the other day when I spoke to him that this will be the *seventh* innovation in the entertainment business [*laughs*], because he feels, and I kind of agree with him, after hearing about it, that it's really going to be an exciting series come next season. So, with *that*, that is the four lives of General Cooper, plus the fifth life which is yet to come, and it is indeed a pleasure... I really never knew that I would meet somebody like you, General Cooper, and if I could just have *one* life, I would be happy [*laughs*]! Let me introduce to you General Merian C. Cooper.

[*Applause*]

Cooper: Thank you! Of all the pictures he reeled out, the man who wrote some of the best of 'em is somewhere around here, hidin' over in the corner, Frank Nugent. [*Applause*] For one of those pictures, *The Quiet Man*, which Jack Ford directed, and deserved far more credit than me, I was just the producer [*laughs*], Nugent won Screen Writers Award for Best Comedy of the Year, '52 or '53. ...It was very interesting, that year I had the two biggest hits on Broadway playing just two blocks down, *This Is Cinerama*, which still holds the hard ticket run [the record] ... I think it's just over three years on Broadway ... and *The Quiet Man*, which was the biggest grosser of its year, of its kind of picture, by far. So I had 'em both at the same time. I used to stroll from one to the other [*laughs*]!

King Kong's a pretty interesting picture for me... What I really wanted to do was go to Africa and make a picture about gorillas. It was in the Depression, nobody wanted to back it, so I told 'em I'd make it right on the lot and that's how it was done [*laughs*]. This is one of the few pictures that I wrote the original story and directed and produced. My partner Schoedsack directed *part* of it. Edgar Wallace was put on the picture by the studio—he was a great fellow—for the use of his name. He unfortunately died, right up here on Elm Drive. ...In his [book] *My Hollywood Diary*, which is published, he gave me more credit than he did the rest of Hollywood [*laughs*], so I want to give *him* [a plug]!

The gal who actually wrote most of the dialogue had never written a script before. She was Schoedsack's wife, Ruth Rose. ...Ruth Rose, who'd never written a line, wrote most of the dialogue, together with me. I wrote a little of it, but she wrote most of it. Some of it I wrote right on the set ... I had to make up things.

…The French put out a whole book about this picture that somebody must have spent five years of research on, 'cause they found out what they said about it in Germany and … *every* place, all over the world. I used to read French quite well, but I don't as well as I did when I was young. But I read it well enough to understand they did a pretty good job. My wife *hated* it, and Ruth Rose was madder than sin, because they said we'd found a striptease dancer to write the script. They got her mixed up with … what's the other…

Audience: Gypsy Rose Lee!

Cooper: Gypsy Rose Lee [*laughs*]! So this was her first script. …The way a lot of this was done, which I'll tell you afterwards if you want to ask me any questions… There's no man inside of an ape suit, and so I had to go out and act the part of the ape and direct the rest of the picture—*most* of it. Schoedsack did quite a bit and I did quite a bit. We were partners on it. Actually, the hero of it for *me* was a fellow who died just year before last, died when I was making *The Best of Cinerama*, which I made in '62, wasn't it, honey? End of '62. And this is Willis O'Brien, who was a technical genius. Actually, in this picture, we had to "invent" 11 new processes. …There were a lot of technical things which I won't bore you with now, but… Let's look at the picture, this'll talk *for* me! [*Walks away, then comes back to the microphone:*] I want to say, I wrote the Old Arabian Proverb at the beginning [*laughs*].

Frank Nugent: Can I ask you one thing? How many times did the ape change size?

[*Groans from audience*]

Cooper: Oh, don't say this before the picture! [*Applause*] Let me say just one thing more. I was unmarried when I started this picture, and I was hunting for a girl for it. So Joel McCrea was a young actor whom I'd hired at a hundred and fifty bucks a week as I recall it, and he'd done a couple of parts, and we were going into the commissary and he said, "I know *just* the girl for you." He [introduced me] to a little budding star called Dorothy Jordan, who's sitting there [*indicates Jordan in the audience*]. And I said, "Uhn-uh. I want a blonde." So I hired Fay Wray, who was a brunette [*laughs*], I put a blonde wig on her—and married Dorothy Jordan [*laughs and applause*]!

[*At this point,* King Kong *is shown. After it ends and the applause dies down, Bob Forbes introduces Cooper a second time.*]

Forbes: We have the producer and the director here with us—

Cooper: Also the writer [*laughs*].

Forbes: And the writer, the creator, the man who made… Well, it's your picture all the way through. But I thought it would be very interesting if we had its *star* with us.

The Eighth Wonder of the World (and its number one movie monster), the immortal Kong.

Woman in Audience: Fay Wray??

Forbes: No, *not* Fay Wray. The fellow who was just shot off—

Woman in Audience: No!

Forbes [*indicating a wooden box marked KONG*]: So I went over to RKO, or Desilu, and I have here its star.

Woman in Audience: Bruce Cabot?

Forbes: He's been out for quite a few years, so… [*The box is opened and the* Mighty Joe Young *armature is revealed. Gasps and laughter from audience.*] And he doesn't look the best, but … I thought you would be interested in seeing it, I know *I* was. He's kind of old and dilapidated…

Voices from Audience: "Oh my gosh!," "Really?," "Oh, for heaven's sake," "My God," "This is for real??"

[*Forbes asks Cooper to stand beside it.*]

Woman in Audience: Beauty and the Beast! [*Laughs*]

Forbes: There must have been more than one.

Cooper: Six of 'em.

Woman in Audience: All different sizes?

Cooper: All exactly the same size. And all of 'em so you could move every joint. I did the same thing with sculpture that Disney does with cartoons. Every joint was moved … one frame at a time, everything. Like the fight with the allosaurus—remember, when the gal was up the tree? Well, I had to act out both Kong and the allosaurus for the sculptor. At the same time. So I had to act … I had two animators working on that, I had to act one side, then act the other, and then we repeated it. Any questions you want to ask? [*Remembering Nugent's pre-screening question:*] Yes, there were many different sizes [*laughs*]. Well, that was a big question: The ape was originally supposed to be a scale of 18 feet, 18 inches to 18 feet. This thing [the model] is *supposed* to be 18 inches high.

At Bob Forbes' *King Kong* screening party, Cooper keeps to himself the news that the armature passing as Kong is actually a Mighty Joe Young.

Forbes: The hair is gone off of it.

Cooper: Oh, yeah, sure ... that's pretty dilapidated. But I found that you had to vary the scale. Frank's the only man ever [picked up on that], though. I varied it all the way from about 80 feet to ... the lowest was 18. According to what it would play against. ...If you notice, I'm very careful to play human beings or windows or somethin' that gives size opposite [Kong]. Woods [jungle trees] won't give size, unless you plant the wood against a person first. ...I heard somebody say they liked the shot, there in the woods, where it has a lot of depth.

Forbes: Was that shot at the Arboretum?

Cooper: No, that was shot in a thing from *here* about over to *there* [*indicates some short distance*]. ...I invented a thing, which was not known as far as I know ... I didn't execute it, of course, I had some fine artists execute it. Called aerial perspective. ...I never heard the term, I invented the term so far as I know. I meant, by aerial perspective, just *depth*. So the actual depth in that was a little over four feet. ...I sprayed the glasses [planes of clear glass with jungle foliage painted on them, between the camera and the animated figures] at various distances back. I had three very skilled painters, one of 'em's still alive, he's painting very well now, he retired from this kind of work having made a great deal of money out of pictures and he's now living in Taos—isn't that the place in New Mexico? His name's [Mario] Larrinaga. He did the painting for me ... I don't know if any of you-all saw [*This Is*] *Cinerama*. In the first picture I bridged from country to country with paintings, and that was a real tough job of painting. ...It needed a fellow that could do this kind of work, and a skillful artist together to do it. I'll answer any questions about the picture you want.

Forbes: I'd like to ask one. You were telling me that one scene has been taken out.

Cooper: Yeah. Actually, I saw another, *little* scene out, but the only scene of importance I thought was the funniest scene in the picture. They took it out because they said it was too risqué or salacious or something. ...All audiences from six years old to 60 laughed. Right up there, when I had [Kong] beat his chest against the sun, and the girl's [Fay Wray] back here? Then he turns and picks her up and he sits down. Well, what I had him do was pick her clothes off. That's why she's so disrobed the next... She gets that disrobement [sic], and then I had him *tickle* her a little. And audiences *roared* [*laughs*]! That ran through '52. I don't know if it's in the negative—I've tried to locate the negative of it, I don't know where it is.

Woman in Audience: How long has it been since you've seen the film?

Cooper: Quite recently, as a matter of fact, about three months ago. Against the advice of my wife, who was giving a party for some aviation people. It was Jimmy Doolittle ... and Joe Doolittle, his wife; and then Johnny Allison, who was one of my best fighter pilots in China, he's a major general now, in the reserve, and he's vice-president of the Northrup Company here; and *his* wife, Penny Allison; and ... who was the other aviation fellow we had at the...?

Dorothy Jordan: Ted Curtis.

Cooper: Oh, and Ted Curtis—he had the same job in Europe as I had in the Pacific during the War. He was a major general too. And he brought Fay Wray. Fay's very

Side by side, the two King Kong armatures.

beautiful today—she's kept her age better than any human being I ever saw, she's a beauty. Looks just like her picture, has scarcely a wrinkle on her face. Only she's black-haired [*laughs*]—her natural color. ...I got a projector about like yours, I got my film from the same joint [you got yours] and I made a little speech, we had dinner, with all aviation people. I got up and said, "Now, I know this will bore the ladies, [I know the ladies are not] particularly interested in aviation. I'm going to discuss some pre–World War I techniques, and I have a few feet of film to illustrate..." [*Laughs*] And then I signaled to my son to start it, and ... remember the night scene where Bruce Cabot kisses Fay Wray? On deck? Well, it took 'em about ten seconds to realize [*laughs*], then they screamed and hollered, laughed. Fay hadn't seen it since 1930-something, '33, when it opened. Curtis hadn't seen it in '33. Allison had *never* seen it. The ladies really had a good time [*laughs*]!

Woman in Audience: How did you do the scene with the planes going 'round, when Kong is...

Cooper: Well, that's the only part I played—the pilot you see in the thing, that's me. I was the actual pilot. I shot that out in two ways. I got a fellow who's since been

Cooper secretary Zoe Porter was used to test the unfinished "life-sized" Kong hand.

killed, a fellow name of [Frank] Clarke, who was with Paul Mantz—[Mantz] did the flying for me in *This Is Cinerama*, flying across the country. I shot [the *Kong* airplane footage] out right where Lockheed Air Terminal is. ...And then I did a little bit of it in miniature, which *I* can tell readily but the audiences don't care. But *most* of that's real. Nearly *all* of that plane stuff is real.

Nugent: How did you get the effect of holding the girl in the hand?

Cooper: I'll tell ya. The only thing that was built on scale, and I decided to build 'em to a 45-foot scale, finally. I built one foot—you know, when you see a foot? I built one arm—one *hand*—full-scale. And I built one head. ...I had three men inside the head [*laughs*]. One ran the eyes, one ran the mouth and so forth.

Nugent: Actually, you *did* have a big head.

Cooper: Oh, yes! ...One of the great shots ... I did it with a method I haven't disclosed as yet [*laughs*]. You see the girl in the hand and see the body and King Kong, and you see him take the clothes off. Today, at our house, I have a secretary I'm sure Frank knows, named Zoe Porter. [She's been my secretary] for 30... [*To Jordan:*] How many years, honey? 30 years? Except during the War. [Back during the time of *King Kong*,] she was a little girl in the script department. I'd sent for a secretary and she came, 18 bucks a week or something. So I said, "Get up in that hand!" [to test the lifting mechanism] and she'd do it! So I had them lift this girl ... this was when there were no unions, no guilds [*laughs*]. No *any*thing! So it took her up about 12 feet. I said, "Look scared!," and she still says, "I've never been so scared in my life!" [*Laughs*]

[*Cooper on the jungle and lake sets:*] I shot the borders of the lake. I built that set on the big stage over at Pathé, which was afterwards the Selznick [Studio] and is now owned by Desilu. That's the one over in Culver City. That's where I did the building of the raft and those shots. And I did all that through the jungle, I shot on that same stage over there.

Nugent: How long did it take to shoot?

Cooper: I was actually photographing, Frank, directing it, whatever you want to call it ... it was either 11 months or 13 months, which *was* it, honey? And *usually* seven days a week—there were no rules then, no overtime [*laughs*]. I had the only bad cameraman strike ... at that time—50 percent pay cut [for] cameramen. That was rough days. That was the Depression.

Nugent: Tell me how much it cost and how much it made.

Cooper: I don't know how much it made, Frank, 'cause it's the only picture I ever made that I didn't own a piece of. [*A gasp from an audience member.*] And this was because I was on my honeymoon, and I had a fellow who died last year ... a great friend of mine, but he didn't know anything about the picture business. He signed my contract, which I had set, and listed the pictures [that Cooper would be getting a piece of]. Well, it was purely by accident, nobody meant to cheat me, but [*Kong* wasn't on the list]. I didn't know it for three years, because that same year I made *Flying Down to Rio* and the Katharine Hepburn version of *Little Women*, I was gettin' 20 or 30,000 dollars a week from all these various residuals [*laughs*]. So *I* thought I was gettin' it from *Kong*. When I discovered I wasn't—three years!—the company had been sold by Sarnoff, the fellow that runs NBC now. They owned RKO at that time. And sold it to Floyd Odlum. Dorothy and I knew the Odlums quite well. Where was their ranch, honey?

Jordan: Indio.

Cooper: Up near Indio. I went up and told him ... it wasn't on the contract. I said, "Well, I'm gonna *sue* you for it." He said, "Well, I just represent the stockholders..." This was the only time I ever wanted to sue anybody except [directing his comment to Frank Nugent] on *our* picture, *Quiet Man*, which we at least had, I dunno, five or six million stolen from us. *The Quiet Man*, I was really furious, because this was my own carelessness. *The Quiet Man*, I don't know how many millions, I think they stole at least six millions. The studio owned half and Jack Ford and I owned half ... I owned a quarter and he owned a quarter. We *knew* where they'd stolen it, so I wanted to sue for it. ...And Jack said, "I'm not gonna spend the next ten years of my life in courts and go to the Supreme Court...," so we settled it for $500,000 [*laughs*]. But, you know, we had the biggest hit of the year—the *two* biggest hits of the year. The other one I made more money off of, *This Is Cinerama*.

Nugent: Have you any idea how much *King Kong* has grossed, approximately?

Cooper: Yes, about $11,000,000.

Forbes: What did it cost to make?

Cooper: It cost about 425. 'Cause things were *very* cheap then. 425,000.

Forbes: General Cooper, you told me just before we ran the picture that *King Kong* grossed more on its *second* run—

Left: A giant bust of King Kong, built for closeup use in the movie, stood outside Grauman's Chinese Theatre when the movie made its Hollywood premiere. *Right:* That's *Kong* animator Willis H. O'Brien in the shot.

Cooper: Yes it did. ...Most of you—*all* of you are all too young to even have been *born*, I guess, during the Depression, but *King Kong* opened in New York the day the banks, every bank in America, closed. And *still* ran to capacity. It opened [at Radio City] Music Hall, this was its first picture, and I held the record up until World War II. I held the record, even though it opened when the banks closed. I held the record *after* World War II, quite a while afterwards, in Tokyo... I beat my own record with *This Is Cinerama*. I had the record, for *this* picture. But there was no money during the Depression—I mean, the tickets, you'd get in for a quarter. Now they pay three dollars for a seat, or a dollar and a half, or a dollar, [depending] on what kind of a theater it is. So I hope we don't have those rough times again.

[*On his first movies:*] I lived a very rough life in my younger days. The first picture I made [*Grass*] was a trek in Persia and the second I made in the jungles—

Forbes: That was *Grass*—

Cooper: Yeah, and *Chang* [1927] was the second. And *Four Feathers*, which was actually the first [time] anybody ever thought of shooting something in Africa and then shooting something here in Hollywood. I'd never *seen* Hollywood. First two pictures I made entirely on my own—I made 'em both with Schoedsack. He was the cameraman and I was the director, was the set-up.

Woman in Audience: But how did you happen to get interested in that stuff?

Cooper: Well, I wanted to be a geographer, and I studied the migrations of tribes at the American Geographical Society, 155th Street and Broadway. I worked there eight hours a night while I worked at *his* [Nugent's] alma mater, *The New York Times*... [*Correcting himself:*] Well, I went to *Times* in the night and the other place in the day. So a fellow named Isaiah Bowman, who afterwards became head of Johns Hopkins [University], was the director of the American Geographical and he taught me how to make maps and I wanted to be an explorer and I didn't know there wasn't any dough, and I borrowed $10,000... I made about a hundred a week with feature stories and everything else, and I figured it would take me 20 years to pay it back. And so I paid for 50,000 feet of film, two cameras and all my expenses for 14 months—*almost*. We had to win all the newsreel prizes—we made about $2000. Won *every one*, we didn't miss a one. All the still photography, didn't miss a one of *those*. And I sold six stories to *The National Geographic* and six to a magazine now defunct called *Asia* ... by cable, 'cause they trusted me. And that paid for us gettin' as far as Paris with our film. ...We'd never developed any film, but we didn't have enough money to hire the pros, so we took our year's work and developed it ourselves. Didn't lose a foot of film either [*laughs*]! And then came back, and I was gonna lecture with it. Schoedsack went down with a fella named Will Beebe, to the Galapagos Islands, as his photographer, and I started lecturin' at colleges with it. I was the big geographer. And [Paramount production executive] Jesse Lasky saw it and said, "I'd like to put it in a theater [as *Grass*]." He paid us so much money—I didn't know there was that much money in the world [*laughs*]. And then he said, "Can you make *another* one?" I said, "Yeah, sure." He said, "What?," and I said, "That was made 'cause there wasn't *enough* vegetation. I'll go to a jungle and make it 'cause ... what happens to people when there *is* too much vegetation." And *that* picture [*Chang*], there's a *real* funny story about that one. I know nothing about business to this day, I'm really the stupidest businessman ever lived. Schoedsack even knew less than I [*laughs*]! They had added about 800 feet to *Grass*, so they could get length, and I thought it hurt the picture terribly... So we cut *Chang* and then we burned up all the film ... all the rest of the negative, every foot of it! I didn't know anything about stock shots!

...We ran [*Chang*] for Jesse Lasky in New York at Paramount, up in his private projection room, and he was enthusiastic. That was when they used to get all the salesmen from all over the country, and about two weeks later *they* came in, so they ran it for them. [*Directed at Frank Nugent:*] This was the old Criterion Theater, you remember it?

Nugent: Mm-hmm.

Cooper: Mr. Nugent was a motion picture critic ... criticized many of my films! Not quite that early, though [*laughs*]. He was still in prep school or somethin'. [*Getting back to the story of the* Chang *screening:*] Lasky was very kind, he gave us $12,000 and 40 percent of the picture, 20 percent each. I thought it was 12,000 for *both* of us [to split]—I'd never made $6000 or ever hoped to, in my life. And I found out it was 12,000 *each*. ...I had a friend who flew with me, who was now a lawyer, and he said, "Now, these gentlemen running these motion picture [companies] know far more about it [than you do]. Anything they offer you for your 40 percent, refuse it." I said,

"Okay, I will." So Mr. Zukor [Paramount executive Adolph Zukor], who is still alive, still chairman of the board of Paramount, he was standing by the door, talking to Mr. Lasky. ...I heard Mr. Zukor say to Mr. Lasky, "And do the *boys* own any of this?," and Lasky sheepishly said, "Forty percent..." So the next day they sent for me, Mr. Zukor did, and said, "You know, distributing these pictures has lots of expenses..." [*Laughs*] "And we don't want to see you boys hurt. I'm gonna give you $25,000 for your share." And I said, "I don't want to hurt Paramount. I know you're fair, and maybe it'll never make it..." [*Cooper gets across that he wouldn't sell back their 40 percent of the picture.*] So, this went on for about a week, he finally got up to 100,000 each and I still refused. And we made a *lot* more than that [off the percentage]! ...Schoedsack was gonna kill me when I turned down 50,000 each! That's a lot of money!

Woman in Audience [*referring to dialogue from the movie*]: How did the only surviving native on the boat, blown out from the island, into the sea, and picked up by a Danish captain, and taken to Hong Kong—

Cooper: I never explained it.

Woman in Audience: How did he explain to the captain where the island was? What language did he use? [*Laughs*]

Cooper: Look, how can a thing be sillier than this: I had the damnedest argument with some of my people that were working with me. They said, "All right, you've socked [Kong] with the gas bomb. Now he's gonna appear in a show in New York..." [*At this point, there are too many interruptions and loud comments from the audience to hear everything Cooper says, but the gist is that it would be impossible for Denham to keep the presence of Kong in New York City a secret until his, Kong's, theatrical unveiling: If you took an animal that size into New York Harbor, he laughed, the news would be all over the radio and be the headline of every newspaper. Cooper said that his solution was to simply dissolve from the scene of Kong's capture on the island to the lighted Broadway sign KING KONG, THE EIGHTH WONDER OF THE WORLD.*]

Nugent: That was the same question I asked John Ford one time. I said, "You see all these Indian chases and they're chasing the stagecoach and they're firing at the guys in the seat and the guys in the seat are firing back at 'em. Why doesn't some Indian just kill the front horse?" [*Laughs*] Ford said, "'Cause that'll end the picture right there!"

Cooper: Well, this picture [*King Kong*] is full of those kind of holes. ...One thing that you may not know: Maxie Steiner, who wrote the music for this, wrote the music for *Little Women*, he's won, what?, five Academy Awards, 24 nominations. He *still* says this is his best musical score. You ought to hear this thing play *away* from the picture—this is a very fine score. It has a good love theme, the boy and girl; it has a great theme for the ape; it has about eight themes going.

Two distinctly different heads were made for Kong and they alternate throughout the movie—but most audiences never notice.

Forbes: By the way, there *is* a recording of it out.

Cooper: The only one *I've* heard, it's a very bad one. ...As you know, in *all* recordings, it's not only the music, it's how good the players are and *who's* directing it. A musical director is just as important as the fella directing the picture—maybe *more* so.

Nugent: What still amazes me is that it was about five reels before you saw [Kong].

Cooper: ...[Edgar] Wallace was dead, so I had to write the original story. [Credited screenwriter James] Creelman couldn't write it ... nice guy, but this wasn't his dish of tea. So I wrote the damn thing and I had to build up to [Kong] before you saw [him]. [RKO executive David O.] Selznick said, "...You ought to open right on the excitement. Open on Kong." And I said, "...You got three D's to make you believe in [Kong]: Distance, danger, difficulty." So I tried to make it [Kong's island home] seem far away, it was dangerous to get to, and difficult. By the time you get there, then maybe you believe that an 18-inch ape is...

Nugent: [*interrupts to say that modern TV producers would also introduce Kong right at the beginning.*]

Cooper: And they're *right*. Look, you got people in the theater, and I'm always prepared to bore people for 15 minutes if I can establish my characters. If you notice, in this thing [*King Kong*], I got my love story going, the boy fell in love with the girl, you understood who Denham was, you understood the character of the captain, I got 'em off. So once you got that *chase* going [*Cooper now begins rapping on a table to emphasize the italicized words*], I never had to *stop* to explain a *single damn thing.* 'Cause you *understood* it. I spent not 15 minutes, I spent nearly 40 minutes explaining this, and this is why it's so bad on television, they cut most of that. You jump right into danger and you don't believe [in Kong]. [*Cooper reiterates that TV producers would be correct to bring Kong in sooner, adding:*] In a theater, you paid your buck, you'll stay 15 minutes. TV…

Man in Audience: You turn it off.

Cooper: Thirty seconds to a minute … bing [you turn it off]. I'm that way myself! [*Talking about his new TV venture:*] It's a Western. And it's a new form.

Woman in Audience: I bet it is, knowing you!

Cooper: Yeah, it is—I'm gonna revolutionize the television business. …If I can cast it. I haven't got the foggiest idea how to cast one part in this. I don't know how to cast it. I need a Douglas Fairbanks, Sr., at age 21 or 23, or an Errol Flynn at age 23. I don't know anybody *like* that.

Forbes: Maybe you could do it by miniature! [*Huge laughter*]

Robert Dix

> *I certainly had a chance to expand horizons with the independents. I not only worked as an actor, I co-authored screenplays, I either held the sound boom or helped pack the prop truck or … you name it!*

In the acting world, Robert Dix never attained the heights that his more famous father Richard Dix did; Richard (1894–1949), the strong, silent, square-jawed type in scores of films of the 1920s and '30s, was among the most popular actors of his day, and an Oscar nominee for his starring performance in the epic Western *Cimarron*, 1931's Best Picture winner. Following in his dad's footsteps, Robert did, however, carve out a Hollywood career of his own, one that has taken a number of intriguing detours and side roads. In addition to his acting roles, he has worked behind-the-scenes as a writer and producer on projects that ranged perhaps as far as projects *can* range: from the exploitative 1969 Western *Five Bloody Graves* (ad line: "A Vicious and Sensuous Orgy of Slaughter!") to his own religious-themed TV series!

Born in 1935, Robert (and twin brother Richard Jr.) grew up in the lap of Hollywood luxury as their father continued to work in Westerns and B-grade suspense films (among them Val Lewton's *The Ghost Ship* and Columbia's eerie *Whistler* series). In the wake of his dad's death and battles with his new stepfather, Robert left home while still in his mid-teens, working a variety of odd jobs and then acting with an upstate New York theater group. At age 18, he became an MGM contract player; later, working as a freelancer, he made a number of TV appearances and additional films and worked with such colorful low-budgeteers as Richard Cunha, Arch Hall, Sr., and Independent International's Sam Sherman and Al Adamson.

Long-married to actress Darlene Lucht, a one-time Miss Milwaukee, Robert has recently paid tribute to father Richard by helping to start a website in his honor, www.richarddix.com.

Do you happen to know how long "the acting bug" has been in your family?
My dad Ernest Carlton Brimmer, a.k.a. Richard Dix, was the first family

member who became involved in the entertainment business as such. Dad was from St. Paul, Minnesota, and my grandpa, *his* father, disowned Dad when he, Dad, decided to get in the theater. In those days, y'know, acting was worse than prostitution [*laughs*]! Grandpa said, "You're not takin' *my* good name into the theater!" So Dad took the name Dix from his buddy Ed Dix, who had been drowned trying to save a woman's life—Ed Dix had a lifeguard job in the summer. Dad just took the name Dix and tacked "Richard" on the front end of it and went to New York ... where there were some severe hungry times. He used to tell a story about taking the cardboard out of the shirts from the Chinese laundry and cutting it up and putting it in the soles of his worn-out shoes! So he had some difficult times, but opening night of some play whose title I can't remember, the leading man became ill with pneumonia and Dad stepped on as the understudy, and *boom*, he became a star of stage at that point.

The grandfather who disowned your dad—did he live long enough to see your dad become a star?

Yeah. It's kind of an interesting story: What happened was, Dad got that break in New York, and then he went with a road company out to Los Angeles. I'll make a long story short...

Don't make it too short, if it's interesting!

Well, in those days, there was a theater in Los Angeles called the Morosco, and they had what were called matinee idols. And these were guys like my dad and *his* friend Preston Foster. The two of 'em were referred to as matinee idols—they got that phrase from the fact that housewives would come and watch the plays in the afternoons. Dad was performing at the Morosco and a guy named Jesse Lasky came backstage after one of Dad's performances and said, "Rich, have you ever thought of being in movies?" My dad's answer was, "How much does it *pay*?" Lasky told him, and my dad said, "I'm now in the movies!" [*Laughs*]

Following in the footsteps of his famous actor-father Richard Dix, Robert Dix began his movie career in the early 1950s.

You were leading up to what your grandfather eventually thought of your dad's stardom.

The bottom line was, Grandpa "re-owned" him when Dad became a star [*laughs*]. Of course, *I* wasn't in the world at that time, but I know that Dad bought Grandpa Brimmer a home in Southern California, right in the Hollywood city limits. Then, later, Grandpa's last days were spent at our ranch in Topanga Canyon—Dad had 165 acres there.

Sounds very nice!
 In 1926, Dad and his chauffeur hiked up to the top of a mountain there and looked around, and Dad bought that property and blasted off the top of the mountain and built a beautiful place he called The Haven. Ol' Grandpa Brimmer used to sit up there on a bench for hours, looking out across the Santa Monica Bay and all of L.A. From the top of that mountain, you could almost see a total 360 of the Pacific Ocean, Los Angeles, the San Fernando Valley and that whole area.

Grandpa Brimmer went from disowning your dad to living in movieland…!
 That's correct! Did you ever watch *Everybody Loves Raymond*, the television series? The father in there, Frank, he's just cantankerous. And I think that probably describes Grandpa Brimmer!

And, needless to say, you decided at some point to follow in your dad's footsteps.
 That's right. I had a twin brother, Richard, Jr.—we lost him in a logging accident back in the early '50s. We were identical twins, just ten minutes apart. Even my mother sometimes called me Richard and him Robert [*laughs*]. He always had his heart set on being a doctor, and I always wanted to become involved in the profession my father chose. So I started very young, at 11 years of age, in school plays and little community theater and things like that. As a matter of fact, my twin brother and I did *The Prince and the Pauper* for a community theater in Santa Monica. We were 11, 12 years old, something like that. Afterwards, my dad came to us and said to my brother, "I'm glad you decided you wanted to be a doctor!", and he said to me, "Son, it looks like you got it in your blood." From that point forward, I at least had that encouragement along the line.

Were you the Prince or the Pauper in the play?
 I played the Pauper, and my twin brother played the Prince.

Were either of you in any movies as kids?
 No. We were very much insulated from the motion picture business as children. Dad tried to keep his family life and his business life *totally* separate. There were a few [industry people] that were invited into our Beverly Hills home, which he build in 1934 on two and a half acres there. (Just shortly after he married my mom, they built this home which was essentially our family home for most of my young years.) It was there that, once in a while, a few of the people in the movie business would come in: John Wayne would come to the home, several of the directors that Dad had become close friends with. But very few. It was essentially family and friends.

Friends who weren't in the movie business.
 Correct.

This is the '40s.
 That's correct. I was born in 1935, so I was anywhere from five to ten years old.

I remember vaguely these people coming to the home and playing bridge and having parties and so forth. As I say, a very small number of the people that Dad worked with at Paramount or RKO or within the industry itself, were ever *in* our home. He was quite adamant about keeping the family life separate from his professional life.

Was your mom ever an actress?

No, my mom came from a whole 'nother world. My mother was educated as a schoolteacher, she had her Master's in English, and she was college-educated. My father was not—he never got any farther than the eighth grade. But he was *self*-educated—we had a library full of books and he had read every *one* of 'em. And he was fascinated with the world of academia, and so, *in the home,* Mom and her sorority sister friends and their husbands were more of the nucleus of their immediate friends than any of Dad's [industry friends].

Were any of his wives actresses?

Well, Dad had two. The first marriage was *very* short and she was a model from San Francisco. That lasted only six months. And he'd waited 'til late in life before he even took that first plunge. That wasn't too far behind him before he met my mother, and they were married, and that was the love of *his* life. They stayed married until he passed on. How they got together was, my mother was *hired* by my father, as a script supervisor—in order to corral her, basically [*laughs*].

You think your dad hired your mom as a script supervisor because he had his eye on her?

Oh, no question about it! In fact, I'll tell you a little aside: My dad in those days had a little business. I don't know if it was a tax write-off or *what* it was, but it was import-export and my Uncle Jack McGowan, he was the front guy. In those days, Depression days, they put a little ad in the newspaper and over 500 girls showed up for a secretarial job. It ended up between my mom and another gal, and finally, in this last interview, Uncle Jack took Mom into the back room, where she met Mr. Brimmer [Richard Dix's real name]. My dad said to her, "Miss Webster, both you and this other young lady are equally qualified for this job. But *she* has an invalid mother to support, and I believe that she should have the job." My mother said, "Well, I agree with you, Mr. Brimmer. Thank you for your time," and she started to go. And he said, "Well, you know, my name *is* Brimmer, but I work in the movie business. My name is Richard Dix." She said, "Oh, that's nice"—she'd never heard of him [*laughs*]. Even though he was in the Top Ten at the box office at that time! But she had been so busy with her academic studies that she didn't know who he was. "Nice meeting you, Mr. Dix," and she left. The way Uncle Jack used to tell the story, Dad then stuck his head out the window and watched her walking down the street and said to Uncle Jack, "Now *there* goes a woman!"

So he called her the next day and he said, "I just happened to have this job opening at the studio, as a script supervisor. Do you think you can handle that job?" My mother didn't know anything *about* being a script supervisor, but was willing to try. So she came on the Paramount lot and they got her settled. I don't know what the time frame was, but one day he came up to her and he said, "Miss Webster,

Richard and Virginia Dix (Robert's parents) at their ranch.

would you care to have lunch with me?"—and she said, "No. No, I never mix business with pleasure." So the next day, he came in and he said, "Miss Webster, would you bring your pencil and your pad? I have a letter to dictate to you at lunch." [*Laughs*] The second no he got was when he asked her to marry him. He said, "Well, why *won't* you marry me?," and she said, "Because you didn't say you love me." He said [*with annoyance*], "Well, would I ask you to *marry* me if I didn't *love* you?!" But eventually he convinced her, and later, I came to be.

And when you were growing up, the family had two homes, Beverly Hills and the ranch.
That's correct. It was really idyllic. All the stories you've heard about the old Hollywood *are* essentially true: We were a close community, and people were making big bucks. My dad was making over a half a million dollars a year as a contract actor to Paramount, and that was when the daily wage was, what?, a dollar an hour. If *that*.

If you could get *a job.*
Exactly! So it was the two homes and servants, the 16-room Beverly Hills house had orange groves in front and servants' quarters and an apartment over the six-car garage for the chauffeur.

Did you visit the sets of many of your dad's movies?
Not on many occasions. One that comes to mind is the one where he played Wild Bill Hickok, *Badlands of Dakota* [1941]. And a movie called *Tombstone, the Town Too Tough to Die* [1942], I remember visiting the set. But that was the exception rather than the rule. That was a very special occasion, to go visit Dad when he was working.

Well, did the family at least go out to see his movies?
On occasion, yes, we would. But my mother didn't really like to watch my father kiss another woman on the screen, and there were scenes where he *was* romantically involved with his leading ladies. So that was one of the reasons why we all didn't go see some of his movies [*laughs*]! Incidentally, when we would go to the movies, his way of "wearing a mask" was, he'd pull his handkerchief out, like he was blowing his nose. He'd always have that handkerchief over his face—

In order to get in and out of the theater without people recognizing him?
That's right, that was one of his tricks, so that the people wouldn't be hounding him in a public place.

What's your favorite among his movies?
Man of Conquest [1939], the story of Gen. Sam Houston. I enjoyed Dad's *Cimarron*, too, of course—that's a classic which won the Academy Award as a movie—but my favorite was *Man of Conquest*. It was historically true, factual, and my father did an excellent job portraying the many faces of Gen. Sam Houston. There's a scene where Houston, played by Dad, was retreating, retreating, retreating from Santa Ana; Houston and his ragtag bunch of Texans were outnumbered something like ten-to-one. Even his own men were to the point where they were saying Houston was chicken. But when Santa Ana and the Mexicans were at the bottom of a hill, and having their siesta, and the Sun was behind Houston, he gave a very famous speech where he ended by saying, "Remember the Alamo!" and he pulled his sword

Robert (right) and Richard Dix, Jr. (left), visit their dad (playing Wild Bill Hickok) during the shooting of Universal's *Badlands of Dakota*.

out and got on his white horse and they all came down on Santa Ana's army while they were sleeping. And kicked the *shit* out of them [*laughs*]! That was a very memorable scene. It was that scene that inspired "Duke" Wayne to make the movie *The Alamo* [1960].

Sam Sherman, who is my friend at the Independent International distribution company, has recently, through some associates, digitally enhanced and created better color for the negative of *Man of Conquest*, and there's talk of having another world premiere *in* Houston, Texas, as they did in 1939. I don't know how far along the trail that is, but that *is* a work in progress.

Where did you catch up with your dad's movies over the years? On TV, I assume?

Mainly TV, but there have been fans and friends out there who periodically still send something they've copied off of Turner Classic Movies. I think that's been my major source.

Your dad played a different character in each entry of the Whistler *series of the 1940s.*

That's where his stage training came out. A lot of people in the movie business, even to this day, they get stereotyped into one particular personality-type character, and they can't get out of it or *won't* get out of it. But Dad had the ability not only to do very serious dramatic things, *like* the Whistlers, but also comedy. I have some of his silent films, made back in the late teens–early '20s, and there's one called *The Lucky Devil* [1925] that's really cute situation comedy stuff.

Richard Dix stopped making movies a year or two before he passed away. Was he sick, was that why he stopped?

Yeah. The first heart attack came, I think, in 1946, and he didn't pass on 'til '49. That heart attack took place at our ranch in Topanga Canyon. He and I were playing tennis—he *always* whipped my butt [*laughs*]—but this particular time I could tell he wasn't feeling well. I asked him, "What's wrong?" and he said, "Son, I feel like I swallowed a *piano*..." I've never forgotten *that* line! That was his first heart attack. He had a clot around his heart, and never totally recovered. Well, mainly because he wouldn't slow down. He was used to leading a very active life. The doctors were all saying, "You gotta take it easy, Rich," but he wouldn't take it easy.

Later on, I had a conflict with my mother's second husband, a guy named Walter Van de Kamp [of the famous Van de Kamp bakeries]. Walter and I *just* did not get along. I felt that he was making moves on my mother while my father was still ill and still with us, and it really created a very severe wall between us. And as a 14-year-old kid at the time, I went out of my way to make Van de Kamp's life miserable!

[Laughs] Good for you!

It got to a point where I was eighty-sixed out of the house. We had a fistfight, actually, and I broke his nose [*laughs*].

How was this bum able to be hitting on your mom before your dad had even passed? Was he a friend of theirs?

He was an acquaintance of theirs, my mom and dad had played bridge with him on a few occasions. We ended up on a tour in Europe together—I had never met him before the tour. It was summer, say June of '49, we were 14, my twin brother and myself, and we went with Mom and Dad to Europe with a tour. Van de Kamp was also part of that tour group. My father's heart started bothering him again and he left the tour. I think we were in Lake Como, way up in the Alps, and Dad got to not feeling well. So he left us with the tour in Lake Como and he went down to the Italian Riviera, and eventually we connected back up again when we got to the Italian Riviera. But it was during that time that I saw Van de Kamp making his move. Dad was ill and couldn't defend his interests, so naturally, as his son, in my clumsy fashion I jumped in … and made Van de Kamp's life miserable [*laughs*].

Before and after the marriage.

Yeah!

Did your brother also have trouble with him?

No, he managed to, at least on the surface, get along with Walter Van de Kamp.

But I never made any bones about it. And, frankly, Walter didn't make any bones about the fact he didn't like *me*, because I wouldn't knuckle under to his control issues.

After I broke his nose [*laughs*], I ended up sleeping in the back of a delivery truck in Beverly Hills. There was a friend of my mother's named Homer who had a market on Beverly Drive in Beverly Hills, and through my mom's connection I got this job as a grocery delivery guy. At night I'd just throw my mattress in the back of that panel truck and that's where I lived for a while. I had friends who'd allow me to use their toilet facilities and so on. Then eventually, at about 15, with my mother's help, I *did* get a little apartment. So I went from the one extreme to the other real quickly.

From riches to rags.

It's a tremendous test in life if you go from *that* kind of early life of affluence to being a working stiff. As a kid, you would, as *any* kid would, just take [the ritzy lifestyle] for granted, "This is the way it *is*." The crash that comes after that is a very severe one. And it's not just a one-time deal, it goes on throughout your life until finally, with God's help, you land on your feet and are able to see life in the light of reality. As you know, Tom, Hollywood production people are illusionists [*laughs*], they create a world that is very *un*real. And, I don't care *how* hard you try to keep it from happening, it slops over into the personal lives of everybody involved.

The atmosphere of unreality does.

Yes, sir. And it's lethal stuff. I mean, I don't know how many hundreds, or thousands, of young people I've met around the world, they think they would have it *made* if they would have fame. They just figure that fortune follows. Not necessarily so! I've known a lot of famous people who were right next to me in the unemployment line in Hollywood [*laughs*]. It's a *lie*, it's a misnomer, and it really is dangerous, because it sets an unreal standard for people to think that if they could become *famous*, if they could just have a television series, that their lives would change. How many actors do *you* know that had a series, and what happened to 'em? They're selling real estate in Orange County [*laughs*]! So it's a very difficult, ongoing culture shock thing for somebody like myself, who came from that very affluent background, to go on to become a workaday stiff like everybody else.

How long was your mom married to Van de Kamp?

That marriage lasted 25 years.

Starting not long after your dad passed.

Not even a year after. During all that time that Van de Kamp was my stepfather, I never went back into the family home. I used to meet my mother on Monday nights for dinner, that was our routine. But I never was allowed back in the home—and didn't have any desire to go into it. Until Van de Kamp died, that was the rule we lived by.

You mentioned before that your brother was killed in a logging accident.

Where he lost his life was in a place called Klamath Falls, Oregon, which is right on the border between California and Oregon. He was working at a logging camp in the summertime, to make some extra money; his job was to unload the trees as they came from the woods. He unloaded them from the flatbed trucks into the pond, and from there they floated 'em into the mill. There was an accident, and we lost him.

I found an old article on you that said that, right up until the time just before your dad passed away, he was telling you, about your plans of becoming an actor, "Be sure ... be sure..."

That is correct. He was concerned because the actor's life can be chicken or feathers. But he also had acknowledged that I seemed to have, even as a young fella, a talent in that direction. I mentioned to you my brother and I doing *The Prince and the Pauper*. So he didn't discourage me, but he *did* warn me, yes.

After my father passed on, my mother told me that she had heard from a friend about the National Academy of Theater Arts at Pleasantville, New York, and asked me if I was interested in going. I said yes. So from age 16 on, that became my chosen walk of life. I went to the National Academy and did that "straw hat circuit" thing. The National Academy was kind of modeled after the Royal Academy in London and the lady who ran it was quite the disciplinarian, and we really kept our noses to the grindstone as young performers. I would be studying a play to do next week, I'd be doing a play *this* week and trying to forget one from *last* week [*laughs*]! If I could pass anything on [to wannabe actors], this would be one of the *important* things I would pass on: Get that stage experience. I've seen guys that have just come in through the film industry, and they really don't have any conception of the audience. Which is what you learn by physically working on a stage with Acts I, II and III. I would highly recommend that to *any* young person interested in being in the entertainment business as a performing artist today: Try and get some stage experience.

At this school, you learned and *you appeared in plays.*

That's correct. We had Shakespearean classes, and we had a play every night of the week and sometimes twice on Sundays. It was a very busy agenda, but the training was invaluable for my work as a professional later.

One thing I really would like to say in this interview is, after the loss of my father and the loss of my twin brother, I was catapulted into a "search for the meaning of life" kind of thing. And one of the fortunate things that the National Academy of Theater Arts did for me was to make me a seeker of truth. When you portray a character, you have to realize that no human being is *all* good, you have to see the good as well as the bad and so forth. You have to remember not to carry a prejudgment or a prejudice into investigating anything. And after the loss of my father and my brother, I was on a path of search which ultimately led me to the Baha'i faith. That really was a pivotal point in my young life. The Baha'i writings are universal and non-denominational, and the kind of information found in them became very important to me. Baha'i faith gave me direction that I wouldn't have had otherwise. If I hadn't had that direction in those days, I don't have the foggiest idea if I'd even still be *alive* today. There are so many influences in our society—think of the young people today, put yourself in *their* boots, with all the various different appetites and influences that are out there. You need some direction to keep you on a path that you *know* will lead you to your goal. Sometimes that path may get fogged in. But if you're on a ship in the sea of life, and you've got your compass set, you *know* you're going to reach port, no matter how rough those seas get. [Baha'i] was very definitely a turning point in my life, it literally saved my life, and I just want to go on record with that. Sure, I had the rough seas since then, but with*out* it, I would have been a bird with one wing.

You first got involved with it back in the '50s?
 I declared myself as a Baha'i April 26, 1956. Today I am the Monitor of the Seeker Response System for the Baha'i community where we live. When there are seekers interested in knowing more about the Baha'i World Faith in our area, I respond to them with a Welcome Letter and guidance to our Fireside gatherings. Recently my wife Darlene and I produced an interview program we called *Impressions* for access TV. We had a cross-section of people, from a professor at the local university to the maintenance man at our condo complex, speaking about their life experiences and relating them to their spiritual development. I believe serving our fellow man gives us purpose in life, whether it's in the entertainment business or helping someone to gain an understanding of their quest for greater knowledge of what life is all about. I have always tried to serve at some level, and it's a service I enjoy.

How did you get your foot in the door at MGM?
 At 18, through a friend—the son of the mayor of Beverly Hills, a kid that I grew up with—I got an interview test at MGM Studios and they signed me to a contract. At 18 years of age! This was at the tail end of what I refer to as "the Old Hollywood days" when the studios would slowly groom their contract players. They'd start by putting you in a movie where you'd say two or three lines, if *that*. You'd learn the craft of being an actor, being on a set, learning how to hit your mark and all the various different *mechanics* of the business. I worked my way up from the one- and two-liners in the MGM movies that I did while I was there, from 1954 through '56.

What was your first MGM picture?
 I think it was a movie called *Athena* [1954]. That was with Janie Powell and Debbie Reynolds and a bunch of health nuts and bodybuilders—a musical comedy. I think I had two little lines in it. Another early one for me there was *The Glass Slipper* [1955]—that was the first time I ever had to get dressed up for a period piece, with the wig and the whole wardrobe. Then there was *The King's Thief* [1955] with Cornel Wilde and *Hit the Deck* [1955] with Frank Sinatra, another musical. One great experience, one that I remember with a great deal of fond nostalgia, is that in those days at the studio, you had to attend classes—it was part of being a contract

player. You had diction classes, you had fencing classes, you had singing classes. Three times a week, I had to attend my singing class. Of course I couldn't sing, not even in the shower [*laughs*]. But I would go, and before me was Janie Powell, and after me was Howard Keel. So I would go early and stay late because I just loved hearing these people vocalize and go up and down the musical scale. I was a great fan of those folks, I really appreciated their talent. In fact, as a young kid, I used to watch Fred Astaire. Mr. Astaire had, in the basement of his home in Bel-Air, a whole nightclub set. That's where he would work out his routines, dancing on the tables and across the bar and all that stuff. I went to school with his son Freddie, Jr., and Freddie and I would go in there after school and watch him. Getting to see things like that—*that* was one of the great advantages of being raised in that community. That was something that really was unique.

Of all the movies you were in at MGM, the best-known—by far—is Forbidden Planet *[1956].*

Yes, it *has* become a classic, even though it was just about the one and only attempt (in those days) by MGM to do a science fiction movie. There were several of us contract players on the thing: Jack Kelly, who ended up in the TV series *Maverick*, Jim Drury, who ended up being *The Virginian* on TV (Jim and I were close friends), Earl Holliman and so on. Leslie Nielsen played the commander, and Anne Francis was Altaira. Anne and I shared a couple of dates together—not too serious, but we enjoyed each other's company. In my opinion, Anne was one of the most attractive, *beautiful* young ladies in the industry in those days.

We all were on Stage 31 down there at MGM Studios for a month or so, as I recall, making *Forbidden Planet*, and it was a very interesting experience. MGM had done such a good job of creating the Altair-4 planet surface set that you really felt like you were on another planet when you walked through those stage doors! Three-quarters of the sound stage had this humongous painted backdrop which, in essence, made you think you were looking out into the universe from the planet we were on. I'll never forget, one of my lines was, "Funny to see two moons in the sky, isn't it?"

A great line!

That was when Jim Drury and I were walking the perimeter together. I don't think any of us at the time realized that it would become a classic in the sense that it has. I remember the guy that worked inside of Robby the Robot. He was a little guy, Frankie Darro. One time he got drunk and he couldn't work Robby the Robot. He got inside that thing and he just couldn't do it—there were various different levers and pedals and stuff, that you had to work from the inside of the robot. Finally he had to say, "I can't handle it." Plus, if I remember right, he was sweatin' like a stuck pig.

What recollection of the scene where you're picked up and tossed around by the Id monster?

They put a harness on me and hooked me up to a cable with a spring on the end of it, and then on cue, when that monster was supposed to get a-hold of me, about four guys pulled on the cable and jerked me off my feet, up into the air. Straight

James Drury and Dix are pinned down by *Forbidden Planet*'s Id monster as Leslie Nielsen takes aim.

up. That was a fun thing to do, what the heck [*laughs*]! Both Jim Drury and I got zapped.

You didn't feel it was dangerous at all?
 No. I was ranch-raised and I'd fallen off of horses and done all kinds of stuff. So that didn't bother me.

Why did you leave MGM?
 Television hit with a big bang, and the whole contract concept went out the window. They let me go, along with just about everybody else at MGM who was a contract player. And I was catapulted into a category called the freelance actor [*laughs*]. It took me about a year to get the word out around the Hollywood community that Dix was no longer with MGM. Then finally I started [working again], through a man named Sam Fuller, who became a close friend. Sam had a movie he wanted to make called *Forty Guns* [1957], a true story of Wyatt Earp and his two brothers. I landed the role of Chico, the younger brother. *That* was a job well done and well received and kick-started my career again. Then I did a lot of work for 20th Century–Fox. In those days, Bob Lippert had a couple companies [Regal Films and Associated Producers Inc.] that made pictures for 20th Century–Fox, for the

second halves of Fox's double-bills. It was for them that I did movies like *Thundering Jets* [1958].

Speaking of *Thundering Jets*, just as an aside: I went into the offices near MGM Studios where they were casting, to pick up my script, and in the lobby I met a young man who asked if I would go have coffee with him after we finished our business in the production offices. I of course said sure. His name was Bobby Conrad, he was a singer from Chicago, and he had just bullshitted his way into gettin' a part in *Thundering Jets*. He said, "I don't know the first thing about this stuff. Can you *help* me, Bob?" So for several weeks, if not a month or more, he would come by my apartment and I'd go through line by line and explain how you develop an inner life of the character and so forth and so on. Well, *from* that *Thundering Jets*, he went right into *Hawaiian Eye*, and then after that, *The Wild Wild West* and *Baa Baa Black Sheep* and all of that. It just launched his career.

You played a police detective who gets killed by the monster in Frankenstein's Daughter *[1958], directed by Richard Cunha.*

The first thing that comes to my mind about that picture is, the character I portrayed was named Dillon—Detective Dillon. That was when [the TV series] *Gunsmoke* was so popular, and so of course everybody on the set was saying [*in a Chester-like drawl*], "Hey, Mr. Deee-lon...!" I recall *Frankenstein's Daughter* not as a great movie at all, but a fun thing to do. We had a good crew, a good cast. John Ashley was the lead, and John and I stayed friends for a while. He owned theaters in Oklahoma. So it was good workin' on that thing, it was a lot of fun makin' that movie.

There was also another son-of-a-Hollywood-star in it, Harold Lloyd, Jr.

When I was a kid in Beverly Hills, I used to go over to the Lloyd estate—as a matter of fact, I took swimming lessons there. I knew Harold Jr. from those early days. He was always kind of an eccentric kid, let's put it that way. He was not with the rest of us out playin' basketball or goin' to the beach or any of that kind of stuff. So we didn't have an ongoing, close relationship.

According to a Harold Lloyd biography, Jr. was gay. In fact, he was some kind of masochistic gay who used to come home beaten-up and bloody!

I remember that he palled around with this gal who was the daughter of a well-known character actor, I can't think of his name right now. The two of 'em were ... uh ... kinda "girlfriends" together [*laughs*]. I remember meeting them on several occasions, and somebody finally explaining to me their relationship. So Harold Lloyd, Jr., and I didn't have very much in common. I was more interested in the girls!

You started out with small parts at MGM, and then slightly better parts in Lippert movies. But in the '60s, you started starring in very, very cheap movies. And my question is: Is it better to serve in Heaven or rule in Hell?

As I look back, honestly, I think I would have been better off just serving in Heaven, as you put it. Though I certainly had a chance to expand horizons with the independents. I not only worked as an actor, I co-authored screenplays, I either held

Dix meets a grisly end at the oversized mitts of *Frankenstein's Daughter* (Harry Wilson).

the sound boom or helped pack the prop truck or ... you name it! You wear a lot of different hats when you're out there as an independent company. I think that gave me an overall working knowledge of how movies are *truly* made, from the page to the screen. So I felt that I had a lot broader experience by working with independents.

I was very impressed by David Niven's book *Bring On the Empty Horses*, where he wrote that all his life he had been saying words invented by other people and doing things directors told him to do. He was kind of saying he'd spent his life as a puppet. Looking back on my career after formally retiring from the production end of the business, I certainly did *not* feel that way. I felt that I had learned and investigated and had not had one foot nailed to the floor, as a lot of actors *do*. Let's face it, a lot of actors know their aspect of moviemaking and that's *it*—they don't have the foggiest idea what goes on in the cutting room or the relationship between camera and sound and all the rest of it. *And*, in many respects, I think ignorance is bliss. They say, "Oh, well, that's *his* job," "That's *her* department," and they just slough it off. But to *me*, it's all part of the creative process.

You played Wild Bill Hickok in Arch Hall, Sr.'s, Deadwood '76 *[1965].*
   One of the reasons I took that was because my father played Hickok in *Bad-*

lands of Dakota. As a matter of fact, I was able to get the same wardrobe to wear that he wore when *he* played Hickok.

The very same clothes?
From Western Costume. The labels were still in the vest and the coat and the shirt and all that. So I had a little private trip down Memory Lane by being able to wear Dad's very same costume. That was, again, one of those shoestring independents. Arch Hall, Sr., put the whole deal together and he's the one who approached me and asked me if I wouldn't portray Wild Bill in it. I still remember the walk that Wild Bill did down the main street of the town, and the fact that he didn't shoot Billy [Arch Hall, Jr.] and said to him, in essence, "Go home, son. I knew your dad. You're a good kid. Get out of here." It was nice to see father and son [Arch Hall, Sr., and Jr.] working together, and I wished that I had had the opportunity with *my* dad. If I hadn't lost my dad at the young age that I did, maybe he and I *would* have. I had that thought again when I saw Kiefer Sutherland and Donald Sutherland together on the Golden Globes award show the other night. Here's the son, Kiefer, nominated for his series *24*, and Dad was up there collecting an award for *something*, and it was nice to see two generations represented.

It was about the same time [as *Deadwood '76*] that I began helping develop movies for friends in Hollywood, like *Las Vegas Strangler* [1969] with [producer] Oliver Drake. There was kind of a nucleus of people in the Hollywood community who were trying, after many years of working in the majors, to branch out and do things on their own. I remember *Deadwood '76*, *Las Vegas Strangler*, and I'd include all the Al Adamson things, all the stuff that Al and Sam Sherman and I did. It was a little community within a community, really.

Las Vegas Strangler *I've never seen. Is it a horror film?*
Yeah, I played a guy who had been abused by my mother as a child, and therefore he was ... well, he was *nuts* [*laughs*]. He had this hatred for showgirls, and was committing a series of murders on the Vegas Strip. It was the first time I had an opportunity to play a guy who was reeeally out of touch, and had this mother fixation. Ollie Drake *had* to be pushing 70 then, and he wanted to make this movie. It was purely a commercial piece, and I understand that it did well. Maybe not so much in this country, but elsewhere in the world. One of the sidelights that comes to mind is, we were non-union, and one day some people came on the set—this was in Vegas. "Look out," I heard, "here come the union guys." Being a Screen Actors Guild member, I didn't want to get busted—it was a $500 fine plus something like a six months suspension if you were caught working on a [non-union picture]. So some guy handed me body makeup and a little sponge, and I proceeded to put body makeup on this naked chorus girl while these guys were walking around inspecting the sets [*laughs*]! It was a small sponge, too—I had a lot of work to do there!

Las Vegas Strangler *was the first time you played a nut; I guess the second time might be* Blood of Dracula's Castle *[1969] where you played "The Moon Maniac."*
Exactly. A very similar type of mental illness!

Did you enjoy playing psychos?

Well, let's say it was a departure from anything I had done before. Before that, when I had been cast in movies and TV, pretty much the only characterization I would have would be, like, a Union officer in the Army, or maybe play an Indian-with-a-wig-on kind of thing. But when you actually have to develop the inner life of a character who was nuts, *that* was an interesting challenge. In both cases, I recall, it came off pretty believably—I had people comment in the positive regarding it. It was a stretch for me, and in the final analysis it was good experience. What I remember about *Dracula's Castle* was that it was the first time I had the opportunity to work with John Carradine. I really loved that old man. He was a great guy. I gotta tell you a story that *he* told *me*, a story I'm sure a lot of people have never heard: When Mr. Carradine first came to Hollywood, there were rumors going around that he must be a vampire or something [*laughs*], 'cause he only came out at night. And he told me the reason he only came out at night was, the only wardrobe he had was a tuxedo! Since that was the only clothes he had, he had to stay inside during the daytime!

John and I became quite close, we worked in several movies together. He could recite Shakespeare 'til the cows came home [*laughs*], and he had a heart as big as outdoors. But unfortunately he'd been married a number of times, his wives were all after him for alimony, and he always had to get paid cash under the table so he'd have some walkin' around money.

As I say, my first experience with John was in *Dracula's Castle*. I remember that this was the first time because I was a fan of his, and I really respected the man's talent. We did a scene around a pool table where we had to shoot pool and deliver lines back and forth about the Moon drivin' people nuts—*my* character in particular! I remember being—well, not *nervous*, but kind of on edge, since I was working with The Master. But he made me feel so comfortable, and was so generous with his knowledge and his time.

Where was Dracula's Castle *shot?*

The castle was out in the High Desert country, between L.A. and Victorville somewhere. It was an isolated old structure. There was no ocean near that castle, though in the movie it was made to look so.

How about the actors playing Mr. and Mrs. Dracula in that movie, Alex D'Arcy and Paula Raymond?

I really loved both of them. "The beauty of the Old Hollywood": These were professional performers who were a real joy to be around. Talk about anecdotes: Just having coffee on the set, they could tell you stories 'til the cows came home about their careers. Paula Raymond was a leading lady [in the '40s and '50s] and then had a severe automobile accident, and her whole face had to be restructured. She really was a fine person, a wonderful, talented actress and, really, I had the greatest admiration for her *courage* to come back after that very severe accident. She became one of my favorite people, as did Alex D'Arcy.

Once you get down to the level of movies like Blood of Dracula's Castle, *what about the stuntwork? Does the actor end up doing a lot of his own?*

That was all me on *Dracula's Castle*. On the independents, you don't have doubles or stand-ins or anything like that, you do all the work yourself. I was fortunate to be trained by Jock Mahoney as a young actor. Jock taught us how to choreograph a fight and tuck and roll when you fall. A lot of movies that I worked in in the late '50s and into the '60s which required physical activity, I did all the work myself. There were a few exceptions, but only when the director said, "I don't want you to get hurt. We're putting a stuntman in there." It helped me to *get* a lot of roles, being able to ride a horse, to take a fall, to stage a fight, to take a punch. I could *do* all that stuff. A lot of actors—as we used to call 'em, the "patent leather actors from New York"—didn't have a clue which end of the horse *ate* [*laughs*]!

In the 1960s, Dix became a familiar (and sometimes grizzled) face in a series of exploitative action, horror and Western features.

Where did you come in contact with Jock Mahoney, that you were able to learn all this from him?

It was through a friend. There were several of us involved in Jock Mahoney's stunt group, and some of them went on to make that a *career*. Hal Needham, I think, was one. I was part of that group, which also gave me a nice rapport *with* the stuntmen in the Stuntman's Association and Stunts Unlimited, the two major stunt groups in the Hollywood community.

So you paid to learn from Jock Mahoney, I assume?

Yeah. It was like going to school, and I had to pay some "tuition." We got together in the backyard of his home in the San Fernando Valley—Woodland Hills or one of those communities. The main thing I recall is a big tree in the backyard and a rope, and swinging on that rope and letting go and landing and tucking and rolling—learning how to do that stuff.

Al Adamson has got a bit of a following these days, partly because of the outlandish nature of his movies and partly, I think, because of his well-publicized murder.

Well, I'll say this about Al, God rest his soul: He was very dedicated to the craft of being a director. But ... there weren't that many people that *liked* Al that much. He was out to make a buck, [to the point where] you better have your hand on your wallet. I don't like speaking negatively about anybody who's gone on to the Great Pasture in the Sky, so I'll just say that Al and I had a working relationship that was beneficial to both of us. But I'll also say that it's good to know somebody's qualities, so you can keep an eye on him [*laughs*]! When he was murdered, there were a lot of people who said he had it *comin'*. 'Cause, frankly, you had to work for Al twice: Once when you did your job, whatever you were doing, acting, sound or whatever … and the second time was to get your paycheck. I on several occasions, representing both cast and crew, would have to hunt him down and get those people's money. That's the reputation he developed.

A lot of Adamson's movies aren't any good. Is that because he didn't have enough time and money, or because he didn't have enough talent?

I think it's more in the taste and talent department [*laughs*]! If the work of an independent producer-director has some inspiration and quality, investors come out of the woodwork—they'll come in and help an independent company. Well, Al never had that happen, not to *my* knowledge. Because he didn't want to treat people correctly. Including the money people! Every time he wanted to start something new, he'd pretty much have to go out and get a whole new group of folks to hornswoggle into *doin'* something. He made a rod for his own back, I'll put it that way.

If he wasn't busting at the seams in the Taste and Talent Department, or even in the Honesty Department, why did Dix International Pictures hire him to product and direct Five Bloody Graves?

Al had a friend who put some seed money in—he matched the seed money that *we'd* put in. But *with* the condition that Al direct.

Five Bloody Graves—*which you also wrote—was partially based on the life of a real-life gunfighter, correct?*

Yes, it was. I wanted to do a commercial piece, but I wanted to also base it on true American history. So it was modeled after a little-known gunfighter called Ben Thompson. Thompson was a very interesting guy. It didn't come out in the movie that he was in love with his first cousin, she jilted him and married another guy, and he went West with a death wish. When he was 33 years old, he drank a bottle of booze and blew his brains out. But in his time he was a very, very lethal gunfighter because he didn't *give* a damn. He had such contempt for one challenger that he showed up on the main street of the town naked, with nothin' on except a six-gun. And shot the guy! Of course, *that* didn't come out in the movie in the '60s. You *might* be able to do it *today* [*laughs*]! The major portion of *Five Bloody Graves* was made in a place called Fruita, Utah. It's a lodge with one gas pump, up near Goblin Valley. The people on that picture, both cast and crew, were a really good bunch. Scott Brady and Jim Davis was old pals, a lot of fun to be around.

I found a New York Times *review of* Five Bloody Graves *and a quote that I thought was funny but you might not: "Its sole virtue is that everybody in it gets knocked off, with one inexcusable exception, the guy who wrote it."*

[*Laughs*] That's good, yeah! But, I have to say … I'm not making excuses for the writer! … but after the transition from the page to the screen, it was hardly recognizable as having come from my original screenplay. This was due to the Adamson direction and subsequent post-production work. The original screenplay and what ended up on the screen were very, very different.

Whose idea was it to have the movie narrated by Death [played by Gene Raymond]?

That was Adamson. I never had that in there. After the way Adamson [made the movie], there were so many holes in it that it needed a narration track to explain what the heck was goin' *on* [*laughs*]!

You said that on Deadwood '76 *it was interesting to watch father-and-son Arch Halls working together. Did you feel the same way watching Al Adamson and his actor-father working on* Five Bloody Graves*?*

Yes, and in fact, I enjoyed Al's father very much. Denver Dixon was a very interesting character who dated back to the early days of Hollywood. I liked ol' Denver. I didn't feel the closeness between father and son there, but I wasn't around 'em that much.

Al Adamson's partner Sam Sherman—what memories of him?

Sam and I have always gotten along okay. It's been pretty much a long-distance thing, over the phone; first just business, and then I did visit him one time in New York and saw the Independent International operation there. Sam and I have had a friendly relationship through the years, and still remain friends. Sam is the one guy who always defended Al Adamson one way or another. It wasn't an easy job, but Sam remained his partner and his friend through the years.

Did Sam have blinders on when it came to Adamson's bad qualities?

[*Laughs*] I just would say that he was inventive in justifying Al's behavior!

You had a small part, but great billing, in Adamson's Horror of the Blood Monsters *[1970].*

Many times when I worked in these Adamson movies, I didn't know *what* they were going to be titled. We'd get called to do a scene, some little sequence that *might* be inserted in *some*thing that was untitled at the time. So we didn't even know what name the picture was gonna be released under. This was one of *those* deals: I simply went by the studio and learned my lines and I played a colonel, sitting at a control instrument panel kind of thing. I never saw any finished product, though I heard later of course that it became part of one of his space movies [*Blood Monsters*]. That's all I remember about that particular shoot: just going on the sound stage, doing my thing (which I usually did in one take) and "Goodbye."

You must also remember an actress named Vicki Volante who was in the scenes with you— you have a scene in bed with her!

Vicki, she was a sweetheart. On *Five Bloody Graves*, Al Adamson fell in love with Vicki Volante up in the mountains of Utah, and was pursuing her for quite a

Actress Darlene Lucht (a.k.a. Tara Ashton), a former Miss Milwaukee, not only became Mrs. Dix but also his co-star in *Five Bloody Graves.*

few months after that. That's probably why there were editorial problems on that picture: His mind was elsewhere [*laughs*]!

Did he ever catch her?

Naw, she had a boyfriend and got married and had babies. Another actress,

After playing a small Earthbound role in the movie, Dix (with ray gun) became a heroic central figure on pubicity materials for *Space Mission to the Lost Planet* (a.k.a. *Horror of the Blood Monsters*).

Regina Carrol, finally came along and put up with Al's jazz and married him, and I guess Al had a pretty decent relationship with her for many years until she passed on. But, getting back to your question, I do recall the sex scene with Vicki Volante that you speak of. It's hard to have a sex scene with a bunch of people in the crew standing around. It's something I think of often when I see these intimate sex scenes in movies these days—I think to myself, "If the audience could just see how many people are standin' around that bed, it would take a lot of the pizzazz out of it!"

It was such a surprise to spot you in a minuscule part in the James Bond movie Live and Let Die *[1973].*

Roger Moore [James Bond] and I became friends when we were both under contract to MGM. Those early days in Hollywood, he and I buddied around. Fade out, fade in: Years later, I was down in Louisiana, working on a screenplay about alligator hunting and what those guys do to make belts and shoes and so forth, and Roger and company came through making the 007 film *Live and Let Die*. There was a big full-page ad in *The New Orleans Picayune*, with Roger's mug shot there. So I called Roger's hotel and he said, "Hey, Bob, c'mon over," so I did.

Let me interrupt myself here and say that, to research this idea I had for a screenplay about Cajun alligator hunters, to get the flavor of the Cajun folks down in Louisiana, I got a job as a bartender in a place called The Happy Hour. This is one of those places where the guys pull up in pickup trucks and have the rifles in the back and no shoes on. To them, I was just Bob the bartender, and I served these Cajun guys. It was a very close-mouthed, tough bunch to get to know, but pretty soon, besides leaving me a nickel tip, they got so they'd acknowledge me and say, "Hi, Bob." Anyway, I was *doing* that and then the *Live and Let Die* people showed up and I went over to visit with Rog.

They had a local actor who was supposed to do just a small one-liner in the picture, but it was a big production shot where they had a funeral procession where guys were marching in slow time and blowing the trumpets and the whole deal. There were quite a lot of people involved, bands and extras and traffic control and you name it, and this actor froze—he couldn't even speak, hardly, he was just shakin' in his boots. Guy Hamilton the director, at Rog's suggestion, put *me* in there. So I did just a one-liner where the funeral procession is going by and I ask a black man, "Whose funeral is it?" and he says, "*Yours!*" and sticks a knife in my kidneys and I drop on the ground. Then they had one of these gags where they placed a coffin over me and, now out of sight of the camera, I grabbed hold of some built-in rungs underneath. I hooked onto 'em with my hands and feet so that when they picked the coffin up again, I went up with it and it looked like my body had disappeared.

Incidentally, during or after the shooting of the scene, a local TV guy is standing there with a camera on his shoulder and there's another TV guy with a microphone, and they're interviewing Roger Moore in front of his trailer. Roger gives 'em background on the movie and his character and blah blah blah, and then he says, "Why don't you talk to my friend Bob over here? We were at MGM together…" So the guy swings the camera around and now I start being asked for background on myself and then my dad. As this went on and on, I thought, "Either there isn't

Robert and Darlene's collaborations include the public access TV series *Impressions*, **on which interviewees discuss their spiritual development.**

any more film in that camera, or they're just being courteous." Well, okay, I do the interview, I say goodbye to my friend Rog and I go back over to Slidell, Louisiana, across Lake Pontchartrain from New Orleans, and I get behind the bar, posing as Bob the bartender. And then the local news comes on [*laughs*]. You already know what's gonna happen, right?

I do, but go 'head!

After a few minutes' interview with Rog, they swing around and there's Bob the bartender—talking for about ten minutes on the local news. These Cajun alligator hunters are lookin' at me ... and lookin' at the TV set ... and lookin' at me...! Well, y'know, they wouldn't even say *hello* to me after that. They felt I'd lied and misrepresented myself to them from Day One, and they wouldn't even talk to me any more. 'Cause now, in their minds, I was a spy from Hollywood!

Live and Let Die *looks to have been your last movie credit—am I right about that?*

That is correct, yeah, as far as feature motion pictures. I've helped co-author a few things, I've helped with some production, but, yes, that *was* the last movie I worked in as an actor.

How have you been making your living in the last 30 years, after you drifted away from acting?

Until recently, my family owned a 42-office building in Palm Desert, California, and I was the manager of the building and took care of the family business in that respect. Also, there are 195 condos in this complex here where I live, and I was the pool manager for a couple of years [*laughs*]! I had two or three young college kids that worked under me and we, during the summertime, made it a pleasant experience for the homeowners around here.

Most of 'em know nothing about my having been an actor. That's fine by me. Other than knowledgeable people like yourself, who have an interest and a legitimate background and a purpose, most folks are like, "Did you know John Wayne??" and so on. When Darlene and I go to any type of social gathering, *most* of the time my acting background will come up, there's always somebody there who'll say, "Oh, did you know that Bob was an actor? He's from Hollywood…" That's all it takes, and then, boom, they're off and runnin' with their questions.

I just accept that it comes with the territory if you were involved in the movie business, and I try and get the conversation turned around onto a subject that may be a little more interesting to me personally. Like, "How do you think we can eliminate prejudice in the human family?"

Donnie Dunagan

*When I [beat Boris Karloff at checkers], he was surprised.
I put my hand out. I wanted my quarter!
...I don't think he liked losin' to this little runt, me!*

If one of the horror/sci-fi cable channels had its own version of *Family Feud*, the question "Name the most memorable things about *Son of Frankenstein*" would certainly include amidst its Top Four Answers "ALL-STAR CAST," "KARLOFF'S LAST FILM AS THE MONSTER" and "EXPRESSIONISTIC SETS." Also standing an excellent chance of making the short list would be "DONNIE DUNAGAN," the Dixie-accented blond moppet who was very (*very*) incongruously cast in the 1939 chiller as Peter von Frankenstein, the curly-headed knee-high son of Baron and Baroness Frankenstein (played by Britisher Basil Rathbone and American stage actress Josephine Hutchinson).

Unlike his *Son* co-stars, all of whom continued in the acting profession, Dunagan was gone from the screen after just a few more films. Gone, but *far* from forgotten: *Son of Frankenstein* was resurrected for television in the 1950s and has since aired innumerable times on local TV and cable stations, in addition to coming to home video via VHS, laser and *twice* to DVD; several generations of fans have taken it to their hearts as one of the great milestones of screen horror's Golden Age. And, simultaneously, there has been endless discussion, and controversy, about Master Dunagan's "square peg" casting and Little Rascal–ish performance—one noted commentator expressing the unkind wish that Karloff's Monster *had* climactically dropped little Peter into that boiling pit of sulfur!

But at the same time that some *Son of Frank* fans were quibbling over the particulars of a four-year-old's performance, *all* of them anxiously wanted to know, "What ever happened to Donnie Dunagan?" Include this writer in the ranks of that intrusive bunch: For years we had that burning question in the backs of our uncluttered heads, occasionally asking other kid actors of that era what they knew about him (nada) and dialing up every directory-listed Don, Donnie and Donald Dunagan in this great big U.S. of A. in hopes of locating *the* Donnie Dunagan. Even though it was perhaps unrealistic of us to expect him to remember much about his short stay at Castle

Frankenstein, this curious little figure in Frankenhistory was now, a half-century-plus later, the subject of a mini-manhunt, the "Unholy Grail" for horror movie historians.

Once again, mission *not* accomplished.

Then, in the summer of 2004, the clouds of mystery parted in the skies above Central Texas, when the lone star to have eluded the Universal Frankenstein series' fans made a brief appearance on local TV. News of the event would have escaped the notice of the Dunamaniacs if not for local resident Paula Mathieu and her Los Angeles–based film-restorer son Eric Aijala, who learned of Donnie's 21st-century TV bow and sprang into action. They passed the news of their discovery on to film historian and preservationist Scott MacQueen, who in turn shared it with his friends and contacts at Walt Disney (Dunagan was the voice of *Bambi* in that company's 1942 animated classic) and with your humble correspondent.

"*The* Donnie Dunagan" was not what we had expected, or possibly *could* have expected. For years, fans presumed that he had slipped away from the exotic world of movie stardom into an everyday sort of existence; we found a Don Dunagan with a life story *more* exotic and adventure-filled than any of his co-stars. His 66-year-old memories of *Son of Frankenstein*, as it turns out, are vivid—and he's not like Aunt Fanny! In short, I found myself doing one of the most satisfying and fun interviews in my 24 years of writing. Meet the *real* Don Dunagan—career Marine, champion boxer, combat officer, counterintelligence agent, Green Bay Packer, mathematician, physicist and American Mensa Society member…

I have a feeling that a great deal of the biographical information that came out about you in the old days was bogus—for one thing, your dad was described as a pro golfer, which I bet he was not. So may I ask you just to start at the beginning?

I was born on August 16, 1934, in San Antonio, Texas. It was the apex of the Depression, of course, and my parents were dirt poor. My mom was a blonde, blue-eyed, gorgeous woman without any education at all—I mean, zero education, as was my dad. But she was a published poet at age 19. True story. My dad was *called* a golf pro [in Donnie's old publicity]; he wasn't. He was in fact, in those days, a hard-working helper in a golf shop at one of the country clubs in San Antonio *and*, on the side, he fought bare-knuckles for

The pride of San Antonio and Memphis, Donnie Dunagan poses with the Orpheum Theatre talent show trophies which brought him to Hollywood's attention.

money in what we would call, in those days, smokers. Remember the *Rocky* movie where Sylvester Stallone is in a bar, in a makeshift ring, and he has no style, he has no training, and he and the other guy are just beatin' up on each other? That's a smoker. The term comes from the Irish and Scottish pubs where everybody smokes to the point where you can hardly see. My *grand*father, who was Irish, from County Donegal, was a bare-knuckles boxer 'til he was 53.

Your grandfather on your father's side.

Yeah. That's how he made a living. And *I* boxed. I don't know if this is a gene transfer or just stupidity [*laughs*], but I boxed from age 14 until age 32 and was a heavyweight champion in the Marine Corps for nine years.

Anyway, we left San Antonio—the Depression was just *awful* there. This was early 1937. My mom and dad, and they were dragging me along, moved to Memphis, Tennessee, where my dad had a chance at being an assistant assistant pro golfer at a public golf course. What that means is that you teach folks who have never played golf before, and they're 40 years old. That's a hard coaching job. (I'm sensitive to that, because many years later I played a lot, and tried to coach folks.) Anyway, that's why they went to Memphis. We lived in an extremely poor but *clean* area, mostly with black neighbors. Across the street from us we had very nice neighbors, a family that was related to a man who was then famous and later became even *more* famous, a dancer called "Peg Leg" Bates. One of "Peg Leg"'s adult relatives, I don't know if it was a brother or a cousin, but one of the adult relatives of "Peg Leg" Bates was a street dancer. There was a *lot* of that around. Street dancers would go to the bus depots and the train depots where people were traveling and they'd dance on the street for pennies and nickels. This nice man across the street taught me, with my mother's awareness and permission, to dance. I was barefooted—he had tap shoes, I did not. He taught me how to dance, with a "top hat" and a "cane." Somebody painted a paper bag to look like a top hat, put it on me, gave me a stick as a cane, and I mimicked this marvelous man.

I was three and a quarter, three and a half, and, remember now, we were *poor-poor*. There was a talent show in the Orpheum Theatre, which is now a historic building on South Main in Memphis. I know it's a historic building because my wife Dana and I drove by it a couple years ago and outside they had a nice plaque identifying it as a national historic building. Not because of *me* [*laughs*]! Anyway, this was 1937 and there was a talent show going to be held there, and the prize money was $100. A hundred dollars then, to folks living like most folks were doing, was like two and a half thousand today in "buy power." I'm a physicist-mathematician, so I can convert that pretty quick! So the neighborhood folks, I suspect black ladies, helped my mom fashion, from scraps, a little outfit for me, and again the painted paper bag as a "top hat," and a stick that somebody painted with (I think) shoe polish, so that it looked like a British swagger stick. It wasn't a real tall cane, it would never hit the floor, but that made it easier to twirl. Oh, and they got tap shoes from some white family that had a lot of money; one of the black ladies there cleaned house for that family, and that's where the tap shoes came from. I was taken to this theater, and people were packed in there.

A packed house for a talent contest?

There *was* no entertainment back then. Entertainment was spelling bees (people today would laugh at that) and talent contests and ballgames. *Lots* of baseball. *Every*where, baseball. On every vacant lot, there was baseball.

How old were the other people competing in this talent contest?

It was for any age that had the courage to do it, up to age 13. The other people were all doing song and dance. I had not been in a theater before, not even for a movie, so my eyes must have been coming out of my head. I was standing off to the side, in the wings, behind all these heavy curtains, very dusty, and I was watching these other acts. I thought, "Gee, *I* can't do that!" Don't give me an interrogative on this, but I have the impression there was some girl who had to be 12, 13, a very tall girl, thin, who did a magnificent tap dance. And I thought, "What am I doin'? I can't go out and do this!" I was just a little jerk kid and I only knew one dance. But it was jazzy and cute.

They threw me out on the stage ... I couldn't even see anybody, the lights were blazing ... and I was doing the dance. To a little song called, of all things, "A-Tisket, A-Tasket." Well, I *won* the bloody thing! I didn't realize I had won until they told me about nine times that I had to go back out [to take a bow]—I had to go out with my mom a couple times.

In the audience was a young fellow who was from RKO Studios. I don't know if he was an agent, an executive, I have no idea. (Nor did anybody else later, when I would ask these questions to those few people that survived in the family.) Well, within four or five days, we had packed in two suitcases everything we owned and we were on a train. The man from RKO accompanied us on the train, which took days to go from Memphis, Tennessee, to Los Angeles. RKO put us up in a hotel, they were extremely gracious—my mom and dad had eyes that were twice normal size. And the first thing I knew, at age three, I was in a film called *Mother Carey's Chickens* [1938] at RKO. And then *Son of Frankenstein*, which was also RKO.

Which was Universal.

Universal? Okay, I'm screwed up here. You gotta remember now, I didn't get "into" this stuff until just recently.

Don't apologize. If you wanted to hear from me everything that I remember from the first

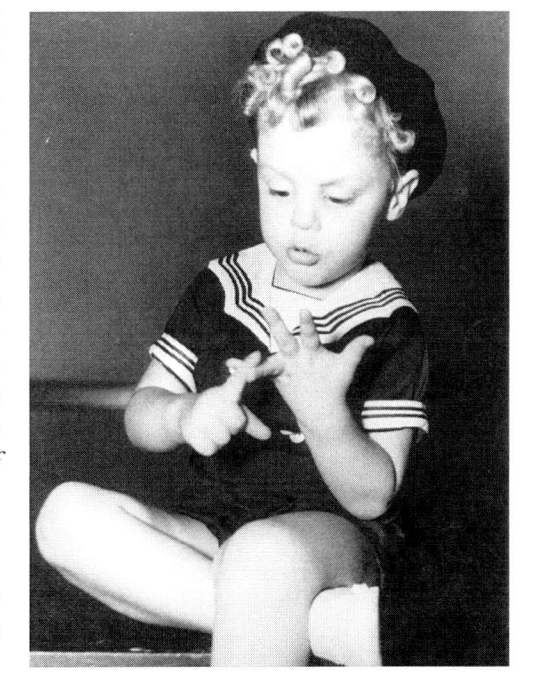

Double-check the math all you want, Master Dunagan, but the amazing fact is that you began your acting career at age three.

10 or 12 years of my life, I'd be done in two shakes. The fact that you remember as much as you do is amazing to me.

Well, from *Mother Carey's Chickens* forward, I remember everything vividly.

What are your earliest memories of Son of Frankenstein*?*

Prior to *Son of Frankenstein*, I didn't know who Boris Karloff was. I met him for the first time in the cafeteria at the studio. He was a broad-shouldered fellow in civilian attire, and very, very pleasant. The *other* people who were there that day were also pleasant. Either the first or the second time that I had time with Mr. Karloff [in the cafeteria], he gave me an ice cream cone; I don't know that he paid for it, but he might have, and he handed me an ice cream cone. Then we sat down at a table. There were three or four people there, and my mom, and somebody told me that Mr. Karloff was going to be playing the part of this big person that everybody didn't like and blah blah blah.

This was their way of making sure you wouldn't be scared to act with Karloff once he was made up as the Monster.

Yes, and that disarmed *every*thing. Later, when I first saw him in his Monster makeup, he laughed at me—"What do you think about me now?" It was just … "easy does it." As I mentioned, he gave me ice cream either the first time, sir, or the second time, and *that's* enough to win me over!

[Laughs] Me too!

Folks say to me, "My gosh, you must have been scared scared scared [to act with Karloff's Monster]." *No.* I had a *ball*! Boris Karloff was a wonderful man. Later I learned from other people, in casual conversations, he was a real humanist. He was a *very* intelligent man, a *very* gentle man, and he had a great sense of humor. He taught me how to play checkers, on the set. We had a whole lot of time "down," waiting for lights to be changed and all kinds of things. "Down time" is boring as the dickens. Borrowing a checkerboard from somebody, I think a man who managed lights, Mr. Karloff, in his Monster makeup and costume, taught me how to play checkers. People were watching, stagehands and folks standing around, and we were having a good time. Now, this is really cute: After about three or four games over a couple-day period, between scenes and rehearsals, we started betting quarters. Now, as soon as we started playing for quar-

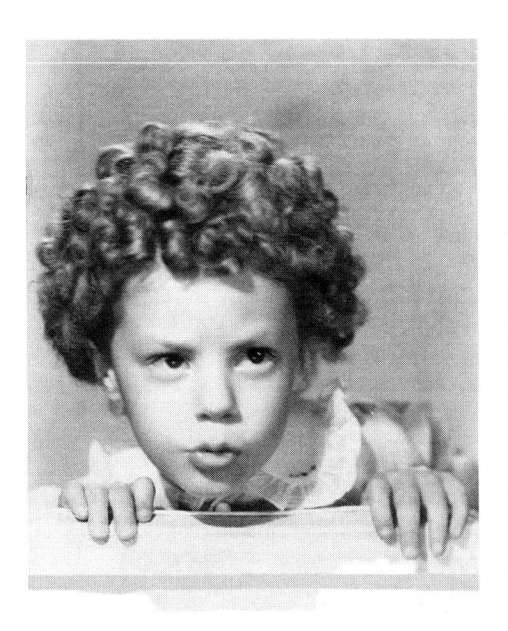

Dunagan was the Universal Monster series' fourth generation of Frankenstein, after Frederick Kerr, Colin Clive (both already dead by 1938 when *Son of Frankenstein* was shot) and Basil Rathbone.

ters, my attention went up [*laughs*], and I won a game. Legitimately. If he had *tried* to let me win, I think I would have sensed it. I won the game. He got to talking, having some fun with people, lost his concentration, and I double-jumped him and I had him locked up! Now, he was smart as the dickens, he could have beaten me easy probably, but he'd been talking, and people were standing around laughing, and he did a couple careless things after about Move 8 or 9.

When I won, he was surprised. I put my hand out. I wanted my quarter! I knew I was making a ton of money but nobody ever *gave* me any money, so I wanted my quarter! He went "Rrrr! Rrrr! Rrrr!" [like the Monster] and people thought he was "playing the part." I'm not sure he *was*—I don't think he liked losin' to this little runt, me! Then he alibied that he was in costume and didn't have any money on him; "I'll give it to you later." Well, the next day, or maybe two days later, we played again for a quarter, with the same borrowed checkers set. I won *again*. Now *this* time he was paying good attention, and I was doing exactly what he taught me to do. Oh, now I was *really* excited, 'cause I've got *two* quarters coming! The people around were again laughing and having a good time about this, and he again went "Rrrr! Rrrr! Rrrr!" I think he really meant it this time—he did not like losin' for poop [*laughs*]! But he was in costume again, and "I'll give it to you later."

"No, I'm gonna go *with* you. I want my quarters!" So he took me by the hand ... people were laughing ... and we went over to what looked like a small trailer inside of the stage. He went inside, "Rrrr! Rrrr! Rrrr!," he came back out and he gave me a half-dollar. I had not *seen* a half-dollar and I thought this was a phony baloney thing he was givin' me [*laughs*]! And I didn't *want* it! He had to show it to people: "Tell him this is two quarters!" And after that, he wouldn't play me for quarters no more [*laughs*]!

Did you get any notion whether he was uncomfortable in the Monster makeup and costume?
The costume was punishing him. I always felt sorry for him, because his costume was heavy and it really hurt him, he was in pain with that. But he wasn't a complainer. He was like a man with a shirt on and the collar's too tight, and he was constantly fidgeting, and once in a while he would mumble to somebody something like, "I gotta get *out* of this thing..." Today a physical costume would not [be as uncomfortable] but in *those* days, sir, I promise you, that costume was real. The costume was extremely heavy, and it did not "breathe." It was exactly what you saw on the film, and it was *murder* on him. He must have lost weight *every day* in that darn thing. And the boots, sir, *had* to have lead in them, because when he walked, *off*-camera, between takes, it was still clunk-clunk-clunk. He had a hard time with them. I can tell you this: When we got through with that movie, my sense was that he did not like that role. And I can *promise* you he didn't like the costume, which had to hurt him physically. He did not like that role but he was a professional man and he agreed to do it, and he did it well. But my sense is that he would probably have preferred to be in Shakespeare, *Othello,* or some*thing.

I can't even imagine how miserable he must have been in that big "hairy coat" thing he wore under those hot lights.

As soon as you'd go under those lights, it was just devastating. We all sweated. There was no air conditioning, and all of us were wringin' wet. I can remember them putting powder on our faces that apparently absorbed or refracted the light. It did not give us any relief, it just kept us from being wringin' wet. When we had a break, sometimes Mr. Karloff would take off some of that costume—he'd take off the vest, which was killing him, and those awful, heavy, lead-weighted boots. That's when I became aware that that stuff was punishing him. You know the old high-top Keds? What he wore during the breaks were kind of like that, they were tennis shoes. Back then, all the tennis shoes were high-tops, but these were cut off, probably with scissors, so they were like house slippers. They didn't stay on his heels very well, like a child's sandals, and I thought that was pretty funny. Under the vest, it seems to me that one time he had a real loose-fitting, very thin white shirt that didn't have a collar. Another time, he had what today we would call a T-shirt. It was during those times that I realized that Karloff was not the big, robust, upper-body-strength guy that some of the grips around *were*. We had grips around there who could've been Mr. America.

What else did you do between takes, to pass the time?

On the sound stages, I was allowed to have a little bag. It had a book or two in it, blank paper and a real ink pen, maybe music sheets of songs I was asked to learn, just nonsense things. I didn't carry my bag around all day, I'd always put it on a chair or somewhere. One day during *Son of Frankenstein* I went over to the canvas chair where I'd put my bag, and laying on top of it was a real expensive-looking box, with an image of a pistol on it. A box almost like you would find expensive collector's pistols in today. And inside was what I thought at first was a cap pistol—it took me a moment to perceive what the dickens it really was, and what it turned out to *be* was a *water* pistol. Now, this was not an average water pistol, this was one spiffy mother. It was gray, it had a round barrel and it was metal, *all* metal—none of this plastic junk today. I picked it up and *almost* started walking around like, "Ooh, ooh, who gave me this, who gave me this?," but I stopped and said to myself, "No, no, no. I'm not supposed to *have* this." I went to the lavatory and I got it loaded. And instead of shooting right *at* people—the only one person I ever shot at directly was a man at Disney who was a jerk, a Scrooge kind of guy—I would shoot it up in the air. The water would come down like raindrops, and people would think that the roof was leaking. Then they'd stop and look around! And I'd sit there like an innocent kid—but having a great time.

You did this to people on the set on Son of Frankenstein.

Yeah, on the last part of it. And every place *else* I got a chance [*laughs*]! It had a pump inside, a classic straight pressure pump, and it took two fingers for me to squirt it.

If you had to guess, who would you say gave you the water pistol?

Mr. Karloff. Oh, I think he was a mischievous guy! A kid can really sense who's uptight and who is a little bit loose, and so I think Karloff may have done that. He had forgiven me for the quarters by that time [*laughs*], and he had a good sense of humor, and I sensed that he was a good man inside. There was a scene where he was in the laboratory where there was a make-believe sulfur pit, and the father Basil Rathbone was going to swing down like Tarzan and knock him into the pit. During part of that scene, I was lying on the floor and Karloff had his foot on me. Now, the two of us had already played checkers and had a good time, and he took me to lunch a couple of times, and we'd walked through the set with him in makeup and me, this little jerk kid, holding hands. So I'm having a good time! Anyway, we got to laughing in this scene because he was ticklin' me with his darn boot [*laughs*]! I was lying down and Karloff had his boot on me, and I could tell he was trying to keep it from pressing on me. His boot was heavy and he was very sensitive to hurting me—for which I'm grateful! But until they said, "Roll 'em!," he would wiggle his boot and *tickle* me.

Dunagan was carefully introduced to Boris Karloff, first *sans* makeup and later in his Monster get-up, so that the four year old would not be afraid to work with him.

On purpose.

Yes! He'd put it down on me and then he'd twist it. I tickle real easy, even to this day. You know something?, when I boxed a lot, I was always worried that somebody was going to discover, in the clinches, that I tickle [*laughs*]! He was twisting it on my back and on my side, and I'd get to laughing. Then *he'd* get to laughing. Then somebody behind the lights would get to laughing. We couldn't stop, and they had to stop for several minutes. At *this* point, I don't think Mr. Lee [director Rowland V. Lee] was too happy, because he scolded both of us. The only time I ever remember getting scolded by Mr. Lee was because I was laughing because I was getting tickled! And [scolding people] wasn't his persona. He was a very gentle and rather slow talker, very deliberate, very personable. I felt a little bad at first, then I realized that he was also enjoying this. But he scolded *both* of us, and everybody *else* who was laughing. Mr. Lee didn't direct it *just* at us, a *lot* of people were laughing. Well, Karloff and I, we were the bad guys, we knew dang well that we were responsible for this delay. Karloff looked down at me just sorta like "We gotta cool it." He didn't *say* that, but he had that kind of an expression on his face. Then we both smiled at each other and we went back to work, and finally got that darn scene done.

Here's a real memory tester: When Rathbone's stunt double swings down and kicks Karloff's stunt double off the edge of the laboratory set, what did he fall into?

A big net on springs. I did not know that until it was all over, when somebody walked me over and held my hand and let me look down. They had a net, and it had big springs (like ones in a car) and it had ropes, and then there was something *underneath* the net, it was probably cushions and stuff. Also, on the edges of this very large net, they also had real ugly machines that were burping out this fog or smoke stuff. During the takes, they had this stuff coming up out of the pit, and it had a bad odor. By the way, they had stunt doubles doing all that, of course, and that confused me. When I would see doubles, I can remember that my reaction was, "What is *this* stuff?" I never did figure that out [as a little kid]—of course, *later* I did. But when I was a kid, I could not understand why we had to have somebody else that *looked* like them.

Rowland V. Lee directed three of your films, Mother Carey's Chickens, Son of Frankenstein *and* Tower of London *[1939]. What other impressions of him?*

You didn't have to be a brain surgeon to perceive that he was in charge. Some people have leadership presence just by *being* there. Years and years ago, one of the interesting things said in the Marine Corps by career sergeants was that you could tell a Marine Corps line officer at a swimming pool in a bathing suit. That was an exaggeration, of course, a complimentary exaggeration. But there *is* something *to* that. Mr. Lee was in charge, and a blind person could sense that in a minute. Now, some people are in charge because they're allowed to give orders and, if you don't obey the order, you go to jail. That's easy—a moron can do that. I used to tell the young lieutenants, I used to hammer them with it: "You lead by example. An idiot can give orders if the person he's talking to is at risk if he doesn't obey. Real leadership is influencing people to do some things that maybe they don't want to *do*." Like charge machine-guns—try that one for leadership!

Well, Mr. Lee had a very natural, calm, dignified presence that everybody seemed to pick up on, and after a few days on *Son of Frankenstein*, I thought he *owned* the whole place! He would move around the sound stages, very casually, checking on people, asking how people were, and I was standing pretty close by—he used to take me along with him. I vaguely remember him talking to somebody who had to be a grip, a guy who had a big ladder on wheels. Apparently this guy's wife had just had a baby and had some difficulty, and when Mr. Lee asked the man about his wife, I thought they were *related*. Then I realized that, no, the grip was a guy who worked there, but Mr. Lee was asking him about his wife *by name*. Now that's leadership. They just thought the world of him. When he would walk by an area where maybe he hadn't yet been that day, the guys handling the lights and the huge, *huge* artificial walls that they had to roll on wheels, they would pause and turn and say [*enthusiastically*], "Mr. Lee! How ya doin', Mr. Lee??" That doesn't happen unless you're a good leader.

Son of Frankenstein producer-director Rowland V. Lee was such a commanding presence, little Donnie thought he was the owner of the studio!

Was Basil Rathbone as friendly as Karloff?

Yes, Basil Rathbone was a cultured, gentle man and he was as friendly as Karloff. He would read poems. They were from European authors, I think, almost all of them. And Kipling—he was a big fan of Kipling.

This was during breaks in shooting, times like that.

That's right. We had a hard time filling in time in the breaks—the breaks were a bore. I mean, [*voice cracking*] a *bore*! Because the lights would be put somewhere, and somebody helping Mr. Lee would go, "No, we need those four feet over here"—they were testing the shadows a lot. That's when Rathbone would read to me.

Did you play checkers with Rathbone?

No. He was *going* to teach me chess. I think I probably did a few moves, but I was very slow, because that was very different than checkers. He may have *thought* he taught me, but the honest truth is that I never played a full game. I did some moves, and he told me what to watch for on the second and third moves, and how you can tell what a guy's "style" is. I didn't know style from peanut butter [*laughs*]—I mean, what do *I* know about style? I don't think I played … if I did, I don't remember a full game. But he did try, and apparently he was very good at it, from the conversations around at the time.

Incidentally, the war [in Europe] was on the minds of a lot of people there on the set. I don't remember what stage it was at the time 'cause I didn't know where Europe was, I couldn't have found it on a map; I don't know if I'd ever seen a globe at that point in my life. But I can remember that Mr. Karloff was very sensitive to the insanity of national wars, and he was making comments about how sad it was that civilized, cultured people were all beating each other up and killing each other. At that age, I thought maybe this was happening, like a crime, in *our* country.

Your mom in the movie, Josephine Hutchinson—any recollection?
Hardly anything, except that she was very attractive and very popular with people. But when the scenes were finished, she wasn't [one of the performers] who would hang around, she would disappear. She was probably a wonderful person, how the heck do I know?, I have no memory of her because *you remember the people between the scenes*. And I don't remember ever *seeing* her between scenes. But, oh, the lady who played the maid [Emma Dunn], she was *marvelous*. She was the "mother" of everybody, she took care of everybody. She was all over the place, she worried about everybody, she took care of everybody, and everybody just loved her.

Lionel Atwill played the police inspector, and you called him "General."
I didn't *like* him. No.

He is kind of an icy character in some of his scenes in the movie; maybe that spooked you.
For some reason, I didn't like him. I avoided him. I didn't like him. That's true. I avoided him.

He later got in trouble with the law. He showed dirty movies at a party at his house, he had kind of an orgy there. Then he pulled a Martha Stewart and lied to investigators about it, and it was the perjury that really got him in trouble. So maybe he wasn't the nicest guy and you picked up on that.
I did, I picked up on that pretty quick. I'll just tell you that I picked up on that pretty quick.

There's a cute moment in the movie where you walk like the Monster. Who taught you to do that?
Mr. Karloff. And Mr. Lee too. We got to laughing in the early takes of that scene, because I didn't do it worth a darn. They said they wanted me to … "*strut*," I think, was the word they used … like Frankenstein. Well, Frankenstein was Mr. Karloff to me—the quarters guy. So I kinda walked like a stiff-legged toy soldier. Well, somebody laughed. Then somebody else laughed. And we had to do *another* one. And Mr. Lee and Mr. Karloff, both, showed me what they wanted me to do. I had to get tutored on *that* one.

What other Son of Frankenstein *memories?*

They kept changing the dialogue, and people were having a hard time. Mr. Lee the director gave me a bonus, a roll of quarters, because I would help folks with their lines! I walked around with that roll of quarters in my hand, like, "Boy, am I rich!" They had to take it away when I did a scene, and I was very sensitive as to who had custody of my fortune. Sixty-something years later I *still* remember who had it, it was some young lady with a big smile. After the scene, I remember people laughing as I was running over to her to get my fortune back!

I think Son of Frankenstein *was still being written as you guys were already shooting.*

That could be.

So maybe the writers weren't changing the dialogue, maybe they were writing it for the first time!

"Cultured, gentle" Basil Rathbone read Donnie poems (and tried to teach him chess) on *Son of Frankenstein*'s Expressionistic sets.

Well, I remembered everybody's lines—I mean, *every*body's lines. And Mr. Lee and Karloff were just delighted that I could, off on the side, coach folks on their lines before the scenes. Because I wanted to get *out* of there! We were in there for *hours* because of all the darn retakes. I remember that on another movie, *The Forgotten Woman* [1939], some of the scenes just made no sense to me, some of the scenes were just silly. I'd think, "Who in the dickens wrote *this* thing?" and "People don't *do* this, this is nuts!" I got hit by a car—in the *storyline*, not actually! I got hit by a sedan in the street and somebody picked me up and carried me off. I was supposed to be in critical condition and I didn't even have my hair messed up! I said, "Wait a minute. I saw a dog hit by a car once, and it wasn't like *this*!" [*Laughs*]

Your old publicity says that you could walk at seven months and talk by 11 months.

We have [San Antonio] articles about that. Neighbors apparently would call the papers about this, and news reporters would come out ... and in some number. When I was somewhere around a year old, someone is alleged to have given me a short sentence in Spanish and asked me to replicate it. I did, and everyone went crazy. So there was a bit of [news coverage], and then later, when I began reading at three and a half, there was some more in Memphis.

Your curly hair in Son of Frankenstein—*is that how your hair really* was *in those days?*

[*Scornfully*] Noooo! No, they curled my darn hair twice a day. What a pain in the neck. I *hated* that, just hated it. On one set one time, probably *Son of Franken-*

stein, I was walking along with big curlers in my hair and some adult was with me, I don't remember who—maybe it was one of my nannies who weren't very good nannies. Anyway, all of a sudden I saw some older boy, and I don't even know what he was there for. He was a foot or two taller than me but still a boy, and he came by with another kid and, as we were passing, he slowed down, pointed at me, laughed and said, "Look at that *sissy*." From that point forward, when they would do that curler procedure, I'd go off and hide, and they had to find me. Later in life, a couple people suggested that maybe that's why I became a boxer at 14, because I didn't want to be remembered as some sissy [*laughs*]!

Several months later, you had a very small part in another movie with Karloff and Rathbone, Tower of London.

In *Tower of London,* at age four or five, my character [Baby Prince Richard] got married to a girl [Joan Carroll] who was about age six. Basil Rathbone was trying to kill me, and others, throughout the whole film, to get control of the British crown. This was a constructed story, *not* much history [*laughs*]!

Walking down the aisle with that little girl was your whole part in Tower of London, *you say only two words in the movie. Did you shoot other scenes that were cut?*

Oh, yeah! I remember being told to pretend that I was afraid that some people were going to hurt me: "Look afraid, stumble a little bit, and run over here…" In another scene, I was watching, in a sneaky way, looking *over* something, looking down on men who were discussing something that I guess was evil. And there was another scene with an adult who was supposed to protect me. There were probably one or two more but I don't remember.

On *Tower of London* I saw Mr. Rathbone angry several times. He would walk around with the heavy script and talk to people who were obviously in charge. And this wasn't just once in a while that I could tell [that Rathbone was angry], this was several times, throughout. I'd be off-camera with other people who were in costume for hours and hours, and it was hotter than blazes, I'll never forget. Hot hot hot. And we sat, and we sat, and we took breaks, and we sat, and we sat. And Mr. Rathbone was angry. Not rude—I don't think he had a rude bone in his body. But he was very upset. And now that I know [that cuts and script changes were being made during production], it's not hard to construct what may have happened, and what happened *may* have been somebody changing the storyline and/or scripting and/or dialogue as we went along. I remember very explicitly that Mr. Rathbone was very "out of character" for him, taking this big pile of typed papers and patting them in the way you do when something's wrong, and then pointing here and pointing there, and big discussions that four or five people would join in on. He was unhappy with that film. *Very* unhappy. I could tell because he was always super-super-nice to me [on *Son of Frankenstein*], and on *Tower of London* he did not have the smiles on, he did not come by or pat me or invite me to ice cream or stuff like he used to do.

Did your mom have a good time on the sets of these movies?

When she was there. After a while, and I don't remember what the threshold

Deserted by his nannies during *Son of Frankenstein* production, Dunagan found new and better playmates in Basil Rathbone and Boris Karloff.

was on this, but progressively [while on movie sets] I was in the hands of tutors—alleged tutors, who didn't tutor. And nannies. The nannies happened to be very young, attractive women who I think were starlet wannabes, and they would evaporate. Fully half the time or more, on-set time, I was by myself. That's why responsible, decent adults like Mr. Rathbone, and a wonderful lady named Fay Bainter on *Mother Carey's Chickens*, stepped in. Those adults became important to me, because I was by myself. My mom was a wonderful person—okay?—but she trusted people. Remember, she came out of an austere environment, so if you had decent clothes on, if you were in a suit, or if you were introduced as somebody who was cultured, her trust threshold was very high. She would turn me over to people and then she would *go*. I learned later that she was off shopping somewhere, Westwood or Beverly Hills or wherever you go. And that's okay—where would I ever get the right to have any feelings [of resentment] about that? But these people to whom I was turned over were frivolous, and I mean *frivolous*, and they would evaporate. So I made my own friends, and I had to learn to protect myself a bit, because there were some not-always-nice people around.

You must remember that [my parents] went almost overnight from managing nickels to having *money*—a new car, a house in Westwood, California, and so on. The money destroyed the family.

The money you earned.

Yeah. It destroyed the family. I'll give you a quick aside on that, one that you might find of interest: We just discovered—"we," this wonderful lady who is putting up with me [Dana] and I—a news article reporting that in 1938, a Los Angeles Superior Court judge ordered a trust fund established for me for one-half of all earnings retro and present, to be put aside until I was a majority age, a trust fund that even my parents could not access. In the article, it articulates that this was being done because of Jackie Coogan's problem—Jackie Coogan made a ton of money [as a child actor] but by the time he was a young adult and married, all of the money was gone because his family squandered it. So now, with a beautiful law firm here in Texas who I trust with my family, and with the help of some judges in California who have been very responsive, we're looking for the old documents from the court and trying to find out what bank that judge directed to be used, and where in the blazes that money *is*. Even if there was only a lousy thousand dollars, and there's more money involved than *that*, but even if there was only a thousand dollars, at two percent compounded for 65 years—click click click *click*. Okay? They're *after* it, and we're going to find out what *happened* to it. And if there's some hanky panky, somebody's responsible for that *some*where!

Jeez, I wish you all the luck in the world on that.

So do *we*! I had some trouble with some fellows called Enron, so I could use some help on this thing!

Oh, shucks—were you an Enron investor?

Heavy. For many years. I got hammered.

What can you remember about providing the voice of young Bambi?

I was hired by Disney personally to be the *model* for Bambi—the big brown eyes, head motions and other gestures, expressions of joy and fear and so on. I can remember posing for the artist at Disney, who was sketching

Five-year-old Dunagan as Baby Prince Richard—and Joan Carroll, who plays his wife (!)—in Universal's *Tower of London*. Most of Dunagan's footage in the 1939 historical horror show got the axe.

furiously, *very* fast sketching. They were telling me to turn my head this way, turn my head that way, "Look frightened!," etc. That preceded auditioning to be the voice of Bambi in his youth—the first two-thirds of the film. For the voice of older Bambi, in the last third of the film, they used an older boy. But I was hired initially as the eye and facial expression model, and *then* hired as the voice.

Incidentally, I don't think that most of the men—and it *was* then mostly men around—were used to having high-speed little guys running about, much less working with them in art production. I often heard someone say, "There is a child in here now…," like to "heads-up" other staff. But the Disney folks were always happy, gracious, over-helpful to me when I was looking for something, or if I had questions—and I suspect I had questions about *every*thing in those days! It was a wonderful experience for a young boy to have.

You recall modeling for the artist; do you remember the voice recording sessions?
There were rehearsals, of course, and a lot of dialogue changed—somebody in Disney was changing the dialogue in *that* one as we were goin' along too! They showed me images of what the baby deer was supposed to be doing, and it was flickering—it wasn't cohesive in motion sequence, like a *good* film. [Dunagan might be describing watching pencil tests.] I had headphones on, old-fashioned headphones, and a man sat next to me and showed me, on something like a clipboard, what to say. And at the right moment he would move his hand in a "Do it *now*!" kind of gesture. I'm sure they're a whole lot more sophisticated now than we were then [*laughs*]. But it worked! I spent more time there in "art mode" than in "voice mode." The voice was easy, and I don't think that took a lot of time. Sitting on a stool for the sketchers—I called them "the drawing men"—that took a bit more time.

Did you meet Walt Disney?
Oh, several times. He met me the first day. Sat down with me and my mom. Easy talk. He asked my opinion on well-known things. He was fun to be with. Later I saw him often. He was one of many who seemed to want to insure that the children in the production areas were well looked-after. Mr. Disney talked to performers a lot, in gentle terms. I had the impression—now, this is just a kid's impression—that he was a tough potato with other people. But with performers and with kids, he was a gentle person. My mom thought he was the most wonderful man.

That's a great photo you have, you and Mickey and Minnie Mouse in the cafeteria.
I remember that cafeteria well. With Mr. Disney frequently entering and using the cafeteria, it seemed to me to be a fun place. People would bring drawings and small models (birds, cows, all kinds of things) to the tables there and have great discussions. I loved it. I moved around like a free-agent spy, and everyone was great to me. It was not a "stuffed shirt" place like some of the dining rooms at the other studios; I rather disliked those because I had to sit still! Mr. Disney's cafeteria for his company-family was a family place. I saw ladies and men dressed like they belonged in the White House, and others with art bibs on, even crew guys in work shirts. It

The voice of young Bambi is flanked by Minnie and Mickey Mouse in the Disney commissary.

was wonderful. I wanted to go all the time and not because of hunger. Mickey and Minnie Mouse staged several photos with me.

And you still had your Son of Frankenstein *water pistol on* Bambi, *you mentioned before.*
    I used it in the cafeteria once. I had to hide it in a cloth napkin to do it—a real clandestine shooter. There was a table with some people nearby, four or five men, and every one of 'em looked like the world had just come to an end. Everybody else in the cafeteria was having a good time and laughing and making jokes, and the men at this table were just *dyin'*, they weren't looking at each other, they were looking down, they weren't even *eating* yet. There was an occasional word or two, but they were just miserable. I got the gun into position and [*makes four squirting noises*] four good squirts, and the water came down right on top of 'em. Well, they jumped up, looked around and pointed up to the ceiling. It was so sunny outside, it would cook your brains, but they were looking for a leak in the ceiling [*laughs*]! One guy went and got one of the managers and came back, and another guy got on his *chair*. The ceiling was not that high, and he was looking up there for the leak! I was laughin' my butt off!

Your friends at that time, kids your age—did they know you were the voice of Bambi?
    Yes, some of the kids around me knew that I had some little contribution to

the film. I recall, loud and clear, all my life, some of their reactions, which were great then and wonderful now: "My dog might have feelings like the deer did"; "I know my cat can feel hurt too ... that is bad'; "People can cause bad things and not know what they are doing"; and one I will never forget: "The Daddy Deer, the big one on the hill—the hunters are lucky he didn't see them. *My* dad would have got those guys..."

When I was ten, I remember seeing two 12 or 13 year olds getting ready to do great evil to a cat who was tied down and yelling for its life. I said, "Did you see *Bambi?*" "Yeah!" "Would Bambi or his mom or dad do that to a little creature?" Long pause. I thought I was going to have to make a run for it. But they looked at each other long. A sharp tool was put back into a pocket. One said, "Sorry." And they got up and left. I untied the cat—which immediately scratched me. Hard. No respect [*laughs*]!

A while back, you said that "money destroyed your family"—do you want to elaborate on that a little bit?

They were decent people, but sometimes that kind of quick cash can ... *distort* things. It just destroyed the family. And then the War [World War II] came along. I want to pass over this if I may. I'll just submit to you, so that I'm courteous to your intellect, [the quick money] and the War, physically and emotionally, and in deaths, just destroyed the family. I was on my own for a lot of time, and [after *Bambi*] I was in an orphanage for a bit of time. From age 13 and a half forward, I was in a boarding house, on my own. And I did well. I was a straight kid, no smokin', no nothin'. I graduated from high school early, and I was going to go to medical school to be a doctor if it killed me, that's all the hell I wanted to do. That was my dream. The only dream that I have had that I didn't fulfill. All these years. I don't mind saying that out loud.

Instead you went into the Marine Corps.

Went into the Marine Corps, fell in love with the Marine Corps, and stayed for 25 years.

What year did you go in?

I get a draft notice in December of '52, to go down for a physical. *Not* to report, *not* to be shipped off, but go down for a physical. I go to the induction center and I've got a towel wrapped around me and I'm standing in line with a bunch of *other* guys with towels wrapped around them, and they're doing things with us one at a time. It's very boring. And out of the corner of this big room comes this guy who's big as a door. I'm not talking about fat, I'm talking about a guy who looks like the NFL in Marine uniform. The rest of the people are dressed in white, boring clothes, and here comes this guy with blue britches on and a white cap, a real spiffy uniform. He comes over and he looks up and down the line and he comes over to me and he says, "Do you play ball, son?" I say "Yes"—I didn't say "Yes, sir." Well, I later learn he was a World War II super-decorated combat gunnery sergeant. A gunnery sergeant in the Marine Corps is like a surrogate god [*laughs*]—and I *was* one later, very young, for a short period of time, before I was commissioned. Anyway, this guy says, "We have a football team, son," and I say [*excitedly*], "You *do*?" He says, "Yes. What do you play?" I tell him I was a fullback. He says, "Come over here…"

Thirty-five minutes later, I'm in the Marine Corps. I'm not kidding! And the next day I'm on a train to boot camp. They gave me a clipboard and put me in charge of a bunch of young men I never saw before, going on this train to boot camp.

How many young men?

I think between 30 and 40, some of whom had been drafted and some who had volunteered. Some obviously came out of some pretty tough circumstances, because a few of these guys didn't have any shoes. Now, wait a minute, this gets hairier! I get to boot camp, and boot camp's a lark! Marine boot camp, physically, can kill you, but I was in good shape and I thought this was a lark! When I graduated from boot camp, they sent me right to D.I. [drill instructor] school, to become a D.I. I was a pfc! Unheard of! I thought that first sergeant at D.I. school, when I reported in there 15 minutes after graduating as a pfc, was gonna have a cardiac! I was the youngest drill instructor in Marine Corps history. True story! Some general somewhere had made a decision, "The Korean War's going on and we're short on drill instructors. Let's see if we can't use a couple of these boys [as drill instructors]." That was an experiment, making me a drill instructor as a pfc. Some officers told me later that they were very worried about how the other NCOs would react to a pfc at D.I. school. But I was a good boxer and I wasn't a wimp, and they treated me very nice. I made some friends that lasted a lifetime. And I became a drill instructor as a pfc. A pfc [*laughs*]!

Did you end up in Korea?

No. When they realized later that I hadn't been through Camp Pendleton training, they sent me to Pendleton. I went through training there and I was put on a ship in San Diego, to go to Korea. The darn ship turned around—President Eisenhower stopped the War. The ship turned around in Hawaii and came back.

And then you came up through the ranks.

I made corporal and sergeant so quick, I couldn't keep my chevrons on the shirt. True story. I didn't even know what was happening to me! I was loving every minute of it. The Marine Corps was wonderful to me. It became surrogate parents. Later—I want to share this with you very sincerely, this is important to me at this stage of my life—I realized later, as a counterintelligence agent, and then a commander, and battalion commander, and other things—I realized later that I was spoiled rotten during my early time in the Marine Corps. I was in the *hands* of … in the *units* of … *led* by … one after the other … the *top* one, two percent of Marine officers. Later, when I was asked in interviews, "Who do you remember [from the Corps]?," I would go through names. And every interviewer would go, "My gosh, that was the top lieutenant colonel," "My gosh, that was the top major," "Gosh, that was the top captain…" Irish luck applied here, or *some*thing, but I went from one top-drawer, well-known leader to another, by just *accident*, I guess. I did my apprenticeships with all these top guys. When people said later, "Gosh, you've done such a good job"—well, I *should* do a good job. I worked for Col. Clyde P. Ford and I worked for Lt. Short and Col. Robert Wise and Col. Bob Monfort and Sgt. Major Sam Pierce, who *should* have been a Marine general, people who were famous in the Marine Corps. I'd have to have been a nincompoop not to be a decent leader after that apprenticeship.

Did you serve in Vietnam?

Three times. I was evacuated each time. In later years, a general named Kenneth J. Houghton would introduce me at big after-dinner shindigs, he was a wonderful guy and a good comedian. He was on the cover of *Life* magazine in 1950, the only time we've had a Marine officer on the cover of *Life*. I worked for him three times in the Marine Corps. A lot of guys were scared to death of him; I loved him to death. We both retired out of San Diego in '77, him as a two-star general, me as a major. Houghton was a unique guy and he had a great sense of humor, he was a great after-dinner speaker, and when he would introduce me as a speaker from time to time, he would do it this way: "And here's this damn Dunagan here—can't hold a job! We sent him into Vietnam and five months later he's in a hospital somewhere, flirtin' with the girls!" So I never finished a tour, because I got zapped three damn times [*laughs*]!

You got injured?

Oh, yeah! I had last rites performed over me three times that I know of. I wasn't a practicing religious person, but they've always put *some*thing on your dog tags, and they put "Roman Catholic" on mine because I had been in a Roman Catholic orphanage I guess. And then [after getting zapped], conscientious people would say last rites over you 'cause you're not breathin' too good! I'll tell you who saved *my* ass more than once was young Navy corpsmen. Nobody is ever gonna say a word adverse to *me* about Navy corpsmen, I'll punch 'em out. I can still get in the ring and coach boxing and I'm 70—I'm not kidding, okay? You wanna find out what real courage is? Find somebody who was scared to death to do something and still *did* it. Young Navy corpsmen are the most courageous people in the whole Marine Corps, and anybody who's really been in combat is not gonna argue with me about *that* one. Navy corpsmen, *scared to death*, most of 'em couldn't load the .45 on their hip, they wouldn't know how, crawling around under fire, puttin' bandages on you while gettin' their helmets shot off, and stayin' *with* you. You know what I'm sayin'? You want to find out where the courage is in the Marine Corps, go look at Navy corpsmen. I've written up an equal number of Navy corpsmen as I have infantry sergeants, they're wonderful kids.

Right before I retired as a major, I was selected to go to the War College at Leavenworth, to faculty. I was going to go, but during October of '77 I got my hands on all the Pentagon Papers that Mr. [Daniel] Ellsberg was courageous enough to leak out. I read *every line*. *No*body read every line. Congressmen didn't read every line. I was a credentialed counterintelligence officer in the Marine Corps and an

After "playing soldier" in *Son of Frankenstein*, Dunagan went on to become a career Marine. (Photofest)

infantry commander at the same time—kind of unique—so I had lawful access to all the super-classified annexes, that were literally in big security safes, that the Pentagon Papers referred to, that weren't included in the Pentagon Papers that were leaked. I studied these in October and early November and I emotionally and intellectually got sick to my stomach. I was so disappointed at what we had done and the lies we told, particularly on bombing targets and results, and lying about where we had sprayed Agent Orange. Some of the guys who were in my last unit had died before they were 45 years old, and when they died, 10, 12, 14 years ago, Washington *still*, then, refused to say that Agent Orange was the agent that it was. Now Washington *has* [admitted it], at last. But of course most of those guys are dead now—how convenient is *that*? I don't mind saying that out loud. Anyway, after reading all that, I was agonizing over this crap that I discovered, and I went back and pulled out all the names of everybody that was lost in the Vietnam War, either in units that I was the leader of, or when I was a junior officer in somebody else's larger unit: 123 in two tours. I then hustled the last-known addresses, "the casualty list" addresses they're called, of all these people, and I wrote every one of those families a letter, in ink, telling them, "This is one standing line officer that wants to apologize to you for the loss of your son in a war that was frivolous and wrong, and I am sorry."

I retired that next month. The Marine Corps tried its darnedest to talk me out

In his military career, Dunagan went from private to drill instructor to battalion commander and Cold War counterintelligence officer.

of it, but I just could not handle… [*Pause*] I had been raised by some very strong people in the Marine Corps that would not pick up a thousand dollar bill on the damn street if it did not belong to them. I was just lucky as the dickens, I had been around nothing but top, incredible people in the Marine Corps, people who could have run General Motors had they not been a battalion commander or something. I got spoiled, I guess, and I had some standards, and the Pentagon Papers just ripped me up. I just was not going to recruit kids and lead 'em again into more of that kind of nonsense. That's one of the reasons why I am *livid* at what we're doing today [the War on Terror].

The letterhead on the letters you send me list your Marine credentials and also say that you're "retired on wounds." Can I ask about that?

Sure, yeah. But [*laughs*], let me preface this: If I had a chance even now to motor 150 miles somewhere to do amateur theater to break back into the [acting] business as an old character actor, I would do it in a *second*. I am *fit*. I work like an animal to be fit. I can do more sit-ups than any 30 year old runnin' around this damn place, and I can still box. And I'm 70 this next week.

Now, having said that to you: I have a gunshot plate at the back of my head. Not a big deal. I have a little bit of a plate on *top* of my head, but I still have a full head of hair despite everything—my haircut covers these. I have a rifle gunshot to my left knee. They were going to cut that leg off in a [Vietnam] field hospital but, because things move very dynamically there, they had made the mistake of not disarming me completely. I was only half-unconscious, I was hearing them talk about taking my leg off, and I threatened to kill 'em. I still had a .45 on me. Then they panicked, and disarmed me. I was about half-comatose because they'd been shooting me up with pain killers. And I had a lot of blood loss, because my leg was literally dangling there—the gunshot had gone right through my knee.

Where did this happen?

Probably on the outskirts of Da Nang somewhere. Well, a *wonderful* Navy surgeon was in this operating tent and he was yelling at them, after they had disarmed me, that they might be able to save my leg with new gadgets, like the Bionic Man got. I don't remember anything else, I must have passed out. The next thing I remember is four days later and I'm up on the third floor of a magnificent Naval hospital on Guam Island, and that's a long ways away from Vietnam. And here is this Navy surgeon! He had talked somebody into letting him fly with me from Vietnam to Guam, and he was there to supervise the reconstruction of my knee. After that recovery, I went back into Vietnam a year and a half later as a commander again, and my leg was as strong as a bull. I could run, I could do the obstacle course, the whole bloody damn thing.

I have another wound in my scrotum sac. I'm functional [*laughs*]—I emphasize that real loud and clear! But my scrotum sac was nicked a little and it opened up and all the fluids passed. A young corpsman did a marvelous job of saving me and evacuating me out at a pretty good speed. I have a knife wound, a rather large, six-and-a-half-inch long knife wound underneath my right ribcage; that was a very violent ... *incredibly* violent night action. I have a gunshot in my left lung and a gunshot in my stomach. And several white marks—fragmentation from enemy mortars and things—on different parts of my body. I have a grenade scar under my chin, a grenade scar on my upper lip and a grenade scar underneath my left eye. Now, these are not offensive scars, okay? Remember, I'm trying to hustle myself back in the business [*laughs*]!

Could you kill me with your thumb?

[*Pause*] I can break an arm that's thrown at me—I don't care who it is—on the way to the ground. And if I *had* to, I could change the attitude of your neck ... quickly ... today!

"Today"—great!

I'm not kidding.

Being part of Bambi *certainly didn't turn you off on guns! Have you ever hunted an animal?*
No.

Did that come from Bambi?
I don't know. I would love to tell you that, but I don't know. I was a shooter in the Marine Corps, so in hunting season it was very natural for a colonel or major or captain with whom I had a good association to say to me, "Listen, let's go hunting." I got a lot of invitations to go to those things, and if I discerned that a trophy hunter was going to be in the party of three or four, I wouldn't go. And *today* I won't. Forget it. Won't do it. The fellows who say they're gonna take this animal they've killed and go dress it and give half of it to an orphanage, or half of it to a church, and then take some of it home to Momma and put it in the freezer—I didn't have any trouble with that. But I never needed to feed anybody, so I wouldn't do it. I went on the hunting trips with a camera, and I would tease the blazes out of them: "After you eat that animal, it's gone. *I* got that animal forever [on film]—ha-ha!" And I loved to take pictures of animals *that they didn't get*. I took several shots of animals (mostly deer) right before the animals heard us or smelled us and took off, and I would flaunt them later. I'd show the pictures to others who had been on the trip, and tell them, "Oh, that one was behind you, you missed seein' it." [*Laughs*] That probably wasn't very nice but I didn't care, I loved doin' that!

Getting back to Son of Frankenstein—*you once told me that you don't remember whether you saw it when it was new, so when* do *you think was the first time you saw it?*
Now, don't laugh at me too hard: I was 46 or 47 years old! It was on television at Halloween time. I was living in Whittier, California, and I had lots of neighbors over to see it. There was probably too much drinking—and I don't drink—and we watched *Son of Frankenstein*. Everybody got a big kick out of it, and I got teased without *mercy*, for weeks afterwards! I was sorry I showed it to them!

You watched it "live" on regular TV.
Yes, sir. With a lot of commercials, as I remember. I got teased—teased in a *nice* way. But I was glad when the teasing subsided [*laughs*]! I was a businessman, and I'd be walking down the street, and some neighbor would see me across the street, with *his* family, and start walking like Frankenstein. And pointing at me, and laughing!

And what do you think of your performance in Son of Frankenstein?
Corny. And I had a Southern accent! So, to answer your question, I saw it for the first time when I was in my forties. In fact, I saw it a *couple* times, back to back. The second time I didn't *do* it with neighbors, by the way!

[*Laughs*] *I'm sure you'll* never *do that* again!
No, I haven't done that again! Anyway, when I saw it the first couple times, I remember thinking that they had a lot of courage: With this dignified European

cast, they had this little kid in there with this loud voice. They kept saying "Speak up!," because I didn't speak that loud then. "Everybody! Speak up! Speak up!" So people were (what you'd call if you were a linguist) "out of voice" most of the time. And as you speak up, your accent is always accentuated. So here's this little curly-headed jerk kid runnin' around there with this *very* deep Memphis-Texas accent [*laughs*]! They had the courage to *do* that!

You say you'd enjoy getting back into acting again today.
    I'd love to have another chance at it. I'm being very frank with you. I would love to have a shot at being in one of these adventure films I see once in a while, [because the actors who *are* in them] wouldn't know what to do with a real .45 if their life depended on it. I could do a character in accent. I can facsimile a real Scotch accent [*Dunagan does the accent for each country as he names it*] ... a real Irish accent ... British ... some French ... some German ... Deep South ... Canadian ... and other accents. I would love to get a shot at a character actor role in a film. I'm 188 pounds, six-foot-one, and I can still box. I don't give a darn if it was some evil character in some film. It would help me get my family out of this ... lost-our-ass mess.

The Enron mess.
    Yes. Forgive me for swearing, but that's where I am.

Well, one thing you could do is go to some of these autograph shows where, if you went with Son of Frankenstein *photos, you could charge 10, 20 bucks a pop and sell a pile of them, I'm sure.*
    People have suggested that in recent times. But I've got an obstruction in this head that won't go away ... and I don't want to try to force it ... of "non-self-promote." My wife had to beat me up for years to let her have, out of boxes in the garage, some medals to display, medals that most men would kill to have. I don't *like* that. I worked for a man in the Marine Corps for about a year when I was a boy, when I was gettin' promoted quicker than I had any right to be. I worked for a man who later would never wear anything [any medals] on his chest, while all the other fellows had all these ribbons and stuff. And I learned later that he had the Medal of Honor, the Navy Cross, two Silver Stars, four Purple Hearts. But unless he was forced to wear them for a ceremony or something, he would wear plain uniform shirts. And he wasn't the only guy like that I was around. I learned to respect that ... *deeply* ... and I just don't self-promote worth a darn. I can't *do* that. This is really hard for me to deal with *you* right now. If that other wonderful man Scott MacQueen had not "warmed me up" for this, I don't know that I could do this *interview* right now!

Well, if you ever change your mind, let me know—I think the reaction would be very good. Frankenstein movie fans have been looking for you for years, never with any success.
    Well, I kept all this quiet—except for the mistake of showing *Son of Frankenstein* to some neighbors [*laughs*]. I never talked about this in 25 years in the Marine

The "Donnie Dunagan issue" of the magazine *Video Watchdog* was a huge hit with readers (and subsequently the winner of a 2004 Rondo Award).

Corps. Only one general, the CIA and the FBI knew, after I was investigated prior to becoming a counterintelligence guy, that I had a film background. I was a rapidly promoted—perhaps *unfairly* super-rapidly promoted recon and infantry commander in the Marine Corps, up through all the enlisted ranks real fast. And that would have been a little bit hard to do that with the nickname of Bambi [*laughs*]. Or the grandson of Frankenstein—I really didn't need *that* one! So I was mute about it. One time Gen. Houghton asked me about it, he said, "Why haven't you talked about this?" [the Hollywood career]. I told him what I just told you, that I could not have commanded men once they'd given me the nickname of Bambi. He laughed so hard he started *choking*! He said, "That's a good idea, Dunagan. Don't let anybody know!" So there you are!

Don and his wife Dana met when both worked at a California memorial park. Dana laughs, "I met the grandson of Frankenstein in a graveyard!"

This is my one selfish moment with you, okay? And I'm going to be a violator of "Don't self-promote": To really portray another person ... that's not easy on a sound stage. And it's a whole lot harder *live*. I've done some live amateur theater years and years ago, Shakespeare and things, for charity, four or five hundred people come and they write checks for the local charity. But apart from that, real acting ... *real* acting ... is tested when you go undercover. You go undercover, and if you fail in this ... you get your throat slit somewhere. I *know* I can still do it [act].

I don't want the film people or you or anybody to get angry at me, but I don't watch many films. I started weaning myself off of that about 1992, '93. Some of the portrayals of action characters has got to make guys who've really *done* it, and their families who *know* they've really done it, nauseous. When you're searching for someone who's armed, you don't go through a door holding a little wimpy pistol with both hands. You don't—you *do not*—get in a gunfight holding an automatic or a revolver in two hands. It arrests your body movement. I've been shot at with revolvers ... I have killed with a .45 ... I'm one of the very few officers in the Marine Corps that has actually shot enemy with a .45. You don't *do* that with two hands! I watch some of these films and I think, "Either they don't want a technical director, or they've got one and don't listen to him." Or, "Those actors have never had a shot fired at them in their life." The first time I got shot at, I pissed. I *pissed*. And when I was on an intelligence assignment in Mexico and I was being shot at by automatic weapons, and the plaster was going off the wall next to me, I had instant diarrhea.

That's what real guys *do*. If you tried to make a film with some of the guys *I've* seen in my life, nobody would believe it. If we ever make an action film that really has those kinds of things in it, the audience would just go crazy. When you throw a hand grenade at a car, the thing doesn't blow up like a napalm bomb—hand grenades don't *do* that. They go *pop*, like a firecracker, and if you're nearby, you've got holes in your body God didn't *put* there [*laughs*]!

Now I'm promoting, so here I am being a hypocrite, but I would *love*, at 70 and trying to be 35 forever (and I'm getting away with it so far), to get a shot at acting again. Either an old grizzled sheriff in a Western, or a character actor of no consequence in some action thing. I never had that aspiration all these years, never even *thought* about it. But *now*, looking at what I can see, the films that my wife drags in here, I'd like to get a chance to penetrate this damn business again.

A couple young adults, art students in the university nearby, did some research and phoned me and said this: "If you can ever make a comeback of any kind, it would be a promotional bonanza. It'd be the record comeback—65 years—of all time, any film artist, any nation in history." Nobody can match that. These kids got on the 'net somewhere and did the homework.

That's brilliant.

Think about that for a second: It would be a 65-year comeback. And I don't look like I'm 70. This is bragging a bit, but I work at it, I don't smoke or drink or those stupid things. People tell me, "*You're* not 70. You're 50." No, I'm 70, damn it! I don't want people to read this and think, "He's an old man, he can't do anything." I'll get in the ring with ya. I kinda move like old Marciano, I don't do the rope-a-dope stuff, but you don't want to let me get in your ribcage, I'll tell you that right now! So I am *eager* to do this, if for no other reason than I made the mistake of trusting some finance people. It's hard for me to say this to you, but we're living more modestly than I did when I was a buck sergeant in the Marine Corps. Now, that's as good a motive as any *other* damn motive, right? I have re-thought doing that kind of thing and I would love to get another shot at it. If I'm no good at it … send me home.

Alex Gordon on Day the World Ended

I [did] an awful lot on that picture. Not only did I get virtually the entire cast ... but also I did any number of other things, down to the office boy, and everything else!

The following is the introduction to this interview as it appeared in issue #229 of Fangoria *magazine:*

On June 24, 2003, fans of classic film history suffered a major loss: Alex Gordon, movie expert extraordinaire, film restorationist and, in the 1950s and '60s, a Hollywood producer himself, lost his lengthy battle with cancer in a nursing home near his Los Angeles home. The passing of the 80-year-old Gordon came as a blow to his friends at *Fangoria*: He was one of the first veteran moviemakers interviewed in this magazine's pages (*Fangoria* #1, 1979) and for several years he wrote the popular column "The Pit and the Pen of Alex Gordon" recounting many of his movieland experiences, from his friendship with Bela Lugosi and early writing collaborations with Ed Wood, to behind-the-scenes stories of the making of his own science fiction–horror films, among them *The She-Creature*, *Voodoo Woman* (both for American International Pictures), *The Atomic Submarine* and *The Underwater City*.

Gordon's lifelong love affair with movies began when he was a boy in London, haunting local theaters along with his three-years-younger brother Richard (later also a movie producer himself). In the late 1940s the Gordons emigrated to New York, where Alex renewed his friendship with a boyhood idol, Hollywood cowboy star Gene Autry. Alex soon had a job as advance publicity man for Autry's personal appearance tours across the United States.

Relocating to Hollywood, Gordon began his own moviemaking career as one of the producers of *The Lawless Rider* (1954), a low-budget Western which he helped stock with veteran players. He next brought his moviemaking talents (and love of the oldtime actors) to a brand-new independent movie company, American Releasing Corp.—later renamed AIP—getting in on the ground floor there and co-producing a number of their earliest drive-in-style releases.

In an interview conducted shortly before his death, probably his last, Alex Gordon recalled the dawning days of AIP and the making of the first SF film he produced, the post-atomic mutant monster mash *Day the World Ended* (1956) with Richard Denning and Lori Nelson.

Before we get into Day the World Ended, *would you talk a little bit about how you broke into the picture business and how you hooked up with AIP?*

When I came out to Hollywood in 1952 after completing a coast-to-coast tour as publicist for Gene Autry's hit show, I became involved with a minor cowboy star-producer named Johnny Carpenter in a movie called *The Outlaw Marshal* [released as *The Lawless Rider*], which was to cost $17,500. Carpenter had financing from private sources and wanted a $10,000 negative pick-up from me on delivery. I arranged for stunt great Yakima Canutt as director and in the cast were Frankie Darro, Kenne Duncan, Douglass Dumbrille and Bud Osborne. The picture, written by and starring Carpenter, ended up costing *$57,000* and everyone looked to me for payment of bills though I was not liable until delivery. The backers put a lien on the negative and I needed a lawyer. Carpenter and I went to Samuel Z. Arkoff, who had helped Carpenter before, but had no movie experience. With Arkoff's help on a deferment basis, we battled for over a year before liberating the picture. A United Artists release was arranged by my brother Richard Gordon, and eventually everyone was paid off.

Where were you living then?

I was living at a place that at the time was called the Gentry Hotel on Hollywood Boulevard. It was next to what *was* the Fox Theater, and then became the Henry Fonda Theatre. It was a clean hotel, properly run and everything, but ... it was kind of a rundown hotel. There were times when I was really flat broke—I remember once when my mother sent me $10 and I was able to eat that day. It was really a bad scene there very briefly after the fiasco with Carpenter, when everybody was calling me at the hotel for money and to pay the crew and all that kind of business. As I pointed out to you, I was not liable, it was a negative pick-up—if they didn't turn over the picture, I wasn't liable for the 10,000. So *why* people were calling me, I don't know ... I guess they thought I was loaded with money! Anyway, there was a very nice guy there, the son of the woman who owned the hotel—he was a cripple and he walked with crutches. He and I sort of had a rapport—he'd wanted a picture of Gene Autry, I'd gotten it for him, all that kind of stuff. At one point I told him, "I've got to go on another [Gene Autry] tour, and it's going to take me about 85 days and *then* some. I will pay you what I owe," which was about 125 bucks, "within seven days of my going *on* the tour. But you have to trust me. Until I get paid my first check [by Autry], I don't have any money to pay you." He knew I'd had my problems, I had explained to him what they were, and somehow he seemed to be sympathetic. *Nowadays* of course, *no*body would! I said, "As security, I will leave you copies of three scripts I'm working on"—three scripts that I did

On an oldtime saloon set at a Manhattan amusement arcade, British brothers Alex and Richard Gordon celebrate coming to America (November 1947).

with Eddie Wood, *Dr. Voodoo*, *The Vampire's Tomb* and *The Atomic Monster*. He said, "That's *fine*." Imagine, just three Xerox copies of scripts [as security]. Although *today* I could buy that hotel if I had those scripts [*laughs*]!

So I gave him the three scripts and of course as soon as I got my first check I immediately sent him his money by express, 125 bucks, and that caught me up. I'm telling you all this just to quickly try to show you how precarious my situation was ... I wasn't getting overweight from food, I can tell you that [*laughs*]!

So there you are, with the debacle of The Lawless Rider *now behind you...*
That's right. Free now from legal worries and feeling a great rapport with Arkoff, I told him about a script I had written for Bela Lugosi, *The Atomic Monster*. We submitted it to Jack Broder's Realart Pictures, a company that was reissuing the Universal pictures with the emphasis on horror and science fiction. Broder turned it down but his sales manager, James H. Nicholson, liked the idea, having had great recent success teaming the original *Dracula* and *Frankenstein* [1931] throughout the country. However, Broder did not offer a deal—he simply took my title *The Atomic Monster* and put it on his Realart reissue of Universal's *Man Made Monster* [1941] with Lon Chaney, Jr.! Arkoff and I sued and pocketed $1000 each in a fast settlement.

That's how Arkoff and Nicholson came together.
Arkoff and Nicholson hit it off and formed a company, American Releasing Corp. [later AIP], with Arkoff and myself heading a split from that, Golden State Productions. Arkoff lived off his legal work, and Nicholson had a shoe salesman acquaintance who helped him financially. I lived off the money I had made with

Gene Autry. No salaries were paid. Obviously product was needed and Nicholson approached Roger Corman, a young would-be director and producer who had made an action film with John Ireland and Dorothy Malone called *The Fast and the Furious* [1954] and was about to sell it to Republic. Arkoff and Nicholson persuaded Corman to give them 30 days to better Republic's offer by rounding up enough guarantees and advances from regional distributors to cover the $66,000 cost of *The Fast and the Furious* and enable him to make one more. Nicholson and I then made a trip contacting these various "states right distributors."

And raised the money to get Fast and the Furious, *and to start Corman off making* more movies for you.

That's right. First Corman made a color Western, *Five Guns West* [1955] with John Lund, and *I* became executive producer of his third film with AIP, *Apache Woman* [1955] with Lloyd Bridges and Joan Taylor. But it soon became obvious that single B pictures like these first three would not work out for the new company—they played bottom of twin-bill programming at $25 per booking. AIP would have to own both pictures in attempting to obtain percentage bookings.

What were AIP's offices like physically in those early days? Fancy at all?

Oh, no, no, it was a very simple office [within Arkoff's small law offices]. Nicholson had his own office and then, in an area that was almost like a waiting room, there was room for a couple of desks, and that's where Nicholson's wife Sylvia and I sat. And that's all it was at the time—that's when they were on Selma Avenue. That didn't last terribly long, it lasted I guess for about a year, until we really got going. Early on, nobody got paid—as I said, there were no salaries paid. Arkoff was still living off his legal practice, and I was living off of the money I'd gotten from Gene Autry, which was 125 a week.

Which was good in those days, right?

Yes, especially since when I was on the tour, he also paid all my expenses, I didn't have to pay *any*thing for hotel or food or anything like that at all. I could put the 125 a week aside and save it. There were two tours a year. But with me starting out a month earlier or sometimes two months earlier, you can see how my money was mounting up. My God, I felt like Trump! But, luckily, I didn't have *Mrs.* Trump to worry about [*laughs*]! Then, too, I was also peddling some imported foreign films to independent distributors. All that gave us a little money, between the proper things. That was all during the period that we were *trying* to set up AIP but hadn't gotten anywhere yet. I didn't get a *dime* out of AIP until about a year after they got going.

And Nicholson and Arkoff in the early days—how were they doing financially?

Arkoff, it seemed to me, really didn't have many clients at that point, although I suppose he did make *enough* to make a living, enough to bring up the kids, and he did have a house and those things. So he must have been making *some* money.

Nicholson was pretty broke. His wife Sylvia was working not only for us but also doing something else, I can't remember now what it was. I was the only one, really, who was having problems making a living, but luckily there was Gene Autry and there were the foreign films that I was peddling.

Who came up with the idea for Day the World Ended?

That was Nicholson. Nicholson came up with the title *Day the World Ended*, and then Lou Rusoff was put on it, to write a script. And to be on the safe side, Nicholson wanted Roger Corman to produce and direct. But he *did* throw me the bone as executive producer for Golden State Productions, because I was doing an *awful* lot on that picture. Not only did I get virtually the entire cast, except for Paul Birch, Jonathan Haze and Paul Dubov—Corman's regulars—but also I did any number of other things, down to the office boy [*laughs*], and everything else! I figured I should get *some*thing there, so Nicholson said, "Well, you can be executive producer on *Apache Woman* and *Day the World Ended*." Then the next picture, *Girls in Prison* [1956], I was the solo producer.

How many days did you have to shoot Day the World Ended?

Bart Carré, our production supervisor, set up a tight ten-day schedule.

Did you have any script input on Day the World Ended?

No, not very much. At that point, I was a little in awe of Lou Rusoff, because he was really the only one who was, you might say, a professional there when it came to actually working on pictures. He had written not only *Terry and the Pirates*, a TV series, but also a lot of other TV scripts. He was a successful writer, he had a nice house in Laurel Canyon and a very nice wife ... and he was Arkoff's brother-in-law.

Roger Corman—what were your initial impressions of him on Apache Woman, *and how did you get along with him on* Day the World Ended?

I first was introduced to Roger when we attended a screening of *Monster from the Ocean Floor* [1954], which I thought, for the money that he brought it in for, was absolutely remarkable. I thought it was very, very good and that he was a very nice, polite, young guy. And a very nice-*looking* guy, properly dressed—he looked like a young executive, not like some guy who was just lolling around like some of the *other* guys who were around in those days, coming around to try and get jobs. And then of course I was impressed by *The Fast and the Furious*, I thought that was a *very* good job.

And, when you got to see Corman in action on a set?

After the fiasco with *The Lawless Rider*, I was ab-so-lute-ly just thrilled and amazed and grateful when I came on Roger Corman's *Apache Woman* set. Corman's set was quiet ... everything was quiet ... everything was efficient ... nobody was shouting ... everybody seemed to know what they were doing ... he had the right people there ... and he was directing very quietly, giving his instructions and so on.

The Mutant (Paul Blaisdell) and star Lori Nelson caught by the shutterbug with producer-director Roger Corman (top) and then—oh-oh!—cavorting while Paul's wife Jackie looks on (bottom).

Later I was told by [*Apache Woman* star] Lloyd Bridges and a couple of others, especially Richard Denning, that Corman wasn't directing actors. Some of the actors were asking him certain questions about their interpretations, and Corman was hazy on that, "Just do it the way you would do it ... whatever you think..." Very rarely did he ever correct an actor, "No, no, that isn't right..." I don't remember him *ever* doing it with the likes of Richard Denning or Adele Jergens or any of the professionals. With some of his cohorts [Corman's regulars], sometimes he would tell 'em, "No, I'd rather you do this, that or the next thing," but not with the pros. And on *Day the World Ended* Lori Nelson particularly needed help [from a director], she was used to getting it at Universal from Jack Arnold and all the rest of 'em. On *Day the World Ended* she was kind of saying, "Gee, Roger won't tell me anything. I'm doing it the best I can, but he's not directing me..." But there was no crisis or anything.

Casting Lori was your idea because she had been in Revenge of the Creature *[1955].*

That's right, absolutely, that and the fact that she had been a star or co-star at Universal. Bart Carré was slightly concerned that a major company actress might possibly show temperament at the primitive conditions and fast schedule, but he need not have worried, we got on very well with her—I don't remember any problem with Lori Nelson at all. Richard Denning had been in *Creature from the Black Lagoon* and Herman Cohen's *Target Earth* [both 1954] and so on. I remember the first time I met Denning: I'd talked to his agent, and Denning had left word for me to come around to his house to discuss the script. He did this that first time, and he did this on every picture after that: When I rang the doorbell, he'd open the door, and he'd have the script in his hand open to a certain page and he would be mumbling the words as though he was memorizing and rehearsing the lines and so on. That was one of his gags—he wanted me to *know* that he was deep *into* it and very interested and conscientious and so on [*laughs*]. He had a great sense of humor. He did that through every one of the five or six pictures that we worked on with him. He was a very, very nice guy, he really was—I can't say enough about Richard Denning. He *was* always up on his lines and he was never late for anything and he was just an absolute pleasure to work with. We got on extremely well with Denning, which is why we used him in so many pictures, including my brother's in England, *Assignment Redhead* [1956]. He turned out to be an excellent actor, a wonderful friend, and in later interviews stated that I was his favorite producer in a way I knew was sincere.

At the time—well, right up 'til her death, Evelyn Ankers was Mrs. Denning.

Evelyn Ankers, of course I fell for her when as a kid in England I saw her in *Murder in the Family* [1938], which was a British sort-of remake of *Five Star Final*, about the family where there had been a killing or murder years before, and a scandal, and now reporters are trying to bring it up again to get a story. That was the first time I ever saw Evelyn Ankers and I thought she was just about the prettiest thing I'd ever *seen*. So I had a *big* crush on her—of course, I never dreamt I would ever *meet* her, let alone anything else. So when it came to *Day the World Ended* I met her for the first time, with Richard Denning, and she turned out to be so sweet and so nice. The Dennings and I became *such* good friends over a *long* period of time—in fact, until he died. I saw him when he was in a wheelchair with oxygen and so on, I was right there virtually to the end. He was probably the nicest guy I ever worked with.

...Well, now, wait a minute, let me say he was up there *with* the nicest guys I've ever worked with, 'cause I must admit that people like Bob Steele, Johnny Mack Brown and of course Raymond Hatton, I wouldn't put them *below* Richard Denning, with all the good will in the world towards Richard Denning. But he was right up there as a very sweet guy. He always felt that he didn't really have the career he *might* have had, because of his war service—World War II interrupted his career. He was just getting there [heading toward stardom] with *Beyond the Blue Horizon* [1942] and pictures like that, but then he had to go to war. And, according to Denning, when he came back, nobody wanted him. He couldn't get interviews or *any*thing, he had a real tough time. He had to go into pictures at Republic and Columbia and so on—the quickies.

Were you ever tempted to offer Evelyn Ankers a part in one of your pictures?
[*Loudly*] *Oh*!! I was after Evelyn Ankers *every* time we met, I *begged* her, I said, "Please...!" She said, "No, no. I've put on so much weight," this, that and the other. I said, "You haven't put on an *ounce* of weight, you look terrific!" I had pictures taken, showed her the pictures, and she said, "Oh, no, no..." She said she never really liked all that stuff she had done and she felt she was typed in horror films.

Did you offer her a Day the World Ended *part?*
Oh, in every picture!

Who would she have been in Day the World Ended*, if she had said yes?*
Ruby, the gangster's moll [eventually played by Adele Jergens]. We first of course offered her the Lori Nelson role, but Arkoff and Nicholson wouldn't go for that, they were really fighting me on that and I didn't want to *start* anything, especially with Richard Denning playing the hero there. I thought, "Well, let sleeping dogs lie."

Did you offer Ankers the role first or pitch her to Nicholson and Arkoff first?
Before I brought it up with Arkoff and Nicholson, *she* said no. But I thought I'd still mention it to Arkoff and Nicholson anyway, and they said, "Absolutely no." So then I didn't want to get further involved, I thought that would be bad, that it might create a bad situation between Denning and them.

I wasn't really all that serious about [letting her play] the Lori Nelson role, I realized that that *had* to be a girl that still looked like a Lori Nelson...

Younger than springtime.
Yes. And Evelyn Ankers already had a daughter [born 1944] and so on. So I didn't *push* it. But certainly she could have played one of the parts in *Girls in Prison* or *Runaway Daughters* [1956] or even in a Western—after all, she'd done that pic-

ture with James Ellison, *The Texan Meets Calamity Jane* [Ankers' last film, 1950]. But she was very unhappy about that picture, she thought she looked terrible, in *Queen of Burlesque* [1946] she thought she looked awful, and so on. I didn't want to make her mad—she *did* have quite a temper—so—

Wait, wait, wait! Did Denning tell you that, or did you see it?

I didn't actually see it, but I *heard* about it, let me put it that way [*laughs*]. I mean, only when she thought she was absolutely right and the other person was absolutely wrong. And of course she was *always* right [*laughs*]! She was the sweetest kind of a person, she *really* was, you couldn't help but fall for her, she really was a very, very thoughtful and nice person and so on. But we never did get Richard Denning and Evelyn Ankers together in the same picture. *Black Beauty* [1946] was the only time they worked together.

How much did Denning get for Day the World Ended?

I signed him for $7500 plus a percentage.

And Adele Jergens wound up with the part you wanted Ankers to play.

Adele Jergens was also one of these very sweet people. We seem to have had very good luck for the most part with our leading ladies. Not so much with our men, but with our leading ladies. She just was word perfect and the first one on the set and helpful with the others and ... just everything you could imagine! So of course we immediately signed her for two more pictures, for *Girls in Prison* and *Runaway Daughters*. And would have had her in *more*, but then I started [making war movies]—I couldn't put her on a submarine [*laughs*]! But she was just a terrific person and very well-liked.

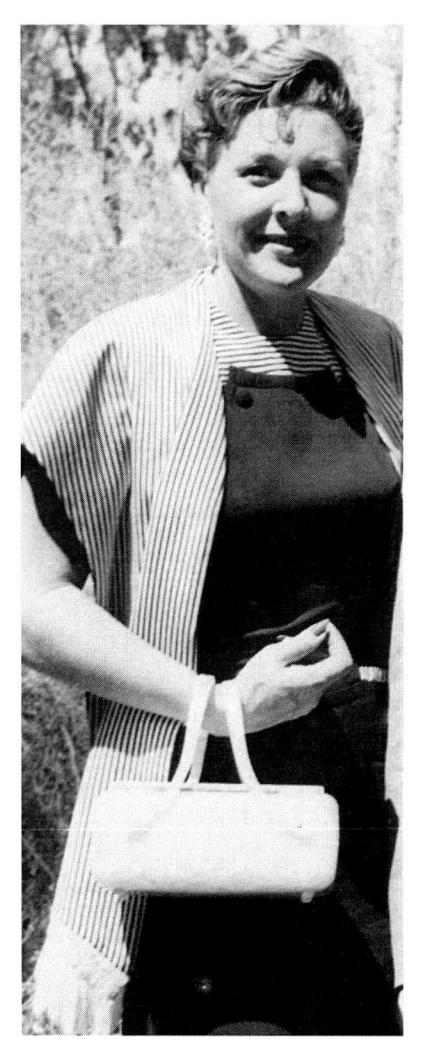

Gordon couldn't entice Evelyn Ankers to appear in any of his movies, but she did visit during the shooting of *Day the World Ended*.

Did you meet her actor-husband Glenn Langan through her at any point?

Yes, and I got him into *The Amazing Colossal Man* [1957]. He wasn't getting any work and Adele said, "Is there any way you can get him into one of the AIP pictures?" [*Colossal Man* writer-producer-director] Bert Gordon knew nothing about actors and didn't care at all, he just wanted to do his special effects and so on. When I brought in Glenn Langan, Bert Gordon thought he would be fine because he was tall and nice-looking and everything, and there'd be such a contrast. So they made a deal with me, they actually paid me to cast both of the Colossal pictures.

I know you could talk all day about Raymond Hatton, who played the old prospector in Day the World Ended.

He was one of my very favorites from the very early days. When I was still in boarding school in England, on Saturdays the Gaumont British people would send over a Western to show to us kids. The first one was a Buck Jones, *For the Service* [1936], and the picture the second week was *Stormy* [1935] with Noah Beery, Jr., and Jean Rogers. The first time I ever saw Raymond Hatton was in that picture *Stormy*, which was about a wild horse.

Hatton had a very interesting career.

Raymond Hatton played leads for Cecil B. DeMille, *Joan the Woman* [1917], *The Whispering Chorus* [1918]—he played the lead in several DeMille pictures, if you can imagine it, in the silent days. And at

Sassy Adele Jergens, another favorite of Gordon's, poses for candids between takes on the movie.

the end of the silent period, he was a team with Wallace Beery, they got co-star billing at MGM. But then he went down to small parts and supporting roles—for example, one scene in *"G" Men* [1935] with Cagney. In the Westerns, though, he was still playing good roles. Then of course he became one of the Three Mesquiteers and he teamed up with Johnny Mack Brown—he regained [a measure of stardom] as a crusty old Western sidekick. But not the kind that does pratfalls!

When I first came out to Hollywood, the very first person I called was Raymond Hatton—I'd corresponded with him and he'd given me his phone number. I remember going to his place, he had a house near the Beverly Hills area, and he said, "Let's have a bowl of soup." We had lunch there at his house—his wife was very nice. They'd been married since the early '20s and they had worked together on the stage, in vaudeville, all that stuff. Raymond Hatton of course had 10,000 stories, but the main thing was he wanted to *work*. I had no way of [getting him work in] Johnny Carpenter pictures, Carpenter just wouldn't pay for people like that—

Raymond Hatton was still with an agent who wasn't going to go below 1000 a week, which is what he was getting at Monogram. And when it came to that prospector role in *Day the World Ended*, Corman said, "Dick Miller, one of my regulars, would be perfect in this role."

As the old prospector?
Yeah [*laughs*]! I said, "Well, Roger, I've got Raymond Hatton, he's a fine actor, he goes back to the DeMille days—" But I don't think Roger had ever heard of DeMille. Roger was not "into" old pictures or old players or anything like that, although he *had* used Chester Conklin in *Apache Woman* and that was *his* idea. So I felt there was a slightly open door there to oldtimers. Roger said, "Well, if you feel that strongly about Raymond Hatton, we'll use him, but he'll have to work for the same money as Dick Miller would." I asked, "How much is that?," and Roger said, "$250 for the picture." So I said, "Well, let me talk to him..."

I took Raymond to dinner at the Nickodell restaurant in Hollywood and I said, "Raymond, I want to get you into American International. It looks to me as though they're going to make quite a few pictures, and I'm going to be on a number of 'em. I think I can get you in virtually any [role] that makes sense for you to play. *But*, I have a problem. On the first picture here, all I can offer you is $250 and I'll tell you why," and I explained it to him. I said, "If you *do* this, and I think it'd be a good idea, on the *next* picture I'm sure I can *get* you your money, a thousand a week." So he said, "All right, I'll *trust* you, Alex. I'll do it." Hatton had a helluva job persuading his agent, but finally he saw the light. So anyway, he did that one, *Day the World Ended*, and then on *Girls in Prison* I got him the thousand and on *Flesh and the Spur* [1957] I got him 1500 bucks and so on. So I kept my word to him. But there was nothing I could do on that first picture *Day the World Ended*; if I'd insisted that Raymond Hatton be paid a thousand a week, Roger Corman just would have said *no*. Roger was king there and rightly so, he put the company on the map, so I wasn't going to fight Roger. But that's how I got Raymond in *Day the World Ended* and then of course used him in almost everything except my submarine pictures. I always had trouble getting 80 year olds into submarines [*laughs*]!

In addition to oldtimers like Hatton, you also cast up-and-comers like Mike Connors in your AIP pictures.
Mike Connors was not my discovery. I forget now who brought him in, whether it was his agent, or if Nicholson knew him—I just don't remember. Mike was just *there* one day and was being introduced to me. He was still Touch Connors then. I was not really familiar with his work, but he certainly looked and acted very nicely and he was a very friendly kind of person. Roger wanted him for *Day the World Ended* and I saw nothing wrong with that. On that picture, Mike Connors and Richard Denning got *very*, very friendly, they just got on extremely well together, and as a result they and their wives would go out, and they had a social life and friendship apart from their work on the pictures [*Day the World Ended* and *The Oklahoma Woman*, 1956].

The Mutant (Paul Blaisdell) buddies up with Gordon, right, and screenwriter Lou Rusoff.

Paul Blaisdell, who made the monster costume and played *the monster—what did you think of him?*

Paul Blaisdell was strictly Nicholson's discovery. Nicholson had been friendly with Blaisdell for *years*, and Nicholson kept having Blaisdell come in to AIP with designs for monsters and so on. Then of course when *Day the World Ended* became a reality, Blaisdell *really* stepped in, because he was a pivotal part of that picture.

There were only two problems: Blaisdell didn't want anybody to *see* the monster, or sketches, or *anything* like that, except certain things he was showing Nicholson. He didn't want anybody else to tell him what to do or what to change and so on—especially Arkoff, who was very opinionated. Then, of course, the bombshell that Blaisdell was going to *be* the monster, to be *in* the monster suit. Nicholson *had* to give way—he couldn't pay Blaisdell anything more than a very minimum [amount of money] at that time—

So it'd be awkward, paying him peanuts and *telling him, "We don't care that you want to play the monster, you* can't."

Right. That turned out to be a slight problem, but not an *overwhelming* problem. For example, when we were getting ready to shoot the scene where the monster was carrying Lori Nelson, it became obvious that it would have to be a very brief shot, because [Nelson] was just too heavy for Blaisdell to carry. I could appreciate that because I'm short myself, and I probably would have had a problem there too. Especially in that get-up. But anyway, we did it, and it came out as it did, which I think was adequate, it was all right.

And Blaisdell personally?

Blaisdell was a very nice man but a very strange person. He wanted everything *his way* and he felt that that was the correct way ... and, frankly, I think he was probably right. But I sort of kept away from that end of things—I figured, "Let Nicholson handle that. Blaisdell's *his* man, he brought him in." That was really Nicholson's area there.

In Sam Arkoff's autobiography, he writes that there was a big guy on the Day the World Ended *set waiting to play the monster when Blaisdell showed up with the little suit.*

That I don't remember at all, and I was on the set all the time, every day, from morning 'til night. The way *I* remember it is, Nicholson made the arrangement with Blaisdell (before Blaisdell delivered the suit and all that), that he, Blaisdell, was *not* going to have anybody else play the monster except him, otherwise no monster suit. I don't remember any big guy on the set, and I certainly feel that I *would* remember. If anybody else had been assigned that role, I probably would have had something to do with the casting.

Blaisdell later played the monsters in your The She-Creature *[1956] and* Voodoo Woman *[1957] and he doesn't do much physical stuff in those pictures—he doesn't carry anybody around or anything like that. Was that because you learned your lesson on* Day the World Ended*?*

That's right. Nothing like that was written into the script.

Would you have preferred that he not *play his own monsters? Would you have preferred having as the monsters a bigger, stronger guy who could have* done *more?*

I don't think "preferred" is exactly the right word, because I had full sympathy for Blaisdell. I felt Blaisdell had a point. I mean, he'd worked for *weeks* on [the *Day*

Lori Nelson seems to prefer the embrace of the *Day the World Ended* mutant to the advances of set visitor Forry Ackerman.

the World Ended monster suit] and I really felt he was entitled to play the monster, that somehow we had to work it out. I think it would have been very unfair if he hadn't played it.

Let me be unfair then and rephrase the question. Would the pictures have been a little better with a bigger, more imposing, more capable guy?

I really don't think so. I think when people saw the final result, the finished film, I really don't think anybody thought about it. I didn't hear any criticism about it, I don't think anybody resented it, because they all had a lot of respect for Blaisdell, making something out of nothing. I think that they felt that he was entitled. Blaisdell was a fine and capable person and he and his wife Jackie worked hard on various AIP films.

Where was the picture made?
  The picture was made in various areas of Griffith Park where we got permission from the people who oversee it. There was a park guy on the set watching that we didn't destroy anything. The scenes in the pond were all done in one day in the trout pond at Sportsmen's Lodge, and we had to do it early in the morning, *before* the restaurant there started serving meals and so on, so that there would be no interruption of the regular work schedule of the Sportsmen's Lodge. We *did* have a situation, and I really don't want to dwell on it because perhaps it's a little indelicate, but it shows what a trouper Adele Jergens was. It just so happened that on the one day when she had to be in the water, and for quite a while, she had a female problem [her "time of month"], and she said to me, "Do you think we could possibly shoot this another time?" I felt terrible, *terrible*, saying, "Adele, to tell you the truth, this is the one day we can *get* into Sportsmen's Lodge—we can't come back, they won't let us do that. It's either today or nothing. And I don't see how we can shoot the scene without you being in the water. But we'll try to do it as quickly as possible..." And she said, "Ohhhh, it's fine, don't worry about it. I'll manage." It was a very brief conversation but I was *terribly* embarrassed to do that to somebody like her. I just felt badly about putting anybody in discomfort, I hate that kind of a situation. But it just gives an example of what a trouper she was—nothing was going to stop her.

And the interiors?
  The interiors were shot at a little studio called the Sunset Stage, on Sunset Boulevard.

The radiation burn makeup—did you think that was well-done?
  Yes, I think that was well-done, considering there was no time, really, to do it. I mean, we're not talking Jack Pierce here!

Nicholson and Arkoff—were they around on Day the World Ended? *Did you get any input at all from them?*
  I never *ever* remember Arkoff on the set of one of my pictures. Or, I should say, the

Actor Paul Dubov survived radiation burns (and being cannibalized) in *Day* to become a fixture in Gordon's movies.

pictures *that I was on*, because on *Day the World Ended* it's really Roger Corman who deserves the producer and director credit. But I never remember Arkoff coming down. Whenever he wanted to discuss anything, he sent for the people to come up to his office. And with Nicholson, he was *always* in his office and working, either with his wife on something, or had guys in there with designs of posters for another picture, or this and that and so on. I *never ever* remember them coming down. I once sort of laughingly said to my wife, "Sounds like they were trying to be like Irving Thalberg"—I understand Thalberg only came down on the set when there was a problem.

The narrator at the beginning sounds a lot like Chet Huntley.
   Nicholson somehow was friendly with Huntley, and he had Huntley do that voiceover, which I thought was very effective. I thought Huntley, who looked like Burt Lancaster, did a very good job on that. Chet Huntley and David Brinkley had the top-rated commentary news show on television at one time.

The movie never tells you exactly who "Tommy" is—the guy Lori Nelson is so worried about. Write-ups either call him her brother or her boyfriend.
   I was always under the impression that the mutant was the boyfriend, not a brother.

Talk a little about some of the behind-the-scenes people.
   [Cinematographer] Jock Feindel was a nice guy. He was a small guy, feisty and so on, and he was fast. Our production manager-assistant director Bartlett A. Carré was a superb oldtimer who had worked as an actor, with Nazimova in *Salome* [1923] and in many Westerns of the '30s. Carré was 90 percent responsible for all the American Releasing pictures he worked on coming in on time and budget, shot in six to ten days on budgets between $60,000 and $104,000. Karl Brainard [property master] and Chuck Hanawalt [key grip] were on *all* our pictures. Harry Reif was the poor man's set decorator. My wife Ruth just went crazy when she saw his cheap furniture in every set, especially on the Westerns. Whenever it was a Western, he used the same broken-down slot machines and so on! Harry Reif had a big cigar and nothing fazed him. If he needed to turn the slot machine into, I don't know, a dispenser for coffee [*laughs*], he'd just do a few things to it and there it was ... and it looked terrible. He did things "for a price."
   [Editor] Ronnie Sinclair's kind of an interesting little story. Ronnie Sinclair was from New Zealand, and as a kid he was an actor. When he came to Hollywood, he had a very strong mother who got him an agent. At that time, his name his Ra Hould, a New Zealand name. Under that name he got into a picture at Republic with Hedda Hopper [*Dangerous Holiday*, 1937] and, on the strength of that, he was signed by MGM. They changed his name to Ronald Sinclair and he was signed as a "threat" to Mickey Rooney, who was getting rather rambunctious. (Well, I guess Mickey Rooney had the right—he was number one in the box office polls by 1940.) Ronnie Sinclair was in *Thoroughbreds Don't Cry* [1937] with Mickey Rooney and Judy Garland and several other MGM pictures, and at Warners he was in *Desperate Jour-*

ney [1942] with Errol Flynn and so on—but what he *really* wanted to be was a director. In order to do that, he decided he had to become a film editor first, and he became a very much in-demand film editor. After *Apache Woman*, he was on every picture that I did where I could get him in, unless it was a studio like Columbia where they had their own editorial department.

Did you like the music score Ronald Stein supplied?

Yes. In fact, I used him on every single picture that I could use him on after that. He was great. What we did, we'd give him $5000 and that would be his and the *score* would be his—he insisted that he would retain the rights to his scores because he wanted to build up a music library, which he did. He would take the 5000, he'd go to either Mexico or Munich and there he'd get a whole orchestra, 20 or more people, sometimes 30, and give us a terrific score, for a price we could afford.

What is "'The S.F. Blues' Solo by Pete Candoli" mentioned in the credits? Is that the number Adele Jergens dances to?

That's it. Pete Candoli was a very big name in blues recordings, his recordings are still sold and have a big following. So he was a name to reckon with. He was later married to Betty Hutton.

Would Day the World Ended *have been better in color?*

I don't think so. I think with that kind of a picture, with a bleak post-atomic situation, I think the black-and-white made it look even bleaker, the way it was photographed and so on. Color might have helped it at the *box office*, if it had been advertised as a color picture. Later, of course, you couldn't *do* anything in black and white, you *had* to have color. But at *that* time, I think it was okay, it didn't hurt the picture.

Did you think Day the World Ended *had average or better-than-average possibilities box office–wise?*

You know, I've got to be truthful with you and tell you that I didn't know. We had high *hopes* for the picture, and we *thought* that it was a pretty good picture when we first saw it put together. As I mentioned before, it wasn't enough for AIP to be getting the $25 bookings as a second feature while a major company picture got the percentages—we *had* to have both parts of the bill, otherwise we weren't going to get any money. When *Day the World Ended* was scheduled for national release, AIP needed a second feature for the bottom half of the program and so they picked up an independent, the Milner Brothers' cheapie *The Phantom from 10,000 Leagues* [1956] with Kent Taylor and Cathy Downs. They became AIP's first double-bill. We were apprehensive, but it turned out very well. The Hollywood Theater at Hollywood and Highland (which is now a Ripley's Believe It or Not museum) never played any picture more than a week—but *Day the World Ended* and *The Phantom from 10,000 Leagues* played four weeks and we saw the lines around the block. That combination did record business across the country on percentage dates and put AIP on the map. From then on, it was double feature programming for a number of years until, like Republic and Allied Artists, AIP tried to get too big and went eventually out of business. But it put drive-in exploitation programs and teenage programming on the screen and outdid most of the other film companies in those areas.

The only thing that bothered me a *little* bit was the Superscope, because I had seen CinemaScope pictures and in those days, nine times out of ten, projectionists ran them out of focus. My wife would try to keep me from doing this but I would go up to the projection room, and I always got into a fight! First I would press the button—they used to have a button at the back of the auditorium and it would ring a bell in the projectionist's booth so he would look down (instead of watching his little television set) and see that it was out of focus, or that the wrong lens was on. And when *that* didn't work, the ringing of the bell (I did it too often and they'd get mad), I'd go up there. And then the projectionist would call the manager and threaten to throw me out! "I'll give you back your money, but don't you ever show yourself in this theater again!" But it was *torture*—that was the reason I never went to see CinemaScope films any more. When it comes to focus, I'm a *fiend* [*laughs*], I can't stand it out of focus, and nine times out of ten, they used to *be* out of focus in those days when CinemaScope first came in.

Do you still find something to raise a ruckus about when you go to the movies?
I haven't been to a movie theater in I think four or five years now, because I don't like the loud noise, the over-amplification—quite apart from the commercials and so on.

Richard Denning was given a percentage of Day the World Ended, *you said.*
Oh, yes! In addition to his 7500, he was given seven and a half percent of the net profit. I'm sure he never saw a dime. Occasionally there would be a question about it and I'd ask Arkoff, and he'd say, "Oh, yeah, I'm sending him checks." Which he wasn't. I never did find out much about Arkoff's accounting practices except that he was the only one who got rich! But Denning never held anything against me. He told me many years later that finally he sold out all his interest in all the pictures to Arkoff and Nicholson—which is what I did too. Denning didn't resent it, really. He enjoyed working on those things.

Did you see the recent made-for-cable remake of Day the World Ended *[2001] or any of your other movies that they've remade?*
I haven't seen *any* of those at all. I have no ulterior motive [for ignoring them], there's no ego or anything like that involved—it's just that I am really ... not ... interested. I just feel with remakes that it never works out—*The Maltese Falcon* [1941] is about the only remake that was superior to the original. I don't think you ought to try and rework [the oldies]. Especially in the way *they* did, throwing in all that sex and violence and bloodshed. In their time and in their place, the old ones were fun and they weren't pretending to be anything that they were not. They were low-budget things for the drive-ins and the young crowds and so on. To try and remake those things in 2001 or whatever ... even though I understand the scripts were quite a bit different...

Completely *different!*
...I think is stupid. I just think that it was a very bad idea and certainly not something I would be interested in seeing or having *any*thing to do with. To call these new pictures by the titles of *our* old pictures, and then do what they *did* with 'em, was not only a cheat all around, but a lousy idea.

How do you feel about Day the World Ended *today?*
Well, the last time I saw the picture, I thought it was pretty good. I mean, you can always find *some*thing [to nit-pick] there, but I say, "Look. For a ten-day picture, in black-and-white, for $104,000, I think we did the best we could." I think it's nothing to be ashamed of.

Day the World Ended
(American Releasing Corp. [American International Pictures], 1956)

A Golden State Production; 79 minutes; Shot in September 1955; Released in January 1956; Presented by James H. Nicholson & Samuel Z. Arkoff; Executive Producer: Alex Gordon; Produced & Directed by Roger Corman; Original Story & Screenplay: Lou Rusoff; Photography: Jock Feindel (Superscope); Music Composed & Conducted by Ronald Stein; "The S.F. Blues" Solo by Pete Candoli; Production Supervisor: Bart Carré; Editor: Ronald Sinclair; Sound: John Speak; Special Effects: Paul Blaisdell; Makeup: Steven Clensos; Wardrobe: Gertrude Reade; Set Decorator: Harry Reif; Property Master: Karl Brainard; Key Grip: Chuck Hanawalt; Script Supervisor: Barbara Bohrer

Richard Denning (*Rick*), Lori Nelson (*Louise Maddison*), Adele Jergens (*Ruby*), Touch [Mike] Connors (*Tony Lamont*), Paul Birch (*Capt. Jim Maddison*), Raymond Hatton (*Pete*), Paul Dubov (*Radek*), Jonathan Haze (*Contaminated Man*), Paul Blaisdell (*Mutant*), Dale Van Sickel (*Stunt Double for Denning*), Tom Steele (*Stunt Double for Connors*), Roger Corman (*Tommy [in photograph]*)

Peter Graves

> *We didn't have special effects, or the money for 'em [in '50s sci-fi flicks]. So we had to flash the outlandish things by quickly, so the audience never got a good, in-focus look at them!*

Peter Graves' biggest claim to TV fame is that, once every week for a full six years, his *Mission: Impossible* team safeguarded the U.S. of A. against looming threats presented by Communist powers, foreign dictatorships, military strongmen and the kingpins of organized crime. This is a record of achievement that should not be taken lightly, but it has unfairly overshadowed his even more remarkable accomplishments of the 1950s: In that heyday of schlock science fiction movies, Graves saved not just Americans but the entire *world* from being devoured by giant grasshoppers (*Beginning of the End*), enslaved by a teepee-shaped monster from Venus (*It Conquered the World*) and annihilated by bug-eyed invaders from the planet Astron Delta (*Killers from Space*). In all three of these movies, Graves was The Man Who Saved the Earth, and 50 years later he is at last stepping forward to relate for the first time a few of his "war stories" from the exploitation movie trenches.

Born and raised in rural Minnesota, the son of a surgical instrument salesman, the actor (real name: Peter Aurness) is the brother of TV Western superstar James Arness of *Gunsmoke* fame. Enlisting in the Air Force upon his high school graduation, he served his tour of duty and, after his discharge, attended the University of Minnesota, majoring in theater. By the time he graduated, brother James had already gone Hollywood and was appearing in supporting parts (*The Farmer's Daughter, Battleground, Wagon Master*), so Peter followed in his footsteps and began looking for work in the movie capital. He also changed his name to Peter *Graves* (the name of his maternal grandfather) to distinguish himself from James.

Graves worked the usual variety of odd jobs while playing parts at the Pasadena Playhouse prior to his first break, landing a co-starring role in Ventura Pictures' *Rogue River* (1950). He was under contract to Ventura throughout the first several years of his career, appearing on loanout in movies like *Red Planet Mars* (1952), as a scientist who has apparently established radio contact with life on Mars, and producer-director Billy Wilder's dark-comic

Stalag 17 (1953), with Graves as the German spy who, posing as an American, has infiltrated the title P.O.W. camp's barracks.

Television stardom in the boy-and-his-horse adventure *Fury*, two renditions of *Mission: Impossible* (the 1966–73 original and a 1988–90 return of the Impossible Mission Force), A&E's *Biography* and other series have made Graves a household name but he remains resolutely down-to-earth and, even after a half-century, has no desire to stamp "Mission: Accomplished" on his career dossier.

How did you manage to land a co-starring role in your very first movie, Rogue River?

In 1950 there was a TV show called *Lights, Camera, Action*, a little show on … well, KNBH it was called in those days, but it was the local NBC affiliate and all the broadcasting was done from the NBC Studios on Sunset and Vine. If I'm remembering right, they had open auditions of some kind, and a gal and I worked up a scene and we did it for them. And they said, "Jeez, let's *do* it" [put Graves and the girl on the TV show]. At that same time, I had acquired an agent, a talent agent who was pushing me around town, and he had put me up for a little independent film called *Rogue River*. The first question that [producers] ask is, "What's he done?" Well [*laughs*], the answer at that point was, "Nothing!" But my agent said, "Listen, he's *gonna* do a guest thing on a little show called *Lights, Camera, Action*." So the *Rogue River* producers watched it, and that seemed to be okay with them, so that got me the *next* interview with them. Or perhaps it was the *Lights, Camera, Action* show that triggered my *first* interview. Anyway, it did have an influence, and we went from there through a series of readings for *Rogue River*. A friend of these producers was Henry Willson, the legendary agent of that time, and *he* came and listened to one of my readings and when it was over, he just turned to them and said, "Hey, you got your guy. Sign him."

For two or three years after Rogue River, *every time you were in a picture, even* Stalag 17, *you were on loanout from Ventura.*

That's right. The producers of *Rogue River*, two gentlemen named Frank Melford and John Rawlins, signed me as a freelance actor to make *Rogue River* and they paid me I think 175 a week to do that. Then they decided to put me under contract—a standard contract of that sort ran for 40 weeks a year. You got paid 40 weeks and you were on layoff for 12 weeks. I started at 125 a week for the first six months and then they had another option which they exercised and I went to 150. They loaned me out for a couple of pictures, and made money on me. For *Stalag 17* they loaned me out to Paramount—they were paying me I think 150 a week at that point and they got *1500* a week from Paramount! So they were doin' okay! At the end of two years with them, they weren't really doing much of anything any more, and my career was getting busy, so we parted in a friendly manner, and I thank them, always, for giving me that first big break.

Red Planet Mars *doesn't loom very large in the movie history books now, but it was your first starring role and it must have been a big deal in* your *life, to get your first starring role.*

Well, *Rogue River* had been a co-starring role—it was with Rory Calhoun.

For his *Red Planet Mars* role, 25-year-old Graves' hair was cosmetically whitened. The real thing was just around the corner.

With special "and introducing" billing, I remember, on screen for you.

I do believe so, yeah. But anyway, *Red Planet Mars* came along and the producers of that film wanted me. I went again, I do believe, on a reading; they had seen other stuff that I had done, and *wanted* me. In *Red Planet Mars* I was supposed to have been a little older character than my actual age at the time [25] so they grayed my temples a little [*laughs*]—even in black-and-white, you *knew* it! *Red Planet Mars* had some pretty good people in it: Andrea King was the leading lady, she played my wife; Herbert Berghof, who played the mad scientist, went on to become a well-known character actor in the film business, and became even *better* known for being an acting teacher. Donald Hyde, who was one of the producers, was the son of Johnny Hyde, *legendary* agent, and the other producer was Anthony Veiller, who was basically a writer, and co-wrote the screenplay. [*Pause*] Boy, it sure was talky, wasn't it?

[Laughs] Well, it was based on a play. A flop play from 1932!

Is *that* right? I'd forgotten that. But anyway, we didn't have a lot of dough for big special effects or anything, so it was a lot of talking, about *what* was going on, where these signals were coming from, were they coming from God on Mars? And it turned out that the signals were coming from this bad guy [Berghof] shooting them up from a hut in the Andes somewhere [*laughs*]. But I enjoyed making it—everything was a new spring garden at that time, Tom. Jeez, just getting started in the business and everything I did was a *thrill* for me, *and* a learning experience. I was, at this point, really in kindergarten.

Getting the part, at age 25, of a middle-aged scientist—did you feel up to the challenge?
I didn't know any better [*laughs*]! I thought, "*Yes*, I can do this," and I thought it [his performance] came off okay.

This was your first time top-billed in a movie but unfortunately it must have had "dud" written all over it—based on a flop play, the plot a weird Cold War thing about God living on Mars. What goes through an actor's mind when he's offered a good part in a movie that's probably not *going to be good?*
Well, at that time in your career, you take everything you can get. You *do* it. You show up every morning at six o'clock and go into makeup and *know* your lines when you get on the set and you go to work. [The actor's life] is an experience of progression, and I think that's probably what I thought of it: "This is another *opportunity* for me to work and to grow." I've never been a great believer in acting school and such things. I know that lots of wonderful people have come out of a thing like the Actors Studio, but [*laughs*] a *vast* number have *not* come out of the Actors Studio to do anything! My belief had always been to *work*, and to work with people who were experienced in it and better than I was. I had a certain amount of confidence in my ability in those days to give a performance, a good performance, and physically I seemed to be one of the sort of young Hollywood leading men of that era. So, man, it was just, "Go ahead! Plow! If this is not a big-budget hotsie-totsie movie, what the hell? Let's go to work!" And that's what we did.

The director of Red Planet Mars *was an art director, Harry Horner—did he have his act together, so early in his directing career?*
Yeah, he was pretty good. I *think* it was his first directing job. But as I mentioned before, we didn't *have* special effects, or the money for 'em. But in those days, an *unlimited* amount of money wouldn't have gotten us much better special effects, because they *didn't exist*. All the computerized stuff that they do today, that [technology] did not exist. So we had to go with the stories and try to make them as believable as possible, and flash the outlandish things by quickly [*laughs*], so the audience never got a good, in-focus *look* at them!

The movie is set slightly in the future and your character has a flat panel widescreen TV hung on the wall of his house. Whoever dreamed that up was 50 years ahead of his time!
A TV like the new plasma ones? My God. That probably would have come out of Harry Horner's head—he was a designer.

According to the Hollywood trade papers, Veiller and Hyde, the producers of Red Planet Mars, *took an option to purchase your contract from Ventura Pictures. I take it they liked you.*

Oh, they liked me, yes. But I don't know that that story's true. That sounds to me more like a press agent dropping something into the trades. It had to be *their* [Veiller and Hyde's] press agent, because I sure as hell didn't *have* one in 1951, I couldn't afford one! Whatever that story was, it wasn't true. In fact, I don't think Hyde and Veiller ever made a picture together again.

When an episode of Biography *devoted to your life aired in 1997, you told a newspaper interviewer that it lingered on the sci-fi stuff longer than you might have liked. How do you feel, honestly, about having all these skeletons in your closet,* Killers from Space *and movies like that?*

Killers from Space—which one was that?

The bug-eyed guys in the cave.

Yeah, yeah, right. Well ... I wasn't too happy about that. Noooo. But obviously nothing *else* was going on [work-wise] in 1953 when I got offered that one. Again, it's that same thing of "This is work. This will get my face on the screen. This will give me more experience as an actor." *And* "I can use the money!" That's a common song that we hear through the years, with almost *every* actor. *If* I had not had a family at that time, maybe I wouldn't have done it. [*Pause*] Oh, *sure* I would have done it, because I wasn't doing anything *else*. And I'm sure I did need the money. If any actor could afford to turn down things and wait for only the right right right right thing to come along, he would only work about once every five years [*laughs*]. And it's hard to *do* it that way! My thought was always, "It's there, it's a job—go to work." So I did.

Do you remember the Killers from Space *director W. Lee Wilder well enough to compare and contrast him with his brother,* Stalag 17's *Billy Wilder?*

Well, W. Lee was the one who did the little pictures and Billy was the one who did the *big* pictures. There *is* a great deal to how you get started in this business, and what early breaks you have that might send you in another direction. *I* began right at the time when the studio contract system for actors was falling apart—the whole business was changing so radically that the studios just weren't *doing* that [grooming contract actors] any more. Some of the studios hung on longer than others. Universal for instance, about the time I started, picked up two young guys named Tony Curtis and Rock Hudson and gave them some good parts in some pretty good pictures. They brought them along carefully as stars, to build to stardom—and those fellows *were* talented. But they also got those breaks. I went into Universal to interview for I-forget-what-pictures over there that might star those guys, and I was always turned down. Because I was a little bit too much competition, perhaps, for them.

I don't know what I'm trying to say [*laughs*], except that life in this business points you in a direction. If I had really been convinced at that time that doing three or four science fiction pictures on the cheapie side would not develop my *career*, perhaps I might *not* have done 'em. Maybe I'd have gone to New York and done a play or something. *But* ... that's the path I took and so be it.

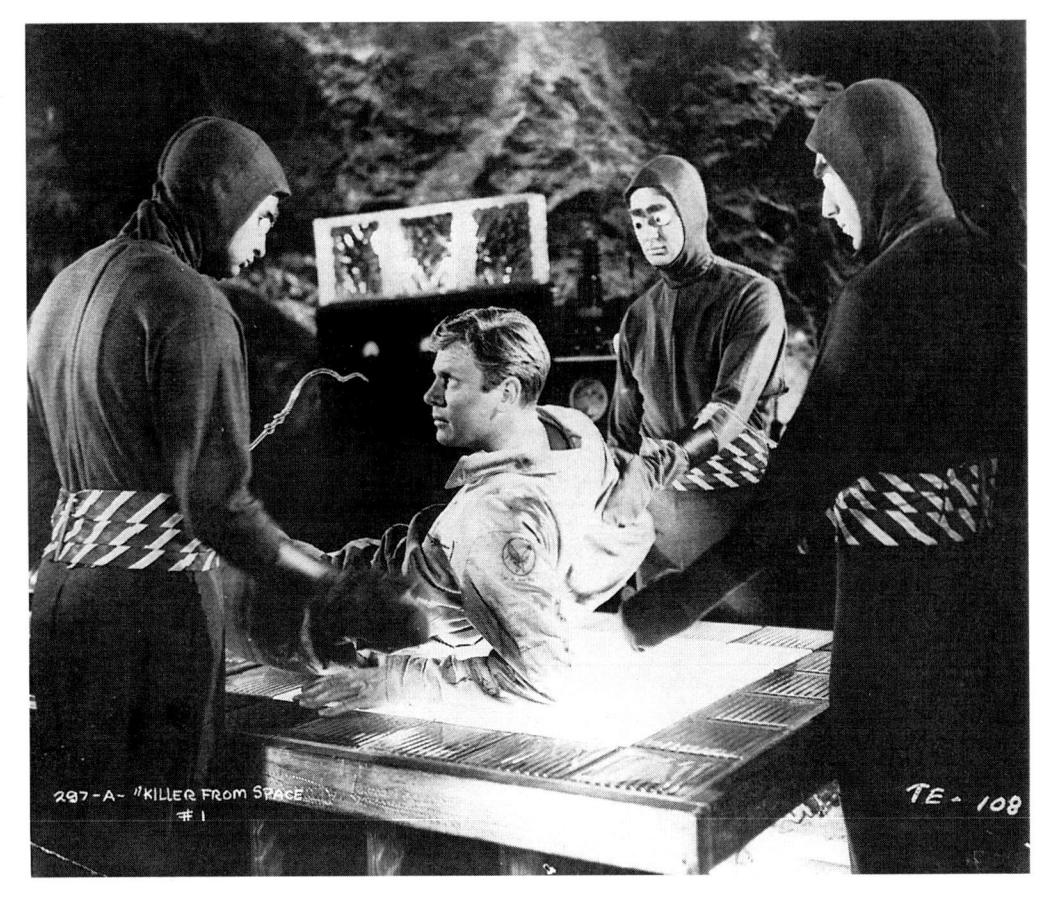

Sawed-in-half ping pong balls sufficed for turning actors into *Killers from Space*.

The reason I was asking about W. Lee and Billy Wilder was because I don't think they got along.

I have a memory of that, yeah, that they didn't talk much.

W. Lee's son Myles, who wrote Killers from Space, *told me that it was shot in six days with his dad's own money, and that they never built sets—for instance, every office scene was W. Lee Wilder's real-life office at KTTV!*

That's my memory of it, yeah. *Killers from Space* was fast work, there was no question about it. As for working in natural sets, I had already done that with *Rogue River*—we shot that whole picture up on and all around the Rogue River, and whatever interiors we had were done in rented homes or buildings or whatever.

What memories of shooting your confrontation scenes with the bug-eyed aliens in Bronson Canyon?

Bronson Canyon was one of the most famous old movie locations in the business. There was such a variety of stuff there, and it was right down the hill from Hollywood Boulevard a couple of miles. The caves had been made by guys who were

"Natural locations" (like Bronson Canyon in L.A.'s Griffith Park) were always popular with 1950s moviemakers on the *Killers from Space* level.

mining or drilling for something, I don't know what, and they presented an opportunity: A clever man with a camera could make it look like the dwelling place of aliens or a subterranean world beneath Africa, or what*ever*! I shot another picture later on, *Hold Back the Night* [1956] with John Payne, a story about the Korean War which we shot mostly up there, and they had to snow it in with artificial snow. So Bronson Canyon was ... jeez, you were workin' in *Hollywood*, man [*laughs*]!

The guys playing aliens with bug eyes—could they see?
    I think they had little pinholes in those things. They were actually sawed-in-half ping pong balls. They cut ping pong balls in half, they painted the iris on and I think they could see to a certain degree. (But they didn't *have* to see much.) I guess that was all the makeup man [Harry Thomas] could do on the budget he had. I suppose they shot some film on different makeups that he may have suggested, and they picked the ping pong balls [*laughs*]!

[Laughs] Makes you wonder what makeups were rejected!
    I didn't like that [the bug-eyed look] at all. I thought it was awful, of course.

I mean, I was a reasonably intelligent middle-twenties guy in those days and I thought, "Boy, this is really some awful corny stuff! But I'm gonna give it my 100 percent because—I'd *better*. I've *got* to. If I do *less* than that, they're all gonna know it and I won't work again even in *this* kind of picture."

Do you recall that it was KTTV where you shot parts of it?
 I would think so—it's just down the hill from Bronson Canyon. The power plant was the L.A. Department of Water and Power, their big power generating plant down in Long Beach, where they use seawater and the tides to run their machinery. Or *did* in those days.

The shooting title of the picture was The Man Who Saved the Earth.
 Right.

You actually remember that?
 Yeah, I do—because the Man Who Saved the Earth was *my* character. Jeez, that was one of the things that attracted me to it, I said, "Hey, I get to save the world." Then they thought better of that and they decided that the Man Who Saved the Earth was Jesus Christ, and they didn't want to presume *too* much. So they changed it.

Throughout your career, when a movie of yours would come out, would you, and the family, go to see it? Even these little things?
 I don't remember doing much of that, no. I would probably see it *myself*—I'm sure I would—because that was all part of the learning experience. But maybe when my children were very young, I didn't *want* them to see something like *Killers from Space*, which would have been scary for them.

Before we get away from the Wilders: In your Biography, *actor Gil Stratton says that* Stalag 17 *was shot in order and that the cast didn't know throughout the shooting that you would turn out to be the bad guy at the end. Did you know from the beginning that you would be the bad guy at the end?*
 Sure. I think Gil made a mistake there, I really do. He may have a hazier memory of the film than I do. First of all, it had been a play on Broadway, and a lot of people in our business had seen it. So everybody should have known. By the way, we didn't start the film with a completed script—hell, we started with only about 20 pages. We shot the 20 pages in the barracks, and then one day we came in and Billy wasn't there and they said, "Just sit down and have coffee, boys…" Then about two o'clock in the afternoon, Billy came down onto the set waving a coupla pages and said, "Everybody sit down at the table and we'll read this." We read through it, and then he said, "Okay, let's get it on its feet and lay it out." And so we'd get it up and block it out and they'd light it and we'd *do* it. Well, we ended up doing a lot of the picture that way!

Appearing in The Night of the Hunter *[1955] and working with director Charles Laughton—what was that experience like?*

A year after appearing in the Billy Wilder classic *Stalag 17*, Graves starred in Billy's brother W. Lee's *Killers from Space*. (Graves, in robe, and co-star Steve Pendleton, in suit and tie, are squatting in front row; W. Lee with black hair and glasses stands behind.)

That was wonderful. I had a good friend then, Millie Gusse, who was the casting director for *Night of the Hunter*. She brought me in to meet Paul Gregory, who was producing the film. I met with him and got along fine and he said, "You should be wonderful for this." I didn't meet Charles quite then because I think he was back in New York at that moment, still in a play or something. Anyway, I was cast in it and did meet Charles and went on the set and had a wonderful time working with him. He was a dream. He was nervous as he could be 'cause it was *his* first time directing on film. He'd start each scene with a full load in the camera; you'd do the scene; and then he wouldn't *cut* the camera, he would just say, "Keep it rolling," and then he'd talk to you and say, "Give me a little more of *this*" or "Give me a little less of *that*" and so forth. Then he'd say, "Now, let's do it again, please," and you might do three or four takes of a scene before he would be satisfied himself and he'd say, "Print it." I remember one time I said to him, "Mr. Laughton, was that good for you?," and he said [*imitating Laughton*], "Dear boy, was that good for *you*?" I said yes, and he said, "There you *are* ... see?" [*Laughs*] So ... there you were! Yeah, it was a very happy experience doing that. I became friends with Paul Gregory, who was, I thought, a brilliant producer, and I later did a play for him in New York [1962's *The Captains and the Kings*].

Laughton was a good director for you then?

Oh, indeedy, sure. I would have worked with him *any* ol' time. And it was my first meeting with Bob Mitchum as well, and *that* was great. He was a very straightforward ... *strange* sort of guy, but very bright. Brilliant in ways. And had this fantastic screen presence. I remember receiving a letter during the shooting of that picture, a letter from some crazy lady back in Ohio who claimed I was the father of her child [*laughs*]! It was "wonderful." And my *wife* happened to open the letter thinking it was a Christmas card or something, and *she* wasn't very happy about that. It took me quite a bit of talking to assure her that this was all nonsense and I'd never been to Ohio and it was impossible, and she did believe me. Then in the next day or two I was on the set with Mitchum and I asked, "*You* must get a lot of letters like this. What do you do about it, Bob?" He said, "I figure if I have a name, I might as well have the game!" [*Laughs*]

You mentioned a minute ago that Laughton was nervous — did he say that he was, or you could just tell?

You could tell. And he would even *say* so: "Oh dear, oh dear, I'm not *used* to this, you know..." But he didn't slink his way through the picture [*laughs*] — no, no! He was an actor's actor and knew what was goin' on. It was just that the mechanics of things maybe stirred him up a little, because he wasn't used to having to deal with that in film.

Those outtakes of Laughton directing the actors between takes still exist, and may come out on DVD some day.

*Every*thing will come out on DVD someday, you may be assured of that! Including ... [*laughs*] ... including Janet Jackson's right breast [during the 2004 Super Bowl halftime show, the day before this interview]!

Roger Corman's It Conquered the World *with Beverly Garland — what memories can you pull up on that one?*

Did I only do one with Roger?

Yeah, and that was my next question. He usually latched onto leading men, used the same ones in a whole bunch of pictures — but you were in and out in one. Did you get along with him?

Oh, sure, he was wonderful, I liked Roger. Last year or the year just before, an organization out here called Pacific Pioneer Broadcasters honored Beverly Garland, the queen of Roger Corman's pictures — she did I-don't-know-*how*-many with him. Roger was there, too, and we had a nice chance to talk again. I certainly enjoyed working with him, he's a very capable guy. And, yes, it was another one of those wacko, shoot-it-in-ten-days jobs. Another fellow named Lee Van Cleef co-starred in that — a very good actor and a good guy. He ran into a problem, I think with booze and stuff, and sorta became *persona non grata* in Hollywood ... so he went to Italy and became a huge star of the spaghetti Westerns! That was great for him. And Beverly was always *wonderful* as an actress, she was a *super* actress, she could do *any*-

Another SF skeleton in Graves' closet: the micro-budgeted one-alien-invasion "epic" *It Conquered the World*. (Photograph courtesy Academy Pictures.)

thing. Indeed, in recent years we have worked together on the *7th Heaven* TV series, where I played the reverend's [Stephen Collins] father, a crusty old retired Marine colonel, and Beverly played his mother-in-law. So we've seen each other over the years, and I've told you about her luncheon at Pacific Pioneer Broadcasters. She's great—she still acts and she runs her hotel [Beverly Garland's Holiday Inn in North

Hollywood] and she's still the same old, great, wonderful, speak-her-mind, loud-mouth dame [*laughs*]! Everybody loves her.

So, yeah, *It Conquered the World* was a happy experience. And, again, Corman certainly always knew what *he* was doing. The one thing that all of those guys had in common was a great ability to plan their work and to know what they could accomplish each day and to juggle that logistical ball of a film schedule and make it work *in* the time and *in* the budget. They all had that and no one better than Roger, who went on and made a career out of making *that* kind of picture. I'm an admirer of his, as is most of Hollywood.

No matter what star of Corman oldies I interview, whether it's Mike Connors or Richard Denning or whoever, they all agree on one thing: He never said boo to the actors and you were always on your own.
I think that's right, yes.

Is that okay, to be on your own?
Well, you get to *thinking* it is [*laughs*]! And sometimes you make some *terrible* mistakes! I think he knew from the beginning that he had hired good performers, and it was best just to let them go within the context of the story and to rely on them. And he *did* so. I remember another very famous, huuuge director named John Ford, for whom I did *The Long Gray Line* [1955], and John Ford almost never said anything to you in the way of acting tips or instructions or whatever. The first scene I ever did in that picture was a scene in the mess hall, with Tyrone Power. It was a meeting between us, and Tyrone Power's character didn't like mine because I was trying to court Maureen O'Hara and so was he. There was something about the scene that I didn't feel was working—*no*body did. We went through a few rehearsals, and I finally had an idea. I said, "Mr. Ford, I think—" And he said, "*Shut up*." He said, "*I'll* do the thinking on this fuckin' set. Just keep your *mouth* shut and do what I tell ya." That was my introduction to John Ford, and [*laughs*]—and the only "instruction" he ever *gave* me!

Did you get to see the It Conquered the World *monster in action?*
I think I did. I wasn't very impressed with it.

Who would ever have dreamed that big movies like The Long Gray Line *would eventually disappear into the past while schlock like, say,* Killers from Space *would attract one generation of fans after another...?*
It makes you worry about the future of our country, doesn't it?

[Laughs] Yeah, it sorta does!
Or the future of Mankind in general! We better get more things up on Mars, because we may have to *go* there! This morning I heard what Jay Leno said in his [*Tonight Show*] monologue last night, about Janet's breast and the fact that CBS pompously said that what happened violated their broadcast standards. Leno said, "*Broadcast standards*?? You just saw a horse *fart* on a woman [in a Budweiser com-

mercial that aired during the Super Bowl], and they've got *broadcast standards*??" I don't know whether you saw that commercial—the horse farted on the girl, and when you see the girl again after the explosion, she's got ... *stuff* all over her face. Now this is just *disgusting*—you know? *That's* part of CBS's "broadcast standards"? Christ Almighty...

So, it's a strange world, yeah. And I don't *know* why, to answer your question about such pictures as *The Long Gray Line* fading away. I looked at *The Long Gray Line* recently, in the last few months, and it's a wonderful film. *The Court-Martial of Billy Mitchell* [1955] was pretty good. *Why* they fade ... darned if I know.

You saved the world from giant grasshoppers in Beginning of the End.

That was another pretty interesting one, with a wonderful actress named Peggie Castle. Bert Gordon directed that. He was okay, he was a good director. Again, these guys have to meticulously plan, and I do believe he did. We shot that, or a good part of it, out at the old Republic Studios. Since it dealt with Chicago and the grasshoppers climbing up Chicago buildings, the first screening of it was in Chicago. The screening was in a theater but the high point of the trip was that we went to dinner one night at the Chicago Stock Yards. The Chicago Stock Yards was a big deal in those days—it was a cattle market and it was all owned by a man named William Wood Prince, who was a million-million-millionaire of his day. There was a wonderful steak restaurant, of course, *in* the stockyards. You didn't get the fragrance of the cattle being slaughtered or anything in there [*laughs*], but you got great steaks! And we had the privilege of having dinner with William Wood Prince one evening. He fell immediately in love with Peggie Castle [*laughs*]! Peggie must have looked very appealing to him—well, she *always* did look appealing!

There were so many good character actors in Beginning of the End.

Yes, yes! I really felt privileged to work with Morrie Ankrum, I'd seen him in films since I was a little kid. Thomas Browne Henry was at that time also a big wheel with the Pasadena Playhouse. His wife taught there, and I think he did too, in addition to having some executive position. He was a good guy. I love working with all of those guys, Morrie and Walter Sande in *Red Planet Mars*, Morrie and Tom in *Beginning of the End*. Oh, and also James Seay. We eventually got him a sort of semi-running part in *Fury*, he played the local sheriff. He became a good friend.

The special effects of the grasshoppers on the hop in Beginning of the End—*in 1957, how well did you think those scenes played?*

I think they played okay. They weren't up to a picture like, say, *The War of the Worlds* [1953], which had a much bigger budget. As I said before, the [B-movie] science fiction special effects in those days were often the quick smoke-and-mirrors stuff. They didn't have any budgets, so they cut up ping pong balls and stuff like that! All of that was ludicrous, but there were a certain amount of people who "bought" it and loved it. Otherwise, Tom, you wouldn't be talkin' to me today! There's still a wide audience out there, around the world, for this kind of stuff.

You had a brief fling at directing in the mid-60s—what brought that on?

I was talking with my brother [James Arness] one day, we talked about directors that we had worked with, and I mentioned that I had thought about directing. He said, "Come on over and do a *Gunsmoke*, for Heaven's sake!" So I did. And I liked it. And it turned out well. And indeed CBS, when they were preparing for their next season of *Gunsmoke*, offered me a deal to do a half a dozen of those shows. At that time [1966], I had just appeared in a pilot for CBS myself, called *Call to Danger*. Then they called me one night at home to say that *Call to Danger* was *not* going to sell and become a series, but they *had* a little series called *Mission: Impossible* that they would like me to join. I liked that—and there went the directing, I *couldn't* accept the offer to do *Gunsmoke* because I was going to be busy with *Mission*.

But then you did *direct some* Mission: Impossible*s*.

That's right, later on in *Mission*, I decided I would direct one of those, and *that* turned out okay. I did enjoy directing, but I felt that my career lay as an actor, and that if I wanted to direct, I should become a director and *only* a director. And I didn't want to do that. So I laid off the directing—didn't try to pursue it at all—and stayed with the acting.

After Mission: Impossible *came and went, you didn't get as many of the villain and weakling roles you often played in your "pre-IMF" days. Did you enjoy doing those? Did you think you did a good job at it?*

Certain of them, yeah. Of course, *Stalag 17* was a very important picture of the day—although Paramount didn't think so! We finished it, and they put it in the vault for a year before they'd release it. They hated it. Billy Wilder didn't hate it, *Paramount* hated it. They said, "Who wants to see a picture about a bunch of guys in a prison camp, for Heaven's sake?" And then in 1953 I think it was, there was a prisoner of war exchange concerning the Korean War, so Paramount said, "Well, we'll let it escape and see what it does." Well, we know what it did [*Stalag 17* was a top-grosser of 1952-53, Wilder received a Best Director Oscar, etc.]! *But*, *Stalag 17* also had the effect, at that time, of making Hollywood think of me as a heavy. In truth, I didn't work at Paramount Studios again until *Mission: Impossible*! Every time I would go there in regard to some picture or other, the Paramount people would say, "Jeez, no, he's a German spy—*we* can't have that!"

In one old interview you said that you've had white hair since your mid-twenties, but in another you said it turned white during Mission: Impossible.

I was *starting* to turn in my late twenties. I remember lookin' in the mirror one morning and there on the side of my hair was a patch of white. I said, "What the hell is *this*?" [*laughs*] and we went on from there—it just gradually changed! The cameraman on *Mission: Impossible*, when he first met me, said to the producer Bruce Geller, "Is Peter gonna dye his hair for the role?" And both Bruce and I looked at him and said, "Hell *no*! White hair is gonna be *it*." So that's what we did.

Your wife talks on your Biography *about you starting to get mobbed once* Mission: Impossible *became popular; and you certainly were offered a greater variety of roles in movies,*

etc., before *Mission: Impossible.*
What are the "downsides," if any, to being the star of a show like that?

No, I don't think there's a downside. I know an awful lot of actors who said [about a TV series], "Jeez, I hate this thing, I'm only doing this for the dough and I can't wait to get out of it"—all of which I think is a lot of ca-ca. It's a job and it's a *good* job, and if it's gonna last a few years, for Heaven's sake, stay *with* it! When you get mobbed, you get mobbed, and you better thank your lucky stars for it. Though it gets tough, sure. It gets tough particularly for somebody like Joan, my wife—yeah, it gets to be a pain for *her*, because I'd be in the middle of the mob and they've shunted *her* off somewhere else, and she can't even get back to me. That's terrible—but that's part of the game.

Mission: Impossible was a different kind of series. My Jim Phelps character, who was supposedly so brilliant and intelligent and suave and sophisticated, [attracted] the usual kind of fan, but *beyond* that, also people with higher standards or intelligence or status in life or what*ever*—they absolutely loved it. I would always get a kick out of walking down the street in New York City and a very well-dressed gentleman with a Chesterfield and a Homburg on would stop and say to me [*in a very quiet, refined voice*], "Very good, old boy..." [*Laughs*] That kind of thing was always a kick.

Graves and his wife Joan (seen here at a 1958 premiere) have enjoyed one of Tinsel Town's most enduring marriages.

How often do you watch your old movies—if ever?

Not often. I've got a lot of them here, but I don't think I've watched anything recently.

If one of your grandkids said, "Grandpa, show me one of your movies," which one would you put on for him?

I'll tell you what I *have* done for them is to play them a videotape of a compilation of musical numbers that I did on *The Dean Martin Show!* Which I got a kick out of and really enjoyed doing—and they turned out pretty well! So I've showed 'em that and they hoot and holler and think that's terrific! "There's Grandpa singing and dancing!"

On-camera hosting stints on *Discover: The World of Science* and *Biography* have helped keep Graves in public view.

From where I'm sitting, it looks to me like you've had kind of a charmed life as an actor. You didn't start in movies with bits, you started by co-starring in one; and I can't think of any other actor who was doing the kind of stuff you were doing in the '50s, who's as active as you are today. What was the key to having gotten where you are?

I guess it's just knowing that the wolf is always at the door [*laughs*]! No, no—I love to work. And there was a point in my career when I got shunted off in the direction of *hosting* shows about different subjects. When a pilot that I had made after *Mission: Impossible* did not sell to become a series, I got a call maybe the next day from Time-Life. They were making a documentary series called *Other People, Other Places*, in which an actual crew and a wonderful German guy went and filmed strange tribes in Africa or China or Russia or talked about deep sea fish or the Loch Ness Monster or what*ever*. They were looking for a host for this series, and I did it. I did three years of those, something like that, and at that moment Time-Life *again* called me and said that they had a show called *Discover: The World of Science* and would I like to host *that*? That was a lot of fun because I traveled a number of places in the world with them, doing that show, and that wound up on Public Broadcasting for two or three years. We would make only about a half a dozen of those a year, and they were wonderful. And then the second *that* was finished, or overlapping actually [*laughs*], came *Biography*. I went to New York and met with these people at A&E—I didn't know what the hell A&E *was*. But I thought it sounded like fun, and I knew it wouldn't stop me from doing films or other things. So I did *Biography* for 15 years—which is not a bad job!

So staying in the public eye with all these hosting jobs is a big *part of your continuing success story.*

Of course it is. Producers always need to see a warm body. If you haven't worked for ten years and they think you're absolutely right for the part but they're not sure that you're *alive*, they don't call. But when your face is around and on the screen and they hear you and so forth, it keeps you "alive" for them. I think that's wonderful. My first movie I made in 1950, and I'm still workin' in 2004—I *like* that. Because I like to work. I don't like to work as hard as I *used* to, no, but I *don't* work that hard now. And what I *do*, I thoroughly enjoy.

Gary Gray on The Next Voice You Hear...

> *If God's voice were to come over the air today, it'd probably be TV.*

It was a bit of a daring experiment for 1950 Hollywood: a movie in which God turns radio monologist for six nights, the Supreme Being at last taking a hands-on approach to spreading His message to all the peoples of the world. Director William A. Wellman's *The Next Voice You Hear...* could easily have become a preachment but instead the MGM production emerged as a heart-warming human interest story by focusing on the emotional upset (and eventual understanding) the voice's nightly 8:30 broadcasts cause in a typical household—the modest Los Angeles home of "Joe Smith, American" (James Whitmore), an aircraft plant worker with a very pregnant homemaker wife (Nancy Davis) and precocious son (Gary Gray).

The Next Voice You Hear... became a highlight in the career of Gray, the 13-year-old child actor whose performance provided the family-friendly fantasy film with some of its best dramatic and "light" moments. Born in L.A., Gray made his movie debut at age three in an uncredited bit in the 1941 Joan Crawford melodrama *A Woman's Face*. Years of small parts followed before he got his first breaks in *Return of the Bad Men*, *Rachel and the Stranger* (both 1948) and *The Next Voice You Hear...*, which earned him an MGM contract. His early-'50s stint at MGM was followed by a decade of TV work and several additional movie roles.

Now a resident of Brush Prairie, Washington, Gray has been retired from acting since the early 1960s. The father of four, grandfather of 20(!) and *great*-grandfather of one, he is a frequent (and highly popular) guest at film festivals throughout the country.

Was The Next Voice You Hear... *"just another picture" when you initially went to MGM to audition for it?*

As far as my mother and I were concerned, it was just another picture that we were going in for. How I got the part: As I recall, they had boiled it down to me and two other kids. I forget who one of them was but the other was Bobby Hyatt. The one kid went into an office and read; Bobby Hyatt went in and read; and at that point, they were ready to hire Bobby Hyatt. But then they said, "Well, there's one more kid out here, we oughta at *least* hear him read." Well, the one other kid was me. I went in and I read, and I wound up with the part. Bobby Hyatt's mother pretty much thought that Bobby had the part, and of course when he didn't get it, she was not happy about it. I can't blame her [*laughs*]!

Who were you reading for?

Dore Schary and Bill Wellman. I don't even know if Dore Schary remembered, but I had worked for him before: He was the head of RKO when I did *Rachel and the Stranger*, so I had met him of course when I did that picture. But that really had nothing to do with me getting the part in *Next Voice You Hear...* 'cause I don't know if he even remembered me from *Rachel and the Stranger*, to be real honest.

With reliable pros James Whitmore, Gary Gray and Nancy Davis heading the cast, MGM (the Tiffany's of Hollywood movie studios) was able to crank out *The Next Voice You Hear...* in just 14 days on a modest $460,000 budget. "If ever a picture rated the must-see lists, *The Next Voice You Hear...* is it," raved *Variety*.

How were you landing parts in 1950? Were both your parents taking an active role?

At that age, you really don't make a lot of choices on your own. I just happened to be lucky 'cause I enjoyed acting, it was fun as far as I was concerned. My dad was a business manager for people in the motion picture business—stars, directors, producers and writers. Jack Benny and Bert Wheeler, clients of my dad's, both told him to get me into pictures, so Dad registered me with Central Casting and the Screen Children's Guild. Then it was just a matter of going on interviews. I felt sorry for my mother, she had to learn how to drive a car so she could take me to interviews 'cause Dad just couldn't break away from work all the time to take me. Those were the days when women didn't all drive, back in the early '40s, and my mother really did not want to drive.

You were a freelancer.

Yes. I always freelanced except for a six-month stint at MGM—I got a term contract because of *The Next Voice You Hear...* I did *Two Weeks with Love* [1950] and *The Painted Hills* [1951] and, after they were done, MGM started letting [their contract players] go. It was like the summer of '50 or '51, and the studios were kinda cleanin' house.

Before I did *The Next Voice You Hear...* at MGM, I had worked there a ton. I had the biggest crush on Elizabeth Taylor that anyone ever had. While I was under contract there, when she'd have picture sittings, publicity would bring me a complete set of the photos, because they all knew I had this crush on her. A few years earlier, after I'd finished my part in a picture called *Three Wise Fools* [1946], right before Halloween, there was going to be a big Halloween party at MGM, in the schoolhouse, just for the kids attending school at MGM. Man, I wanted to go to that party. So Mrs. McDonald, the teacher, gave me a pass so I could come back on the lot for the Halloween party. I went [in drag]—my sister Arlene had real fine hair so she had this fall she used to wear, so I put the fall on and a dress and the whole thing. And, boy, did Mrs. McDonald get upset, she got all over my mother—she said, "I told you that you could bring *Gary*, I didn't tell you to bring Arlene!" Mrs. McDonald thought I was my sister [*laughs*]! Everybody there thought I was a girl except for *two* people. One was Jane Powell, the other was Elizabeth Taylor. I'll bet neither one of 'em remembers this, but I'll remember it forever: They sat me up on the sink in the kitchen area in the back of the schoolhouse and they were putting makeup on me, putting my lipstick on and doing my eyes [*laughs*].

When I was doing *The Painted Hills*, I was having makeup put on by ... I think it was [William] Tuttle. And, oh!, my heart was just *breaking*, 'cause Elizabeth Taylor was going to get married to Nicky Hilton. I was 13 and she was 18. "Gary," he said, "by the time you're old enough to get married, she'll have been married five times." And, you know what? He was only off by *one*, I think [*laughs*]. She got married for the fourth time right after Jean and I got married in 1961. *He* knew her really well [*laughs*]!

The stars of Next Voice You Hear..., *James Whitmore and Nancy Davis—what memories of them?*

Ordinary flash thunderstorm ... or God's wrath? Davis, Whitmore and Gray huddle in fear as they make up their minds.

It's funny, when anybody asks me about Nancy Davis, the things I always think of first are her brown pedal pushers. My mother and I went up to her apartment, which was just off of Pico somewhere, and I can still picture her in brown pedal pushers, sitting cross-legged on a Hollywood bed. We were sitting there running lines and things. For some reason, that's what I remember more than anything about her! She was always extremely nice to me on the set. She was just an everyday kind of gal.

And this picture was a break for her, too.
Oh, it was a *big* break for her, that's right.

And James Whitmore?
James Whitmore is exactly what he looks like, he's just one heck of a nice, everyday guy. We used to play catch a little bit out in front of the sound stage. Several years ago, back around '95, one of the guys from the Memphis Film Festival, Steve, went to a play and saw James Whitmore. After the play, he went backstage and saw Jim and told him that he'd seen me at this film festival, and Jim said, "Jeez, I'd love to talk to Gary." Steve went home, called Ray Nielsen [organizer of the Memphis Film Festival], got my phone number and then [*laughs*] went back to see the show *again* the next night in order to go backstage again and see James Whitmore again and give him my phone number. Of course, all this is unbeknownst to me. I'm sitting here at the house in Brush Prairie one day and I get this phone call: "Is this Gary Gray?" When people do that to me, I always think, "Oh, it's a salesman," so I said [*cautiously*], "...Yyyyes." And he said [*cheerfully*], "Jim Whitmore here!" I can still hear it in my mind's ear, "Jim Whitmore here!" And we had a nice conversation. He's just a *really* nice guy.

William Wellman—how did you feel about him as a director?
Oh, *man*. They don't come any better than Bill Wellman. He could get things *out* of you that maybe you didn't even know you had. He was really good. Remember the one scene where God asked if He had to perform such miracles as making it once again rain 40 days and 40 nights, and then outside our house the rain and thunder and lightning starts? Bill Wellman told Nancy to scream ... but during all the rehearsals, he never told James Whitmore or me or *any*body that, in the take, she was gonna scream. Then we did the take, and she screamed. When you saw us all grab for one another, let me tell you, that was *real*. *We* didn't know it was coming. *She* did, but *we* didn't! It scared *every*body [*laughs*]!

You have a number of good scenes in the movie—what's your favorite?
The scene where Nancy Davis and I are sitting at the breakfast table. I'm sick and I'm staying home from school, and James Whitmore goes out to get in his car. I pantomime him opening the car door and slamming it and getting a rag and wiping the steering wheel and throwing it in the glove compartment and so on—everybody who talks to me about *The Next Voice You Hear...* seems to really like that scene. And there's one scene that was really, really simple. It's at the very end of the pic-

Dore Schary (in suit and tie), the producer of *The Next Voice You Hear...*, later wrote an entire book about the making of the off-the-beaten-path drama. He is flanked in this shot by Gray, Davis, director William A. Wellman and Whitmore.

ture, where Jim Whitmore is taking Nancy Davis to the hospital to have a baby and they don't know I'm in the back of the car until I poke my head up. Jim Whitmore says, "I thought I told you to stay home," and I say, "I'm going *with* you." It was a simple little thing, but I like it because it seemed so true-to-life, something typical of what a young kid *would* do and say under those circumstances. By the way, Jim Whitmore was related to Lillian Bronson, who played Nancy Davis' aunt in the picture.

How were they related?

Well, at *that* time they weren't. But eventually she *was* his mother-in-law, because she was the stepmother of one of his several wives—I don't know which wife it was. She was a sweetheart, Lillian Bronson. I worked with her, oh golly, I bet four or five different times anyway. She was in *Next Voice You Hear...* and *Two Weeks with Love* and *Father Is a Bachelor* [1950]—we worked a lot together. Just a *really* nice person, and a great actress. There were a *lot* of good people in that picture. Remember Sherry Jackson from *The Danny Thomas Show*? She had a little silent bit, a close shot of her in the church at the very end. Jim Hayward [playing an aircraft plant security guard] was around forever—I worked with him a couple different times. Doug Kennedy [Whitmore's barfly friend Mitch] lived right across the street from my girlfriend Sandy Jones, so we used to go over there and baby-sit for him! I thought there were a lot of great character actors in that picture.

Why doesn't the audience get to hear God's voice?
Because they didn't want anybody to stand up and say, "Hey, that was (let's say) Charlton Heston!" They didn't want anybody to know that voice. Plus, it kept you in suspense.

There's only one *part of the movie that I think is dated, that doesn't quite ring true any more, if it ever did. That's when James Whitmore comes home with a snoot-full and you practically go into shock. Educate me, was it really that awful in 1950?*
I think it depends on your upbringing. My mom and dad were teetotalers, as Jean and I are. If I saw my dad come in like that, I don't know *what* I'd do. It all depends upon whether you'd seen your folks drink, and maybe get a little boozy occasionally. If you were raised in a household where that was not the case, it might *be* a big deal. Incidentally, I still have the model plane that I was working on in the movie. Jim Whitmore comes home drunk so I leave, I go over to Art Smith's, and when Jim finds me I'm sanding down a model plane. I still have that plane, with Bill Wellman's signature on it. I just asked if I could have it, and if he'd sign it. And he said yes.

Incidentally, it was well known that "Wild Bill" Wellman did not like women on his sets—hairdressers, wardrobe women, *movie mothers*, etc. The first day of shooting, Mr. Wellman saw my mother and wanted to know who in the hell that woman was. When he was told that it was my mother, he knew that there wasn't anything he could do about it—the law required me to have a guardian on the set. By the end of the shoot, Bill Wellman and my mother were really good friends due to the fact that my mother was anything *but* a movie mother. My mother would go to the back of the stage, as far away as she could get from the action, and sit and read or do needlepoint all day. I can honestly say that she was never really thrilled about the motion picture business. She *was* thrilled, however, when Jean and I decided to get married, and I made the decision to get *out* of the industry. In fact, my mother helped me find a business to buy so that we would have a steady income.

Where did you see the picture for the first time?
I think it was on Pico, at the sneak preview. That was in the days when they *really* had sneak previews, when they didn't advertise that they were gonna have sneak previews [*laughs*]. Today they'll tell you way in advance what movie is going to be sneak-previewed, and where, and they'll run an ad in the papers! But in the old days, at the last minute they'd just put on the theater marquee **MAJOR STUDIO SNEAK PREVIEW TONIGHT AT 8 P.M.** and you wouldn't know what picture, or even what *kind* of a picture it was going to be. You'd pay to see whatever double-bill the theater was running—it was always a double-bill in those days, the late '40s–early '50s. You'd see the double-bill and a newsreel, and then the sneak preview was kinda thrown in.

A glimpse behind the scenes: The filming of the thunderstorm sequence is watched by dozens of crew members and set visitors (and director William A. Wellman, seated in front of camera).

So if you ended up in a theater that was hosting a sneak preview, you'd see three pictures in a row.

Up to three pictures, yeah. And that was the first time I ever saw *The Next Voice You Hear....* The audience reaction was very good. What the studio representatives used to do is, they'd pass out "comment cards," and after the movie the viewers would rate everything and give the cards back. I remember that Bill Wellman and Dore Schary and the studio representatives who were involved were real thrilled when they were picking up the cards out in front—they were very happy with the results.

Who else from the picture was there?

Nancy Davis and James Whitmore. The first time I saw Nancy Davis afterwards was when I was about 15. My girlfriend Sandy and I had gone to the premiere of *Bwana Devil* [1952] and Ronald Reagan and Mrs. Reagan, Nancy Davis, sat directly in back of us. Sandy still has a scrap of paper with Ronald Reagan's name on it, that he signed there that night. Then the next time I saw them was about 1964, when I was a member of the Young Republicans and he was speaking at a

Goldwater rally. I have not seen *her* since. But I received a note, hand-signed, from both she and Ronald Reagan when I came to the Memphis Film Festival for the first time in 1995. Later on, Jean and I went up and saw Ronald Reagan in his office in Century City. That was quite a thrill.

How did you manage that?

It was so funny. At that time I was national sales manager of American Products, a swimming pool equipment manufacturing company, and I was at a convention, I think in Chicago, and my friend Mike Fitzgerald [Michael Fitzgerald, film historian and author of *Universal Pictures* et al.] called me. He said, "You're going to be in California next month, you ought to call President Reagan's office and tell them you'd like to come in and see him." I said, "Yeah, *right*, Michael, he's gonna see *me*." Mike said that the Reagans used to watch all their old movies when they were in the White House and he assured me, "*They* know who you are. Would you mind if I sent 'em a Fax?" I said, "Michael, I don't care *what* you do." [*Laughs*] "I just don't have time right now to do anything." And I forgot about it.

I'm sitting at home in Brush Prairie about, I don't know, three weeks later and I get a phone call—again, kinda like the one from James Whitmore! "Gary Gray?" "…Yyyyes?" "This is President Reagan's office. We understand you're going to be in town and you'd like to come up and visit with the President." I said, "Oh, I'd love to!" So they made the arrangements and then, when I got to California, Jean and I went up and saw him and talked to him. He was in very good shape—he looked good and he sounded good. But I opened my big mouth and embarrassed Jean to death: I was showing him a photo from *The Girl from Jones Beach* [1949] that I was having him sign, a picture that had him, Virginia Mayo and myself in it, and I said, "I gotta tell you, when we did this picture, I was a lot more impressed with Virginia Mayo than I was *you*!"—Virginia Mayo was gorgeous in those days. Well, he just broke out laughing, he thought that was hilarious! "Yeah," he said, "she was *awful* pretty, wasn't she?" Jean was trying to find a crack in the floor she could crawl into [*laughs*]!

What major movies have you had better parts in, than Next Voice You Hear…?

Boy, I'm not sure. Maybe *Rachel and the Stranger*. It's a toss-up between that and *Rachel*, as far as I'm concerned. There are a couple Bs that, as far as my performances go, I look back *now* and think were noteworthy. Those are *Gun Smugglers* [1948] with Tim Holt and a Republic picture called *Streets of San Francisco* [1949]. In both of 'em, I start out as a bad kid and turn good, and you get to see the change.

What is the movie you're most asked about?

Actually, probably *The Painted Hills*, because of Lassie.

If God's voice did start coming over the radio, for real, how well would your movie match up with what you think would happen in real life?

Well, if God's voice were to come over the air *today*, it'd probably be TV—the TV would probably go blank and you'd hear the voice. But I think the reactions

The family that prays together: Whitmore, Davis, Gray and Lillian Bronson's lives are changed by the Voice.

would be pretty much the same in real life [as in the movie]. You'd have a lot of people saying that it was a phony. You'd have a certain amount of people who would believe right from the get-go. But in the long run, if it continued the way it did in the movie, and they couldn't trace it to a source, and different people heard it in different tongues, I think the reaction would be pretty much the same.

Incidentally, the movie starts on a Tuesday because they did not want to tie it in to any particular religion. So far as I know, the seventh day doesn't normally fall on a Monday, for any religion. I think in Judaism, Friday is their holy day; and Seventh Day Adventists is Saturday. The rest of almost the whole Christian world is Sunday. The movie had it so that the Seventh Day fell on a different day, so that nobody could look at the movie and claim, "Oh, that was for *us*."

I know The Next Voice You Hear... *is a message picture ... but what is* the message?

They talk about everything in the picture: faith ... understanding people ... peace ... you name it, they talk about it [*laughs*]. But basically it's about two things. Number one, be thankful for what we have. And, number two, live the Golden Rule. Do unto others as you would have others to do unto you. There are so many little messages throughout the picture, but I think if you lumped 'em all together, that's kinda what you'd come up with.

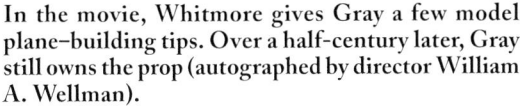

In the movie, Whitmore gives Gray a few model plane-building tips. Over a half-century later, Gray still owns the prop (autographed by director William A. Wellman).

The Next Voice You Hear... was a big success for Dore Schary. Later on, when he wanted to write a book about the making of a single movie [*Case History of a Movie*, 1950], *that* was the movie he used as his example. It started out to be a B production, a "two-week wonder," and that's what it *was*—it was a real quickie for MGM. But I think it was also a great, great picture with a great message and I'm proud to have been a part of it. The other big plus, of course, was being able to work not only with Jim Whitmore and Nancy Davis but with one of the all-time great directors, "Wild Bill" Wellman. It is a picture that I think everyone should see. It certainly would help our country if more people would live by what is taught in that motion picture.

The Next Voice You Hear...
(MGM, 1950)

83 minutes; First day of production: February 21, 1950; Produced by Dore Schary; Directed by William A. Wellman; Screenplay: Charles Schnee; Story: George Sumner Albee; Photography: William Mellor; Music: David Raksin; Editor: John Dunning; Assistant Editor: Greydon Gilmer; Art Directors: Cedric Gibbons & Eddie Imazu; Set Decorator: Edwin

B. Willis; Associate Set Decorator: Ralph S. Hurst; Production Manager: Ruby Rosenberg; Recording Supervisor: Douglas Shearer; Sound: Conrad Kahn; Assistant Director: Joel Freeman; Camera Operator: Neal Beckner; Gaffer: C. A. Philbrick; Script Supervisor: Bill Gale; Grip: Leo Monlon

James Whitmore (*Joe Smith*), Nancy Davis (*Mary Smith*), Gary Gray (*Johnny Smith*), Lillian Bronson (*Aunt Ethel*), Art Smith (*Fred Brannan*), Tom D'Andrea (*Harry "Hap" Magee*), Jeff Corey (*Freddie Dibson*), George Chandler (*Motorcycle Officer*), Douglas Kennedy (*Mitch*), Tim Hawkins (*Red*), Jim Hayward (*Arthur*), Thomas Browne Henry (*Doctor*), Marjorie Hoshelle (*Sweetie*), Milton Corey, Sr. (*Minister*), Mary Bear (*Nurse*), Donald Kerr (*Hot Dog Man*), Mickey Little, Frankie Darro (*Newsboys*), Grace Lord (*Elderly Woman in Church*), Fred Hoose, William H. Vedder, Howard M. Mitchell, Michael Barret (*Men in Church*), Helen Eby-Rock, Rhea Mitchell, Donna Boswell (*Women in Church*), Sherry Jackson (*Girl in Church*), Tommy Myers (*Boy*), Douglas Carter (*Father*), Bob Alden (*Soda Jerk*), Louis Merrill, Chet Huntley, Cecil Brown, Wilson Wood, Lyle Clark (*Radio Announcers*), Frank Gerstle, Frank Cady (*Plant Workers*), Eula Guy, Billy Bletcher (*Newspaper Customers*), Jim Pierce (*Myron*), Jack Sterling, John McKee, Rush Williams, Dwight Martin

Arch Hall, Jr.

I can honestly say, as I fast approach my sixtieth birthday, that I have been blessed with a most interesting life. Looking back, I wouldn't change a thing! I've had some pretty wild adventures over the past 37 years, flying four-engine jets to far-off, exotic places with strange-sounding names, in both peacetime and war.

Places with names like Phnom Penh, Da Nang, Saigon, Bangkok, Mogadishu, Tehran, Beirut, N'Djamena, Managua, Maidugari, Entebbe, Islamabad, Shanghai, Shenzhen and Ṣanā', to name but a few.

Prior to that, however, I had some great adventures far closer to home. At the corner of Lincoln and Olive Avenue in Burbank was Fairway Films, where we lived, worked, loved, laughed ... and cried sometimes ... making movies.
—Arch Hall, Jr.

From the late 1950s through the mid–'60s, Arch Hall, Sr.'s, Rushmore Productions and Fairway Films provided a string of highly exploitable features aimed at the teenage drive-in market. The movies ranged from j.d. melodrama (*The Choppers*) and the kooky, *King Kong*–like story of a lovesick caveman haunting the desert outside twentieth century Palm Springs (*Eegah*), to the near-brilliant psychodrama *The Sadist*, and they involved an assortment of new talent even *more* diverse: Ace cinematographers Laszlo Kovacs and future Oscar winner Vilmos Zsigmond, man-mountain actor Richard Kiel and offbeat auteur Ray Dennis Steckler, among many others. But the Burbank-based company's most visible attraction was its top (and only) star, Hall's teenage son Arch, Jr. Emoting from under a formidable mop of blonde hair, he headlined the aforementioned productions and most of the rest of the company's wildly eclectic output.

Arch, Sr., a real-life South Dakota cowboy turned B-Western badman of the 1930s and '40s, began his producing career in 1959 with *The Choppers*, easily convincing 15-year-old Jr. to take on the starring role of the leader of a car-stripping gang. Sr. and Jr. subsequently starred together in *Eegah* and *Wild Guitar* (both 1962) before Jr. had his finest hour (and a half) in the title role in the harrowing *The Sadist* (1963), giving a nightmare performance as a depraved thrill killer terrorizing a trio of schoolteachers stranded at a remote auto salvage yard.

In his first-ever career interview, Arch Hall, Jr., reminisces about these productions and unflinchingly paints a far-from-rosy picture of the dog-eat-dog independent movie scene of the 1960s.

[No opening question.]
I was born in Van Nuys, California, December the second, 1943, while my dad was in the Army Air Corps. I grew up an only child in what I suppose you would call, in modern-day psychobabble jargon, a minimally dysfunctional, typical middle-class family. We moved around a lot in Southern California during my growing-up years. It seemed I was always changing schools and having to make new friends. Not a lot of fun for a kid.

Where are some of the places you remember living?
We first lived on Babcock in North Hollywood, then in a wonderful old Spanish-style house on Beverly Glen, south of Ventura Boulevard in Sherman Oaks. Then in about the third grade, we moved to a small, nondescript house in Palm Desert. I attended grades four through six at Palm Desert Elementary School. During the seventh grade, it was back to North Hollywood, where I attended Madison Junior High, then we moved to Sun Valley where I went to Sun Valley Junior High. Then back to Palm Desert until I graduated from Coachella Valley Union High School in Coachella. That was in the summer of 1961, when we filmed *Eegah*.

Were you at all interested in acting when you were a kid?
To be perfectly honest, I had little interest in becoming an actor. At the time, I was far more interested in how to impress a slender young Native American girl whom I had a terrible crush on. I would try to offer her rides to school on the back of my "chopped" 1947 Indian Chief motorcycle. But her family didn't like the idea of a white boy with a loud and scary-looking motorcycle, pursuing their 14-year-old daughter. I *did* participate in high school drama class one or two semesters, but it seemed really boring most of the time.

And you'd describe your family back then as middle-class, you said.
My dad always did the best he could to be a good provider. My mother and I never went hungry, but living was "tight" at times. I remember having to buy used clothing at thrift shops before it was trendy to do so [*laughs*].

Your dad grew up on a South Dakota cattle ranch.
That's right, and he was a true, real cowboy. He came out to Hollywood not too many years after Yakima Canutt, the famous Sioux Indian stuntman. Canutt rose to fame doing spectacular stunts—he did stirrup drags, where you'd fall out of the saddle and get dragged by the horse, and he would do the old stagecoach scenes where it would be a six up or an eight up and the horses were running flat-out and Canutt would be down with the horses jumping forward, one pair of horses at a time. Well, my dad did some of those things, too—he was *that* good of a horseman and he hung out with people like Yakima Canutt and such. My dad did a lot of that

Eleven-year-old Arch Hall, Jr., with his dad in a 1955 at-home shot. In 1959, Junior would star in the first of Senior's movies, *The Choppers*; a few years later, part of their second film *Eegah* would be shot in that very house in Palm Desert—74-165 *Fairway* Drive.

trick riding stuff where he would ride flat-out and then he'd jump from one side of the saddle to the other, he could do *all* that. He wasn't always overweight and a middle-aged guy [*laughs*]!

My dad landed acting gigs in many early Westerns starring John Wayne, "Crash" Corrigan and Gene Autry, starting back in the '30s. Being that he was the "real deal," a real cowboy, he naturally could ride and shoot better than most of the so-called cowboy stars. Sadly, he never managed to land a starring role in those days. I remember him telling me that one time he felt he was on the threshold of breaking through in his acting career when his father fell ill and called him home to help run the family cattle ranch in Philip, South Dakota. Physique-wise, my dad was a hell of a guy in the early days. He had a 29-inch waist and he was 6'2", with big wide shoulders. He could have been a handsome leading man-cowboy star-whatever. I think he felt most comfortable as a cowboy [actor] in those days, but he could have gone into other things as well.

He stopped acting in Westerns right around the time you were born. What jobs do you remember your dad holding as you grew up?

After the war, my dad worked in radio in the L.A. area. Next he had a few years of modest success building houses in the San Fernando Valley. He called his company Cozy Homes with an office and model home on Laurel Canyon. Several partners were brought in, most of them taking advantage of Dad's dislike of business details and screwing him royally! Then just prior to the making of *The Choppers*, on the advice of a singing cowboy-friend named Kelly Walker, he became the owner of a small trucking business, aptly named Hall and Company—a sort of play on words [haulin' company]. My dad knew zip about the trucking business and it nearly wiped us out in more ways than one. One time he was driving, himself, a heavily loaded dump truck down the steep grade on Barham Boulevard. He was coming down the hill, just before you get to Warner Bros., when the air brakes failed! He whizzed through the red stoplight at the bottom of the hill at over 100 miles per hour, with 14 tons of hot asphalt, barely missing cars!

The South Dakota Badlands, circa 1919: Arch Hall, Sr., his sister Caroline (later the mother of *The Sadist*'s Helen Hovey) and his older brother Joseph as kids.

What gave Senior the idea to produce his first movie, The Choppers, *in 1959?*

I can really only guess at this, and my guess would be that at 50 years of age, he was beginning to feel that life was passing him by. He realized that he might never have an opportunity to accomplish what he really wanted to do—and

Hall Sr. as a kid with his first pony in 1917. *Bottom:* Hall Sr. as a young cowboy on the Pine Ridge Indian Reservation.

Hall Sr.'s many B-Western roles included 1939's *Overland Stage Raiders*, an entry in the Three Mesquiteers series with John Wayne.

that was act, write and produce movies. I can't be sure, but I think he was feeling a sort of a midlife crisis. He probably enjoyed being a writer and maybe an actor more than actually producing, but he realized that nothing was going to happen unless he kind of invented his own gig. That's *my* take on it, anyway. We never had a direct conversation about it, but I certainly know his appreciation and his love for the business—he did love the business. So [by making *The Choppers* and the other films] he finally returned to doing what he wanted to do. It may not have been on a grandiose scale, but he didn't have the means to do it on any other terms. What he lacked in finances and everything, he sort of made up for by finding interesting and talented people to contribute. I'm not necessarily including my*self* in that bunch [*laughs*], I'm saying others—graduates of cinematography schools and talented immigrants like Vilmos Zsigmond and Laszlo Kovacs and people like this.

Whose idea was it for you to star in The Choppers?

My dad wanted me to do it. He said, "Why *not* you? Why some stranger?" My father was very persuasive—and so I also said, "Yeah ... why *not* me?" I think he followed with something like, "That's my boy!" At the time, I was pals with Bobby Diamond, the kid star of *Fury* [a popular TV series]. I recall asking Bobby if it was hard to act and he said, "Fuck, no! It's easy." I thought it was no big deal. It was like if your dad was a plumber and he asked you to join him on a big plumbing job—does that make any sense to you?

The Choppers was shot where?
The interiors were shot inside my dad's office at 2221 West Olive Avenue in Burbank—an office at what was to become the Fairway complex. The office, if shot in one direction, was the police station with Tom Brown. From another angle, it became a "different" interior. Exteriors were shot on location at an auto salvage yard on Branford, a block or two off of San Fernando Road.

Speaking of Tom Brown, few people know that he was a highly decorated hero of World War II and the Korean War. He had just finished *Adventures of Smilin' Jack* [a 1943 serial] when he parachuted into Occupied France as a commando, helping the French Resistance. Burr Middleton [who plays Snooper in *The Choppers*] visited Tom during the last few days of Tom's life. Burr saw the tremendous display of Tom's wartime medals and decorations on a plaque beside his bed in the hospital. When asked how he was doing, Tom responded in his cocky signature high-pitched voice, "Aww, I'm okay, kid, I just got a little touch of cancer, that's all." Tom may have been small in stature, but he was a giant of a man in the courage department!

How did you enjoy the experience of starring in a movie?
For the most part, it was just what you might think it to be—a total blast! However, I made some serious mistakes. One day at the junkyard, the cameraman had this very heavy blimped Mitchell [camera] hefted up on his back and he was shouting for someone to move Bill Rolland's Model T that I drove in the movie. When nobody responded to assist him, I said, "I'll move it for you, sir," and I started it and drove it maybe 15 feet tops. Well, that did it! The Teamster boss came over, asking me the obvious: "Did I just see you move that car, kid?"

"Of course," I answered truthfully, "because none of you guys would help him." Well, the union shut down the set for a couple of hours and only agreed to return if, for the next two days, they were paid at "golden time," which is double pay or something Here my dad was going broke making this fucking movie and now I had just caused him more grief with the Teamsters Union. I felt awful! Worse yet, the Teamster guy laughed at me. I remember telling my dad, who seemed close to losing control, "I'd like to take your .45 and shoot that fat bastard that keeps smirking at me."

"The story goes" that your dad started making movies because he wanted to make you a star; you were reluctant, but did it to please him.
I think there is some basis of truth to that, but grossly oversimplified. Any reluctance I may have had was just the father-son sort of Yin and Yang thing. If he said black, I said white; if I said black, he would say green.

There might have been more than a little vicarious interest on his part to live through me—what he wanted to do years earlier in Hollywood, maybe? There was also some jealousy from me on the attention others got from him. Sure, I think my dad sincerely wanted me to be a success—be it in low-budget movies or anything *else* for that matter.

Was the role of Jack in The Choppers *the kind of role that could help make a 15 year old a star in those days?*

Becoming a teen star by portraying a glorified car thief? In 1959, I sort of doubt it, don't you?

What did you like, and not *like, about your first movie experience?*

For the most part it was great fun, driving a car that was featured in *Hot Rod* magazine and all. But remember, I was just 15 and hadn't even gotten laid yet, so let's keep this all in perspective, okay [*laughs*]?

How quickly was it made?

The Choppers was shot rather fast, a matter of weeks. This was the *only* film my dad ever made under union guidelines. It ended up going way over its projected budget, costing well over $150,000. That may seem like chump change in today's dollars but keep in mind, the follow-up movie *Eegah* came in at under $35,000. *The Choppers* was financially devastating and almost broke him.

Did you get to see rushes—if they even had *rushes on* The Choppers*?*

Yeah, we saw rushes once or twice. I *think* the first screening to the general public was at a theater on Magnolia in Burbank. I always can defer to Burr Middleton. Burr is the grandson of Charles Middleton, who played Emperor Ming in the old Buster Crabbe *Flash Gordon* serials. Burr is blessed with a fantastic memory and can recall every detail of *The Choppers*. During the Clinton years, Burr gained attention on *The Tonight Show* as a dead ringer for Kenneth Starr! He's made a living for years acting and doing voiceovers, both here and in Japan.

The Choppers *was made in 1959 but I'm told that Senior couldn't get it released at all until after* Eegah *was finished two years later and double-billed with it.*

My dad was of course involved in other endeavors, and after he took this first shot at making a film, he just had to "retreat" and get his bearings to figure out what his next move was going to be, based on what he perceived as his options. Also, he did meet a lot of resistance when he tried to peddle *one* film *a cappella*, so to speak. It was an on-the-job training thing for him, and he was learning not only how corrupt and crooked the whole independent distribution business was, but how really no one would share any information. My dad had to blaze his own trail. And it wasn't a very pleasant trail. In 1961, after he had finally made another movie [*Eegah*] and could provide a full double-bill, *then* he had more power and leverage. It took him a couple of years to figure out how to deal with the people in the world of thieves and charlatans of independent film distribution.

He had no *offers for* The Choppers*?*

I think there were some offers, but some of them were so pitiful that he couldn't

Hall Jr. film-debuted as the leader of a gang of teenage car strippers in *The Choppers*, shot in 1959.

believe that that was what the industry was offering up. Later on, he realized that in fact, that *was* how the industry was. I think the initial shock of learning that he was up against a den of thieves was very disheartening. My dad was *not* a particularly strong businessman. He was of the mindset that people are just basically good at heart. *Wrong*!

The bills kept rolling in and the bank notes came due and it seemed *The Choppers* had become a sort of "vanity" production. I think he quickly lost his faith in the myth that independent distributors had good character. Later on, it only got worse! After *Eegah*, he had possibly more leverage, but was also deeper in debt and had finally reached the point where he was *ready* to try to deal with the independent distributors. He tried to get ideas from everybody. At the time, I was sort of dating Susan Sherman, the beautiful young daughter of famed Hollywood director George Sherman. On one occasion, my dad asked George if he had any ideas. I think this was out of desperation as Sherman didn't have any background with the distribution end of the business.

The Choppers *is a "Rushmore Production"—your dad had a lot of fondness for his South Dakota roots, I sense!*

It goes far deeper than you could possibly imagine, his love and passion for

South Dakota and the Badlands and Mount Rushmore and all these things. His early days were heavily influenced by Native American beliefs, beliefs in nature and in the importance of personal character in all that one sets out to accomplish in one's lifetime. He learned to speak Sioux on the reservation and was accepted by the Oglala Sioux in an unprecedented manner. Watogola Oakshilla—"Wild Boy"—was his adopted Sioux name. At one point he was working at radio station KOTA in Rapid City and caught national attention with his live interviews of aging Oglala Sioux leaders, including an old man who was a scout for Sitting Bull and Crazy Horse at Little Big Horn.

Did you see much of South Dakota as a kid?
 Only on summer visits—a couple of visits when I was like 10 and 11 years old. We went to the family ranch down near Wall, South Dakota, where the famous Wall Drug Store is. It was a little town called Owanka—it's probably not even on the map. The Hall Ranch was there. I was too young to have a driver's license but my uncle let me use an old World War II military Jeep that was now a ranch vehicle. Ten years old and driving that Jeep was way cool for a kid! Remember, this was near Ellsworth Air Force Base. Ellsworth was a Strategic Air Command bomber base. On weekends the aircrews would go out in their B-36s but, rather than fire their 50 caliber machine guns during these flights like they were *supposed* to do, they'd just throw the unfired ammunition out of the planes because they didn't want to clean the guns when they got back, they wanted to go into Rapid City to party. The guns were clean when they left and they were clean when they came back! Well, I would drive this Jeep around the Badlands and *find* these belts of ammo and I'd load 'em in the Jeep—I ended up with hundreds of rounds of 50 caliber ammunition. I would "de-link" the 50 cal rounds and place them each individually in a tree with the primer facing me, then go back about 25 yards and shoot the primer with a Sears, Roebuck .22 auto-loader rifle. When the rounds went off, they sometimes blew the tree apart! So, yeah, I did all *kinds* of crazy stuff! Being able to drive a tractor, and a Jeep—it was just great fun being around the ranch. But I also saw how much hard work it was, too. I learned where the Hall Ranch *first* started, which was not where it was at *that* time. My dad and his father and mother lived in a dugout, an area dug out of the side of a mountain, with just a lean-to kind of piece of tin over it. It was one of the most primitive places to live you could imagine.

Getting back to something we started talking about a minute ago: "The books" say that your dad produced these movies for the purpose of making you a star, but you're saying that the truth is that he was going to make these movies with or without you.
 That's absolutely true. He was bound and determined to make a movie, and I think he felt that I was definitely gonna get the first shot at the lead. But I know that if I would have refused to do it, somebody *else* would have done it.

If you had said no to The Choppers, The Choppers *would have got made, and a couple of years later* Eegah *would have got made, and everything would have happened just the way it did—except you wouldn't have been in 'em.*

That's probably a true statement. He probably would have been very disappointed in me. But, nevertheless, *he* was gonna be in the movie business, and that was that. You see, he truly *loved* the business … even though it wasn't so good to him. Once he began producing low-budget movies, his revelation was how crooked the business was on the distribution level. It was just so difficult. There was really no way to follow up on anything [make sure he was getting a fair shake], 'cause nobody had the money to go around to all these cities and find out what was really going on at all these theaters and drive-ins where their movies were playing. I would say that these movies actually played maybe five times as much as they did according to the [cooked books].

And on top of the distributors cheating people like your dad, moviemaking is just simply a damn expensive business to be in.

Of course. The lab made the 35mm prints, they'd make a whole run of prints, and they were very expensive, even black-and-white prints. People told my dad that they'd play his movies but they wanted to open in 30 drive-ins and walk-in theaters in a city and so they needed at least 30 prints. Or 50 prints. Or 75 prints. My dad would ask, "Well, can't you just take *ten* prints, and then rotate 'em?," and the answer would be no.

Even though still a teen, Hall Jr. knew that singing and playing the teenage hero in *Eegah* were not exactly star-making opportunities.

Then [after a movie was in release] you had to pay off the lab for those prints before *you* made any money. So the little money that came in from distributors went to the lab and it went to the bank for loans, until *that* was paid off, and *then* the movie generated a little bit of money for you ... *possibly*. It was *not* a good business business-wise, and it was embarrassing for my dad to say that. But he was not the greatest businessman. He enjoyed the creative aspect of the business more, and that's where I think he shined. In the businessman part ... mmmm ... not so good [*laughs*]! I'm not so good, either, at that part. That's why I've kinda been an employee all my working career.

Did you get paid to be in these movies, like a regular actor would?
Yeah, I think I got a little bit now and then. But it was nothing that was like an agreed salary or a contract or anything like that. I was just expected to do it because it was, basically, a family effort. Some of the things I got out of it were some pretty neat toys or "perks," like I got a Harley-Davidson motorcycle out of *The Nasty Rabbit* [1964].

Any idea where the idea for Eegah *came from?*
It came from my dad. He had ideas for a lot of strange and bizarre stories; in fact, before he offered *Eegah* to Richard Kiel, my dad told him about this idea he had for a movie called *Striganza*, which was pretty far-out. In fact, I think it was a little bit distasteful to Richard, even though he was without a gig at the time! So, yeah, my dad came up with all sorts of crazy, off-the-wall things. Even back in his radio show days, some of those shows used to have a lot of comedy and almost a Spike Jones kind of a mentality, and they would swing from one direction to another.

And your feelings about starring in a second picture, Eegah, *now that you had an idea what it entailed?*
You know, again, it was sort of like growing up in a family where your dad's a plumber, and you learn from time to time how to do plumbing and related skills. I never really gave much thought to it. I don't want to give a non-answer but that's honestly the truth.

Richard Kiel—your first impressions of him?
Well, my first impressions are probably like most people's first impressions: I was a little leery of him, as he was a physically intimidating fellow with his tremendous size and all. Of course, he was very young at the time, but he still was as big as he is today. And a little frightening. But Richard Kiel is a smart guy with a tremendous interest in history and things. When it behooves him, he doesn't speak much ... and when somebody that big doesn't speak, it can be even *more* intimidating. He may or may not have divulged this to you, but I remember that at one time he used to be the sales manager at Star Lincoln Mercury, an automobile dealership in Glendale. He was the person that the salesman brought the prospective buyers to, to close the deal and to ring up everything and to make sure the contract was correct. When

Eegad! Hall Jr. goes toe to mega-toe with king-sized caveman Richard Kiel in the low-budget favorite *Eegah*.

people came in and he stood and shook their hands, lemme tell ya, they were more than a little intimidated about buying the car! At that point, they didn't want to do *any*thing but sign the paperwork and get out of there *alive* [*laughs*]! And I think Richard "played" that a little bit, once in a while! But he's a very kind person and a very gentle person. I have the highest admiration for Richard, I was so happy to see his successes through the Bond films and other films—I see every film that he does. I'm on very good terms with him and I admire his intellect and his spirit.

Marilyn Manning was the leading lady of Eegah. *Where did she come from, and what did you think of her?*
    She was a secretary in the office of a chiropractor who was a tenant of my dad's in the greater Fairway complex. In *The Sadist*, Marilyn did quite a good job. There wasn't much to playing a deaf-mute-type character in that, but I thought she did a good job. In *Eegah* ... I dunno. I think it was reeeally bad casting, because here you have a kid, *me*, who is a very young-looking 17 years old, and his girlfriend who, with a lot of heavy makeup on, looks like she's 35 [*laughs*]. *That* didn't make any sense to me, or I think to anyone *else* at the time! But you just press on, go straight ahead, read your lines, hit your marks and don't make any complaints, I guess.

Was there too much of an age difference for you and Marilyn Manning to have much in common?

No, she was very friendly. We tried to do the best we could with *Eegah*. But there was not a lot of preparation, not a lot of rehearsal time or takes. If something wasn't exactly right, unless it was *grossly* wrong with something in the background wrong or lighting changes or something like that, it was pretty much gonna be a take!

Shooting Eegah *out in the desert—what were you putting up with out there? Spiders, snakes, scorpions?*

Basically, all of the above [*laughs*]! We were shooting in the California Low Desert in summertime 1961, and there were sidewinder rattlesnakes, which are little pygmy rattlesnakes—there were nests of them at the bases of greasewood bushes all over the place. Scorpions built their nests there too. There were spiders and red ants, vinegarroons, chuckwallas, all sorts of things that make people very uncomfortable when they crawl across ya [*laughs*]. I had lived in the desert and of course I was used to most all those things and it was not a big deal to me. But I think Marilyn Manning was terrified of creepy things like that.

What precautions were taken?

None. There was no time or budget for anything. None of us actually were bit by anything other than I was bit by a scorpion just before the shooting started. I had kind of a sore hand, but that was about the extent of it. I don't think I made any comment to anyone about that—my mother knew, and I *think* my dad knew. I also recall the scene shot day-for-night in the desert, where Marilyn and I are supposedly sleeping on the ground near the dune buggy. Well, the area chosen was on top of a nest of scorpions, with many pissed-off scorpions trying to sting us!

Was that your *dune buggy you were driving in* Eegah*?*

Yes. It started out as a 1939 Plymouth sedan! At one point the poor gas welds on the shortened frame broke, collapsing the windshield into the seat and trapping me, Marilyn and my dad in there. After we were extricated, I welded plates alongside the frame to reinforce it somewhat, but it still didn't hold well and broke again later on.

Even at that age, you knew how to do that kind of stuff?

I mostly liked working on motorcycles. I had an old 45 c.i. Harley and my prize, a 1947 80 Indian Chief, which my friend Al Scott and I bought from an elderly Mexican widow in Indio for $5. Can you believe that? Al is one of my best friends, a lifelong friend. He played my brother in *Wild Guitar* [1962].

Richard Kiel told me that you were working out in the desert when you got word that the raw film stock you were using was no good!

That was pretty scary. "Short ends" are short rolls of unused raw film stock, supposedly still good. We would come by those and use them. For the most part, they were actually pretty reliable—except there were no guarantees, you bought 'em "as is." And of course, as Richard explained, there was the disaster which occurred in the midst of the desert, where we got the message from the lab that the film we had been using was bad. I don't recall how many days we'd filmed using bad short ends, but I think it was two or three. They tried a variety of different processes to correct it, to somehow salvage it, and I'm not sure how much was salvaged and how much had to be re-shot. It was time and money wasted.

And still the movie ended up costing under $35,000.
  I believe that is correct.

Why in the movie do you sing songs to your girlfriend Marilyn Manning titled "Vicki" and "Valerie," when her *character name is Roxy?*
  [*Laughs*] That doesn't make a lot of sense, does it?

Even as a kid, I thought to myself, "Poor Roxy has *to be wondering who Vicki and Valerie are!"*
  Yeah, probably a normal person would. But not in a Fairway International movie [*laughs*]! My dad wrote those two songs—I think he'd had an idea for *another* movie that never came to fruition, and *that* was the movie those songs were really written for. Those were his babies, he liked those two songs. His desks, at the office *and* at home, were covered not only with yellow pads filled with free-streaming ideas, but also completed and half-completed screenplays and story ideas and novels and songs and poetry and abstract things that he would come up with. He would just reach around and get things and work on 'em and then put 'em aside and go to another idea. He was the only one who really knew what was going on, or what was coming up next, or what he was *thinking* about would be the next production project.

The big head of hair we see on you in all these movies—was that a popular style, or—
  I think it's basically called a poor haircut. Or lack *of* haircut [*laughs*]!

Were any of the crew members also in Eegah?
  The drunk who came out of the motel by the swimming pool and fainted when he saw Eegah was Bob Davis, one of the sound men. The lady with him happens to be my mother, and the little dog running around happens to be my dog Chipper, a little Hungarian Puli. Don Schneider, the associate producer and editor on *Eegah*, plays the old man in the restaurant who's small-talking with my dad and makes a comment about me and Marilyn Manning dancing.
  One of the members of my band in *Eegah*, the one I get into the scuffle with, was my very close friend Deke Lussier. I think I first met him in junior high school—his father was a screenwriter for years [Dane Lussier's film credits include the *Donovan's Brain* adaptation *The Lady and the Monster*, 1944]. Deke and I were both self-taught guitar players; we used to set up a couple of amps and play guitar at parties in the Palm Springs–Palm Desert area. I looked too damn young to buy booze,

but Deke had this rugged, sort of acne-scarred face along with a resonant, deep voice. This, combined with his uncanny skill learned in Drafting Class at making fake California driver's licenses, scored us beer and whiskey when we were only about 14 years old. This made us both extremely popular among the teenagers of the Low Desert!

Deke always had an amazing talent for composing songs, coming up with killer lyrics ... maybe he got it from his dad. Deke later changed his name to Deke Richards and became one of the top songwriters and record producers for Berry Gordy, Jr., of Motown Records. He produced and wrote for both the Jackson Five and Diana Ross, to name just a few. Deke is now retired from the active music business as far as I know—he got fed up with the L.A. and Detroit scene. He now lives on a tranquil lake up in the Seattle area.

Did you have a band in real life during these movie days?

Yeah, sure did—The Archers. It changed from time to time but the band that really was the most impressive had as its nucleus Alan O'Day doing keyboards, vocals, harmonica; myself on guitar and vocals; one of our high school dear friends Ernesto Gurrola, a fantastic drummer; and Joel Christie, a bass player and vocalist. A strong, incredible vocalist. He not only had his own [singing voice] but he could mimic almost like a John Byner. He could sing a Johnny Mathis song and sound just like Johnny Mathis, or some of the great blues singers like Bobby "Blue" Bland, or James Brown with all the yelping. Unbelievable talent. Dobie Gray was in my band as well. Dobie got out of the pop music thing and got into country music and he did very well. He still tours and records.

Two unbelievably trivial questions, even for me. One, at the beginning of your fight scene with Richard Kiel, was that a real rock you threw at him? It looks like you got *him.*

Of course it was a real rock! We couldn't afford a fake Hollywood rock [*laughs*]! Ask Richard if I got him or not.

And, two, how come we see scenes of Hall, Sr., and his daughter Marilyn Manning at home ... but when Eegah later invades the house, breaking down a door in the living room takes him right into the rest room corridor of some restaurant?

No one's ever asked that before! I think modern film buffs are more observant and less tolerant of irregularities these days. What can I say? It's a poor cut! But keep in mind it might have been the best they could do [editing-wise] with what they had to work with.

Anything else you can recall about the making of Eegah*?*

The worst, most punishing thing of all was working on a sound stage that was rented for the cave interior scenes. I believe it was off of Argyle in Hollywood. There were all sorts of problems. A man came in to help dress the set, and some carpenters tried to make it look like a cave, and the more they worked on it, the worse it got. They put up some canvas that was painted to resemble the inside of a cave, but it just didn't look right and everybody shook their heads. Finally the set dressers camouflaged a lot of it by getting some huge bags of graphite, which is like pencil lead, and throwing graphite all over the place. We were walking in that black stuff and it was in our eyes, it was on our skin, it was in our hair, it was just everywhere. A god-awful mess. At one point the cops and, I think, the fire marshal showed up and said there wasn't any permit, and requested that everyone vacate the premises—we were rousted from the sound stage. We left for like three or four hours and the cops went away and then we re-congregated and kept on shooting. We had rented the sound stage for (I think) two days, and so much of that time was spent building the set in there—it was wasted. So, after the set was built, we had to just shoot right to the very last moment. It was pretty miserable. I couldn't keep my eyes open. I remember being so tired that when I was riding a motorcycle home to the Valley, even with the wind in my face, I was falling asleep. I'd been up for about 44 hours—I think that was the total by the time I tried to lie down and go to sleep.

Was your dad up for that amount of time also?
Every bit of it. And everybody was getting cranky—it had an effect on *every*body's temperament, as you might imagine, because of the sleep deprivation and the lack of food. A lot of people were allergic to all the graphite that was being thrown around everywhere. If anybody had any propensity for orneriness, including my*self*, it came out—I was just sick and tired of the whole thing, and I began to fall asleep while holding a handheld mike boom! It was even worse for Richard Kiel, Marilyn Manning and my dad, who were in every scene. It just went on and on and *on* and on and on. We really should have called it a day and come back another time, but that couldn't be done because we didn't have the money. And once we ruined the whole building with that graphite, I don't think anybody would have permitted us to come back even if we'd *had* the money [*laughs*]! Everybody knew that, so we had to make our stand and finish the cave sequence.

Your dad was the voice of Eegah.
That's right. There was some dubbing-to-screen-playback done down in Hollywood at a recording studio but it became way too expensive, so that was abandoned and we reverted back to a homemade system at Fairway. Alan O'Day and I did the recording with our trusty Wollensaks. We used a Movieola in one of the editing rooms, turned around backwards so it could be viewed from outside the office through the glass window, thus reducing the noise of the Movieola. This was always done late at night, of course, to minimize traffic sounds, and we placed the mike as close as possible. My dad called upon his old radio announcer's voice, washed through a Fender reverb tank, and brought Eegah's voice to life. He focused seriously on Richard Kiel's mouth and movements on the screen preparing to dub the voice, sometimes even throwing in some words in Sioux that somehow, as crazy as it sounded, seemed to fit the scene. There were times it would crack Alan and me up so much, we couldn't contain our laughter and we would blow his take. He might give us the evil eye at first, then laugh himself. It was so utterly ridiculous, he couldn't seriously get pissed off. Once, after an all-night session, Alan sped up the tape rather

Composing cue music for *Eegah* at Fairway's studios are Hall Jr. and pal Alan O'Day.

than slowing it down, to make Eegah sound like the singing Chipmunks. We were simply so tired we became silly.

When Eegah *went into release, double-billed with* The Choppers, *you toured with it.*
 That was my dad, Richard Kiel and myself. We went to Ohio, to West Virginia, to Kentucky—my dad did most of the driving. (The car was his white 1959 Caddy Coupe de Ville—a true classic!) We drove all over, primarily the big cities that had the multi-drive-ins. The tour was based around going to the various cities where the pictures would be playing and going cold turkey into radio stations and television stations and announcing who we were. This created sort of a major ruckus in the offices, of course, with a seven-foot-two giant in a caveman costume carrying a big club! With my dad sort of running interference, we found ourselves in a matter of minutes either on our way *out* to the parking lot, ushered by security, or immediately ushered *onto* a live set, where we were interviewed, whether it was a television morning show or a radio program in progress or what*ever*. For the most part, it was very successful. It was a little nerve-wracking, but it was impressive to see how, if you had the chutzpah to just walk in raw and present yourself, for the most part people will accept you and say, "Come on in, let's talk. We don't know who you are or why you're here, but we're gonna find out!" [*Laughs*] I couldn't believe how bold my dad was, sending us into situations "cold," with no prior coordination. But 99 percent of the time, it worked, and both Richard and I gained great personal confidence and also respect for my dad, who *made* it work.

How did you enjoy performing at drive-ins? Was that your first time doing that sort of thing?

Yeah, and it was sort of miserable, because you get pressed into a corner—you have no real band, you have nothing, you're standing up there in some cases just with a guitar and an amp and it's freezing cold or you're sweating in the heat. And of course the sound is not gonna be right, and you're talking through a loudspeaker or whatever. But, y'know ... we just *did* it, and we didn't cry in our beer over it afterwards. It was a little crazy, but people were impressed that somebody they saw on the big screen suddenly was on top of the snack bar—"What the heck is going on *here*?" They'd crowd around by the hundreds and listen attentively, and it was sort of a captive audience. It was fun ... but it's more fun looking back on it than it was *doing* it.

It was primarily drive-ins, where I'd stand on the roof of the snack bar or on the back of a flat bed truck trailer. But we did old theaters [hardtops] in downtown areas as well. Sometimes there would be an emcee, who might be a local radio personality or might be the theater manager. And in some cases it might be my dad. There would be a contrived entrance for Richard Kiel, who'd come down the aisle unannounced, carrying the big club and wearing the caveman costume.

And the beard?

The beard was not a good-enough beard to wear, so he went without the beard. And that made him more of a handsome caveman rather than kind of a grungy...

Homeless caveman!

[*Laughs*] Yeah, right! Of course the crowd would turn around and they'd just *scream*, because he was so impressive. It was a campy thing and he had fun with it. If there was anybody who was like a bully or a smart-aleck teenager or something, Richard would walk right up to the guy and put his hand on the guy's shoulder, and of course that was the end of that [*laughs*]. Once he laid that big paw on you, you knew who was in control of the situation! He did it in a fun way, but at the same time it quelled any sort of problems. He also did that later when he worked as a bouncer in the San Fernando Valley, in some country-Western bars which were pretty rough places.

It was a little bit corny but people enjoyed it and it seemed to work just about every time. At a drive-in, on top of a snack bar, it was a little more dangerous, trying to climb up on the roof and then standin' there, in a light rain, trying to play an electric guitar when probably you're gonna get shocked from an electrical short or something. But, you know, people had respect for that, and they'd give us a round of applause and they were real appreciative of it. They knew this wasn't *Gone with the Wind*, but they enjoyed the fact that somebody was following up and taking the trouble to come out to their home town and make a personal appearance. In most cases, it was a lot of fun and the people were really nice. In very few cases, there would be drunks or something like that, but that's the same as you're gonna run into *any*where. It was always different, nothing was exactly the same twice. We just walked in and tried to do the best with each situation, with what we had, the weather, the lighting, the lack of a decent p.a. system ... we just sort of made it work. It was an education.

Your dad worked behind the scenes on Eegah *using the pseudonym "Nicholas Merriwether" and then acted in it using the name "William Watters"—what's up with that?*

Yeah, my dad used a whole collection of names, including Nicholas Merriwether, the one I've adopted to write under. He used Nicholas Merriwether, he used William Watters, he used a *lot* of different names. He didn't want the credits of all these movies to say Arch Hall, Arch Hall, Arch Hall, because then people know you're the next thing to a one-man band, doing just about everything yourself. He wanted to make it look like there was more to the production company than one or two guys stayin' up late at night [*laughs*]!

Incidentally, my dad researched our family origin during several trips to England—that was later on, during the early '70s. He brought back the Hall, Watters and Rolfe family coats of arms, which I have on the wall in my office today. Interestingly, the Watters coat of arms has a human hand at the top. The story goes that, when coming ashore in the West Indies, it was by royal decree that the land would belong to the man who first "laid a hand" on the soil. William Watters' launch was losing to another boat and was floundering in the surf. When it appeared certain that another boat would beach first, not the boat Watters was in, Watters severed his own hand with a sword and then told the strongest man in his boat to hurl his hand up onto the beach. Thus Watters was the first man to "lay his hand" on the soil of the new land.

The Fairway offices were on West Olive in Burbank, you said.

Yes, and my dad owned the property. It was a long U-shaped two-story building with many small offices. Only about two of 'em had running water or a bathroom in 'em. (There was a men's room and a ladies room down below.) Most of the offices were maybe 16 to 20 feet square, with one entrance, and a wall air conditioner. They were all rented pretty much all the time. Very low rents, maybe $35–65 a month. To this day it still is a nest of film production subcontractors. I found out just the other day that rents currently start at $650.

It's no longer in the family, I'm sure.

No longer in the family.

You've mentioned a couple times that money was often tight—but, watching these movies, I always had the idea your family was well-off. The family coat of arms used as the Fairway logo—

Well, you don't have to be rich to have a family coat of arms [*laughs*]!

I guess not. But the idea of a guy, your dad, making movies for his own son to star in, shooting in places like Palm Springs, and just the way your dad carries himself in these pictures—I got the idea he was quite the fat cat!

Well, at one time he was I think rich on paper with property. Post–World War II he purchased quite a lot of property and he had a lot of rental property, which was in fact the entire property that became Fairway in Burbank. Also, on Ventura Boulevard in Studio City, he owned a long stretch of buildings and vacant lots and things, which are now of course totally built-up. He owned several houses and commercial buildings around. Primarily it was just property that he had bought in earlier times, in the '30s. Of course, over the years, property in the San Fernando Valley appreciated dramatically. He had borrowing power, based on all this, to… [*Pause*] To basically put himself into hock, by producing these movies.

Starting around the time of Eegah, *and for a couple years afterwards, Senior kept announcing that movie you mentioned a while back, a horror-type picture called* Striganza.

Striganza was a dark kind of a thing, and pretty gruesome too, having to do with cannibalism and all that sort of stuff.

Would you have been in it?

I have no idea. But I'm sure, if Fairway did it, there would have been *some*thing for me to do! Keep in mind, too, that on these pictures I sometimes ran the sound recording equipment, I ran the booms, I learned how to load the Arriflex camera magazines, etc., etc. Everybody did a little bit of everything.

As we discussed earlier, if you'd refused to star in these movies, somebody else *would have starred and they all would have been made without you. But it crosses my mind that the one picture that* might *not have been made without you is* Wild Guitar.

Yeah, that's true. My participation and the participation of my friends in the music business was so integral with that. It would have been tough to find anybody else who'd put into it that much elbow grease. We worked from morning 'til late at night and got up in the morning and started right back in again. We used a mix of all sorts of old, very substandard recording equipment and microphones, Sears, Roebuck Wollensak recorders recording tape-on-tape—crazy stuff that doesn't seem to make any sense. But we learned that when everything is reduced down to an optical track, the fidelity is not very good *anyway*. If you can filter a lot of the noise and things out, fine, and if you *can't*, it sort of adds character to it [*laughs*]! It's one of those crazy things where somebody nowadays would say, "You can't do that. Forget it." Well, I'm here to tell you that it worked. My colleague Alan O'Day and I spent many a night up there at Fairway with Wollensaks, cleaning the heads, because they'd get all loaded up with iron oxide, realigning 'em, reducing the speed to make voices lower and so on.

Wild Guitar was an interesting project and a lot of fun. Many of the *Eegah* people worked on that, including Ray Dennis Steckler [who plays a bit part in *Eegah*]. Ray directed *Wild Guitar* and he played Steak, the notorious "enforcer" who works for Mike, the villainous record producer [played by Hall, Sr.], and Ray brought in some of his friends to play those mock Three Stooges characters. It was a big project and it was a lot of fun. It was all done right there at Fairway.

The interiors too?

For the most part, yeah. The diner scenes were shot in a diner over in the neighborhood of Magnolia Boulevard in Burbank, a real diner with the old red patent leather revolving stools and the malt machines and all that. That was the real deal.

I thought Wild Guitar *was a good vehicle for you. If you enjoyed making any of your movies, I bet that would have been the one.*
   Yeah, it was fun—it was *great* fun. In retrospect, we could have done a lot better on this, that and the other thing, but in general terms, it was fun. The story had elements of silliness and it had elements of drama. It was interesting. Whether or not it plays well *today* is another thing, but when it played throughout the country in the mid-'60s, it was well-received. People hissed at the villain and threw things and cheered and laughed. It definitely had its audience.

Did any of your songs play on the radio or come out as records during your heyday?
   Only in connection with promoting of the movies, I believe.

Who if anybody did you emulate singing voice-wise?
   I don't have much of a voice as far as range or style or anything. I would love to be a blues singer. I'm not. I just don't have it. In those days, I sort of emulated, like, Rick Nelson ... white boy, rockabilly-type music. I can handle *that*, but anything that's more complicated than that is beyond my capability!

Was the plot of Wild Guitar *supposed to make viewers think of Elvis and Col. Parker, or were "all similarities strictly coincidental," as the fine print always says?*
   I think that was honestly coincidental.

If as a result of these movies, you could have become either a major-studio Hollywood actor or a popular singer ... which would you have chosen?
   None of the above. I would have preferred to become a writer.

Did you tour with Wild Guitar?
   Sure did. And it was even more punishing than you could imagine. It was much more punishing than the *Eegah* tour. Of course, we toured with much more musical equipment; however, *again*, our act was still crippled because we didn't have a bass player. When a band doesn't have a bass player, it leaves a sonic deficit. It was Alan O'Day,

The "Fairway family" gathers for a group shot in the company's parking lot: Hall Sr. (squatting, with hair dyed white for *Wild Guitar*) and, left to right, Rod Moss, unknown, Ray Dennis Steckler, Al Scott, Hall Jr., and Alan O'Day.

[drummer] Dave Sullivan, myself and [*Wild Guitar* leading lady] Nancy Czar, who was a trouper.

And your dad.

And my dad—at times. Sometimes we did some things on our own. Most of the time, we drove a brand new 1963 model Greenbriar. Do you remember the Chevrolet Corvair? It was one of *the* most dangerous cars ever, according to Ralph Nader. The Greenbriar was the window van version of the Corvair van. It was a great vehicle, way ahead of its time and very reliable. Rear engine design by Chevrolet. No air conditioning, of course. We drove it across the country and all the way back to California with our p.a. system and musical gear and all that stuff, we drove the hell out of it, and it never gave us a lick of trouble.

There was an incident that was rather tragic, where we came across in the middle of the night, down in Mississippi or Louisiana, a terrible accident. There were bodies and people lying all over the road. Alan O'Day recalls me being rather heroic, but I don't recall that—I remember it being rainy and that there *was* an accident and we helped people, but I don't remember the details. *He* said that I carried some people who were very badly hurt off of the highway, carrying them over to the side of the road. Nancy of course was there and did *her* part, too, to help.

Nancy Czar—she was the vocalist on the tour?

Well, and dancing too. She would do some pseudo-go-go dancing and sometimes get people from the audience up there—she'd pick on some shy farm boy, some handsome young kid, and get him up there to dance with her. We just tried to create fun but we didn't have much to work with, only our imaginations. In some cases where we played outside and it was really cold, it was hard to play guitar, and for Alan to play the keyboard—your fingers are freezing. It was not really conducive to being comfortable to play! We got sick, of course. I remember being in motels where we were all coughing because we had colds. And yet we still had a great time.

Getting a movie "in the can" was only half the battle for Hall Jr., who was then often called upon to tour with it. Along with him on his *Wild Guitar* personal appearance tour were co-star Nancy Czar and his Fender Jazzmaster guitar, given to him by the legendary Leo Fender.

What was the double-feature there? Wild Guitar *and...?*
I can't remember if it was *Eegah* or *The Sadist*. It was another Fairway film.

The Medveds and Elvira and the guys on Mystery Science Theater—*all of them, and a lot of others, have been taking potshots at your dad's movies, and at* you, *for years now. What's your reaction?*
Hey. If you can't take it, you shouldn't be in or around the business. If somebody makes a real nasty, vicious sort of a personal remark, I think it's unfortunate that they feel they have to do that to maybe get a laugh out of somebody. But ... I don't care. They can think anything they want to. They were not back there then—most of them probably weren't even *born*. By the way, I know they are experts and all, but how many low-budget movies did the Medveds make? They don't have any concept of what it was like. These movies were, in some cases, lower than low-budget, they were *no* budget. It was almost ridiculous. At one point, Warner Bros. offered my dad a position as a producer because they saw that this guy was working with *nothing* and he was coming up with *some*thing. The movies may not have been the greatest quality, but by God he was coming up with *some*thing and they were playable and they were out there in the drive-ins and so on. Somebody has to acknowledge that. These movies of my dad's were not trying to be *Gone with the Wind* or anything, they were just trying to be entertaining cannon fodder for the drive-in audiences of the '50s and '60s.

Okay, we've settled that the potshots don't faze you. How 'bout all the nice *things that have been said about your work in* The Sadist, *how do you feel about that?*
That's the only movie that I really am rather proud of.

Director Joe Dante says The Sadist *is one of the best low-budget pictures of the 1960s.*
Well ... thanks! I agree with him!

He calls it "one of the most underrated B-movies ever" and "a brilliant example of the kind of tension and intensity that can be generated—in broad daylight, no less—on a shoestring by the right combination of people."
The end product, even though it's dated, even though it was filmed with a lot of haste, *still* stands pretty darn good on its own merits. I worked real hard on it. And James Landis, the writer-director, worked with me on that real hard. In some cases, I think, he wanted something else [performance-wise] from me, but I had long talks with him. Afterwards he told my dad, "Y'know, Arch, Jr., really surprised me. He had it in him, and he actually did some things with the character that *I* didn't even think of. He took it to another level—he thought of it as a different physical character than I came up with." So, yeah, of course I like when people say I did a good job on something ... *every*body does. *The Sadist* is the one that I feel most proud of. It could have been done in color and it could have had a lot of effects that would have been more dramatic, they could have done slow-motion effects, Sam Peckinpah kind of schtick and stuff. They didn't. But it still came out a little unsettling and a little bit scary, even to this day. Where most of the time if you play some-

Arch-villainy turned out to be Hall Jr.'s forte when he played the brutish, animalistic Charlie in director James Landis' nightmarish nail-biter *The Sadist*. (Pictured: Hall Jr., Marilyn Manning.)

thing made in 1962 in black-and-white, it's awfully hard to stay awake during the thing [*laughs*]! *The Sadist* still gives people the creeps, which means the story keeps people interested. Well, it also means that there *was* a story in the first place—a lot of modern movies don't even *have* stories much any more. Maybe big stars, but no stories. *This* had a story, and it was eerie, and it scared the bejeezus out of people.

Any memory of how your dad and Landis got together to make this movie?

That's a good question. *Some*body put 'em together, probably somebody turning Landis on to my dad, who had a production company. Landis did a lot of different things, he used to write and sometimes direct TV shows—he did several episodes of *Combat!* with Vic Morrow. He was always trying to look for a gig and to *do* something.

What was he like?

An extremely talented guy. Sometimes he didn't have the temperament for some of the extracurricular tutoring that I required—I needed a lot of it compared to somebody who was an accomplished actor. But he came through for me. I liked Jim very much. I remember he worked well with [cinematographer] Vilmos Zsigmond, he and Zsigmond were very compatible. One kind of "drove" the other one. They would converse as far as how to improve something with another camera angle, or change something, and there was never any argument between the two.

What were your initial impressions when you first read the script? It was certainly unlike anything you'd ever done.
 I thought it was tremendous. I thought it was fantastic. I also knew I might really be in over my head. But it was exciting to think that I was gonna get a chance to *do* it. It made me a little bit nervous too, because I realized, "I'm gonna have to come *up* with something this time. This isn't just walking through and reading throwaway lines, this is a real character. To be believable, I'm gonna have to have some help." And I *did*, I had some help, so…

From Landis.
 Yes. *And* other people, too. Landis briefly reviewed for me the case of Charles Starkweather [a teenage thrill killer of the late '50s], to draw the parallel to his screenplay, and to help me get a grasp on how to portray the role. That helped a lot, too. Another thing that helped was, I didn't change out of the clothes. I tended to get out of the character when I got out of the clothes; and when I got back in the clothes, I wouldn't be in character for a while. Landis told me, "Don't change the clothes. You seem to take on the persona of Charlie Tibbs when you wear that Levi jacket and everything, but when you *don't* wear 'em, you start talkin' like Arch Hall, Jr. I don't *like* that." I said okay.

So, between takes, you didn't get out of the jacket.
 If I was gonna read lines to someone from off-camera or something like that, and I didn't necessarily have to be dressed in the costume, I'd take it off—and for some reason it didn't work any more [*laughs*]. Call it a lack of experience, or whatever, but I had to be in my outfit to do the voice and the character.

Were any other actors ever considered for that role? Or were you always it?
 To be perfectly honest, I think Landis started out with a rather low opinion of me, as far as having the capability of pulling this off. He wanted some young fellow who was kind of a New York Method actor—certainly older than me, and I'm sure much more experienced. Landis wanted him to come and read for the part. So I know that there was at least that one guy, and maybe others, that Landis had in mind. But he was gonna give me a shot at it, of course, and obviously my dad wanted him to give me a shot. Landis did realize, however, that it wasn't a very even playing field. If I was just given the lines to read without any sort of preparation, without him helping me devise the character, then probably I wouldn't stand a chance against somebody who was a serious actor. So he worked with me, and the *more* he worked with me, the more he sorta liked how I was comin' up with things. Sometimes I would kind of overdo it and he'd say, "Well, you gotta back out of *that* a little bit, that's a little heavy." But sometimes I would overdo things and he'd laugh to

himself and he'd say, "Y'know, you overdid it, you didn't do it the way I told you to do it, but damned if it didn't *work*. I *liked* it." So I think I created a different character than he had originally thought of. He and I both were responsible for whatever my performance was in that movie.

All this early trial-and-error stuff—this took place where?
At the Fairway offices. I was just reading lines in front of several people, Landis and my dad and maybe one or two other people—I can't remember who they were. At first Landis was trying to give me an accent or something, and *that* didn't work at all, so we changed that. And we finally developed this twisted character.

Were you acting opposite somebody there, or just reading lines?
When there was [back-and-forth] dialogue, it would be with Landis. Other times it would be just reading lines that *he* would feed me and I'd mimic—it was like monkey-see-monkey-do, "Read it like this," "You're going too fast, slow it down," "Give me several beats before you say that," "Give me a facial grimace or *some* kind of a look, and *then* come up with the line…"

Did you feel that whatever headway you had made in the "teen idol" category was now going right out the window?
Not really. This was a heckuva lot more fun, and it really *meant* something. Being a musician was very serious to me, but as far as the movies, *Eegah* and the other pictures … I really didn't have any belief that those were going to be any sort of a vehicle that would carry me anywhere. I knew it was a long shot, but I thought there was a chance that the character in *The Sadist* and the movie itself could be something for not only *me* but, more importantly, I wanted it to be something for my dad, so that finally he'd have a movie that people would take *him* seriously for. And for Jim Landis, too. Landis would remind me, he'd say, "Hey, this is my script, this is my story, this was mine from the time it went to paper, and I want it to be right." So I felt I had a lot of weight on my shoulders and that I had to pull this off. And if I *didn't* pull it off, I was gonna certainly disappoint a lot of people. The whole movie hinged around how bad this guy was—he was a hideous, sadistic person, and if that didn't come off, it was all for nothing.

Where was the junkyard where you shot most of the movie?
That was actually not a junkyard, it was a ranch that was dressed as a junkyard. It was a man's property over in the Newhall-Saugus area, north of the San Fernando Valley. A contract was signed and they brought in dozens of junk cars and dressed this area like a wrecking yard—which it certainly looked like when they finished. When they brought in all these old wrecked automobiles, the man's wife started to balk. Even though there was a signed contract, she just went ballistic. She thought their ranch was being ruined. It was a little crazy, but there was a constant daily thing where the man who owned the property had to calm her down, and then we would come in with all of our people, but then she would come around and be very upset. I felt sorry for her, but if she didn't want it to be messed up, she shouldn't

have agreed to it. Actually, I *don't* think she agreed to it, I think her husband did, and then he never told her. I believe that, afterwards, the place *was* cleaned up rather well, to her satisfaction, and it cost a lot. All the cars had to be taken out and the oil that had drained out of a lot of 'em had to be cleaned up.

What about some of the other people in the cast?

Don Russell played the older teacher *and* was also the production manager on the picture. He was great, I liked Don a lot. He was very professional, as was Richard Alden. Richard Alden was supposed to be a physical education teacher, so he would take weights and he would really pump his muscles up with 'em prior to going into a scene. It helped his shoulders and arms, he looked very buffed out and very fit— which he was. And it helped his character. Helen Hovey is my dad's sister's daughter ... that'd be my cousin. She now has several children and lives in the Washington D.C. area. She was actually a very, very talented person but, much like me, she was never involved in any movies or anything until she was thrown into *The Sadist*. I thought she came off rather well, portraying sort of a prudish schoolteacher. It was easy to play against her—and against the other actors as well, they were all good. It raised the bar a little bit for me, I had to come up to their level, as opposed to some of the other pictures where I was interacting with people who were probably as inexperienced as myself. Incidentally, Helen Hovey is the "Vicki" I sing about in *Eegah*—Vicki is actually part of her hyphenated name, she's Helen-Vicki. And Valerie [the title of another song in *Eegah*] is her sister. The lyrics of those songs were written by my dad, who liked to use family names—that was one of his "things." But of course in the application, in *Eegah*, it didn't really make any sense because I was singin' 'em to my girlfriend Roxy [*laughs*]! But, you know what?, it was like the Emperor's New Clothes: Who was gonna *tell* him that?

What is it like doing menacing scenes with your own cousin?

That was really difficult. I felt very uncomfortable about it. Landis sensed this, he sensed me sorta dropping out of character and being a little hesitant to be aggressive and mean-spirited physically around her. So when it came time to do the scene where I molest her, he said, "We won't rehearse it, we'll just *do* it. I'll tell you what I want you to do, and I want you to do it with force and with conviction. Don't hold back. Don't pull any punches." He said that right in front of her, and then he asked her, "Do you realize that that's the only way it's going to be believable?" She said she understood. I felt very uncomfortable doing something rough like that with a lady, especially my own relative, but Landis was good—he sensed [problems] before they happened. He could feel how you felt and he would step in and say, "When you do the scene, *don't* hold back," or what*ever*.

In general, were there a lot of takes?

No, there weren't. Some of the more difficult scenes, yeah, we did shoot a few takes of those, but nothing that was ridiculous. If it wasn't happening, we would usually have to go into remedial training [*laughs*], and then come back and hit it again.

Sadis-isn't so!: Hall family member Helen Hovey is threatened by Marilyn Manning (*top*), then by her own cousin, Arch Jr., in *The Sadist*.

What kind of accent is that you're affecting?

Y'know ... I don't really know! It was just kind of an affectation of that character, it went with the face and the costume and the dirty blonde hair and everything. It sort of came, it developed, with help from Landis and from ... *every*body. When I'd try something, I'd get, "Yes, that works" or "No, that doesn't work." "Do that more," "Do that less," "More of this," "Less of that." I zeroed in on the voice and the mannerisms and the face and everything by trial and error.

Were the scenes of you shaking up the Coke bottles meant to be as sexually suggestive as they came out?

Actually, no. Shaking the Coke bottle was not meant to be a sexual thing, just one more aberrant thing for Charlie to do, a disgusting habit, making the Coke fizz. The sexual meaning of that, the sexual movement ... I'm not sure that was even perceived by Landis at the time. He just wanted Charlie to have one more quirk—something that a normal person probably wouldn't do, but a sadistic halfwit *would*. I believe Landis came up with that, and of course he showed me how to do it and how to kind of twist my face a little bit and so on.

What, if any, psychopath movies had you seen at that point that might have influenced your performance?

Probably none. Of course I did see, like everybody saw, Alfred Hitchcock's *Psycho* [1960], but that didn't really have any bearing on *The Sadist*. I don't think I really had *any*thing [to draw from] at that point.

The only character I can think of who came anywhere close to Charlie was Richard Widmark in Kiss of Death *[1947].*

I saw that movie much later and appreciated his performance. But not prior to *The Sadist*.

Helen Hovey speaks with an accent in the movie—did she have that in real life?

Slightly. And I don't know, really, what kind of an accent you could call it. It's almost a British accent, but not quite. I thought it really added to the character, it added to the prudishness and the innocence of her.

Your dad produced the movie but somebody named L. Steven Snyder gets on-screen producer credit.

My dad [produced *The Sadist*] kinda *through* Snyder. Snyder was a distinguished-looking guy, wavy gray hair, and he certainly *looked* the part of a producer, but I don't think he functioned very well in that position. Snyder had nothing to do with the movie business, he was an accountant ... and as I recall, he was not very well-received. He was a nice guy—a real nice guy—who was one of the tenants in my dad's building, he had an accounting service. But he somehow, and I don't really remember the details how, but he was somehow sucked into the vortex of Fairway [*laughs*], as everybody *was* who came down the street or the alley or the boulevard, and he became the producer, officially. As far as really *doing* the job of producer, I think he did not do too much because he didn't get along with Landis very well. Snyder was a detail-oriented, anal-retentive kind of person, Landis was a real left-brain, creative person, and they mixed like water and oil. Landis could be very temperamental if he didn't get his own way...

Your dad and Landis got along okay?
For the most part, I think they got along marvelously. Both of them wished they had more of a budget to work with.

Are you really 6'1", as you're described in the police broadcast we hear in The Sadist?
No, 6'2". I'm the same height as my dad.

What makeup was involved?
My eyes are sort of deep set anyway, and the makeup lady Joan Howard darkened them with makeup products, to give the eyes maybe a more dramatic look to them. Joan's boyfriend at the time was [co-star and production manager] Don Russell And Joan's son Gregory Von Berblinger, a very young man at the time, worked as an assistant to Vilmos Zsigmond—Zsigmond took a liking to him. Zsigmond trained him on how to operate the camera, measuring focus, loading magazines. Greg was working desperately hard to learn the business, to learn Zsigmond's thought processes, how he made decisions, his style. Greg later became a cameraman on his own, a director of photography of music videos, commercials and movies.

A couple of the things that happened during the filming of *The Sadist* were rather unique. There's a scene where I'm terrorizing Helen and Don Russell—I'm waving the gun around and they're sitting on the ground up against the door of a car. We needed a bullet hole to appear in the car door window right over their heads, as if I'd shot the window to frighten 'em. They attempted to do that with a pneumatic air gun firing a piece of black wax—they hoped the wax would look like a bullet hole when it hit. They tried it four or five times but, with the critical eye of the camera, it was unacceptable. After each try, Vilmos would turn and look at Landis and just shake his head no—"This is not working. It doesn't look like a bullet hole, it looks like a piece of wax, which is what it *is*." Zsigmond was absolutely right and he was critical in stepping in and sticking to his guns and saying, "This is crap. This is not gonna cut it." The guy shooting the wax would try it different ways, different colors, different speeds of the projectile, but nothing made any difference, it simply wasn't happening. Landis even said, "Nothing *will* look like a gunshot except a gunshot."

"Well," my dad said, "I'm a pretty good shot. If you want *me* to shoot, and if the actors will agree to it, I'll fire a live round right above their heads." Everybody looked at each other like, "That's pretty crazy!" Especially the actors! My dad told 'em, "Look, if you don't feel comfortable with this, that's fine, we won't do it. But I'm an old cowboy and, I guarantee you, I will not miss." The actors agreed, so the fellow who owned the property went and got a rifle—not just *a* rifle but a high-powered rifle, a 300 Winchester Magnum, bolt action rifle. My dad took the rifle, removed the scope so as to use only the "iron sights" and he leaned up against something, probably one of the old wrecked cars. A tiny little X was put on the window precisely where they wanted the bullet to go. The "cue" to fire was Landis tapping my dad on the shoulder. Zsigmond had to put earplugs in, because this was a tremendous high-powered rifle. When those go off, there's a supersonic concussion!

Landis tapped my dad on the shoulder and he fired and a hole appeared in the center of the X! Helen and Don's reaction was of course very realistic—they were jolted, and it was captured on film. After Landis yelled "Cut!," there was applause from cast and crew. My dad carefully unloaded the weapon and handed it back to its owner, then smiled as Zsigmond was grinning from ear to ear! To think of anybody doing that on a modern-day film would be total insanity, with all the possibilities of injuries to the actors and bystanders, lawsuits and everything. This was a live round fired right above people's heads from a distance of probably 25 feet away. It's one of those crazy things that just happened. It was Fairway at its best!

In the scene where you kill Don Russell's character, how were you able to fire the gun so close to his face?

The weapon that I had as Charlie Tibbs in *The Sadist* was a Colt government model .45 automatic. In the scene where Charlie shoots the teacher in the face at point blank range, we of course used blanks, blanks that were downloaded [underpowered] so they wouldn't have so much high velocity wadding that could blind someone. Yes, it was certainly taking a chance, firing a gun that close to Don's face, so I tried to be very careful and I made sure the bore was not pointing at his eyes. I wanted to avoid injury to his eyes, at all cost!

It probably ended up on the cutting room floor, but at one time there *was* a very quick flash cut of a primitive sort of a special effect that Jim Landis went to great lengths to achieve, to add more horror to the scene. Landis was quite familiar with weapons and the kind of wounds that they would inflict. Well, shooting a man in the face at close range with a .45 very easily could make some ugly wounds! Landis said, "I want this to be as vicious and as realistic as possible," and he wanted it to look like some of Don's scalp lifted up. Don wore a wig, and then a plastic skull or an animal bone underneath the wig, all painted with theatrical blood. The wig had a monofilament fishing line connected to it. When I fired the gun, Landis wanted the wig to come up and the bone to be exposed. There was even some brain matter—I believe it was cow brains. I mean [*laughs*], it was pretty graphic! Even by *today's* standards, it would probably be permissible but it would be pushing the limit.

But unfortunately it became a time-waster, if I can put a tag on it. It simply couldn't be synchronized. I mean, it *kinda* came off, but it was not the big, "high drama" thing that I think Landis wanted it to be. I remember Zsigmond saying, "It's just not working. I know what you want, but it's not gonna happen this way." There also was concern about the censors, because back in those days, the censors were very, very strong. It *was* too graphic but Landis felt that in time, the shot would be *not* too graphic and it would help add to the horror of the situation. In the television version of the movie, it's definitely gone, but in the original theatrical version, it *may* have appeared just for a fraction of a second.

So Don Russell had on his head a piece of plastic or bone ... and then on top of that, blood and brains ... and then on top of that, a wig. And when you fired the gun, somebody else yanked the wig up.

Yes. *And,* Landis also wanted a squib to fire on top of the skull, so that blood and brains would fly out. I'm tellin' ya [*laughs*], Landis was really *into* it! We did it several times and it was *not* in sync. Don Russell was *very* courageous in letting all this be done to him!

[Laughs] You ain't kiddin'!

I don't think many actors would have allowed this! He wore a face shield—safety glasses or something—to protect him from the blast of the blank. Remember, a blank fires a lot of residue. Not only wadding comes out of it at high velocity, but burning powder as well. It can go right into your skin and continue to burn and make a powder tattoo right into your face. Even though you're not firing live ammunition, people can get hurt with blanks, as we've learned all through the years with moviemaking. That's why it's so carefully guarded now, with an armorer, and actors are not allowed to just goof around with firearms.

In the movie, it really does look like your gun is pointed right at his face when you fire it.

It was a cheated angle. You probably cannot see it, because it was acceptable to Zsigmond—he said, "It looks perfect." But I was not shooting at his face because, as I said, the wadding and the powder residue [are dangerous], even from low-powered blanks.

So you shot slightly to the right of Russell's face.

That's correct. And one time he got some residual powder, and Joan Howard had to come over and administer first aid to him. I was really sorry about it, but ... it's one of those things that happens. It was kind of a "flier," a piece of powder that came out of the muzzle and it didn't come *straight* out, it flew out at an angle. The wadding was never a problem, it was just this little piece of powder that came out— I believe it burned his cheek.

The shot of the car headlight being shot out—obviously a real bullet there, yes?

Absolutely. Fired by my dad. Then there was a scene where I fired live ammo. The .45 automatic that was Charlie's weapon, that weapon will not cycle unless you're firing a live projectile—live ammo. Which at times we did, we *did* use live ammunition. There was a scene where I was chasing Richard Alden and he went running through the broken-down shed and I was firing indiscriminately *at* him, but trailing him, knocking pieces of rotten wood out. Those were live rounds, not blanks.

*Jeez, it sounds like every*body *in this movie had a set of brass balls on 'em!*

[*Laughs*] Richard Alden would run out of the shot, and then I would run in and fire a volley of rounds into these rotten boards that he had just passed. Those were live 230-grain ball government ammunition. *Again,* something that you would never, *ever* see, something that would never be permitted today!

The characters Charlie and Judy in *The Sadist* were based on true-life killer teens Charles Starkweather and Caril Fugate and their 1957-58 murder spree. Here Charlie (Hall Jr.) prepares to bump off two unsuspecting highway patrolmen.

The shot where you're firing the gun down toward the ground, supposedly at an off-camera Richard Alden—you're firing shot after shot in the same "take" so those had to be real bullets too, no?

No, they were blanks. Remember, I had *two* guns in that scene, I had Charlie's .45 and I also had the dead highway patrol officer's weapon stuck in my waistband, a revolver. When the .45 was out of ammo, I reached for the revolver, and *that* was the gun I fired repeatedly when Alden was down. A revolver can fire blanks with no problem.

Who played the two motorcycle cops?

I believe they were off-duty California Highway Patrol. Those fellows had done some extra movie work prior, as I recall.

And who were the bodies of the man and woman in the shed?

The lady was Joan Howard. I believe she did the post-mortem makeup on herself and the guy. The man might have been the owner of the property. As I mentioned, he was a pretty good guy, but his wife thought we were all stark raving mad.

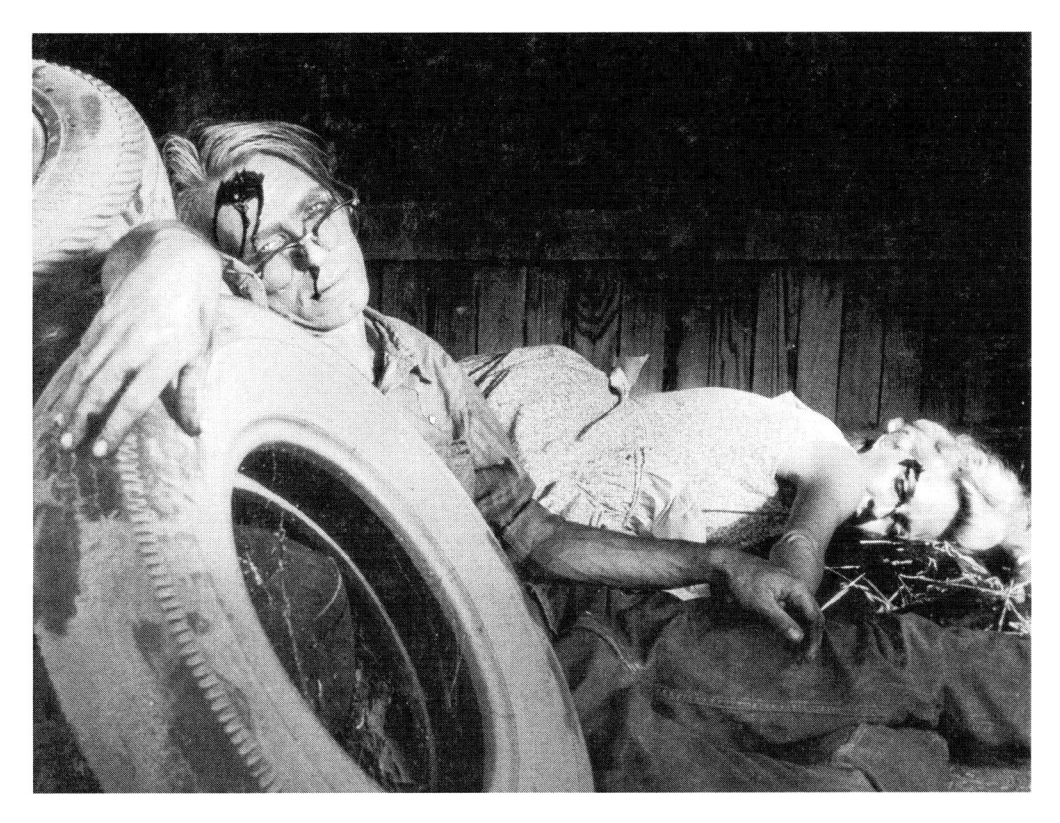

Appearing as victims of The Sadist *are makeup artist Joan Howard and the owner of the property where the movie was shot.*

The other thing in *The Sadist* which is worth mentioning is the snake pit scene at the end. I was chasing Helen and I fell through the rotten boards into the pit. What that pit *was* was an abandoned mine shaft. They put some boards over the opening and I ran and then fell through the boards into the pit, which was maybe six or seven feet deep. It was a pretty good fall—I hurt myself a couple times doing it.

Did they at least put empty boxes or something down there for you?
I think it was an old pad from a chaise lounge. But I missed that because I was goin' too fast [*laughs*]. Then the scenes with me and the snakes were shot a few miles away, in a [passage] that was dug out of the side of a wash or riverbed—they dug it back fairly deep. Those were real rattlesnakes, and other types of snakes too. But the rattlesnakes had their mouths sewn shut with clear monofilament line. They would strike at you, but of course they wouldn't inject any venom 'cause their mouths wouldn't open. They were all handled by a professional snake handler.

We ran out of light one day while filming this scene and everything was shut down, and when we came back early the next morning to resume, the snake handler did not show up on time. Everybody was there and was getting a little bit antsy, because time was wasting. Landis came over to me and he said, "The snake guy left his truck here all night, and the snakes are there in boxes. Do you mind if we go over there and we just dump these snakes in and we start shooting now, with*out* the snake guy? I mean, all *he's* gonna do is dump 'em in and just sit there anyway, right? Do you have any problem with that?" I said, "I guess not." So they went over and got these boxes full of rattlesnakes and they dumped 'em in the pit. Zsigmond was in there too, with the camera.

These snakes were rather cold—it was chilly overnight, and they weren't moving very much. A couple of them were striking at me and hitting my boots and the side of my leg, but they were still sort of sleepy. We were stirring them up with sticks and throwin' dirt in their faces and everything, trying to get 'em to rattle and strike at us. We were drinking coffee and doing this about maybe ten or fifteen minutes before this pickup truck rolled in and the snake handler came out and he was ab-so-lute-ly furious. He said, "What are my snakes doing out here? What are you doing? Are you people out of your *minds*?" Of course Landis and Zsigmond and I turned around, and he said, "You got that kid in there with live rattlesnakes that *don't* have their mouths sewn shut!" I dove out of the pit and he went in there with a snake-catching device and he grabbed 'em.

So where were the snakes with their mouths sewn shut?

They were still in boxes on the truck! It was an innocent mistake, but, really, none of us had any business messin' around with poisonous snakes. First of all, they were the wrangler's property and we were using his stuff; and, second, we didn't know what we were doing. He said, "You're just damn lucky that kid [Arch, Jr.] wasn't bitten. These snakes are still sleepy and they're cold. *That's* why they didn't bite him. But they'd have bitten him as soon as they warmed up." And we were stirring 'em up with the sticks and the dirt, thinking they were safe [*laughs*]. I guess I lucked out on *that* one.

Sewing a snake's mouth shut—is that what's done for snake scenes in movies?

I'm not sure. The animal rights people might say that's terrible and cruel and all that, but if you have rattlesnakes striking at you and bouncing off of your body, trust me, you'd rather have their mouths sewn shut!

Well, I'd just rather not be there in the first place [laughs]! This dugout you were shooting in—could you have just walked out at any time if you'd wanted to?

No, the camera was pulled right up too tight, and the director was in there, and people standing around with lights, right up in the opening of this dug-out area. So there was really no way to get out until you asked everybody to move back, move the camera back, move the lights back. You couldn't just jump straight up and get out of it.

What was Vilmos Zsigmond like between takes?

He was great, totally professional, and I had the most admiration for his talent. He was funny sometimes, he cracked jokes, but when he got his race face on, he was deep into his craft. Without meaning to tell any tales on him, he then had an old Studebaker, and there were some times when he slept in his car at Fairway, so we could start out earlier the next day, or so he could get some sleep and then start in the evening if it was a night shoot. He was never temperamental, nothing was a problem with him. Well, it really *shouldn't* have been: He was a combat photographer coming from the Hungarian Revolution, so he had certainly seen worse times than Fairway Films [*laughs*]!

By the way, that's another thing about my dad: He would give people a shot. People who were having doors slammed in their faces any place else they went. There was a time when *nobody* would give Vilmos Zsigmond the time of day. Well, he certainly has carved out quite a career, as we all know [Oscar wins and/or nominations for *Close Encounters of the Third Kind*, *The Deer Hunter* and *The River*]. But at one point, he couldn't *do* that. He had to be sponsored by a producer to make his application to get into the cameraman's union and all the other unions that he had to be in. My dad went to bat for him, and was his sponsor right through the whole process.

I think Zsigmond did an excellent job on The Sadist.

I agree. One of the things that the people holding the purse strings get very upset at is having a lot of camera movements. They take so much time. But my dad and Landis said, "We've got to let Zsigmond do what he feels he can do." So nobody restricted him. If he felt like there needed to be a camera set-up or dolly shot, a different angle or whatever, no matter how long it took, it was done.

Zsigmond said on a DVD audio commentary for The Sadist *that an early title for the picture was* 12:01.

Absolutely correct, that was what Jim Landis titled his screenplay.

When you were making the movie, was it 12:01 *or* The Sadist*?*

I believe the shooting scripts had *12:01* on them. It was later changed to *The Sadist*.

Zsigmond also said it had a $33,000 budget and three weeks of shooting.

That sounds right.

Before the credits start, when we see those crazy eyes in the dark—is that you?

Yup. And my dad narrating. He sort of inherited that narration job out of just, "It's one more thing that has to be done." Landis didn't have the voice for it, and he liked my dad's voice, and that was *it*. My dad was blessed with a terrific voice and could speak with dialects and so on.

The gasoline that Richard Alden pumps in your face—obviously, just water…?

It was water that was colored with strawberry food coloring, to give it that gasoline [look]. Even though it was water, it had a pink cast to it. In black-and-white it probably wasn't appreciated, but Landis was such a stickler for details that he wanted it to look like gasoline.

Cast and crew of *The Sadist* break to pose for a souvenir photograph: Unknown, Alan O'Day, Dave Sullivan with clapboard, Rod Moss, Joan Howard, Marilyn Manning kneeling, the man-and-wife property owners, Richard Alden, Don Russell in chair, unknown, Vilmos Zsigmond, James Landis squatting, unknown, Helen Hovey and Hall Jr.

Why didn't James Landis go farther in his career?
   [*Pause*] I don't know. He had a wonderful talent. Jim Landis was a perfectionist and had very little time for those who were not of the same mindset. I think he resented actors who thought they wanted to change dialogue and stuff like that ... which is pretty normal for a director, I would say. Yes he had a temper that could flare up, but he certainly was a talented man. *The Sadist* was personal for him because he wasn't just the director, this was his story, the whole thing was created by him. To say he was extremely passionate about it would be an understatement—he was *so* into it. It would make people tired to be around him because he never came down, he was ... just so intense. Zsigmond could keep that same intensity up as well, but some of the other people couldn't take it. Of course, the whole atmosphere around Fairway could be pretty intense. You could say that in *some* ways it was laid-back and it was relaxed, but in *other* ways it was pretty hardcore, because we'd shoot things all day long, all night long. The worst it ever was for me was the time I went 44 hours without sleep on *Eegah*. It had gone so far that I had started to hallucinate!

What memories do you have of seeing The Sadist *for the first time, all put together?*
   I was pretty proud of it. Of course, when you're that close to something, you sometimes can't see the woods for the trees. After it was shot, I was in there in the

editing room with [editor] Tony Lanza—we had Movieolas at Fairway and all of the sound effects and so on. So I had been sort of desensitized to it, I knew it forwards and backwards. Any place you started it, I knew it from there on. But the first time I saw it in its final form, with the general public watching at the same time, *that* made me feel pretty good, because people were reacting who had never seen it before. When you see somebody watching it for the first time and *they're* getting a kick out of it, or they're scared by it, or they're uncomfortable, or they make "Ewwwww!" noises or comments—*then* you realize, "Hey, this has *got* something." And I definitely felt that. Like I said before, *The Sadist* was the movie that I was the most proud of being a part of. Yes it was a low-budget movie, but definitely it was a scary movie, and of course that was exactly what Landis *wanted*. He wanted it to come off that way.

I don't know how appropriate it would be to tell the following story, but it's one of the all-time funniest things that ever happened at Fairway. Late one night, during post-production of *The Sadist*, the band was rehearsing new tunes in the largest vacant office at Fairway, located upstairs, overlooking Olive Avenue. It was me (Fender Broadcaster guitar and vocals), Alan O'Day (Wurlitzer electric piano, Hammond organ, harp and vocals), Joel Christie (Fender bass and vocals) and either Dave Sullivan or Ernie Gurrola on drums. It was like three A.M. and the Burbank police had already come by once after noise complaints were called in by neighboring residents. We had stopped for about ten minutes, then cranked up again. It wasn't too long until there was a loud knock on the door. We immediately thought of course that it was the cops again, so we stopped and quietly opened the door. Well, it wasn't the cops, it was this skinny white guy from Arkansas, asking if he could jam with us on the harmonica. We being hospitable Fairway-ites, we invited him in. At the conclusion of this driving blues shuffle, in which we allowed this chap to play an extended solo on his harmonica, after the last crash of cymbals had faded away, our guest from Arkansas suddenly felt compelled to pull down his pants and show us his bloody underwear while laughing hysterically! Apparently, he and his girlfriend heard the live music while driving by and pulled into Fairway's parking lot, where they proceeded to have sex in his old pickup truck while Arch Hall, Jr., and his Archers entertained from above! The fact that his girlfriend was having her period must have been some kind of down-home Arkansas humor! We let them wash up in the public restroom and then told them both to move on. They told us they were headed for Hollywood [*laughs*]!

*After Marilyn Manning was in those three Fairway movies [*Eegah, The Sadist *and 1964's* What's Up Front!*], were you ever in touch with her again?*

No, never, and I don't know if she stayed in the business or *what* her aspirations were.

According to "the books," The Sadist *was originally double-billed with Ray Dennis Steckler's* The Incredibly Strange Creatures Who Stopped Living and Became Mixed-up Zombies *[1964], but Steckler felt that your dad was favoring* The Sadist *and he wasn't happy about it.*

The founding father of Fairway Films, Arch Hall, Sr., as he appears in the far-out comedy *The Nasty Rabbit*.

That I don't know about. But if I may be so bold, I'm not sure *The Sadist belonged* on a double-bill with *Incredibly Strange Creatures*, that just didn't make any sense to me from the get-go. I think it was demeaning to the quality of *The Sadist*. Landis would probably agree with me on that, and Vilmos Zsigmond too.

I have lost track of Ray over the years, although people *have* run into him and he's made comments about me—nothing unfavorable that I know of! I liked Ray, he was real talented, he worked his tail off, did a lot of different jobs, and I thought he was capable of finding his niche in the business. I don't really know where it all ended up for him ... but I do know that some of the things that he came up with were pretty far-fetched! I mean, if I can allow people to take potshots at a lot of the Fairway films, I can maybe take a potshot at a couple things that *Ray* did. They're pretty far-out! But I think he had fun with 'em. Ray Dennis Steckler added a lot of talent and a lot of hard work when he worked around my dad, but I don't think they saw eye to eye on a whole lot of things.

How in the world did James Landis go from The Sadist *to* The Nasty Rabbit*?*

I think he needed a job. It's pretty simple: A lot of actors that we admire, sometimes later are seen in something not quite up to par, and you kinda cringe [*laughs*]. Well, it goes the same for directors, writers or anything else. I think Landis needed a gig, plain and simple.

Mischa Terr, the star of The Nasty Rabbit—*what was his story?*

I can't remember what his actual background was except obviously he was really Russian. I believe he was involved in music production—*serious* music, classical music. But he was a ham, of course, and he just *loved* playing this bumbling spy. I think he might have been a partial investor in *The Nasty Rabbit*, just like a fellow named Millard B. "Tex" Collins was on *The Choppers*. It was hard for my dad to turn away [investors]. Even people to whom he *probably* should have said, "*No*. There's the door, please leave now." When somebody came along and opened his wallet and said, "Y'know, I wouldn't mind havin' my name in the credits as assistant producer..." and threw down some cash, it was very hard for my dad to say no, because we *had* no money, or very *little* money, to work with. So he'd say, "If you're really serious, yeah, you can be assistant producer," or what*ever* it was. Was Millard B. Collins reeeally an assistant producer? Absolutely not. He kind of bought his screen credit.

Was The Nasty Rabbit *your dad's idea?*
   Yes. As crazy as it sounds, I had a lower opinion of *The Nasty Rabbit* years ago than I do now. In recent years, I've seen it on cable, along with strangers watching it, and they *laugh* at it. They're laughing at the gags, as ridiculous as they are ... but they *are* laughing. There seems to be a market for just about *anything* [*laughs*]! It was just something that was ground out. Remember the old comment, about how you never want to go to a sausage factory to see how sausages are made? Well, it was sort of the same at Fairway! Some of the things that were done there were done with some cleverness and perhaps some elements of talent and devotion ... and other things were done with less [of those elements]. We were *trying* to do everything as best we could, but they're such diverse projects, and there were crazy and different people involved in each one. The common thread maybe were some of the actors in front of the camera, but a lot of the people *behind* the camera were all different and trying different ideas. Some of the experiments worked, some of 'em ... boy, *didn't*. They didn't work at *all*. And of course you can see it.

I can see where someone would think making a movie like The Choppers *would be a good idea, I can see* The Sadist, Wild Guitar, *even* Eegah ... *but what was the thinking behind making something like* The Nasty Rabbit?
   I think it was a product of, "We have to come up with another film idea." It was the Cold War era, so of course in the movie there's the Soviet submarine and the threat of the Soviet Union and all that ... which [in real life] was certainly not *funny*. Then there's the idea of an impending germ warfare attack and the use of biological agents, and that's certainly not very funny stuff, as I'm sure you would agree. But what if you *made* it funny? What if you had a bumbling Russian secret agent [Terr], and then a bunch of other intelligence services from different countries like Israel and Japan and Mexico, and our CIA, that were funny also? In real life, our CIA is pretty funny at times on their own [*laughs*]. Trust me, I've done some ancillary work around them!
   As I said a minute ago, having just recently seen an audience look at it for the first time, I know that people still laugh at it. And so ... what can you say? If it works, it works. It's not the best thing *I've* ever been involved with, but, again, *that* was the movie where I ended up with a nice new 1964 Harley-Davidson FLH, which was a wonderful bike. I had that for several months, until it was stolen in the '65 Watts riots [*laughs*]!

Where were all the ranch scenes shot?

At a ranch in Topanga Canyon. The interiors were mostly shot back at Fairway again.

You had a sound stage there at Fairway?

Of sorts, yeah. For years there used to be a drugstore there—my dad owned it. In fact, he even *ran* it, back in the late '40s. They sold the wax lips and the wax things with the colored water inside, and one of the little girls who used to come in there was Natalie Wood—she lived right down the street. Well, years later the drugstore interior was ripped out and it was soundproofed with Fiberglas and all kinds of soundproofing material applied to the inner walls, and it became Fairway's soundstage-of-sorts. The exterior of the building is still there but I have no idea if that's been restored to be a working building or an office, or if it still looks the same inside.

Deadwood '76 *[1965], a Western made on location in South Dakota—one of your dad's more ambitious pictures, no?*

Yes it was. But misguided—I really think so. It was much fun to do but … *Deadwood '76* was Fairway's biggest mistake. A tragic miscalculation. I think at that point my dad should have stayed in the genre of exploitation and not tried to go too "legit." Low-budget Westerns weren't really hot then. Even big-budget Westerns were bombs at the box office. Yes, sadly, *Deadwood '76* was … ill-advised.

In one scene I worked with Bobby Means, who was a real Sioux and about my age. He is Russell Means' brother—Russell Means is now quite famous in Hollywood [as an actor] and also with AIM, the American Indian Movement. Bobby Means was the Indian I had the fight scene with, the one trying to kill me with a knife. It got pretty realistic—in fact, I've still got the scars to prove it. There was a rubber knife used when we jumped on the ground, but on the ground when the camera was close-up, only a real knife would pass. We didn't have anything other than Bobby's real knife, and it was razor-sharp. I got cut up pretty bad. He was a little over-aggressive. I'm *pretty* strong, and at one point it took every ounce of strength I had to keep him from killing me. And, worst of all, it doesn't even look that spectacular as a fight scene! We were both trying to be actors, but nevertheless, he was so "adrenalized" in wanting to fight… [*Pause*] It's hard to explain, I can't really set the mood of the whole thing. He was a very nice guy, but it was a situation where I was still a white guy and he was an Indian, you know what I mean? It was getting pretty real, I assure you…

What other life-threatening scenes do you recall?

Almost being gored by a buffalo in the Black Hills, in Custer State Park! How's that for life-threatening? My dad said, "You know, Arch, this is not *real* safe to do, it *is* sort of … like … dangerous … but if you would like to ride your horse through that herd of buffalo over there, we'd like to shoot that. How do you feel about that?" Buffalo are very unpredictable, and they can take a horse down in just a matter of a

Hall Sr. reacts with dismay to find Jr. the victim of a lynching in the finale of the Western *Deadwood '76*, the last Fairway Films production.

second. But I said, "...Sure. I'll try it," and I went over and did it. There was nobody around—if one or two of the buffalo *had* made an aggressive move towards me, there were no cowboys or wranglers or anybody who could have dispersed 'em. The horse was real scared—horses don't really feel right around buffalo either. Horses, I think, have an innate fear of the buffalo. You could feel it, the horse was getting really skittish and real nervous.

Was Richard Kiel correct in telling me that Deadwood '76 *lost enough money that it put a big dent in your family's finances?*

Yes, sad to say, Richard was absolutely correct. Over the years my dad had, for lack of a better phrase, kept pouring money down a rat hole, to keep Fairway alive and to keep it running. Then his line of credit pretty much played itself out. It's sort of like when you try to use your ATM card and it's refused because it's maxed out. Believe me, that's where it ended up. He was maxed out. My dad was rather embarrassed to admit things like that. Frankly, I am too. But what little money was still trickling in was going directly to the bank, or going directly to Technicolor, or directly to MGM—the labs that made the prints.

It must have been really tough.
It was so depressing to me at the time. This is the part of it that's not very glamorous, but I remember my mom crying, opening envelopes [from distributors]. My mom would take in the returns, the money generated by a film when it would play in the theatrical run—she'd open the mail, many times I would too, to help her in the office. For example, there would be a playdate for *Eegah* or a playdate for *Wild Guitar* or a playdate for *The Sadist*, or what*ever*, and it would be $12.50 from (say) Cleveland, Ohio. And it had played at a double drive-in there all weekend long! I'm sure you're old enough to know what a drive-in looked like; well, there were also a lot of twin drive-ins, really big. And they were *all* packed, usually, on weekends. Fairway product would play there at a double drive-in all weekend long, and we'd get a check for $12.50. And the $12.50 check that came in, in many cases, was no good.

Oh my God...!
And if it was deposited and it cleared, most times it went directly to pay for prints and things like that. Did it generate anything for my family, for my dad's business? *No.* [*Pause*] It's pretty brutal to say that, but I want you to keep it all in perspective.

*How did any*body *in the independent film biz survive back then?*
I think my dad survived because of the money that he had invested in his earlier years, when he bought real estate and property. *That* was all put on the block to borrow money to make *movies* with. After he had made *several* movies, then the revenues from those movies became collateral for *more* movies, or whatever. It sort of snowballed. But eventually, like I said, it reached the point where you stick your ATM card in and it says, SORRY—NO FUNDS AVAILABLE.

Was there no way to keep an eye on the distributors in those days?
There was just no affordable way for an independent producer to audit or refute the reports that were submitted by the distributors. One time my dad hired a private investigator to audit exhibition records of a Midwest distributor. The P.I. reported the playdates and counted cars entering several drive-ins. My dad compared the P.I.'s data with the reports that were submitted for the same period by the distributor. What the report revealed was shocking! Tens of thousands of dollars were taken in over a weekend and yet the distributor's report read, "Three days multi-drive-in, $12.50 per day per title." My dad realized these distributors had *all* independent producers by the balls! They had no guilt about lying right to your face. I remember my mother crying a lot during this period, as my dad would sit behind his desk and drink. And his drinking was on the increase.

One day he said he had *had* it and was going to pay a surprise visit to one of the worst offenders in the Deep South. Keep in mind this was all before 9/11 and airport metal detectors. My dad took a Colt .45 automatic pistol with him on the trip—it was the same pistol I carried on *The Sadist*. A day or two before he left on the trip, I spent the afternoon cleaning it for him. I also bought a box of fresh ammunition at a North Hollywood gun shop, loading several magazines for him.

My dad returned after a week, telling my mother and me of a meeting in which the Southern film distributor wined and dined him, and he lost the focus of his mission, and didn't confront the guy. (My mother thought the booze had a lot to do with it.) However, before he left to return to California, he told the guy he should consider himself a lucky man, as he had brought a gun with him in his briefcase and had been in a mindset to do whatever had to be done, to impress upon the guy that he'd better clean up his act when dealing with Fairway Films. "Strangely," the revenue that followed from this distributor after my dad's trip jumped ten times higher for a few weeks. But it soon slipped back to the same pitiful levels. My dad commented, late one night, months after the trip, that he should have pistol-whipped this asshole. I think he felt guilty about drinking with him instead of kicking his ass! I said, "It wouldn't matter. Nothing matters with these pricks." They were all crooks and they wouldn't change. They were too used to having a license to steal!

Later on, toward the Fairway finale, my dad hooked up with a very bright guy named Jerry Kurtz, a former B-52 pilot. Kurtz helped him promote and package the films, developing a long-needed marketing strategy. Jerry Kurtz was a good man. He and my dad connected. Incidentally, when Kurtz and my dad began the Vanguard Group to package and market the Fairway films to the TV market, there were major objections to the Don Russell death scene in *The Sadist* as well as objections to the title itself. That's what led to the name change to *The Face of Terror*. The network censors had real teeth back then and if they gave a thumbs down, it was *no deal* on the little screen.

Did Senior go into another line of work after that, or was that the point at which he pretty much retired?

Wellll ... he certainly was offered work. Like I said, he was offered a job as staff producer at Warner Bros.—an offer which he declined, causing my mother to again break down and cry. His knack for actually finishing films for pennies had finally caught the attention of those who controlled the purse strings around town and they felt that, if given a decent budget to work with, this Hall guy could really keep costs down. My mother was so happy when she heard about this, because she was thinking, "Maybe we can get out from under this enormous debt, maybe we can get square with the bank" and so on. Well, he just nixed the whole thing with a phone call, he said, "No. I'm not interested." It was a shocker. That crushed her. At the time, I didn't understand why he nixed it, but I do now: He just didn't want to work for anybody else. He would much rather be the chief cook and bottle washer, the jack of all trades and maybe master of none—but at least he was in charge of his own destiny. I don't think it was any dream of his that he was gonna hit it big and be a multi-jillionaire—it was not *that*. It was just the idea that he wanted to be his own boss. He wasn't very good at being an employee under somebody's thumb.

I think my dad *could* have done other things [after the end of Fairway] but, no, he really didn't do too much after that. He did try to write some stories, and he worked with Richard Kiel on some [unrealized] projects. And he worked with *other* people on stories and ideas and scripts and novels. Even poetry. But they were things that were not really commercial successes.

Once Fairway went under, was there any thought on your part of looking for acting jobs at other places, or was that the end of it?

Actually, it happened way before that. One of my dad's old friends, Clete Roberts, a newscaster and a local television personality in Los Angeles for over 30 years, was a pilot and had a hangar and several airplanes up in Santa Paula. He was over one time having lunch and he sensed in me kind of a feeling of... [*Pause*] I won't say despair, but ... a little depressed. Clete later took me aside and said, "You know, I sense you're kind of bummed-out around your dad. The business is not going too well, and you and your dad are sometimes a little at each other's throats." I said, "I don't mean to *be* that way, but you're pretty right. I guess things *aren't* going too well." He said, "Well, why don't we go flyin'?" So he took me over to Santa Monica and we rented a little airplane and went up and flew around Malibu. Clete said, "What do you think of this? This is pretty nice, isn't it?" And, I'll tell ya, from that moment on, I was hooked just like you'd sink a hook in a blue marlin. I knew that was what I wanted to do. And I told my dad that, I said, "Clete took me up in this plane" and "It was so neat" and "Jeez, that's what I want to *do*, Dad, I *know* it. I know that's what I want to do." He looked at me like, "...You gotta be shitting me! What do you see in *that*?" Because he always thought that I should be interested in the same things that *he* was interested in. If he liked something, then I should automatically like it because I'm Junior. Well, that's not really true—you can have an offspring that doesn't want to do what *you* want to do. I think he was a little bit ... I dunno, maybe a little bit *upset* with Clete for doing that, thinking that maybe if I'd have hung around a little bit more, maybe we could have done more movies or whatever. I personally thought that [the moviemaking] had best be put to rest as soon as possible, because it was taking a toll on his health.

So there was still a plan, at least in his *mind, to do more movies after* Deadwood '76.

He loved to write and to make the movies and to work in the hotbed of seething activity during the production of a film, but after the movie was made, again I'll say it, my dad was not a businessman.

I wish my dad could have seen his dream come true and been really successful at what he loved to do. The pictures weren't blinding successes, but he still was totally involved and had the

After the fall of Fairway, Hall Sr. (left, with his son) lived in a Newport Beach retirement home a few blocks from John Wayne.

great times and had a great nucleus of people around him, *like* the Jim Landises and Vilmos Zsigmonds and these people who kinda got their push-start with him. There was a genuine feeling of camaraderie at Fairway Films and my dad just loved being in the center of all the action. Some of them, as we have learned, went on to great things, some of them maybe petered out along the way.

If there were 40-year-old movies out there with my whole family participating in 'em, I think that'd be kinda magical—that's my perception anyway. Now what's the reality? How often do you look at these things?

Quite often. My oldest son Wayne, who lives in Southern Utah and has a towing business and a family of his own, *he* was very close to my dad, his grandfather, and he has all these films. He can show his daughters, my father's *great*-granddaughters, what their great-grandfather looked like—his daughters of course were born after my dad passed away. So it's become a vehicle of not so much what it *is* itself, but, "That's your grandpa!" and "That's your great-grandpa!"

I don't remember what my father sounded like, and now there's no way to find out. And my grandfather and great*-grandfather—fuhgeddabout!*

It's true. In that respect, it had nothing to do with *Nasty Rabbit* or all these crazy things, it's just the idea of, "*That's* your great-grandpa!," and the little girl looks up at the screen of the TV and says, "Wow…!" For *that* reason, it's really cool. These films keep playing and playing and playing on cable, and it's just amazing. In the '80s, I had a pilot friend who, when passing through Bangladesh on a U.N. charter flight, saw *Eegah* dubbed in Hindu, playing in a dirt floor theater with pigs and chickens running about! If anything, there's more of a growing interest in these films, every passing year!

The acting—was it fun right to the end, or did it ever get old?

It was fun. And, for good, bad or indifferent, trust me, I was really tryin' to do it to the best of my abilities. So, yeah, it was fun!

You spent the greater part of your aviation career working with the Flying Tigers.

I started with the Tigers June 19, 1967. Prior to that, I was working as a co-pilot for a little outfit in Burbank, flying military passengers in DC-2s and DC-3s—I worked for that outfit for about six months before I got hired by Tigers. Flying Tigers was a Los Angeles–based air cargo company that was started after World War II, in 1945, by some pilots and a couple of California bankers, but mostly pilots of the original AVG [American Volunteer Group], which was Claire Chennault's famous Flying Tigers that flew in China against the Japanese Air Force during World War II. Tigers was a small company but a global company, about 6000 employees, flying domestic cargo—major cities in the United States as well as overseas, *and* military. I flew for them from 1967 to 1989, when they were purchased by a major cargo carrier. I did some interesting flying with Tigers—I'll never forget it. I've been all over the world, and to places that are so bizarre [*laughs*]. But it was a total blast. It was like somebody throwing the keys to a four-engine jet to this kid from Burbank and saying, "Here, take this out and fly it all over Asia and Africa, sometimes in the middle of wars and everything. Don't bend any metal and don't hurt yourself, but have fun, kid." It was sort of like barnstorming with heavy jet aircraft—it was an incredible, incredible experience. I miss it so.

Did your mom and dad divorce, or were they just separated toward the end?
They never divorced, but were not living together for many, many years.

And he died in 1978.
He died from a massive heart attack. I got a call from my dad's girlfriend, that he had had a heart attack at her condo and I was to come quickly. I was sort of in shock. My dad and I were, you might say, estranged in many ways, but other ways we were *so* close. My wife Le-Thanh and I got in my car—I had an old '68 Cadillac El Dorado with a 472 engine, and that thing had *power*. We were driving flatout until the traffic was bottlenecking a little bit. I was kind of shaking, and she was patting me on the shoulder, when I heard a siren, and here comes a paramedic ambulance coming from the opposite direction, going towards the Newport Beach Hospital. As it passed, I turned my head and I could see my dad on a gurney inside.

I did a turnaround in traffic, with people honking, and I chased the ambulance. When I got to the hospital, they had him in an emergency room, and I sat outside until they came out and they said, "He didn't make it." They tried everything, but … it was just his time. His girlfriend said he was laughing and talking and joking up until five seconds before he had the heart attack. He got quiet and he put his hand on his chest and he walked towards the door—he said, "I want to get some air…" She knew something was going on so she followed him out—"Are you okay? Are you okay?" He walked outside, he took one or two steps and then keeled over. Fell like a tree. When he hit the ground, I think he was basically gone.

My mother felt it was best to bury him in California, but I knew he would want to go home to South Dakota, the land of the mighty Sioux. So I took him home. Le-Thanh and I took him back on Western Airlines—he rode in the belly and we rode in the same airplane, topside. I had a funeral director there take him, and then there were a few days of confusion in Rapid City when I didn't know what to do—I'd gone there with little preparation, without having a list of contacts set up in advance. I got a-hold of his old boss Helen Duhamel—the Duhamel family is a very, very wealthy, influential family in Rapid City that owned the radio station my dad used to work at, KOTA. She supported my dad in his shows about Native Americans and all. Understand that Mrs. Duhamel was one of the pillars of the social community, respected by *every*one, including the governor. She asked me, "What would he really want?" There was a long pause, then I told her, "I think *you* know most of all."

"Something to do with his beloved Sioux?" she answered. "That's a tough one," she said, "but let me work on it." She made some calls and got a-hold of representatives of the Tribal Council, who were already in some kind of session down in Chadron, Nebraska. Le-Thanh and I waited for three days in a motel for the issue to be brought before the Tribal Council, then we received a call that the Council had voted. The vote shocked even lifelong South Dakotans: The vote was to give *full* honors and respect to my dad, a white man, by presiding at the graveside service. Representing the Sioux Nation was a large entourage headed up by the ranking Sioux Chief, Frank Foolscrow, who spoke both in English and Sioux through an interpreter. A ceremonial burial blanket was even ordered made. I knew in my heart it was exactly as my dad would have wanted it—exactly!

My dad was buried beside his mother and father at the Masonic Cemetery in Philip, South Dakota, with Chief Frank Foolscrow and many Indians from Pine Ridge and Rose Bud. There were about 50 in attendance at the graveside service. Old cowboys and retired ranchers that lived their whole life in that area and had known my dad, they came up to me and introduced themselves and said, "Arch Jr., in my entire life of living in South Dakota and being around Native Americans, I have *never* seen an outpouring of the Sioux over a non-Indian. This is unheard-of, it's unprecedented. I just want you to know that this is *truly* a special event that I'll never forget." Even though my dad's life led him far from South Dakota and the land of the Sioux, his love and respect for the Sioux was never forgotten.

You recently wrote your first novel, Apsara Jet, *a racy thriller with a pilot caught up in the world of narcotics trafficking in Southeast Asia. What got you into writing?*

Reflecting and reminiscing about my dad (and nearing my sixtieth birthday, which would mark the end of my airline career), I suddenly wanted to write an adventure novel. I can't explain it. Maybe it was a midlife crisis thing? Or just realizing that in 2001, I was now the exact same age as he was in 1965? Whatever, I felt I had to do it. My dad didn't talk about it a *lot* but I knew that he enjoyed writing, and I just sorta kinda wondered if I had any of that in me. Then at the same time, I had a curiosity about the differential of popularity among successful novelists. There's a disproportionate amount of success being enjoyed by female writers writing romance novels. You know the ones that I'm talking about, the ones with the covers featuring Fabio in repose, holding a girl with long flowing hair in the wind on top of a balcony. Those authors—usually they're ladies—are so prolific, and very successful. I wondered, "Why isn't there anything written in that vein for *male* interest?" Of course there *is*, there are the Tom Clancys and the Michael Crichtons, but sometimes they get so techno that I think it leaves a lot of people a little bit cold. I thought maybe I could write about subjects and areas that I know about, that I am somewhat of an expert on—like aviation and Southeast Asia.

I of course began by making all the mistakes that fledgling writers make, like throwing everything out and starting from scratch every few days. I did that a couple times until finally I started seeking advice from some *real* authors, who said, "Look, just write and don't look back until you're through with it. *Then* go back and do anything you want to do with it." Eighteen months later, I finished my first manuscript. It was interesting to get back into something that was in an artistic vein, a creative vein, whatever you might call it. Music is one thing I'm still involved with, but writing a novel seemed far more personal and deeper. My first book, *Apsara Jet*, is today considered a regional bestseller in both Thailand and Cambodia. It's never really been reviewed anywhere in the United States and it's never really been released anywhere via major distribution, even though it's available on Amazon.com and all that.

Many who have reviewed *Apsara Jet* overseas have commented about its screenplay potential. It has been read by some notable people to date, one being John Travolta—he wrote me a nice note saying he enjoyed it very much and wished me well. I was a little bit disappointed that Travolta didn't pick up on it 'cause I know he is an avid aviator. The book's main character, pilot John Jackson, *is* somewhat of a dark character. Frankly, *Apsara Jet* is pretty hardcore. It would take someone as bold as Quentin Tarantino to make it into a movie. *Reservoir Dogs*, *Pulp Fiction* and *From Dusk Till Dawn* prove that Tarantino can think outside the box.

Why did you use the nom de plume *Nicolas Merriweather on* Apsara Jet?

I wanted to dredge up one of the old names that my dad used to use, and that was one that I liked very much. (I spell it a little bit differently.) I like the name, it's just a cool name. Also, it sounds a little bit British, and that's helped me in certain venues where Americans are not well-received. I may write under Archie Hall some time later. If my dad taught me *one thing* it's that, if you have the inspiration and the talent and you want to do something, it doesn't *matter* what you call yourself. If people like it, they like it, if they don't, they don't.

Hall Jr. gave up low-budget stardom for high-flying real-life adventure, including many years with the legendary Flying Tigers. In a recent shot, he poses with a copy of his first novel, *Aspara Jet*.

When I got to the point in the book where the lead character John Jackson mentions that his father came from South Dakota and spoke Sioux, I of course said to myself, "Archie's writing about his own dad."

There are certainly elements there that I did take from my dad, that's an absolute fact.

On page 6, Jackson wonders what his late father would think of his, Jackson's, failures and weaknesses, and wonders if his father would still love him. Was that based on anything that you and your dad had going on?

Wellll ... that's a possible mixture of real feelings. My dad was very disappointed that I sort of abandoned the acting thing and went my own way. It was my life and he wished me well and all that, but he was not real happy with it. So, yes, those are fictional situations in the book but there are elements of real emotion and reality mixed in. Having Jackson wonder how his father would feel about him if he were a failure ... that was just trying to tug at the readers' heartstrings a little bit.

Have you got more story ideas in your head?
Absolutely. I'm full of 'em. Or I'm full of *it* [*laughs*]!

What do you want to close with?
Just to say that I never heard anybody have anything bad to say about my dad. That he ever cheated them, or that he was a scoundrel, or that he ever did something bad in a business deal. At least, nobody's ever said that to my face. Other people in the business, you can hear *reams* of information about how people got cheated by them. My dad knew all those people and he never signed up to be that way. He was pretty straight-up. I don't think any actor or any employee who worked with their sweat was ever stiffed by my dad. Maybe some people volunteered to work for *free*, but nobody who said "I'll work for you for so-much a week" ever got left hangin' or was cheated out of their wages.

Another memory: I remember we'd all be sitting around the Fairway compound with a group of people like Vilmos Zsigmond, Alan O'Day, Dobie Gray, Joel Christie, Ernie Gurrola, Ray Dennis Steckler or whoever was around at the time, and we were all hungry and we had little or no money. "Big Arch" would say, "Well, that's enough work for tonight, let's all go eat." We'd go to a restaurant up the street called the Tally Rand, a Denny's-type place on Olive Avenue in Burbank that had become Fairway Films' own "studio commissary" by adoption. We'd all go there and eat together, like a big family, and of course "Big Arch" would pick up the tab. That's why I say, it was a *family* kind of a deal more than a company. It's hard to convey all the feelings that surrounded Fairway at the time. I would definitely describe it more as a family operation. Even the people who weren't family members were still regarded as family. People would come up and tell my dad, "We need to go get some sandwiches," "We need some film," "The wheels broke on the camera dolly, we gotta run out and find some tapered roller bearings," and he'd have people runnin' in all directions. Everyone, and I mean *every*one, pitched in at Fairway Films. Wonderful memories.

Stephen Kandel on Chamber of Horrors

> *Every episode [of the* House of Wax *TV series] would have involved a horrible crime. Dismemberment, rape, Jack the Ripper, impalements, horrors ... that was the idea! Think of Hannibal the Cannibal as a regular!*

The setting is Baltimore, circa 1880, and a killer prowls the foggy night streets: Jason Cravette, a mad blue-blood who once strangled his bride-to-be with her own hair and then forced a clergyman to perform the wedding ceremony anyway. With the help of Anthony Draco and Harold Blount, criminologists and operators of a local wax museum Chamber of Horrors, Cravette had been apprehended, tried for her murder and condemned—but en route to prison, he escaped. Now he stalks the city again, deadlier than before: During his getaway, Cravette had to hack off his own shackled right hand, which he now replaces with a series of grisly instruments of murder.

This was the bizarre plot of the TV pilot for *House of Wax*, a proposed 1966 Warner Bros. series starring Cesare Danova and Wilfrid Hyde-White as the sleuthing showmen and guest star Patrick O'Neal as the homicidal (but otherwise impeccably mannered) "Baltimore Strangler." Gruesome, sometimes verging-on-kinky, the Hy Averback–directed shocker was deemed too strong for TV, and the idea of a series was scrapped. But to salvage their investment, this unsold pilot episode went back onto the sound stages and was expanded for summer theatrical release as *Chamber of Horrors*. (The plush-looking Technicolor production also featured the gimmicky "Fear Flasher" and "Horror Horn": Intercut flashes of blood-red, with accompanying electronic-sounding screeches, fill the screen just prior to the film's "four supreme fright points," giving timorous audience members fair warning and a chance to avert their eyes from the coming carnage!)

This terror tale, with all of its ahead-of-their-time dashes of the grotesque, was the brainchild of 38-year-old Stephen Kandel, a New York–born television and movie writer whose résumé reads like a Baby Boomer's dream list of must-see TV (*Sea Hunt*, *The Wild Wild West*, *Bat-*

man, *Star Trek*, *Mission: Impossible* and many more). Now East Coast–based and still writing for the small screen, Kandel here recalls the 1960s Horror Series That Never Was.

Were you under contract to Warner Bros. in 1965 when the House of Wax *TV series was first proposed?*
No, I was a freelance writer. I had just done a Western series, *Iron Horse*, for Columbia, and now I was doing a pilot for Warner Bros., when Hy Averback contacted me. They had this idea of spinning off a TV series from *House of Wax* [1953], which had done very well as a feature.

You think this was Hy Averback's idea?
Well, Hy Averback was the only source *I* had. It may have been [writer] Ray Russell's idea. All *I* know is, Hy contacted me 'cause I'd created that series which he liked, *Iron Horse*. He called me up and he said, "We got this project to spin a series off *House of Wax*. You interested?" Sure! *You* know … I'm a hired gun! So I toddled over to Warners and we made the deal, and they gave me Ray Russell's… [*Pause*] It wasn't really a treatment, it was just some *ideas*.

Some ideas for the series.
The idea was really an insane one, but that's okay [*laughs*]. The idea was to combine the functions of Sherlock Holmes with the proprietor of a wax museum. It was one of these ideas that sounds great … *in a meeting*. "We'll have all the gaslight atmosphere, and fog, and *more*. It'll be centered on a sense of the macabre. A man who has traced the convoluted thinking of insane killers is the ideal detective to search out…" blah blah blah—*that* was the pitch.

That was Ray Russell's idea?
No. [*Laughs*] Oh, no, no, no, no, no! That was the *pitch*. The *idea* was simply to do a series based on *House of Wax*, which was the story of a wax museum operated by an insane proprietor—it wasn't much clearer than *that*. When you have an idea this dim, the input is immense! It was like so many other projects: Ev-er-y-bod-y pitches 20 cents worth in, and soon it sinks! In this particular case, there was a lot of discussion, and if you saw the picture, a lot of it ended up on the screen, which is why the picture went in 17 different directions. What I contributed to the story was the idea of a mad murderer who collects a corpse made up of the body parts of the people who sentenced him to hang. That was supposed to be the spine of the picture.

Anyway, that was the situation: I was given this rather inchoate series of notions, and then I worked out a storyline. Hy and I talked about it, and I *think* [associate producer] Jim Barnett was involved in some of the meetings too. Remember, this is going back quite a while! And I was doing two other shows at the same time, so it's a little vague. I have written so much television that it all blurs.

Did you ever meet Ray Russell?
No. Well, I *may* have, as another face in the crowd, but I don't remember that.

You need to understand how scratch this was. Hy said, "Did you see this picture *House of Wax*?" As a matter of fact, if I remember correctly, he said, "Did you see this piece of shit *House of Wax*?" Well, that was his nature, the casual denigration of a project he had not done [*laughs*]. I said, "Yeah, I saw it." And he said, "Okay! Now you know what we're lookin' for!"

You really make it sound as though "Turn House of Wax *into a TV series" was just about all* the "direction" you got. Did Ray Russell's work on the project, preceding yours, really produce *that* little?

I don't intend to low-ball Ray Russell, but you must understand the compartmentalization that's a norm in development TV. I knew vaguely that Ray Russell had done some work on it, but I never saw any pages, talked to him, or heard anything more than a few offhand references to earlier groundwork. For all I know, he wrote a complete teleplay; if so, I didn't see it. *I* got a memo, a lot of verbal chitchat, a screening of *House of Wax*, a walk through the sets and away I went.

Did you like Hy Averback?

Oh, sure. He was a lot like Sheldon Leonard, for whom I wrote *I Spy* for a couple of years: New York, funny, brash, irreverent and frequently abusive. We got along loudly and well.

House of Wax, a Stephen Kandel–scripted television pilot, failed to hook a network and was expanded for release as a feature film, *Chamber of Horrors*, instead. Pictured: Patrick O'Neal. (Photofest)

What did you think of the casting of the series leads?

Bi-*zarre*. In Cesare Danova, Warner Bros. thought they had a great romantic hero—Warners had this dream that Cesare Danova could become another Fernando Lamas, another Latin leading man. But … running a wax museum, and going to upscale Baltimore social balls? It's a stretch! An odd piece of miscasting. I think he was a pay-or-play.

"Pay-or-play" means that the studio has promised an actor, a writer, a director—whomever—a specific sum of money for work…

…and if the work doesn't materialize, the money is nevertheless paid. So it's customary to find some work for the payee to do. I once in my dubious career had written a tender and affecting story

Patrick O'Neal put his best heel forward as the diabolical Jason Cravette, strangling one victim with her own hair, in *Chamber of Horrors*.

about a young girl who is taken under the wing of a traveling priest. Then the studio called me up and said, "Listen, we've got a pay-or-play deal with a collie." So the girl had to be changed into a dog [*laughs*]. You laugh! But I did it! Of course it made the incipient romance, which was testing the celibacy vows of this priest, somewhat more peculiar, but ... if you don't adapt, you die!

A year before this House of Wax *pilot, Universal shot a pilot for a series called* Black Cloak, *in which a turn-of-the-century criminologist, Leslie Nielsen, and a dwarf assistant would crack supernatural cases. Two "period" horror series about a criminologist and a dwarf assistant just a year (or less) apart strikes me as quite a coincidence.*

As far as I know, nobody involved in *Black Cloak* had a hand in *House of Wax*. As for there being a dwarf in both ... well, there was for a while a dwarf vogue, and it included the idea that you can put a dwarf [in a series] instead of a woman. That removes the romantic entanglement question for the lead. There have been a number [of dwarf characters on TV], *House of Wax* did not feature the only one. I remember, years later, the TV series *Man from Atlantis* briefly contemplating including a *mutated* dwarf as a sidekick [*laughs*]. So I think it was just great minds coming to the same dim conclusion.

What memories of the guest star in your House of Wax *pilot, "Baltimore Strangler" Patrick O'Neal?*

He kind of enjoyed it. He chewed a lot of scenery! This was a television show made on a budget and on a time schedule that made it really difficult for an actor to find his character. He played it silky and ... hammy. But ... y'know ... okay, *sure*! He was a better actor than that performance, and some of the pieces worked better than others. But that's the nature of the beast.

He had a good part. Heck, he had a better part than Vincent Price had in the original House of Wax.

He did have a good part. But, as I said, he didn't have enough time to develop it. Warner Bros. said, "We're giving you this jewel, this *House of Wax* set," and the necessity of exploiting that set threw the dramatic structure all to hell and gone. We *had* to include the waxworks, and all that prating by Wilfrid Hyde-White [the wax museum tour guide].

I found an old review where the critic wrote that O'Neal played it "with an aristocratic leer reminiscent of William F. Buckley, Jr."

[*Laughs*] Oh, *very* good! Oh, that is great, absolutely! Anyway, as I've been stressing, *House of Wax* was done under time pressure. They had been diddling around with this project for a while, and the network was saying, "Come *on* already, where's the script for the pilot?" My reputation included speed—as a matter of fact, it may have included it as a primary virtue! So I wrote it fast, and everybody said, "Oh, great! Let's go!," and they went ahead and shot it. At which point, the network said, "We can't put this on the air!"—it was too bloody. Jack Warner said, "Release it as a feature," and the rest is history.

Which network was it made for?
I think it was ABC.

And they shot on the same set as the movie House of Wax?
They certainly did. That was one of the main economic underpinnings of it. All the stuff existed, it was made for that feature. They got the House of Wax on the cheap, because Warner Bros. already owned it.

Was it going to be an hour series?
Yes. And every episode would have involved a horrible crime. Dismemberment, rape, Jack the Ripper, impalements, horrors ... that was the idea! Think of Hannibal the Cannibal as a regular [*laughs*]! I would have been a regular writer on the series—I would have been *head* writer.

Did you get to watch them shoot much?
No. There is an absolute rule in Hollywood, "The less they [the writers] know, the better." The writer is not encouraged to be on the set. When *I* produce a series, I go the other way, but I'm not feeling threatened, I guess. Essentially, writers are advised to turn in their pages and go away. And for some unknown reason, writers are *not* encouraged to talk to the director, which is true insanity. *But*, that's the structure of the business.

I watched the movie again just the other night, and I noticed that a shot was missing—a shot which sent the network over the edge. It was a cut from Patrick O'Neal's cleaver hand descending at the judge [Vinton Hayworth], to a piece of rare roast beef being sliced in an upscale restaurant. It was *very* effective—at the screening house where we tested the pilot, with an audience of civilians enticed in off the street to watch and rate the show, there were screams. Which was the *idea*, I thought! But the network said, "*That's* it! *No* chance!" Jack Warner, because of this flap, saw it, and he said, "Hell, [we'll make it] a feature." And he said, "Let's put some more money in it." Eleven cents [*laughs*]! I wrote more and Hy Averback shot more. I wrote, for instance, the wedding scene at the beginning, to help pad it out.

You must have had to pad it out a lot, *to get it from an hour TV show to 100 minutes, or however long it is.*
With the initial pilot, we *thought* we could get an hour and a half on the air, and about an hour and a half's worth of material was shot. So it wasn't that much of a stretch, to make it feature-length. You ... not *always*, but *generally* shoot more than you need and then you edit it down, after you test some of the material. On that series I mentioned, *Iron Horse*, I threw in everything I could think of, including a pet gerbil [*laughs*], which perched on one character's shoulder. (The guy complained bitterly, 'cause he had gerbil shit running down his arm.) And the test audience *loved* the little beast, so it became a regular! If they hadn't loved it, we would have cut it out.

Did you think Hy Averback was a good director for this kind of material?
He was okay. But, again, remember, a director of television, especially then, and especially at Warners, had ironclad limitations. I did a whole series for Warners called *Harry O* and it was a constant battle with the studio, which had imposed bizarre limitations on that series. Which was a very *good* series, I must say.
Something else I was reminded of, re-watching the movie the other day: There was originally a much better underwater sequence, and I don't know what happened to it. You see the Strangler [at the bottom of the river] wrap that chain around a rock, forcing his hand on top of the rock and chopping it off. Just then, a cloud of little fish comes by, attracted by the blood. And that's *it*. The last thing you see is the anchored hand on the rock, bleeding, and the fish swimming around this cloud of blood. Which I thought was a great shot.

So that was actually shot?
I shot it! Hy didn't care, he said, "All right, look, we're out here [in the studio tank] anyway. If you want to try and sneak a second unit shot..." I said, "Yeah, let me take a whack at it." That was in the days when I had a fantasy that I might direct ... before I actually tried to direct and discovered that "fantasy" was the correct term! So, yes, there were things that were shot that [weren't used], like the roast beef slice and a better amputation scene.

Was that the one and only scene you directed in the thing?
It wasn't even a scene, it was a *shot*, a *shot*, a *shot*. A second unit cameraman and

En route to the death house by train, O'Neal hacks his way to freedom—but at a gruesome price.

a second unit director (me!) got together, set up the shot, I told him exactly what I wanted, and said, "See if you can get it."

Did you still have Patrick O'Neal in the tank, doing that for you?
   Oh, no, no, no. Christ, no! We were not gonna get the star, he was busy working. This was a shot of a clothed arm-wrist-hand, shackled, and an axe coming down. The hand was the "star"!
   Another thing they cut out was the cat apparently eating the corpse of Patrick O'Neal's first victim, the bride he strangled with her own hair. He puts her on the bed and he leaves, and we see there's a cat sitting on the bed. At the last moment, the cat leans over and licks at the body—there's a trickle of blood out of the side of her mouth. It's like a kiss. Then later, when the police come in, the shot was designed to make it look as if the cat was eating. Locked in a room with meat, what's a cat gonna do? When the police come in, the cat springs away from the corpse, and they react with horror. I thought, what the hell, pull out all the stops.

I like the fact that there's slow motion when Patrick O'Neal fires a gun from inside a fake hand, killing Wayne Rogers.
   The slo-mo when the gun goes off, I *loved* that. I think I specified slo-mo in the script but I cannot say for sure, it may have been the director, Hy, who came up with that. There again is an instance where there may have been a cut. The young detective [Rogers] says to Patrick O'Neal, "Put your hands up"—and O'Neal's hands, *two* of them, come into view. The detective says, "My *God*, that's impossible!," or words to that effect.

It's impossible that O'Neal again has two hands.
   Yeah! The detective realizes he is looking at a man with two hands, when he knows that the killer only has one. O'Neal says, "Well, perhaps you have the wrong man…," and the detective is stunned and lowers his gun slightly. Then O'Neal fires and the hand explodes.

I love it!
   I loved it too! But then, of course, writers love their own work. Anyway, I don't know what happened to that version, which as far as I know was shot. I didn't edit the film.

The dream-like courtroom scene with the weird colored backgrounds and echo-chamber voices—was it suggested in the script that it be shot that way, or did someone else come up with it?
   Yes, it was suggested in the script.

Were Suzy Parker and Patrice Wymore in the pilot, or did they come in when it was being padded out into the movie?
   They came in for the movie, I'm pretty sure. They were just added touches to tart up this pilot as a feature film.

The back lot theater used in Warners' 1953 horror classic *House of Wax* was seen again in *Chamber of Horrors* with Cesare Danova and Wayne Rogers.

And Tony Curtis in a cameo, as a gambler playing cards with several beautiful women in a brothel.

That was Jack Warner. Jack Warner's idea was, "I'm taking this crummy little failed television pilot and making a feature out of it." His problem *never* was a loss of ego! The actors who now came in, playing small parts or cameos, were there because they were working on something *else* at Warners. They just strolled through, and they got five grand or they got a car or *some*thing, just for doing two minutes. And the idea was that the audience would go, "Oh my God, that's *Tony Curtis!*," and wild excitement ensues.

[Laughs] But what does "Oh my God, that's Tony Curtis!*" do to the mood and atmosphere you're trying to build up in a horror story?*

This picture was a potpourri. This was a corpse put together from parts of other pictures [*laughs*]! Anything to make it "go." And it *went*! They were *right*! Go figure!

The Fear Flasher and the Horror Horn—why were those put in there?

Somebody had done a movie called *The Tingler* [1959], which included a gimmick whereby a mild electrical shock was wired in some of the seats in the theaters that played it. That produced a certain amount of press, so the idea was to emulate *that*. The Fear Flasher and the Horror Horn was a takeoff on the actual electrical pulse in the theaters, on that other film.

Were they added for Chamber of Horrors *the movie, or would we have seen that in the first episode of* House of Wax *if the series had come to pass?*

Oh, it would have been the show's trademark.

We'd have seen it every week.

Yes. I really resisted that, and I got absolutely nowhere. Finally I said, "Look, let's use it only *in the moment* when something horrible is gonna happen, so the audience is cheated of its vision of the exploding viscera? They see the Fear Flasher instead and it enables them to visualize what's hiding behind that red glowing splash on the screen." They sort of went for that. So, yes, the Fear Flasher and the Horror Horn would have been seen and heard every week. But hopefully done with a little more delicacy … a little *less* delicacy not being *possible*! [Author's note: In the film, the Fear Flasher and Horror Horn ended up *preceding* the "four supreme fright points."]

Kandel today.

Chamber of Horrors was released as a feature, and for some benighted reason it continues to play on the [TV] airwaves—God only knows where, but undoubtedly between two and four A.M. I get residual checks regularly. It's one of my pleasant surprises that there seems to be an infinite human appetite for *schlock* [*laughs*].

What did you think of the thing when you first saw it?

I thought it was a hoot then. It was an off-the-wall idea, *never* to be taken seriously. But I could have lived without the Fear Flasher and the Horror Horn.

And what are you up to these days?

I'm doing relatively little. I have a play that's going to workshop, *if* the gods smile, in another few months—a musical. And I'm writing a little television from time to time. It's always movies of the week because I can't do a series without moving back to L.A. which I'm not gonna do, because my kids are all in the East. Let me tell you a telling anecdote. I'm out in L.A. about two years ago, for a meeting on a movie of the week, and a youngish, early-thirties network executive is late to the meeting. Finally he arrives and he says, "Oh God! Sorry I'm late!," introductions all around, he gets to me, I'm introduced, he *stops* and he says, "Steve Kandel? I thought you were *dead*!"

It broke me up!

Chamber of Horrors
(Warner Bros., 1966)

98 minutes; Released in September 1966; Associate Producer: Jim Barnett; Produced & Directed by Hy Averback; Screenplay: Stephen Kandel; Story: Ray Russell & Stephen Kandel; Photography: Richard Kline (Technicolor); Music: William Lava; Art Director: Art Loel; Editor: David Wages; Sound: M. A. Merrick; Set Decorator: William L. Kuehl; Unit Manager: Sherry Shourds; Makeup Supervisor: Gordon Bau; Supervising Hair Stylist: Jean Burt Reilly; Assistant Director: Sam Schneider

Patrick O'Neal (*Jason Cravette*), Cesare Danova (*Anthony Draco*), Wilfrid Hyde-White (*Harold Blount*), Laura Devon (*Marie Champlain*), Patrice Wymore (*Vivian*), Suzy Parker (*Barbara Dixon*), Tun Tun (*Senor Pepe De Reyes*), Philip Bourneuf (*Insp. Matthew Strudwick*), Jeanette Nolan (*Mrs. Ewing Perryman*), Marie Windsor (*Madame Corona*), Wayne Rogers (*Police Sgt. Tim Albertson*), Vinton Hayworth (*Judge Walter Randolph*), Richard O'Brien (*Dr. Romulus Cobb*), Inger Stratton (*Gloria*), Berry Kroeger (*Chun Sing*), Charles Seel (*Dr. Hopewell*), Ayllene Gibbons (*Victoria*), Stewart Rose (*First Police Officer*), James Drake (*Second Police Officer*), Jack Shea (*Gross*), Jean Carson (*Girl on Street*), Annazette (*Prudence*), Clegg Hoyt (*Bartender [New Orleans]*), Paul Sorenson (*Bartender [Baltimore]*), Barbro Hedstrom (*Florabell*), Robert Goodwin (*Negro Coachman*), Lyle Latell (*Trainman*), Ray Kellogg (*Officer Manton*), Tony Curtis (*Mr. Julian*), Philo McCullough (*Man*), Nedra Rosemond (*Maid*), Cherry Stucker (*Woman*), Harry Ellerbe (*Judge Train*), Ralph Roberts (*Doorman*), Fredd Wayne (*Charles Benton*), Monty Margetts (*Dowager*), Napoleon Whiting (*Servant*), Al McGranary (*Senator Dixon*), Buddy Van Horn, Richard Farnsworth, Michael Lally (*Stunt Doubles*)

Carolyn Kearney

> *All that horrible makeup, making me up as a corpse.*
> *It was just a very terrifying [experience], because*
> *everything was very realistic.*

In the late 1950s, Universal, Hollywood's legendary studio of horrors, seemed to finally begin running out of steam after 30 years of nearly non-stop monster movie production. Among the minor movies found at the tail end of this remarkable run, one stands out as ghoulishly imaginative: 1958's *The Thing That Couldn't Die*, a low-budget chiller combining threads of witchcraft and satanic possession in its far-out story of the disembodied but still-living human head of a fifteenth-century devil worshipper, found buried in a copper box on a modern-day California ranch. Among the innocents upon whom this undying Thing imposes its evil will is Jessica, the forked stick–wielding teenage girl who re-discovered it, played by Carolyn Kearney.

Born in Detroit and raised in New Orleans, Kearney acted on the stage of the Pasadena Playhouse and other theaters prior to her horror debut in *The Thing That Couldn't Die*. In total she made just four features but compensated with many TV roles, from *Playhouse 90* to *Lassie*, and including several of the top anthology horror series of the day: *Alfred Hitchcock Presents*, *The Twilight Zone* and, most memorably, *Thriller*, as the young wife of Dick York, menaced by Boris Karloff and a trio of resuscitated corpses in the chill-bump classic "The Incredible Doktor Markesan."

Twice-married (now to an advertising executive-writer) and eyeing a return to acting, Kearney here recalls severed heads, walking dead men, coffin confinement and other offbeat highlights from her brief but busy Hollywood heyday.

How did you get the co-starring part in The Thing That Couldn't Die?

My agent at that time was William Morris, which was a very big agency. I didn't have *that* many credits, just a *few*, but William Morris took me on, and they asked me to go for a [*Thing That Couldn't Die*] reading at Universal. I said, "Oh, great!" At that time, the picture was called *The Water Witch*. I went over there—I remember sitting at a big desk and doing a reading for the four or five men who were also sitting around this desk. The producer-director Will Cowan was one of them. I read for the part of the "sweet" Jessica, Jessica as she is at the beginning of the picture. Then of course, later in the picture, once she falls under the spell of the disembodied head, she turns into that wild kind of person. After I read for the "sweet" Jessica, one of the gentlemen asked, "Now can you be a *mean* Jessica?" I said, "Well, just a minute." I went into a tiny little ladies' room and I changed my hair—I wet it all up and pulled it back, and when I came out, I looked sort of maybe a *little* seductive, a *little* wild and a *little* weird. One of the gentlemen, I think it was Will Cowan, said, "You've got the part"—I got it right there on the spot. I was dating a writer-producer named Harold Jack Bloom at the time, and he thought it was a good thing to do.

What memories of your castmates?
　　The gentleman who played the head in it, oh, what a wonderful actor. An extraordinary English actor who's since died, Robin Hughes. He was just very "true," he was very honest with his acting, and he *listened* to the other actors—he was, as I am, a listening actor. Because if you can't listen, how can you react? He did Shakespeare—at the drop of a hat, he would go and do *Hamlet* or *Richard III*. He loved to entertain between takes so he would go into his characters, into different soliloquies that he remembered from the different stage plays that he did. He was a truly brilliant actor and he should have gone much further than he did. He passed away about ten years ago, 15 years ago.

When he was doing Shakespeare, was he in his horror makeup?
　　[*Laughs*] Yes! You have to picture him with the horror makeup doing Macbeth and the other Shakespearean characters that he was brilliant at! [Co-star] Andra Martin was great, I liked her. She married Ty Hardin, and divorced him, and then she married the gentleman who owned the May Company, the big store here in Los Angeles. She married him and then divorced him as well! The man who played my boyfriend, William Reynolds, he was fine, a very upstanding and very stable actor. I liked him, too.

Nineteen fifty-eight was bad times for Universal, not much production going on. Does this ring a bell?
　　There really *wasn't* a lot going on around there, '58, '59. There were *some* movies being made, but not a lot. My gosh, nowadays it's *so* busy, with the tour and all of that. It's just an extraordinary place to go now.

As you mentioned, for most of the movie you played Jessica as sweet, almost child-like. But also emotional and angry a time or two.
　　I remember reading the script three or four times, and beginning to understand the simplicity of this young girl, and the *fear* that she had. I think she didn't trust men at *all* once she began to think about them, and think about how they could hurt her. When she was thinking simple and direct and honest, everything was fine.

The minute that fear came in, then she had to protect herself by acting a certain way, which was mean and hostile. But, really, she was not. She simply wasn't very stable in her feelings.

I couldn't help but notice what a small waist you had in that movie.

Yes—*thank* you [*laughs*]! It must have been about 23 inches. Edith Head once said to me, "Carolyn, you have a *very* small waistline." And *she* was a tiny lady, she was like five foot.

During production, the title was The Water Witch *and so you were playing the title character. Were you disappointed in the title change to* Thing That Couldn't Die?

I wasn't disappointed, not really. Because it really didn't change my part. Oh, another thing I remember is walking up and down all those hills [dowsing]—my feet were so hot! Oh, God! But, boy, when you're [a beginning actress], if you're told to walk up a *volcano*, you're gonna do it [*laughs*]! Me, anyway, *I* would do it. I would do it *today* if I could! Except I don't think I *could* walk up a volcano any more!

The Thing That Couldn't Die featured Carolyn Kearney as a "water witch" whose supernatural dowsing abilities lead her to the titular, long-buried Thing.

What do you remember about the scenes with the disembodied head?

In one scene, Andra's character asks me to open a hatbox on a bed—I open it, and that's when I see the head for the first time. And Robin Hughes was actually under the bed, and his head up through the bed and *in* the box. Will Cowan the director didn't tell me that, because he wanted to get my reaction. He wanted me to react to seeing this horrible head looking up at me from the box. Of course, the reaction *was* very honest and believable, because it scared me! There was no acting there!

They were able to keep from you the fact that he was under the bed?

Exactly! Then when I looked, it was very scary. Of course, at the end of the picture when I was walking around carrying his head in my hands, it was a prop made of some soft material—very icky! But I had to do it. It gave me a really ... *strange* feeling. When the headless body stood up in the coffin, the guy was wearing an outfit that went up over his head and covered his head. The shoulders and neck of the outfit came up over his head.

Do you recall seeing the movie for the first time?

It was a preview or a premiere on Hollywood Boulevard, in an old movie theater that's still there. I think it was playing alone—I don't know *why*, because this was not a major movie [*laughs*]! It was so ... *different*. I guess we didn't use the word "campy" then, but maybe we did. It was so ... kind of ... ludicrous. At the time we made it, I believed it—I couldn't have done it if I didn't believe *in* it. Now, looking back, it's funny in many ways. But also good.

What was the audience reaction?

There were a lot of gasps. Harold Jack Bloom, who I later married, took me to it, and he was just so proud of me. He sat there with his arm over my shoulder, and *he* liked it. And he was hard to please—very, *very* hard to please!

Kearney restores the devil worshipper's head to his body in *The Thing That Couldn't Die*'s horror highlight. (Photofest)

In Universal publicity, they made out that they discovered you—they said you were a student in New Orleans when they went there in 1957 to shoot Damn Citizen, *and they gave you a part in the movie. But you were in Hollywood for at least a couple years already by 1957.*

The real skinny of it is that I came to Pasadena Playhouse in 1954 or '55 to go to the College of Theater Arts, Pasadena Playhouse. I studied there, I was in a class with Dustin Hoffman and Gene Hackman and some marvelous actors—they were actually a little ahead of me. It was a wonderful school. I went there and I studied, and I got on the Main Stage. The first one was *Man on a Stick*, which was with Stuart Erwin ... the second one I believe was Maxwell Anderson's *Winterset* ... I worked with Edward Everett Horton in a play called *The White Sheep of the Family*. I was the "white sheep of the family"—the only cat burglar in the family [*laughs*]! Have you ever heard of Gilmor Brown, who founded the Pasadena Playhouse in 1909? He was an extraordinary director and a humanitarian, and he also cast me in an "in-house" movie, a movie about a young girl, me, going to the Pasadena Playhouse. It was really terrific and it was "good film" on *me* when I was very young, 19 or 20. Gilmor Brown wanted to show off the Pasadena Playhouse, not show *me* off, but I was *in* it, it focused on me, a young person going into his Playhouse and going to classes and getting on Main Stage. [Author's note: In 2004, Kearney was named Woman of the Year by the Pasadena Playhouse Alumni Association.]

THE GRAVE CAN'T HOLD IT
...nothing human can stop it!
...it rose from the crypt to slake its monstrous thirst for beauty...*and the power to rule the earth!*

THE THING THAT COULDN'T DIE

WILLIAM REYNOLDS · ANDRA MARTIN · CAROLYN KEARNEY · JEFFREY STONE

"For a while I was afraid it was going to be the thing that wouldn't end." — *The Los Angeles Times* reviewer.

During your early days in Hollywood, where were you living?
 My mother didn't want me to stay in Los Angeles–Hollywood by myself, she was very, very worried about me. The only way I *could* stay here was if I lived at the Studio Club [a rooming house for young actresses], a big, big building on Lodi Place. Now, you couldn't get a room at the Studio Club unless you had a job in the movies. So I got a wonderful part in *The George Burns and Gracie Allen Show*, their television show. It was really great, I got a recurring part as their son Ronnie's girlfriend and then I got the room at the Studio Club. This was the beautiful part: It was very inexpensive to live there. At the Studio Club, it was 27.50 a week. *With* that, you would get a room, maid service, your linens changed every week, and you would get breakfast — no lunch — and dinner. Two meals a day, beautiful meals. And all for 27.50 a *week*. That was really extraordinary! My room, Kim Novak had stayed there a few years before. Ruth Buzzi taught me how to cook Italian — she was a wonderful cook.

And then movie parts started coming along, like Hot Rod Girl *[1956] and* Damn Citizen.
 In the interview for *Damn Citizen*, they asked, "Where are you from?," and I

said, "New Orleans." "Oh!," they said, "this movie is going to be *done* in New Orleans." But by this time I had lost my [Southern] accent, 'cause I had played all kinds of stage roles. I got wonderful work at the LaJolla Playhouse as well, playing an English girl in Graham Greene's *Potting Shed* with Gladys Cooper, Cecil Kellaway and Leo G. Carroll.

Jeez, them, *Edward Everett Horton, Stu Erwin—you kept getting cast opposite the oldest people on Earth, didn't you?*
   [*Laughs*] Yes! But, you know what?, I learned so much as a very young girl, I was like a sponge. I had to change my accent to an English accent for *Potting Shed*— *every*body was from England except *me*, I was the only American. I think of *Bridget Jones's Diary* [2001] with Renee Zellweger, because *she* had to play an English girl amidst all those English actors. *Me* when I was very young at the LaJolla Playhouse, I also had to become English.

Then after that you did Damn Citizen.
   And for *that*, I had to get my *Southern* accent back [*laughs*]. They flew me and the whole cast to New Orleans, and I was desperately afraid to fly—ooh, I was so afraid. But I knew I *had* to do it, it was a *job*. I got over it, and I went there, and I did the part. I played the part of a young drug addict—a drug addict *prostitute*!

How did you know how to play a drug addict? I'd like to think you'd had no real-life experience with drug addicts!
   Not at that time, I didn't. For *Damn Citizen*, I went and read a lot about it and I researched—she was a heroin addict. They had to put all the little dots on my arm with makeup. And I thought very sad thoughts, because I always like to work from the inside *out* and to think about it and to understand the character. I truly thought heartfelt thoughts, thinking what the person must have gone through before she would become a drug addict. When I was in New Orleans doing *Damn Citizen*, I got the key to the city. They gave me that and they also gave me a wonderful plaque, 'cause I was raised in New Orleans and they thought it was really neat that a person would come back and make a movie there. It was a thrill. It was beautiful to go back to the city where I was raised and to have that experience.
   Then I came back to Los Angeles and I was dating Harold Jack Bloom. He was a producer and writer, he was nominated for an Academy Award for *The Naked Spur* [1953], and he did *Dragnet*s and, oh gosh, he did a lot of things. I ended up marrying him, a lovely man. He just passed away.

Are you a widow now, or did you divorce him?
   We were divorced but he remained a friend of mine throughout my whole life. We had a son together, Charles Bloom, who's now living in New York, a composer and a writer of musicals. Harold and I were married for several years, and then we went to live in Europe when he was doing some movies there. Just a lovely man, a wonderful man...

You're making him sound like the nicest guy you ever divorced!

[*Laughs*] I *know*—that's exactly right! But at least we remained friends, there was never any animosity. It just didn't work out: I was quite young and he was a lot older, and he had *never* been married. But we had a wonderful son together, and that's so important.

You also worked in TV—in fact, you worked a lot more in TV than you did in movies.

Oh, *so* much TV, including *Playhouse 90* and a whole bunch of *Matinee Theater*s. I was fortunate enough to be in *all* of those [kinds of series] in "the golden years of television." They were three-camera shows, and oh my God it was really hard, because you'd fall over the cables and everything [*laughs*]! But you had to *do* it! Being on *Playhouse 90*, *Matinee Theater*, it was just like being on the stage.

One of Kearney's earliest film credits was an "in-house" Pasadena Playhouse production which followed her through her dramatic studies there.

I asked you about your movie Young and Wild *[1958] the first time we talked and you said that was fun to do. That was the last word I expected to come out of your mouth, because I think the movie's almost...*

Mean. It wasn't really fun to do—I don't know why I said that it was. It *wasn't* fun to do, because I was injured in that. Scott Marlowe [the main juvenile delinquent-villain]—oh, he just threw me around. There were three fellows ganging up on me, Scott Marlowe and his two cronies. Thank God I lived through it! I remember going home and having black and blue marks ... oh, God. I don't remember totally the text of the movie, but I remember they terrorize me throughout. In the scene at the end where they're pushing me around in a cabin—I hated that, I hated it, I hated it! And I *was* scared of these guys, I was so scared of 'em, I didn't want to talk to 'em. In the breaks between shooting the scenes, I remember staying pretty much to myself because they were *always* very terrorizing and angry.

They stayed in character?

Yes, they did. Consequently, I didn't want to have very much to do with them, other than when I was doing the work. Ooh, they were just very "into their parts."

On TV, you were on Alfred Hitchcock Presents, *in an episode called "You Can't Be a Little Girl All Your Life."*

Oh, that was good, wasn't it? That was with Dick York, and I later did a *Thriller* with Dick York too. He was just an extraordinary actor. Alfred Hitchcock himself was on the set—I remember that very clearly. He didn't like my hair *this* way and he didn't like my hair *that* way—oh, he was so specific about different things that he liked and he didn't like. He was a very hands-on director, even with the television show.

He didn't direct that episode, though.

No, he didn't direct it, Norman Lloyd did, the actor-director. Incidentally, there's a book out by Stephen Rebello, *Alfred Hitchcock and the Making of "Psycho,"* and if you turn to page 62, it says I was considered [for the role of Lila] in *Psycho*! "Actress Carolyn Kearney, a 'Doris Day lookalike,' had caught the director's eye while playing in a *Playhouse 90* drama. Instead of newcomer Kearney, however, Hitchcock cast 29-year-old, Oklahoma-born Vera Miles." That's in that book. Isn't that exciting?

When did you first find out that you were up for a part in Psycho? *When that book came out?*

I dimly remember my agent mentioned *some*thing, that Alfred Hitchcock was interested in me for that particular part in *Psycho*. And then, of course, Vera Miles got it. As I told you, when I did my *Alfred Hitchcock Presents*, Hitchcock was on the set a *lot* and discussed things with Mr. Lloyd. I called them "Mr. Lloyd" and "Mr. Hitchcock"—I remember *always* as an actress I would call people Mr. or Mrs. That was very important to me. In New Orleans, we were always taught to call people Mr. and Mrs. When I was dating my future husband Harold Jack Bloom, I was *dating* him and at *dinner* with him, and I would say, "Mr. Bloom, would you please pass the salt?" [*Laughs*] It's *true*, Tom! That came so natural to me, because I went to Catholic school and all that business. I was taught to do that and I *did* it.

And did Hitchcock talk to you about your hair, or to the hairdresser?

He talked directly to me. [*Sighs*] It would have been wonderful to have been in *Psycho*. But I missed that.

You were also in one of the best episodes of Thriller, *"The Incredible Doktor Markesan."*

Thriller was unbelievable. With Boris Karloff, and all those very strange gentlemen [the reanimated corpses]! I read the script, and—my gosh, the idea of working with Mr. Karloff...! One thing I vividly remember: In the script, the *husband* was going to be in the coffin for the last shot of the episode. Dick York, *he* was supposed to be in the coffin.

And you would have been the one to find the coffin and see him sitting up in it.

Exactly. But at the table reading for it, they changed it to the wife—they were saying that *I* had to be in the coffin. Do you know what table readings are? We had table readings on many of the shows I did, *Dr. Kildare*, *Bonanza*, *all* the shows that were worth their salt have table readings, 'cause the table readings are what gives you the foundation, the feeling that you'll be able to do the show. Everybody in the cast goes to the studio in the morning and each actor has a copy of the script. We're meeting together for the first time, usually on a sound stage that has no sets, it's just chairs and a table. No makeup, no hair, no nothing. And then you read from the script, all the way through—no analyzing, no asking questions, no *anything*, just reading the lines. From page one right to the end. Then we'd read it through a second time, and that's when the director would come in and give different directions. Then the third time, generally, *we* could ask questions, "Do you think she would do it this way?" and "May I try this?" and so on. Three times in one day. The next day we would get our blocking. We were on our feet with the scripts, on the sets, and the director gave us our blocking. The third day, we did it for the camera.

Anyway, they told me at the table reading for *Thriller* that the script had been changed and it was now my character, the wife, who was going to be in the coffin. I'm a person who says, "The show's got to go on!" in my head, and in my heart, but … getting in a *coffin*? I said, "Gee, when I got this script, it was the *man* that was in the coffin." They said, "Yeah, we decided to change it." I said, "Could you *please* put some holes in that coffin? Because when that lid comes down, it'll be terribly scary, I would *think*"—I was thinking ahead. And they said, "Are you kidding? That coffin is $1800—we're not gonna ruin it!" [*Laughs*] I thought, "Oh, God…" I asked, "Well, how can you get that coffin lid off of me quickly? I don't like the idea of being in it." They said, "We'll put a string on the coffin, and the minute it closes, *then* we'll pull it up." Of course, when we did the shot, the string broke! Oh, God, it was so horrible! But then the people came and got it off of me.

Plus you wore a lot of makeup in that shot, to make you look dead.

Yes, all that horrible makeup, making me up as a corpse. It was just a very terrifying [experience], because everything was very realistic. Oh, *every*thing was—I can remember it to this day. I remember Dick York and I walking down that hallway, and they had cobwebs and all kinds of things. The sets were filthy and dirty, and ratty, and just really, really awful … ugh!

My mother was visiting from New Orleans, and she came on the set the day I did the scene in the coffin. And she *fainted*. That poor lady! She just couldn't believe it. I didn't get to [warn] her, 'cause they weren't supposed to do that scene that day. But then they changed things around and *did* want to do that scene, and my mom saw me in there and she just completely fainted. On the floor! "Mom, Mom! What's the *matter*?" It was very, very real, and very creepy. It was a scary television show to do.

What was Karloff like?

Oh, gosh! I'd have breakfast with Mr. Karloff and his wife every morning. *Every* morning he invited me to have breakfast with them in his limousine, and I just couldn't believe it. He would have tea, I remember. Oh, what a gentleman—just exactly the opposite of what you'd expect from the person who played the Frankenstein Monster and all those other horror parts. He was *so* lovely to his wife and he would take his wife's hand and help her out of the limousine. Of course, he wasn't a young man when he did *that*.

It was the best of times (working with her horror hero Boris Karloff), it was the worst of times (claustrophobic Kearney had to be sealed in a coffin): *Thriller*'s "The Incredible Doktor Markesan."

I would have thought she'd be helping him *out of the car by that point!*

[*Laughs*] That's right! But he was just so gracious and attentive and loving to her. And as an actor, when you would get on the set, he really knew his p's and q's, he just really knew his spots. And, the old saying *is* true, you're only as good as the actors you work with. I've been very fortunate working with [good] actors. Remember *Ben Casey*? I had some terrible experiences with him, the gentleman who played Ben Casey.

*Vince Edwards. I never hear any*thing *good about him.*
 Oh, you don't? Oh, he was totally ungracious and totally unprofessional, in my view. Whereas Mr. Karloff was just totally professional: He knew everything he had to do, he knew what *you* had to do, he knew the *lighting*, he knew if the makeup wasn't the way he felt that it should be. He was the master of horror. I learned so much about terror doing that film, I can't *tell* you how much I learned. When I wasn't working, I would stand on the sidelines watching him, just watching "the craft." Everything was so spontaneous-*looking*, because he had crafted so much of it before he did it. I'd be sitting behind the camera, or standing behind the camera, or sitting or standing in the corner, just to watch true genius at work. And I learned a lot. He should have never died. He was one of the people I felt ought to have gone on and on and on and on. I guess maybe he's doing the same thing up in Heaven, who knows? I believe that!

And you rode to work with him in a limousine and had breakfast during the ride?
 Oh, no, no. To get to the studio, I drove myself, I didn't get to go in the limousine. (It would have been *nice*, but I didn't!) I would drive myself, and then when I was there, in my dressing room, he would say, "Miss Kearney ... would you like to have tea?" "Oh!" I said—and then I couldn't talk any more! I'd mumble out an "Excuse me...?," and he would say again, "Would you like to have tea?" And we would have tea and scones in his limousine, *with* his wife.

He would go sit in his limousine to have breakfast?
 Yes, in the limousine, which was on the sound stage. I was, like, so overwhelmed. He was so lovely and nice and kind, and his wife was so sweet too. They were "up in years" then, as some older people say!

Why would anybody get into a car to have breakfast?
 I don't know but he did. I can't imagine why. That *was* weird! But it was charming and I just couldn't believe it, because I remembered the movie *Frankenstein* [1931] and the Monster and the little girl and them throwing the flower petals in the lake, and then the Monster throwing *her* in the lake! We *all* have that memory of Boris Karloff playing Frankenstein, right? Just the most extraordinary Frankenstein! And now here I was having tea and scones with Mr. Boris Karloff!

Do you know who co-wrote Frankenstein *and was originally supposed to direct it? Robert Florey, your director on that* Thriller.
 Robert Florey, *oh*!, he was a master. We don't *have* those people any more—darn! He and Boris Karloff would talk to each other, quietly, and then come very prepared on the set. They seemed to get along, they were very fine technicians.

Did Florey work with the actors much?

Yes, he took time to work with each actor. Robert Florey was the kind of director who truly wanted to take time, and he did especially working with Boris Karloff. And remember the corpses? Oh, gosh, each one of those gentlemen [Richard Hale, Basil Howes, Billy Beck] had like a hundred years of experience, it seemed [*laughs*]!

It must have been creepy, even between *takes, having those guys underfoot all day.*

Yeah, it was creepy, because they of course stayed in costume. Once you get there at five o'clock in the morning and get your makeup and your costume, it's really too hard to take it off. So you keep it *on* until just before you go home at night. I remember at lunchtime they could open their mouths just a teeny, teeny bit [to eat]. Or drink a milkshake or something through a straw. I don't know if they were movie actors or theater actors, but they too were total craftsmen and total professionals. What a wonderful experience I had on that. I was thrilled to be on *Thriller*!

And another "fantastic TV" credit, Twilight Zone's *"Ninety Years Without Slumbering."*

Yes, with Mr. Ed Wynn, who was quite elderly then. You're right, I did work with a lot of older people [*laughs*]!

You're still *younger now than all those guys were back then!*

I played a pregnant girl in that, his granddaughter. In the story, Ed Wynn was an old clockmaker who thought that, the minute that his grandfather clock stopped, he was going to die. Many of us have in our lives something a little *like* that. I have a ring that's like 105 years old, a beautiful ring from Cuba. My grandmother gave it to me, and I always think of it as something that brings me good fortune. And so *this* gentleman, Ed Wynn, thought the grandfather clock was his lifeline, and if *that* would run down and stop, he would die. By the way, Ed Wynn being up in years at the time, when he had to go up and down the stairs [on the set], I had to help him.

You're not talking story-wise, you mean you actually had to help him.

Right, because he was having trouble. He would lean on me, and then he would say, "Oh, but you're pregnant! I don't want to hurt you." I said, "But Mr. Wynn, I'm really *not* pregnant, I'm *playing* pregnant. You can lean on me any time you want to!" "Oh, that's right, that's right!"—he laughed, he *liked* that. I just had a big ol' pad in my tummy, to make me look pregnant. I had actually just *had* a baby, so I knew how it felt!

So I do remember he had a hard time going up and down the stairs, up and down the stairs. The director [Roger Kay] had him do it quite often, and he was getting very winded, and I said, "Well, let's take a little time out and take a breath," and so we did. I remember that he was very eager—he *had* to be pushing 80, but he was eager and he was interested. I think that's what kept him going, his eagerness and his interest.

Did you get to meet Rod Serling when you did Twilight Zone?

Rod Serling *was* on the set, 'cause he was also the producer. He was there and he was very protective of Ed Wynn. He wanted to make sure that Ed Wynn had his chair and he wanted to make sure that Ed Wynn was well taken care of and that they didn't work him too hard. Roger Kay didn't do any of that, but Rod Serling was very instrumental in making sure that he was well taken of. Roger Kay was a little frenetic, and not taking the time that Robert Florey [on *Thriller*] and some of the other directors did. Roger Kay was sort of "rushed," and you can't do anything good if you rush.

Keenan Wynn, Ed Wynn's son, was also there to support his dad. I think he was worried about his father, because his father was in ill health, and Keenan Wynn was like, "Now, Dad, I'm gonna be right here…" Remember the scene where Ed Wynn's character dies, and you see his spirit rise up from his body, and then there are two Ed Wynns, the spirit and the body, having a conversation? On the set, Keenan Wynn was actually the person that Ed Wynn was speaking to in the scenes where [in the finished episode] Ed Wynn was talking to "himself." Keenan Wynn came in and did that. It was great to see father and son working back and forth and back and forth. *Twilight Zone*, my main memory about that show is that I just so enjoyed doing it.

You kinda lucked out. Not a lot of the actors appearing on Alfred Hitchcock Presents *got to meet Hitchcock, not a lot of the actors on* Thriller *met Boris Karloff, and not a lot of the actors on* Twilight Zone *met Rod Serling—but you met all three of 'em!*

I met all three of them! I was fortunate, you're right—*very*, very fortunate. Not everybody got to meet those people because they were often just the hosts. I'd also met Rod Serling when I did a *Desilu Playhouse* called "The Time Element" [a 1958 time-travel fantasy scripted by Serling]. William Bendix had the lead, and I remember he was very "ready"—he had all his lines learned! And Jesse White was always joking around and being very funny. Rod Serling was on the set all the time—I don't know why, but he was there.

In recent years, you've helped form a group called Benzodiazepine Anonymous.

Yes, with a psychiatrist named Dr. Ronald G. At one time, I was addicted to Xanax and nearly lost everything. I started taking the drug after becoming extremely claustrophobic as a result of being trapped in my room on a train, in a train accident on my way east. I went to a doctor, and he said, "Oh, take Xanax. It's not addictive." And as you've read in all of the papers and see on television, it's actually *very* addictive! There are many doctors who are *wonderful*, and there are also many doctors who give these pills out like they're candy. And they can not only cause physical damage, they can affect your mind, your judgment. They affected my mind and my emotional well-being. I was addicted to *that* for about two and a half years. I'll send you a copy of the book *Prescription Drug Addiction*, in which I wrote an essay for the chapter "Voices of Recovery" and tell my story.

A founder of Benzodiazepine Anonymous, a 12-step program for recovering addicts, Kearney—seen here with husband Alan Hirshfeld, wearing glasses, and sons Charles Bloom (left) and Tom Hirshfeld (right)—is hoping to juggle her BA work and a return to acting.

And an attack of claustrophobia started all this? I guess you were *the wrong person to ask to get into that coffin on* Thriller*!*

[*Laughs*] You're right! The train incident was how I got addicted to Xanax. This dependency took away my dreams and my belief in myself. My therapist and psychiatrist seemed uneducated about the dangers of this drug and they said I'd have no trouble getting off it. I entered a treatment center in August 1987 and my stay was 40 days. My "birthday" is September 15, 1987—that's my "recovering birthday," my "sobriety birthday." I made 15 years in August 2002.

In 1989, in L.A., I co-founded Benzodiazepine Anonymous, a 12-step group for those recovering from addiction to benzodiazepines. We have speakers, doctors and psychiatrists and recovering people, come to speak. It's *very* much like AA, because AA was founded by a doctor and a lay person, and BA was founded by a psychiatrist, Dr. Ronald G., and a lay person, me. I worked with this marvelous psychiatrist for seven years and wrote the steps and the goals and the code of ethics and principles. I started it all over the country, it's really helping a lot of people and it helps *me* on a weekly basis. I'm so proud of the work that I do. And I also want to return to acting—I do *so* want to return.

If you had to choose between continuing on with Benzodiazepine Anonymous and resuming an acting career, what would you do?

I wouldn't choose, I would do them both.

[Laughs] That's cheating! You have to pick!

I would do them both because I *can* do them both. I'm still young enough to do them both, I still have the energy to do them both. Hundreds of people [in the Benzodiazepine Anonymous program] depend on me, and I surely wouldn't want to give it up.

Ken Kolb

A giant roc is bad enough but, no, it's gotta have two heads!

Plumas National Forest, California. Meadows. Stands of conifers. Sparkling lakes. The twitter of birds. Five hundred forty miles from the fleshpots of Hollywood geographically, but *worlds* away by any other sort of reckoning. Just don't tell the chipmunks that they've got a little bit of Hollywood right there in their sylvan midst.

Ken Kolb called this area home for 23 of the 25 years that he wrote for television. His job entailed making the commute to LaLaLand innumerable times but he did it with nary a chirp of complaint because he loves the surrounding million-plus acres of National Forest as much as he "*haaated* L.A." Not surprisingly, it's still his home decades after his retirement. And today in his country-style home overlooking a mountain valley (and about 40 head of cattle), he takes a long look at his short but nevertheless impressive list of genre credits: In 1957 he wrote the mythological monster adventure *The 7th Voyage of Sinbad* and, almost a decade later, some of the best early episodes of TV's one-of-a-kind Western adventure-SF-fantasy *The Wild Wild West*.

A native of Portland, Oregon, Kolb was a skin magazine scribe and a forest fire lookout in the early 1950s when he got the unexpected opportunity to "go Hollywood" and do some writing for the TV series *Medic*. Doubtless setting some sort of record, he arrived in town, worked on his first *Medic* script that same day and saw it go into production just hours later! A Writers Guild Award winner for one of his subsequent *Medic* teleplays, Kolb got the job of scripting *Sinbad* through its producer Charles Schneer, and cooked up fantastic perils for Secret Service sleuths Jim West and Artemus Gordon (Robert Conrad and Ross Martin) at the invitation of *Wild West* creator Michael Garrison. In addition to his scores of teleplays (*Dragnet*, *Have Gun—Will Travel*, *Ben Casey*, *Honey West*, *Hawaii Five-O*, more), he is also the author of the novels *Getting Straight* and *The Couch Trip*.

Did you grow up in Northern California?

No, for my first 18 years, I was in a rain-induced coma in Portland, Oregon [*laughs*]. Somehow while in this state, I managed to go through grade school and high school. World War II was still in a very active stage when I got out of high school. A Navy recruiter came around and selected the best and brightest of us to take a test, to see if we could become radar technicians; I was one of the four who passed. So I became a sailor, a Navy radar technician second class, and went to sea on the USS *Sicily*, which was a CVE 118. An escort carrier, 550 feet long, very tough for planes to land on—I think we lost six planes over the side. It's hard to land on those things when they're moving up and down in a heavy sea! I did not see action except the endless war between the officers and enlisted men. And I was on the losing side [*laughs*]! But us radar techs knew things the officers didn't know, so they could not impose really obscene duties on us, like getting up and standing watch at midnight.

I got through two years of the Navy, as a radar technician, and I realized that, *as* a radar technician, I would *always* be second class. There were guys there who had more knowledge of electronics, and more feeling for it, in their screwdriver hands than I had in my *head. They* would read the instruction manuals for entertainment. I would be reading Jane Austen [*laughs*]. When the gear broke, *I* would be the one who went and got the instruction manual and started looking for the symptoms in it, and *they* would have the back off the gear and have it fixed. So instead of being an electronics engineer, I went to Berkeley on my G.I. Bill as an English major. What I loved to do was read and write, so I thought, "Well, I'll read and write for a living." Sure enough, that's the way it turned out. I met a cute little kappa delta at Berkeley—I met her in my freshman year, she was my roommate's date. In our sophomore year, she was *my* date. Emmy and I were married 50 years the other day. And we still like each other!

After I got out of college, I was makin' a meager living writing magazine stories for the T&A magazines—*Playboy, Penthouse, Adam, Cavalier, Esquire*. Emmy was a registered nurse, and she was able to support us during my thin times. We also did a couple of seasons as forest fire lookouts, up here in the Plumas National Forest—a really formative experience. We liked it so much the first year that we did it a second year, and then came down with her eight months pregnant and me with no visible means of support. At that point, I went to a cocktail party with an old fraternity brother who had been working while we had been hanging around at the lower rungs of the economic ladder. (I just never wanted to have a steady job, I wanted to be a freelance writer.) Anyway, I went to this party, and there was a guy there who was name-dropping. He said, "I just got back from Hollywood, and my buddy Jim Moser is desperate for a writer down there. I hear you're a writer."

And that's how you got your foot in the door in Hollywood?

That's right, I called Jim Moser. San Francisco was Jim's home town and he had a nostalgia, a soft spot for it—and that's where I was calling from. Jim was desperate for a writer for a TV show he had originated, *Medic* with Richard Boone as "Conrad Steiner, Doctor of Medicine." He said, "Tell you what: Why don't you risk 25 bucks? That's the price of a round trip plane ticket. Come on down and talk to me." So I went down and I talked to him for about an hour, and by midnight I was in an adjoining office working on a [*Medic*] script that was gonna be shot in the morning. And we got it done.

You were diddling with an existing script, or you started one from scratch?

We were diddling with an existing script. Jim was a little on the stressed side by then. He was kinda living on dexies and alcohol, and had difficulty really focusing on what the problems might be. *I* was fresh and I could see 'em. So I read a script that they were comin' to shoot in the morning and I worked on it until ... well, probably until around one o'clock, at which point Jim came in and said, "Hey, the Formosa's gonna close in an hour"—that was the bar right next to the studio there. He said, "We gotta put some *gas* in the tank!" So we went next door and put a *lot* of gas in the tank [*laughs*]—J&B Scotch was his weapon of choice in those days. Then we came back and took a couple more dexies and went to work on the scenes, and by morning he had a shootable script. Which was good, 'cause they were coming to *shoot* it [*laughs*]. So I had a job. Then my son was born, needing a herniotomy, and sure enough I wrote another script and paid for the hernia operation, and I wrote a third script ... and suddenly I had a job writing scripts on *Medic*.

You had a job on Medic, *but you lived hundreds of miles north.*

Exactly. Jim Moser said, "Listen, this is too awkward, you goin' back and forth. I'll give you a contract for *ten* next season, if you'll move down here. It would be good if we could help each other on the writing." As I told you, he was stressed out, he was doin' an awful lot himself and living partly on alcohol and partly on speed. He needed some help and I'm that kind of guy—I knew my way around the alcohol and speed departments! So Emmy and I packed up our three-month-old child and moved to Los Angeles, where I found us a little place. The movers unloaded everything we owned, and the baby cried, and the man came and connected the phone, and Jim called me up and told me the show was cancelled [*laughs*]!

By that time, incidentally, I had acquired a crooked agent named Murray Rosen, whom I can easily call a crooked agent because he's dead and would otherwise sue me. I've never met anyone who knew Murray who didn't say, "Did *you* know Murray? How much did he *get* you for?" [*Laughs*] He was a genius at that. He found me working in the back office at the *Medic* plant and asked me who my agent was. When I said, "I just got here," he said, "*I'm* your

Even in his TV-writing prime, nature lover Ken Kolb says he could only bear Los Angeles for about four days before beginning to get "the horrors!"

agent. How much are you getting for this? I will get you *more*." And, sure enough, he was the one who had negotiated the deal for ten.

Anyway, I had a crooked agent who was not unwilling to lie about my paucity of credits. (I had three credits on a dead show, which is like having measles, mumps and whooping cough!) He called me up one morning and asked, "Do you know Charlie Schneer?" I said I'd never heard of him. He said, "Well, he produced a picture, *It Came from Beneath the Sea* [1955], and now he's gonna make a new picture—" I interrupted, "Murray. Gimme a *break*. I wrote *Medic*. I write docu-dramas." He said, "Wellll, come on down and meet him, and we'll just tell him you're too busy. Maybe someday he'll want to make a *good* picture. Get to know him." So I went to Columbia, the big office building on Sunset and Gower, and met Charles Schneer and shook hands and "How do you do, Mr. Schneer?" An unexceptional-looking man. Slightly shorter than I am, and I would call myself of medium height. A suit, a tie. *No* giant cigar, none of the props of the idiot producer at all. But a very sharp look behind the horn rims.

Did you know at that point that he was looking for somebody to write a Sinbad picture?
No, I didn't know 'til I got there. Incidentally, I don't know what Murray told Charlie my credits were—he probably fabricated some other credits for me. Murray was much more comfortable lying than telling the truth [*laughs*]! But Charles was not a dummy, he knew I had very *few* credits. Charlie kind of looked at me and then said to Murray, "So ... what do you think he's *worth*?" I said, "I just came to say I'm very sorry, I'm too busy at the present time. I hope that we can get together on another occasion," and I went for the door. But by that time, Murray and Charlie were in negotiations [*laughs*]. Murray was on the edge of the desk, and he had a-hold of Charlie's sleeve, and Charlie was saying, "I can't put him on week to week, he might not pee a drop for weeks." Murray said, "So make us a flat deal," meaning you get paid [a set price] for a treatment no matter how long it takes. Charlie said, "The guy's a nobody, he's a nobody!" Murray said, "If he was *some*body, you couldn't afford him, Charlie. He's a genius, he got a Writers Guild Award." I guess Charlie had heard about that, and saw a chance to pick a green grape here. A guy with no earning capacity, but great genius [*laughs*]. I said, "I'm sorry, I'll see you later," and I went out and sat in Murray's convertible with the top down, in the sun, on a smoggy, hot summer day for about 10, 15 minutes—it *seemed* forever. Just looking up and down Gower Street and *not* seeing a bar sign *any*where [*laughs*]! Finally Murray came bustling out of the building and he said, "How long would it take you to write, let's say, a 35-page treatment?" My private thought was, "About three days"—I usually write ten pages or so a day. But I said, "Oh, I dunno ... I could do it in a week." Murray said, "I can get you 1500. But take at least *three* weeks—Charlie doesn't like to think he's payin' more than 500 a week!" Well, that was 1500 more than I *had*. That was when our rent was $150 for the month, and so that was going to be better than the baby and the wife and me being out in the street. By *far*. Also, this was toward the end of that year's TV season, there wasn't much doin' in television land. We had no visible means of support and, God, we were trapped in L.A., which is *bad* for two San Franciscans! So I said, "Okay, how can it hurt?," and sud-

The 7th Voyage of Sinbad would be a financial success, writer Ken Kolb felt—but he wasn't especially sure he would enjoy *seeing* it.

denly I had a gig to write a 35-page treatment, a story outline for an untitled movie based on the public domain figure Sinbad. Charlie was great for public domain [*laughs*]!

I took three weeks. I had a treatment written at the end of the *first* week, and then I read an old stack of *Saturday Review of Literature*s left by the previous prisoner in that office at Columbia. And I was delighted to be paid 500 a week to sit in that air-conditioned office, and have a toke now and then, and blow it up the message tube. (The windows were high-up and hermetically sealed.) Anyway, Charlie loved the treatment and then we had the same kind of salary discussion and Murray asked me, "How long will it take ya?" [to write a screenplay] and I told him some lie and he said, "I'll see what I can do." I ended up writing treatment, first draft and second draft and one polish, the whole thing took 11 weeks, and I got $5500 altogether. $500 a week, that was good wages.

Had you ever read The Arabian Nights?

I read that while I was in grade school because I was hospitalized a lot—I was a sickly kid. I had scarlet fever with double mastoid infections and I had a ruptured appendix and so on. So I read *The Arabian Nights* while I was in ... about the sixth grade, I think.

How soon after your first meeting with Schneer did you meet Sinbad's *stop-motion animator, Ray Harryhausen?*

As soon as we made the deal, practically—within a couple of days. In that same office at Columbia, Ray showed me pictures of the Cyclops and of the two-headed giant bird and of the skeleton, 8x10 glossy blow-ups from his pencil sketches. He said, "I can animate this ... this ... this...," and he showed me all those pictures, and then Charlie said, "Now it's *your* job to tie all this together with Sinbad."

Harryhausen saying, "The movie has to have this monster, it has to have that monster"— that's all the "story input" he had?

That's all he did. He had no idea of what kind of story might [utilize all these monsters]. After I talked to Ray and saw the pictures, I didn't see him again until between first and second draft. I went out to his place in Pacific Palisades and that was the point at which we started talking about how I might change the writing so as to make it easier for him to do the animation.

In an interview, Schneer said that he hired you and then "together we built a story line around Ray's drawings."

[*Pause*] Well [*laughs*]... Yeah, well, y'know, if *that's* the way Charlie *remembers* it...! Naw, he never offered *any*thing. Charles was a guy who would say, "We can't do *this*," "I can't afford *that*," "Ray, can we afford this??" Charles was more ... the *limiting* factor, because he understood what everything would cost. He had a dynamite eye, and I respect Charles ... but he didn't help with the story at all. If he *thought* he was helping... [*trails off, laughs*].

Anyway, that's how it started, I was given some 8 × 10 glossies of Ray's sketches of monsters that were going to people this thing. There was the Cyclops and there was the dragon and there was a skeleton and there was a two-headed giant roc ... to which I objected at first. I mean, a giant roc is bad enough but, no, it's gotta have two heads [*laughs*]. *My* job was to spin a tale around these sketches of Ray's—to create a story that tied all of them together somehow. So all of the monsters were Ray's creations, but what they *do* in the movie was entirely up to me, and in what order we met them and so on. And, of course, you've got to have a princess. Once I had the idea of shrinking her down [to doll size] and Sinbad having to go through all of the different monsters to get the final ingredient for the potion to restore her to full size, then it all was easy. I knew that, if Sinbad and his men were on this island and every time they turned around there was a monster at their ass, they had to have some good reason to stay around [*laughs*]! In *The Arabian Nights*, treasure was the thing, but here, treasure was not enough—we needed a better reason for Sinbad to have to stick with it. And having a bride no bigger than his thumb seemed like pretty good motivation!

What did you think of Harryhausen?

Ray's a sweetheart. And a nice balance to Charles. Ray is kind ... gentle ... imaginative ... none of which I would apply to Charles! Charles, I would say he is shrewd ... bright ... aggressive ... very capable ... *un*imaginative. But a producer doesn't *need* to be imaginative if he's got Ray [*laughs*]!

So you and Harryhausen became friends.

I would say so. Well, we had a certain bond: We were both being exploited by Charlie [*laughs*]!

Setting aside the fact that you were happy to be providing for your family, did you enjoy the experience of writing 7th Voyage of Sinbad?

Yeah, I enjoyed the experience; in retrospect, I *am* glad that I was out of a job and able to do it. The time was made easier, and the movie was made better, by the association of John Kneubuhl, a really marvelous writer. And a wonderful person. John was in a Columbia office on the same floor, just down a couple of doors, writing a picture for [producer] Bryan Foy, the least attractive of the Seven Little Foys [*laughs*]. John was writing a dope smuggling picture of some kind, *The True Story of Lynn Stuart* [1958]—it was taken from a tell-all book by a mother who'd turned her son in, in order to break a giant dope ring. John was having a lot of trouble with Bryan Foy, and I was having a certain amount of trouble with Charles Schneer ... I think I had a better story in mind than made it onto the paper. But at any rate, John and I would commiserate. We would meet for lunch, we would go just up a block and a half, across Sunset, on Gower, to a restaurant called the Naples. Whereupon we would have a martini, and then we would decide whether or not we would have lunch or whether we would have *more* martinis [*laughs*]. So we would get drunk and work on each other's movies. He gave me a number of interesting suggestions, and I'm sure a few of them were incorporated into the script. It was a help. I would not have been such a happy camper, and would not have written such a good movie, without John, and I would like to credit his memory on that. He died of prostate cancer about three, four years ago now.

You said a minute ago that you thought you had a better story in mind than what made it onto the paper. Care to elaborate on that?

I might have had some ideas at the time that I thought were great, but ... finally it got to the point where, if I had two choices as far as story was concerned, and one of 'em was bound to prompt a question from Charles, then I did it the way I thought would get the least static from him.

As you were writing it, how much potential did you see in a Sinbad picture? Did you think it would be any kind of a hit?

I thought it would be a financial success, but I didn't even think I would particularly enjoy *seeing* it. Although, y'know, I kind of fell in love with some of the minor characters. And I liked the villain, I liked Torin Thatcher. He was the best actor in the picture by far, I really enjoyed his performance.

Without wanting to sound like I'm trying to butter you up, I think half the fun of watching Torin Thatcher is relishing some of the great dialogue he has, and the deliciously evil things he does—in other words, your *contribution.*

Well, he carried it off. His was the most important part, because if the villain in this was not credible, then the whole thing would have fallen apart. He played it just right, I was impressed with Torin's work.

Kolb didn't think the Spanish-speaking actors in *7th Voyage* were good for spit. The Cyclops disagrees.

Whose idea was it to have a boy genie in the movie?
    I think that was Charles. He had heard of *The Arabian Nights* and he knew there was a magic lamp in it, so I suppose he thought, "We may as well use the whole thing, it's public domain." I wasn't especially crazy about the way that whole genie business turned out. What I had in mind was fantasy, and we were stuck with filming a real live boy. So the genie was not my favorite part of it.

It was too bad it had to be played by a real live boy because…? How would it have been different if you'd had your druthers?
    I didn't think of the genie as having a gender. I thought a genie would be genderless, not such an intentionally cute boy. But it worked, it's a bit of business that you need in a picture like that. In a magical picture, [the hero] had better have *some* magical aid.

Why was Sinbad *shot abroad?*
    Because it was cheap. This is where Charlie was brilliant: He was the first guy to open Spain under [Francisco] Franco. Franco had never dealt with the American movie companies, but Charlie was able to make a deal with Franco and his was the first American movie company to go there and film. I don't know what kind of arrangement Charlie made with Franco but, for instance, the Caliph's palace room in the movie is the room where [in real life] Columbus asked Queen Isabella for the money to get the three ships. The Alhambra, all of that—millions of dollars worth of scenery for peanuts. They got total cooperation, because the Spaniards were starved for dollars. Once I found out Charlie was planning to shoot in Spain, *I* sug-

gested the caves of Arta, on Majorca. So that's where you see the dragon, is in the cave.

Had you been there?
I had been to Majorca in my travels as a writer, before marriage. After college, I'd gone to Europe to become an expatriate forever, "I'm tired of this filthy, degrading culture over here!"—I was gonna do a Scott Fitzgerald–Ernest Hemingway. And I discovered I was 30, 40 years too late! But while I was living on Majorca, and that was like 1951, I lived extremely well for $50 a month. A haircut was a dime, shoes were $1.50, handmade from local leather, and so on. Anyway, I had been to Majorca and I knew about the caves of Arta, and so it's in the caves of Arta, on the far side of Majorca, that the dragon and the Cyclops have their memorable meeting. The caves were a great plus, and of course the Alhambra was a great plus, and so were costs in general. So … it worked out well for everybody.

You did not *go over with the production?*
I did not go. In fact, they only took about four [actors] that could speak English, and so all of Sinbad's crew were Spaniards that they hired—and probably none of them spoke English. They had to memorize their lines phonetically. Well, you don't get quite the same sharpness in dialogue when it's just a bunch of guys spouting memorized sounds [*laughs*]! I was very disappointed in the scene where there's a wine creek on the Cyclops' island: I had what I thought was a fairly amusing scene of the crew members scarfing up the wine and debating what might be on this island that makes it so weird. That whole scene was lost because there was too much dialogue for the Spanish guys to learn phonetically, it just didn't work. So they cut some dialogue, and the rest of it [the dialogue that the Spanish actors did deliver], it seemed to me, fell rather heavily on the ear!

When you finally saw 7th Voyage, *what did you think?*
I got pretty much what I expected. I could visualize the extras just off-camera throwing buckets of water on Sinbad as he steered his ship through the storm—I noticed that the "ocean spray" came by the bucketful! In other words, I could see "low budget" sticking through from time to time. And, as I told you, I was unhappy that all of the minor characters, whom I thought I had given some sparkling dialogue, were all just grunting it in pidgin English. So *that* part was a disappointment. But the special effects work was certainly not disappointing at all. I had very few complaints with the film. In fact, I was impressed with what Charles had done in the way of getting the natural settings in Spain. I had assumed I was working on a low-budget production, since *I* was low-budget at the beginning of it. Actually, I think the guy that got paid the most, probably more than Ray and me together, was the real loud music man, Bernard Herrmann. Our leading lady Kathryn Grant, a very inexpensive Columbia contract player when we started the picture, had become far more famous during the course of it [by marrying Bing Crosby in October 1957], so the composer-conductor for the picture had to be a bigger credit. That was all right, it put me in good company!

Kolb felt that Sinbad needed an excellent reason to run a gauntlet of monsters. Restoring a doll-sized princess (Kathryn Grant) to full size was the key.

I must say, I have mixed emotions about my *7th Voyage of Sinbad* "fans." I'm surprised to be remembered for *7th Voyage* because ... well, because it was strictly a lunch pail job that I didn't *want*. I took that job, not because it was a childhood dream to write a movie about Sinbad, but because Emmy and I lived in a very unglamorous place, a little apartment two blocks off Fairfax on Willoughby, which is fairly near the heart of the Jewish ghetto, and we had a three-month-old baby crying, and Daddy had to put some food on the table. *That* was my motivation. I had *no* idea that it would be "alive" this many years later, that it would achieve a kind of cult classic status. It has kind of slowly turned into a classic, while I've turned into a relic [*laughs*].

Later on, when I worked for Charlie again, which we need not delve into *too* much, he felt bad, I think, about raping me so badly for a shootable script in 11 weeks for 500 a week. So he did employ me a couple of other times with less successful results, and probably salved his conscience by that. And *mine*, as far as *that* goes. I bear him no ill will. I mean, he paid what I was worth in the market at that time. Every time I see *7th Voyage* run, I think it would be nice if I had some kind of kickback. But the Writers Guild at that time had not envisioned the breadth of the market now. We couldn't foresee, say, a couple dozen movie channels broadcasting 24 hours a day, and home video. Oh, well. At any rate, it was a good deal for me *at that time*. Later, I feel like they got quite a bit for their money. But so did I ... so did I. And, God knows, my agent Murray Rosen needed the commission, because he was so far in debt [*laughs*]! They came and swooped down on Murray while I was still working for Charles, the D.A. came and got him.

Without delving into it too much, what did you subsequently write for Schneer?

Charlie had bought the rights, from Richard E. Byrd's widow, to his book about the five months he'd spent in total isolation in Antarctica. It was called *Alone*. I was given an office at Columbia, in the heart of the hive there, without windows. One wall with a door, and the other three walls were bookshelves, on which sat a copy of *Alone*—and nothing else! I used to receive people with one little light over my desk and one little book that said ... *Aloooone* ... on the shelf [*laughs*].

The movie was never made, correct?

The movie was never produced. You can imagine that [writing a movie about] five months in Antarctica poses even more problems than the movie about Lindbergh's solo flight across the Atlantic [*The Spirit of St. Louis*, 1957]. *That* made a lousy movie too—a guy [James Stewart] talkin' to a *fly* [*laughs*]. There were no animals, not even any insects, under the icecap, so...! At any rate, that one didn't work out to be a movie, but Charles paid me for it. In fact, now that I think about it, if you wanted to prorate all of the other projects, Charles has paid me well enough over the years. But we used to have irritating arguments ... arguments that I felt he did not really understand the gist of. He would see something visually in his mind, something that would really look good on screen, and he'd ask, for example, "Okay, when Sinbad goes onto the island, why can't *this* happen?" And I would say, "...Because that has no relation whatsoever to the story!" You can't be importing monsters from another film, just for Sinbad to meet them! And then somebody told him about *motivation* somewhere along the line. I came back drunk one afternoon from a long lunch with John Kneubuhl, and Charles had left an urgent message for me to come in. I went in. Charles asked, "Hey ... in the end ... when the Cyclops and the dragon fight ... what is their motivation? Why do they fight?" [*Laughs*] I said, "Charlie, haven't you read *The Arabian Nights*? They're like cats and dogs. Cyclops and dragon, cat and dog." "Oh ... okay. Okay. As long as there's a *reason*. There's gotta be a motivation..." So [*laughs*], I found Charles wearing in regard to questions about the script. But on the whole, I've got to admire him. He gets ten dollars worth for every buck he spends. That's a great art in a producer.

You also wrote another Sinbad movie for him.

We later tried to do another picture that never got filmed because Charles had a falling-out with the then-head of Columbia, Frank Price. Frank became head of Columbia at the wrong time for another picture that Charles had in mind, which was called, God save us, *Sinbad on Mars*. (I told Charles that it'd sound like more fun if it was *Sinbad on Venus*!) Ray was happy with it, Charles was happy with it ... Frank Price was not happy with it. I think whatever Charles might have done at that time, Frank would not have been happy with it. So it just never happened. But I'd been paid off. In fact, I had been paid for that much better than I was for *Sinbad*!

Were you sorry it didn't get made?

You know what? I did have fun doing it, and I am sorry it didn't get made. If

Caught between a Roc and a hard place, Sinbad must contend with the mythical bird on his amazing *7th Voyage*.

you read the *Writers Guild Journal*, you'll see that most of us who are in the business for any length of time find that Hollywood *makes* about one-third of what we *write*. And usually the worst third [*laughs*]! There's always some reason why the best scripts don't get made!

Harryhausen's subsequent mythological movies—me, I don't think any of 'em are nearly as good as 7th Voyage, *script-wise.*

Script-wise I think not either, but I would *naturally* think that [*laughs*]. I do think it's a better story than the others. It seems to me the others are somewhat obviously constructed for the special effects passages. It's like a little string accompaniment to the major percussion that goes on ... a thin thread of story.

Did the success of 7th Voyage *do you any good?*

Yes, it did—a financial success of any kind never hurts your credits in Hollywood. And I'll say this for Murray Rosen: The next thing he got me after *7th Voyage* was *Have Gun—Will Travel*, which was a hot TV show. I wrote about five originals and six rewrites for [producer] Julian Claman, who loved me, and suddenly I not only had finished a movie at Columbia, I had credits on a hit series. And

Kolb suggested the caves of Arta for the Dynamation donnybrook between the Cyclops and the dragon.

from then on, it was just a matter of not layin' eggs. Once you're in, if you're competent, you don't fall out again. The Guild has maybe 6500 members, of which probably 2000 at least have had *one* credit. You can make *one* mistake [*laughs*], but you better be good in the beginning because they feel they're risking too much money on you. It's easier to go with the safe hack, who will not give you anything really interesting but will give you a shootable script. And I became exactly that over a period of 25 years. I wrote from '56 to '81, and in '81 I was a dependable hack. There was going to be nothing to alarm the sponsor, the network or anybody else about my script, it would cause no arguments from top to bottom, it would be on time and under budget. And I'm glad they decided I was too old and that I got booted out [*laughs*]. It was journeyman work that was less and less satisfying. I worked for 25 straight years, from '56 through '81, until my list of credits had begun to indicate how old I was, and it was a nice monetary career.

During most of the time that you were writing for TV, you lived in Northern California.

I've been up here 45 years in August [2002]. Twenty-three of the years that I worked in L.A., I did it by commuting by plane from Reno—it's an hour flight from Reno. When everything on TV was half-hour, I would go down and I would get *Dragnet*, *Have Gun—Will Travel* and *Court of Last Resort* [assignments]—I was writing for all three of them at the same time. Then I would come up here and do one a week, and then the fourth week I'd go back to L.A., clean up whatever needed to be cleaned up and take home *another Dragnet, Have Gun—Will Travel* and *Court of Last Resort* [*laughs*]. Half-hour was paying 1500 at that time so I was still taking home about 4500 a month, which has always been more than enough here.

I'll tell you how I'd work. I'd talk on the phone to a producer, say the producer of *Wagon Train*, and we'd arrange a meeting, and then I would think, "Jeez, I better be thinkin' of a story for *Wagon Train* ... let's see ... lemme think..." But since I had a very pleasant life up in the country, and many activities that were much more fun than sitting looking at a blank page in the typewriter, I tended to *not* think about it until I *had* to think about it. When I would really do my thinking about it was on the plane [*laughs*]—on the plane, I *really* began to think it over. And especially after I was in the rental car on the freeway—then I was *really* givin' it some thought! That's always been my [m.o.], I write real fast when it's almost due. I've always sent first-draft copy, and it's almost always been shot. Unless, of course, something goes wrong. I once wrote a *Rifleman* where Lucas the Rifleman and his kid drive into town in the wagon and, while Lucas is shopping for goods, along comes this stray dog and jumps up in the wagon with the kid. "Oh, Dad, can I keep him? Can I keep him?" "Yeah, okay, all right..." And the dog turns out to be in the early stages of rabies. It was an easy script, we had bad guys in it, we had plot and subplot, we had the shootout and so on. The only problem with it was that, two weeks after the script was done, Ralston Purina became a sponsor. And all of a sudden, there was no such *thing* as rabies—"Don't give us any stories about rabies, for Christ's sake!" [*Laughs*]

You wrote some excellent episodes of a series that, in my book, was one of the best of the 1960s, The Wild Wild West.

My friends Gene Coon and John Kneubuhl were both real influences on that show. *And* [*Wild West* producer] Mike Garrison, of course. Mike was truly one of the most interesting producers I've ever encountered. A funny, funny guy. And gay as your Aunt Hattie [*laughs*]! *Not* in speech or in manner or anything else. I think I was on my third *Wild Wild West* and we were talking informally in his office after hours when a neighbor of his, an executive of some kind I guess, came in to see him. "Mike," he said, "a word to the wise: We've had reports of prowlers in the neighborhood. I know you often come home quite late, and I wondered if you had thought about getting a gun permit and carrying a gun." And Mike kind of looked at him funny, and said, "Well, no, but I always have my *hatpin*." [*Laughs*] And I could see he *meant* it! So working for him was fun. He was not afraid to try *anything*, and that's why it was fun to write for him. If you could make it seem halfway credible, he was willing to go *with* it. *He* knew it was a fantasy show, *he* knew it was *The Man from U.N.C.L.E.* out West. And *Man from U.N.C.L.E.* was never too highly rigid in reality [*laughs*]!

How did you get involved with Wild Wild West*?*

I got involved because, probably my best friend among the writers down there [in Hollywood] was Gene Coon, who was one of the early producers of *Wild Wild*

West. He later was a full-time producer on *Star Trek*. He was a great guy, a Nebraska farm boy who had been a Marine combat corps correspondent. Gene and I went to work together on the same show, *Medic* with Richard Boone—Jim Moser gave Gene his start, as he did me. Jim was good about finding young writers who really knew what they were doing. Anyway, Gene was working on *Wild West* and he told me, "Hey, I'm having a good time here, why don't you talk to Mike Garrison?" So I went in and talked to Mike Garrison, and I liked him of course. He was a very engaging guy. Big, imposing, powerful build, deeply tanned, shaven head at a time when that was rather unusual. And, again, gay as your Aunt Hattie. His young inamorata was Joe Kirby, who [in the *Wild Wild West* credits] always had the credit "Assistant to the Producer." Joe Kirby looked like a sweet little Frank Sinatra at about 19 [*laughs*]. Wore fuzzy sweaters and fuzzy socks, and was altogether a real nice guy. *And*, he used to sit in on meetings and had some useful suggestions, as far as *that* goes. They were very much an item. But that didn't concern me one way or another. Mike used to treat me very well indeed. He would have a star's dressing room for me when I flew into L.A., so I stayed on the lot there, in some comfort. In the mornings, I'd go see Mike, and we would have a… [*pause*] …a Salem [*laughs*], and talk about the show. Then we would go out and get in Mike's golf cart and go traveling around the lot to see what sets were standing. I would then come up with an idea for a story that [would utilize] a lot of those standing sets. That was how the one with Ida Lupino, "The Night of the Big Blast," got done. We found some Gothic standing sets, and I said, "Hey, why don't we have James West be Frankenstein's Monster? And Dr. Frankenstein can be a *woman* [Lupino]." That was a lot of fun to do. We opened with the "creation" scene, the thunder and the lightning and the sheet-covered form being endowed with life. And when Ida pulls the sheet off it, it's [a robot facsimile of] James West. Actually, I don't think West appears too much in that episode.

It is *a very "Artie-centric" episode.*
Yes! And that happened because Bobby Conrad wanted to go to the Kentucky Derby, and so he was only going to be available for two days of the shooting. It worked out fine, it was easy enough to shoot his part in two days. That's the one where Artie has a love interest, isn't it? Mala Powers.

Who was Ross Martin's real-life girlfriend.
Was Mala Powers his girlfriend at that time? I didn't remember that. Anyway, I thought the whole thing really worked out great. And Ross Martin always loved me. He didn't remember the names of writers a great many times, but he *did* remember me because I gave him the episode with the romance in it! It worked like gangbusters: I mailed in exactly what came out of the typewriter, and I called Mike Garrison a week later and said, "Hey, what's the problem? I haven't heard from you." He said, "Oh, didn't anybody tell you? We're *shooting* it!"

You mailed it in from home.
Yeah. It was my custom to mail in a script and give people time to digest it and

decide how they wanted to change it, and then I would fly down about every fourth week—once a month was about all I wanted to go. That's the way I worked for 23 years.

What was the key to writing a good Wild Wild West?
Getting a decent premise. A good premise to start with; and then keep in mind that Bob Conrad could do anything in the way of action that you could write; and create a disguise character for Ross Martin, knowing that he could advance the plot when necessary. That was always the plan for the *Wild West* writer: Artie can carry plotlines, whereas James West can carry action. Bob Conrad had a tendency to toss off the line as he was diving to swing from the chandelier, and a lot of times the plot point would get lost [*laughs*]! Also, since *Wild Wild West* was a one-hour show, you knew you were going to have to write four cliffhangers. You set out to leave it at a high point each time, so people who go to the bathroom will come back to the same station. I never found it difficult.

Your first Wild West, *back in the show's black-and-white days, was "The Night of the Burning Diamond."*
I had a posthumous collaboration, as we call it, with H.G. Wells on that. There was a short story ["The New Accelerator"] by Wells that I had always liked. In Wells' story, two characters drink an elixir that enables them to move so swiftly that they literally disappear from sight.

And you adapted that for Wild West, *making Robert Drivas a villain who moves so fast he's invisible.*
That's right. I like working with the dead, they're very cooperative. I did a *G.E. Theater* with Guy de Maupassant.

Oh? What was he like?
Guy? He was very French [*laughs*]! He, too, did not make any unreasonable claims about the way we were mangling his story. That was a *G.E. Theater* for Ronald Reagan ... and I'm still asking forgiveness for helping make *him* famous! Anyway, H.G. Wells' "The New Accelerator" was a great little story ... and I'd been in Hollywood for a few years by this time and so my conscience had rolled over and gone to sleep ... so I had no qualms about adapting it for *Wild West*. But I *did* say, "Hey, it's fine with me if you credit Wells for the story and give me the teleplay." They said, "Why would we *bother*? It's not the kind of idea that could only occur to one person. The estate of Wells would not bother to sue us in any case." And I don't think Maupassant got credit on the *G.E. Theater* either. So, working with the dead, it gives you a better residual [*laughs*], and it gives you an easier story conference. Everything you suggest, why, somehow or other, the famous writer who created the idea has very little to say!

At one point in "The New Accelerator," the characters talk about another concoction, a Retarder that would slow people down so that they'd be almost at a standstill while the world went on around 'em—which is what happened in "The Night of the Sudden Plague," your next Wild West. *Were you ripping off Wells a second time, consciously?*

No, I do not recall that. Stopping to think back, I have to admit I don't recall ever seeing "Sudden Plague." Because, for one thing, up in Northern California here, we live in an area where, for many years, for most of the years that I was working in Hollywood, we were living in a valley between two mountain ranges that pretty much destroyed the old regular rooftop TV signal. We got ABC poorly, and that was it. And *Wild Wild West* was a CBS show. For many years, I didn't see anything that I wrote for CBS or NBC. And I was a much happier camper as a result [*laughs*]!

What were Robert Conrad and Ross Martin like to work with?

Conrad was guts, *all* guts. He was a very physical little guy. At one point, in fact, CBS had to get a court injunction, or maybe just threaten to get a court injunction, to stop him from fighting a young black welterweight well known around Los Angeles. Conrad was going to fight him during the hiatus, during the off-season. Well, look at it from his point of view: On camera, every time he hit somebody, they'd go down. So he had, I think, a somewhat unrealistic attitude about how much talent he might have [*laughs*]! CBS was afraid this black fighter might really damage their goods severely, but Bobby was not afraid. He thought it would be good for the show if he went in and beat a pro fighter. And it might have *been*, if he could have beat him. But I think the consensus was that he'd get all of his teeth knocked out! Anyway, that was one of the things that occurred while I was working on the show, they had to stop Bob from fighting a pro boxer. That should give you an indication that, as far as doing set-up stunts [for the show], Christ, he was not afraid at *all*.

And personally?

He remembered that he had been a milkman out in the San Fernando Valley, he remembered that at four A.M. he was hefting big cartons of milk up onto his shoulder and delivering 'em around the Valley. And so he was not a typical star at all. Bob was the soul of cooperation during my time with *Wild Wild West*.

Ross Martin?

Ross Martin would have been at home on a desert island with just a mirror [*laughs*]. Ross was an actor's actor, all right, he was not "off stage" a lot—he was *on* stage most of the time. And it was always a mystery to Ross why Bob Conrad was the lead in the show. In Ross' eyes, he was every bit as handsome as Bob, and he couldn't fathom why he was called the second banana. Ross was an actor, Ross was very self-centered, and he found it a hard thing to understand why Jim West was considered the hero of the show. And he had already had some success as an actor, and so he was not as cooperative as Bob. Bob Conrad was getting his first big break, this was the first time he'd really tasted stardom, and he was anxious *not* to screw it up.

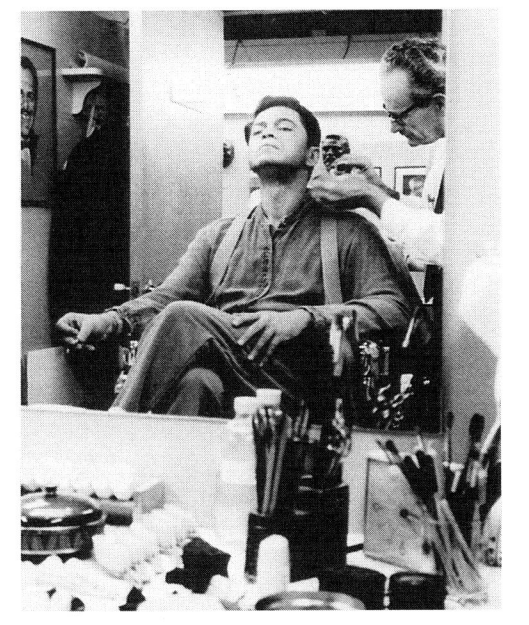

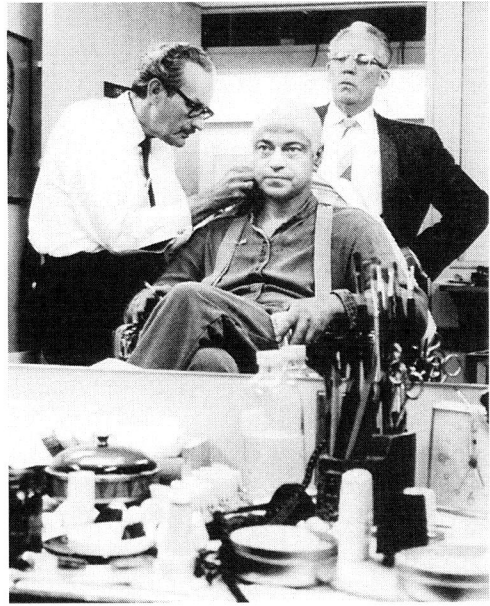

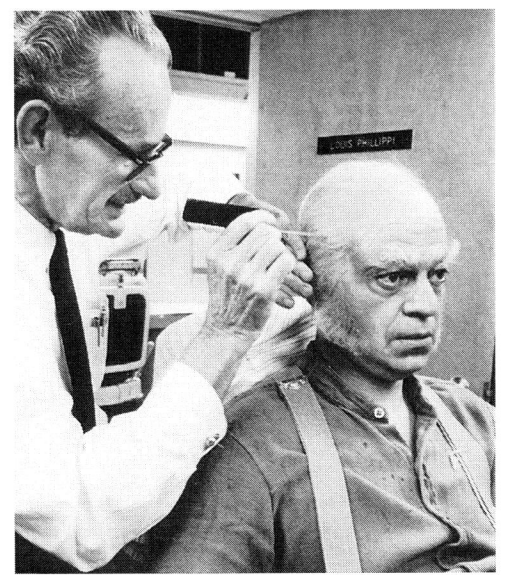

Ross Martin insisted that each *Wild Wild West* episode involve an elaborate character makeup. But maybe he just liked the mirrors.

Approximately how long to write a Wild Wild West *script?*
A week.

How much were you paid per script?
I think it started at 4500. *That* was a good weekly wage—more than I ever made loading boxcars. That was right after I got my Master's in English [*laughs*]—my Master's enabled me to get a job loading boxcars in the Oroville cannery! That was really the last back-breaking work that I did, and it made me very grateful to be able to write a *Wild Wild West* in a week and get 4500 bucks for it.

Were any of your Wild Wild Wests *challenging to you at all?*
I was stretched a *little* bit by one. They had been running seriously over-budget on a couple of episodes, and Mike Garrison called me and said, "Hey, get your ass down here. We gotta do 'a ship in a bottle.'" A ship in a bottle is something that looks very big if you're up real close to it—but as you draw back, you see that it was not that expensive to construct! Mike said, "We gotta save $50,000 on this episode.

We can build *one* set, and we can have three speaking characters besides Jim and Artie." And so that was an exercise all right! But I built a beautiful ship in a bottle: It was called "The Night of the Colonel's Ghost" and it was a ghost town with a lot of hanky-panky and unseen voices and unseen events. Things happening that never require speaking parts. I don't remember how it all went, but it was all ... it was all bull [*laughs*]. And yet it *worked*! In the episode, by the way, was a girl with a big rack [Kathie Browne] who wasn't much of an actress at all. I remember sitting with Mike and Bob Conrad watching dailies, and [the consensus was], "Wow ... she's a visual plus, *but*..." And there was a point at which Mike said, "We gotta cut this scene short. Ken, can you give us a line to get rid of her in this scene?" I looked and I told him, "Let her say, 'I think I'll carry these things [her boobs] back to the hotel.'" Bob liked that—he thought that was so funny, he fell out of his seat.

I ended up enjoying that episode because it saved the requisite amount of money, and nobody really *noticed* [all the cut corners]. That's where a lot of beginning writers go wrong: They do not have an eye for the budget. If you let your imagination go, you begin to think in terms of 30, 40 people milling around in a scene. You have to remember that speaking parts cost money. You have to know how to get by with just a few sets. That probably had a lot to do with my success down there.

"The Night of the Ready-Made Corpse" with Carroll O'Connor?
Carroll O'Connor had not been Archie Bunker yet, but he was already known as a good actor. In the episode, his name was Lavender and he was an evil mortician who specializes in giving criminals a new life: He finds someone who resembles the criminal, kills him off, buries him under the criminal's name, and then does a little plastic surgery on the criminal and turns him loose. Carroll was perfect as the mortician. We were watching dailies again, and Bob Conrad watched this scene with him and Carroll O'Connor. And when it was almost over, he said, "That son of a bitch can upstage me with his *back* to the camera...!" And it was true, because that's who *I* had been watching throughout the scene [*laughs*]. Bob did not have that mysterious thing called *presence*. Some guys, when they walk on-camera, *that's* who you look at. Not too many actors have it, and not all the *stars* have it either. Jack Webb had presence. When Jack Webb's in a scene, he's the guy you watch. He was a very limited ... a *breathtakingly* limited actor [*laughs*]! Almost on a par with Ronald Reagan! But it came natural to Jack, he had that in person. When he entered a room, that's where the attention focused.

I believe you wrote seven Wild Wild West*s.*
I wrote two in the first year and I wrote about five or six more the second year, but somewhere in the course of that, Mike Garrison fell down the marble stairs in his big new Bel-Air mansion and killed himself. I'd flown to L.A. expecting to meet with Mike at ten o'clock but when I got there and phoned my agent Sam Adams, he said, "Mike Garrison *died* last night." It happened late at night: There was a flight of stairs that *had* been carpeted when Mike moved into that place in Bel-Air but the carpet had been removed because he found out that the staircase was Carrara marble or something like that.

Too nice to hide under carpeting.

Right. When he went down the steps, he hit his head, and that was that. Most people knew he was gay and naturally didn't care, 'cause he was not at all swishy, he was not at all faggy, he was a big, tough, blustery guy. And funny as hell too. I never told him anything that he didn't "get." I never suggested anything that he couldn't immediately pick up and see how it would work dramatically. So it was a great pleasure to work for him, and it was a genuine loss when he went down the stairs.

Then there was a rough period [for *Wild Wild West*] in there, because CBS's idea of replacing a guy with an I.Q. of 150 was to get two guys with 75 each. For a while, the show really struggled and I didn't do anything for it. Then Bruce Lansbury took it over. I knew Bruce from some other show that I'd done for him, and we got along fine. Bruce is like a fine old English gentleman—he is the brother of Angela Lansbury. I found him easy to work for. But the show was changing then. Fantasy was going down the tubes [ratings-wise] and Westerns were getting great ratings. So, since Westerns were great and fantasy was bad, CBS constantly struggled against us doing any fantasy. But [fantasy] *was*, literally, the key to the show. When there got to be less and less of that, I got less and less interested in writing it. Also, it wasn't as much fun to work for Bruce as it was for Garrison. We didn't have "Salems" and we didn't have the rides on the golf cart, and I didn't get to stay in a star's dressing room on the lot, I had to go back to staying in various motels. God, I stayed in every motel in Hollywood and North Hollywood over the years.

[Laughs] You make Hollywood sound so horrible!

The nice thing about writing, it's the only job you can mail it in, you don't have to be there. And I didn't *want* to be there! I *haaated* L.A., I could do about four days in L.A. before I began to get "the horrors"! And it's cutthroat. I met people down there that I really wouldn't want to know. *Including* my first agent Murray Rosen [*laughs*]! Who, by the way, made two or three comedy albums after he got out of jail. After he served his time in Chino, he became a nightclub comic, because he could no longer get an agent's license. So he became a nightclub comic and he was pretty good at it, and he did a record called *Busted* about his stay at Chino and some of the adventures he'd had there. He of course had immediately become the prison librarian and the projector operator for the movies. This was a guy who could land on his feet, *any*where! He made a fairly decent living selling the key to the library rest room to various guys who wanted a place to meet their lover [*laughs*]! The locked rest room in the library became Murray's whorehouse! And he found out how you could get homemade alcohol—somebody was *always* brewing alcohol in prison—and he got so drunk while he was running the movie projector that he missed a reel change and burned up some film, which caused a minor riot. Cons watching a movie are impatient when it quits! Incidentally, *Busted* [came out during] the anti–Vietnam War time, and Murray makes it sound on there as though he was busted for being a war protester. Not so. *Not so* [*laughs*]! When he went to jail the first time, he had swindled all 13 of his clients, for various sums. He got us all, every single one.

When he went to jail the first *time?*

He got two to five the first year, and so he was out in the minimum time because he was well behaved, he was a good Chino librarian. Then he and his former cellmate went into business in Beverly Hills and printed up some checks, and one of 'em would go out and cash the checks while the other one stayed at "the home office" and okayed the checks! "I'll go in and pass this check and I'll tell 'em, 'Hey, if you're worried about it, call my company,'" and he'd give 'em the number. Murray and his ex-cellmate took alternate days of phoning and cashing!

Why did you retire in 1981?

A couple of reasons. For one thing, by that time, the tendency in television was to have more and more people involved. A lone writer on a script became less and less frequent. And to have a lone writer who's living five, six hundred miles away from Hollywood, up in the wilderness, doesn't appeal to most guys who are very nervous about their jobs. Everybody who's getting paid too much (which is almost everybody in town) has this deep-seated fear that they're gonna make a mistake and then be back at their job in the car wash, so nobody wants to take chances. And so nobody wants a guy who lives that far away, and doesn't even have a writing partner.

Also, years before I got out of it, they said, "Listen. Try to remember, the average mental age of our viewers is 14 years." Well, by the time I was retired at 55, I had children too old to understand the 14-year-old mind! It was time that I was bumped, because certainly I was rapidly losing contact with the TV-watching audience. And the shows were getting worse and worse and worse. Just before the strike of '81, I remembered that the strike *before* that had lasted several *months* and so I took assignments that I didn't necessarily want. I signed up to do a thing called *B.J. and the Bear*—a truck driver and his monkey and his seven beautiful partners. Count 'em—seven god-damn women, that you could *not* tell apart, and they each had to have a part in the story. I don't know if my show was ever made or not—I would hate to think so [*laughs*]. But I do remember having to write a *B.J. and the Bear* before the strike hit, and thinking at that time, "I wonder how much longer I can go on *doing* this." And the answer was ... not at all! I *never* went on after that, because around that time, the price of a freelance writer rose about twice as much as the price of a staff writer. It became a lot cheaper to put two guys on staff than to have one freelancer. So after the strike, I didn't work.

I could have become a story editor and kept up the flow of income, but it suddenly occurred to me, "Hey ... I don't really *have* to keep doing this." I have a fortune cookie fortune on my wall here that says, "Your problem is not a lack of talent, it is a lack of ambition." I cherish that, it's a genuine character reading! Had I been a more ambitious man, I could have stayed in Hollywood and been very, very rich by now, and probably been on my third marriage and my second liver transplant. But I'd rather have the same wife and the same liver, and live much more modestly.

Not enough people are able to know when enough is enough. Emmy and I were happy on a forest fire lookout, and that's like a 15-square-foot cubicle of glass on top of a mountain peak, so ... it depends on what it takes to make you happy or contented. We've certainly, certainly had excellent lives here. We were able to go around the world with our three kids, and ... it's been a very nice career. But I really don't actively promote it any more. I think I can still write ... but I don't *need* to [*laughs*]. I'm a writer in recovery! I've been thinking of starting Writers Anonymous, for people who don't write any more. And when you feel in danger of writing, you phone another writer and he rushes over and gets drunk with you!

Robert L. Lippert, Jr., on Lon Chaney, Jr.

"You fuckin' Chaney, I'm gonna kill you! I'm gonna kill you!"

In 1953–54, Robert L. Lippert, Jr., produced two of Lon Chaney, Jr.'s, rarest '50s films, *Bandit Island* and *The Black Pirates*. The former, made to cash in on the 3-D craze, was a nearly plotless cops-and-robbers yarn with hold-up men Lon, Jim Davis *et al.* on the lam from the law; the real stars of the 27-minute short were the cars, boat and helicopter coming out of the screen at audience members. (The color short may no longer exist, but most of the footage was reused in a later Lippert feature, the black-and-white *The Big Chase*, 1954.) The latter title, *The Black Pirates*, filmed in El Salvador, starred Chaney as a village priest who defies Anthony Dexter, a ruthless pirate aware that buried treasure lies beneath the site where Chaney's church has been erected.

Lippert's memories of working with Chaney Jr. are as vivid as they are hilarious. The son of motion picture exhibitor-indie movie producer Robert L. Lippert, Sr., Junior was in his mid-twenties and a jack of all trades in the early 1950s: assistant film editor to Oscar-winning Elmo Williams on *High Noon* (1952); producer of some of his dad's company's movies; and even a stunt double within one of the pictures he produced! For his first (and last) directorial effort, *Bandit Island*, Lippert also devised the slim plotline with considerable help from Chaney; Lippert so enjoyed working with the actor that he rehired him the following year (1954) for the South American–made pirate picture. Now, on their fiftieth anniversary, Lippert shares his impressions of the great horror star.

Whose idea was Bandit Island*?*
Bandit Island was a short subject. I think it was the third 3-D thing made: Arch Oboler made the first 3-D [*Bwana Devil*, 1952] and then Warner Bros. came out with a 3-D [*House of Wax*, 1953], and then my dad jumped in and said, "Let's make some 3-Ds." So Lippert made *College Capers* [1953], which was about ... remem-

ber, way back in the '50s, panty raids? That was a comedy. A guy that has an Oscar produced and directed that, Elmo Williams. Boy, he'd run if I told anybody! Then Senior says, "I want a 27-minute 3-D short, and I want it to be nothing but action." And then he says to me, "*You* do it." I ask, "When do you want this done?" He says, "I want you to start in two weeks." I say, "Oh, you're full of shit, for Christ's sake! Are you crazy?" It was going to be my first directing job, producer-director. That was *Bandit Island*.

Who came up with the plot of Bandit Island? *Your dad said, "Gimme 27 minutes of action," but who came up with, "Let's have the bad guys pull a robbery, let's have the cops chase 'em," etc.?*

Partly it was Lon. I meet Lon through an agent named Hal Gefsky. Lon's a *hell* of a nice guy. I tell him, "Look, Lon, I've never directed a fuckin' thing before in my life, I don't know where I'm goin'. But I'm a film editor." He has nothing going on right then, so he says, "I'll *gamble* with ya," and he takes the S.A.G. minimum. You ask me who came up with the plot of *Bandit Island*, well, it was myself, my film editor Carl Pierson and Lon. We just got together and had lunch for two days, and decided to have this robbery, the chase, the train and the helicopter and stuff. We all worked together on it, the three of us. Carl Pierson was an oldtimer who knew Lon many years ago at Universal, he even knew Lon's father.

I don't have much in the way of credits on Bandit Island. *I don't even know who wrote it.*

There *was* no script written [*laughs*]. There was no dialogue in it, it was all action. Carl Pierson knew action, and of course Lon knew action. A lot of the stunts and stuff were Lon's idea. Lon had a couple of stuntman friends that went along with us on the picture.

He lined up some of those stuntmen for you?

Yeah, he knew them over the years. He knew *every*body. Lon instigated a lot of the stunts and he did some of 'em himself. I was surprised. We had car chases, a helicopter and everything. Twenty-seven minutes of action ... and no fuckin' story [*laughs*]. The bandits pulled a robbery and took off so they wouldn't get caught. Senior wanted all these 3-D gimmicks thrown at you, so we had to go action, everything coming at you, you duck in the audience. We shot the thing in four days, with all these gimmicks. We had these two cameras, they were very bulky, huge. Two Mitchell cameras facing one another. You could hardly move 'em, it took four gaffers to move these damn things. It was tough to get action shots.

Walk me through a day's shooting.

We get in the cars—probably a total of five cars, the camera car and cars for the crew and everything. With Lon and everybody. I have my cameraman Gil Warrenton, great cameraman, action cameraman from the '30s. And we get in the cars at the place that was robbed and we say, "Okay, where are we gonna go from here?" "Let's go down Sunset, it's picturesque." So we go down Sunset Boulevard. We had to fill 27 minutes. And then we say, "What are we gonna do *now*?" We all discussed it, the cameraman, one of the gaffers, a couple of the stuntmen, myself, Lon, [actor] Jay Lawrence, a couple of the other actors: "Suppose we were in this circumstance..." This is how it went. Those were the good days of Hollywood. We went all the way down Sunset—

Shooting film as you go.
As we go. And we ended up at ... I forget the name of the pier, it's toward Malibu. There's a pier everybody uses out there for motion pictures.

And, obviously, no sound equipment.
No. We put the sound in later.

I'm gonna guess that you didn't get permits to do what you did.
None [*laughs*]! I also got fined like hell, because I was not a member of the Directors Guild. I told everybody, "Oh, I'm a member, I joined..." I think it cost $1500 to join in those days, and *I* didn't have the money. And the old man was not gonna give me any money!

If the goal was just mindless action and 27 minutes of 3-D, why did Bandit Island *even need "name actors" like Jim Davis and Glenn Langan and Lon Chaney, Jr.?*
Jim did it as a favor to me. And Lon just happened to be a good guy.

In addition to his stints in the movie business, Robert L. Lippert, Jr., has also worked as a builder, in the hotel industry (the Thunderbird Motor Hotel chain) and as a restaurateur.

I hear that Lon liked his nips. Ever a problem?
No. He *did* take quite a nip out of the bottle—he was half-drunk half the time, if you wanna know the truth! But no problem at all. He did the work. He never held things up. He could be half-loaded, brother, but he knew what to do and he was there. He *never* held up any production that *I* know of.

So he was that way on Bandit Island.
Oh, God, yes. And, boy, the crew loved the guy. He was a no-bullshit guy. He knew as much about all the other guys' jobs as *they* did. He was very knowledgeable.

Probably from having the father in the business.
Possible. And growing *up* in it, sure.

Was the editor, Carl Pierson, one of the guys running around with you?
Carl was with me, because he was our film editor, and this was my first directing job.

Carl directed a couple of the early John Wayne movies—we're not talkin' A's, we're talkin' B movies now, eight-day wonders. Carl broke me in with the film editing, and he broke me in as a director. He stood right beside me to make sure I got all the coverage. Gil Warrenton and Carl Pierson were around and they protected me. They were oldtimers.

One of my favorite moments is when Jim Davis and Jay Lawrence run across the railroad yard and they just miss being hit by a train.
We did that at the downtown train station in L.A. Gil Warrenton had made so many earlier pictures there, he knew the ropes, and he says, "Bob, let's go talk to this guy…" So we go talk to some guy, and we talk to the engineer, and we give 'em a carton of cigarettes and we explain what we want to do. To get that shot of Jim Davis and Jay Lawrence just missing being hit by the steam locomotive, what we do is, we actually have the steam locomotive back up. You put the camera down and you back up the train. In the lab you reverse it like the train's coming *at* you.

So the camera is on the tracks, the train backs away from the camera, and then the two guys run backwards across the tracks?
Yeah.

That's brilliant.
The engineer later got hell from his boss for doin' that, because it wasted some time. And *we* got a letter from the Union Pacific, or some damn place, saying, "Please don't use our train yard any more!" [*Laughs*] We just went ahead and *did* it, the train yard and the pier and *all* that stuff. In those days, you didn't need permits and all this crap they have today.

I bet it was a lot of fun back then.
Oh, it *was* fun!

Who were your stuntmen?
What's-his-name. Roberson.

Chuck?
Yeah.

There's a Lou Roberson listed in the credits.
That's his brother. They're both in it. Lou takes the fall out of the helicopter. Chuck does some stuff, but I don't remember what. And Lon jumps out of a railroad car, like, headfirst, into the camera, so it'd look like he was jumping out into the audience. The guy was amazing, physically, at his age.

How much did Bandit Island *cost to make?*
Oh, God, I hate to tell ya [*laughs*]. *Bandit Island* cost less than $30,000. Remember, we were making B Westerns for Lippert for 75–100,000.

The Lon Chaney, Jr.—starring short *Bandit Island* was later expanded into the feature film *The Big Chase*.

Did you get to see it in 3-D?
   Yes, but only a couple of times.

How did the effects look?
   Beautiful. Gil Warrenton, you couldn't find a better cameraman. Anyhow, we finish *Bandit Island* and, about eight, nine months later, Senior says to me, "God

damn it, make a movie out of it!" True story! This is maybe a *year* later, almost. So I call a couple of the guys who were in *Bandit Island*, get 'em for this new picture *The Big Chase*—we have to check their haircuts and all of that [to make sure the old and new footage will match]. We write a story to kind of tie the whole thing together, and that becomes *The Big Chase*.

I've seen that but I've never seen Bandit Island.

Well, *Bandit Island* you have to see in 3-D. *Big Chase* was *not* a very good movie.

Why weren't the added Big Chase *scenes shot in color? By adding a half-hour of color footage, Lippert would have had a color feature.*

That was my old man. We had budgets.

What if anything did you have to do with The Big Chase?

I coordinated the story and I also worked as an editor on it. Fred Freiberger did the script. Fred just died [March 2003], by the way.

Glenn Langan and Jim Davis, both featured in Bandit Island, *came back for* The Big Chase, *but not Lon.*

Not Lon.

You worked with Chaney, Jr., a second time on The Black Pirates, *made in El Salvador, and also written by Fred Freiberger.*

Thirteen families owned 99 percent of El Salvador in those days. Seven of the families, headed by Alfonso Alvarez, a very wonderful man—he was the biggest coffee man—decide to form a production company and make a movie down there. One of the families knows Anthony Dexter—he's very well-known in Latin America because he had played Valentino [in *Valentino*, 1951]. The Salvadorians are represented by a man down in El Salvador called Clarence Simmons, and he contacts [agent] Hal Gefsky. Hal gets me involved, and Lon too. Then Chaney, who was a scream, says, "I wanna play the *priest*..."

Robert Clarke, the star of The Black Pirates, *told me that Chaney was contacted about playing one of the lead heavies, but for a change of pace he held out for the role of the village priest.*

And so he plays the priest! I'm down there trying to organize the locations, the hotel rooms—I'm doing a production manager's job, because we can't *afford* one. In those days, we didn't have all these assistants that they have on pictures today. When I made the B movies, I had no Assistant This and Assistant That, we did it ourselves. I can't believe the crap that goes on today in Hollywood.

It's depressing being on modern sets, seeing scores of people all doing next-to-nothing day in and day out.

It's terrible. The most boring thing in the world now is working on those sets.

Back in the '50s, we had to do 20, 22 pages of script a day, and we had to do an average of 50 camera set-ups, on *all* the pictures of Lippert.

The Black Pirates was low-budget again.
We didn't even have enough money for a pirate ship [*laughs*]! You saw in the movie, it's a shitty movie anyhow, at the beginning we showed a rowboat coming in from the ocean and the pirates gettin' out! No ship! They were fun days, I'm tellin' ya, because you could get *by* with things like that. We made that whole god-damn thing for $108,000 in color. That's the total budget!

Every morning during the filming of *Black Pirates*, an astrologer was consulted. Near Lake Ilopango, a nice beautiful lake right near the center of San Salvador, there was an office building, and Clarence Simmons would go down to the astrologer's office and talk to the astrologer because the 13 families, they lived by astrology. The astrologer foretold whether it was going to rain or not, the weather and so on. The families financing this picture, they picked the middle of the god-damn rainy season! It was their money, so they picked the time. We were told every day whether we were gonna go out and film or not, by an *astrologer*. I did not go, I thought that was ridiculous—Jesus Christ, I had *enough* problems down there!

The families insisted that the astrologer be consulted.
That's right. Every day. The astrologer, he's like a fortuneteller, and we had to go according to his schedule. Crazy. Those were crazy days. Then there was Col. Bolones, who was running the country, he was the boss—an army colonel. We had a Gefsky actress, some American B actress, signed up for the picture. She comes down there to co-star in this thing, and she's there two days when Col. Bolones invites her out to his mansion. He wants to go to bed with her. And she says no. She comes right back from his place and the next day they take her to the airport and she's on the airplane—he kicks her out of the country! And we're starting to shoot in two days! We get on the phone to Hal Gefsky and he says none of his clients want to go there because the revolution's starting.

The revolution in Guatemala, right "next door."
Right. Anyhow, my co-producer down there gets a replacement, the Mexican actress Martha Roth. A very capable, good actress.

When the colonel wanted to kick that actress out of El Salvador, did you consider going to him and appealing to him to change his mind?
No. Not at all. I kept away. Remember, this is right at the beginning of the revolution in Guatemala. Col. Castillo Armas and Arbenz. The National Guard in El Salvador was on alert—and they're tough mothers. They're really the army, but they call themselves the National Guard. And they didn't like Americans too well. Gil Warrenton and I, just before the main crew came in, we were in the center of El Salvador, near the Cathedral, and there was a big student demonstration. I had never been to one before—I was a young guy. I remember Gil said, "Lippert, we better get the *fuck* out of here." And then the National Guard started shooting the students.

In an old newspaper clipping I read that the cast and crew of Black Pirates *would frequently see soldiers armed with rifles and field packs in the vicinity.*

When we didn't work one day a week, we'd get out on the road and drive places, La Libertad, Lake Ilopango, Santa Ana, and you kept having to stop [at roadblocks] because, remember, there was a war going on. Those National Guard guys, a lot of 'em are young guys, and they know how to shoot. And they're tough. They didn't give a shit *who* you were.

Who was with you, riding around and encountering these roadblocks, on your days off?

Lon ... Robert Clarke ... Gil Warrenton ... and Allen Miner, the director. This was his first job.

Were any of you armed?

I always was armed.

How about Lon and the others?

No. I had a handgun they didn't even know I had.

And you and Chaney Jr. got along well again on Black Pirates.

Lon and I became very close friends. There was Lon, Robert Clarke and Martha Roth—I loved her, she was a helluva gal. We also had some other Mexican actors. And we had a ball. Lon was a great guy. Don't laugh, but he said he was impotent at that time. He was drinking too much. Every god-damn night, we were into Casa de Puta—those are whorehouses. We'd all go to the cathouse, not to get laid, but to drink, and to get away from the local people. We wanted our privacy. We did that every night.

Including Chaney.

Oh, Chaney was there. He was an instigator [*laughs*]! And, brother, it didn't take much persuasion for *me*.

Why did he mention to you that he was impotent?

The booze.

No, but ... why *did he tell you that? If it was me, I* wouldn't *have told ya!*

I don't think he wanted to lay these girls. They were Indian whores. They weren't your typical whores, these were for *every*body. In those days, the thing you had to worry about was gonorrhea.

So maybe he just didn't want to get involved with them.

That's right. He'd rather drink. Tell stories. He was a great storyteller, he could go on and on and on and on.

So do you think he was impotent, or he just said that as an excuse?

I think he just said that as an excuse. But, I got news for ya, [impotency] can

Chaney Jr. played a man of the cloth in Lippert's The Black Pirates, *but he remained the carouser and practical joker off-camera.*

happen when you drink a lot of that fuckin' tequila! Down there, he drank a good tequila. I forget the name of it. It's not popular up here because it's expensive, but it was good.

Were Robert Clarke and Anthony Dexter also at the whorehouse?
   Yes, oh, yeah. Bob Clarke was a nice guy. A gentleman. And Anthony Dexter was always a gentleman.

Where did you stay down there?
   In the annex of a hotel, the second floor. No rooms down below, but maybe 30, 40 rooms upstairs. Forty rooms with a 25-gallon hot water heater. 25 gallons for 40 rooms! Shit! Fred Freiberger and I are rooming together, nobody could have their own room. Fred's doing rewrites. Murder's your number one cause of death down there, so on the hotel annex, there's big wooden doors, about 12 feet high, and each door four feet wide. It opens to eight feet by 12 feet. To get in, you gotta knock on the door and then the guard inside opens a little window *in* the door to see who's there. He knows if you're a resident, and he lets you in.
   Oh, I gotta tell you a story—that damn Lon Chaney, I could kill him, because he was responsible, the son of a bitch. When it doesn't rain, we're shooting in the jun-

gle, we're in the village of Panchimalco, which is about 40 minutes outside of the city of San Salvador. This is Indian country where the god-damn Indians, they don't even know what electricity is. They don't know what a *movie* is, they've never *seen* one. These are *real Indians*! There's an old church there, we get out there because of this old church of around 1600. And there are a lot of snakes down there, Jesus Christ—fer-de-lance, bushmaster, little snakes, big snakes. And bugs! You name the color of a bug, they *got* it! One morning, along comes this big fuckin' bushmaster—that snake is about 12 feet long, and it's thick as a banister rail. One of the cameramen kills it.

How?

I don't know how, I wasn't there when they killed it, I saw it later. Fuckin' Lon Chaney, he doesn't like snakes, and Fred Freiberger's a New Yorker, he's scared pissless. He didn't even want to go out on location because of the bugs. Anyhow, it's so hot down there that time of year. In order to get out of there, Fred and I make excuses about one-thirty, two in the afternoon. We go back to the hotel, take a hot shower, and then Fred and I lay bare-ass nude on top of our beds. Fred and I had too much to drink the night before and we're taking a nap—a dead, dead sleep. Nothing is gonna wake us up.

Chaney knows this, Chaney and the cameramen and all these guys—*they* know that fuckin' Lippert and Freiberger are sneaking off and taking hot showers and getting some sleep! These sons of bitches, that fuckin' Lon Chaney, he and the camera operator, I forget his name, they get that fuckin' snake they killed that morning and they bring it back to the hotel and they sneak it into our room. They put it between the two beds, between Freiberger and me. Then they sneak back out, and now they're *all*, most of the cast and a lot of the crew, outside the room. Then they knock on the door.

I put my foot down to go to answer the door, I step on something, and I see this fuckin' snake. And it doesn't look dead to *me*! I don't remember touching the hotel floor—I *fly* to that god-damn door. And as I'm running to the door, I see Fred going out the *window* [*laughs*]! Right out our window! There's no glass, just shutters, and it drops about 15 feet to the outside sidewalk—the windows are 15 feet up. And he's got no clothes on, he's bare-ass nude! I open the door and they all start laughing, "Ha ha ha ha!" And Freiberger ... now, this is a guy who did a lot of stuff, *Star Trek* and all, he was the head writer—he's in the middle of the god-damn main street of the city of San Salvador, knocking on the god-damn hotel door to get back in, trying to cover himself up with his hand! The natives out there don't know *what* the hell is goin' on, and the guard at the door won't let him in, he's thinking, "There's a gringo nut out there with no clothes on, we're *not* gonna let him in!" This was funnier than hell. I start laughing ... but then I get mad! "You fuckin' Chaney, I'm gonna kill you! I'm gonna *kill* you!"

You figured out it was his idea?

It was *all* his. He put 'em all up to that. I don't think Freiberger ever talked to him again.

How many people outside your door when you came charging out?

I'd say 12 to 15. Chaney was in his monk's outfit [*laughs*], he was in costume. They *all* were, they just came from the set. Then there was another thing with Chaney, and *this* almost got us killed. We're gonna do a scene with Chaney and Eddie Dutko, who's playing one of the pirates. Eddie is actually one of my assistants, but we also shaved his head and made a pirate out of him. And in the scene, he shoots Chaney, the priest. Well, the fuckin' natives are gonna *kill* Dutko! *Really.* They get the machetes out, they chase him, they're gonna kill him, because he shot a priest! Lon was so believable when he took the bullet, the natives thought that he was killed. Like I told you, these villagers never even *heard* of a movie, they thought we actually shot a priest.

These are just terrific stories!

I'll tell you another funny story. The generator breaks down, and we can't operate our lights or camera on our locations, Lake Ilopango or Panchimalco. Well, Chaney's a knowledgeable guy, and he says, "Bob, when we flew in, I noticed that when the planes land, the [airport people] put an air conditioning unit right up to the airplane"—in those days, there was no air conditioning on the airplanes. So he says, "*That's* a big generator." So, would you believe, we bribe a fuckin' government guy and we take that airport generator for two weeks! For two weeks, when the planes landed, they didn't have air conditioning, because the generator was out in the village of Panchimalco! Lon was the one who spotted it. He was a fix-it-up guy, he could fix things. None of us thought of [using the airport generator], but *he* did.

Closing comments on Lon?

He was a good actor. *Of Mice and Men* [1939]. This guy was an actor. Then that god-damn *Wolf Man* [1941] came along, and then he couldn't live it down. Because he did a hell of a job, if you remember. My father later made two with Lon Chaney, *The Alligator People* [1959] and *Witchcraft* [1964].

I know nothing about him except that all the crews, the working guys, knew Lon, and they had nothing but good things to say about him. He was a regular guy. He was not a bullshitter. What *I* liked about Lon was, he never told stories on anybody. Well, he told stories, but never *bad* things. I never heard him say anything bad about anybody. He told some *funny stories* about guys, but not bad things. Like he would never say, "Oh, that guy's no good" or "He's a bullshitter" or something like that. He never did that. He never downed anybody that I knew of.

Jan Merlin on The List of Adrian Messenger

> *While I was on the Universal lot one day,*
> *I got a call from my agent asking whether I'd be interested*
> *in doing something rather* weird *and* strange.

Even in the 1960s, the Golden Age of gimmick movies, it was an outrageous ploy: A stylish, high-gloss murder mystery in which the faces of some of its most famous stars would be *so* completely concealed under latex masks and makeup that, as new characters appeared on screen, the audience often wouldn't know if the actor they were seeing at any given moment was (a) Kirk Douglas, (b) Robert Mitchum, (c) Tony Curtis, (d) Burt Lancaster or (e) Frank Sinatra. What the film's producers *also* did not want moviegoers to know was that the answer was often (f), "None of the above."

These five superstars were top-billed in director John Huston's *The List of Adrian Messenger* and part of the challenge of the twisty 1963 whodunit was to penetrate their disguises—but in truth, two of the five did not actually appear in the body of the movie itself (other, lesser-known actors played their parts). Nor did Kirk Douglas, *Adrian Messenger*'s central character, play *his* own multi-face role from start to finish. In the film, set in England, Douglas co-stars as George Brougham, a creature of pure evil who, to clear the path to a fabulous inheritance, turns mass murderer (107, counting train and plane wrecks!), donning a series of elaborate disguises to achieve his nefarious ends. But nearly all of Brougham's dastardly doppelgangers were actually played, in the strictest anonymity, by character actor Jan Merlin.

A native of Manhattan's Lower East Side and a Navy veteran of World War II (an amazing ten battle stars), Merlin "didn't know how to do anything but shoot torpedoes" when in 1946, at age 21, he enrolled at the city's celebrated Neighborhood Playhouse. Early stage and TV work included a supporting role in the Broadway smash *Mister Roberts*, a highly praised performance in an Off-Broadway production of Patrick Hamilton's *Rope* and a co-starring stint in the sci-fi kid's show *Tom Corbett, Space Cadet*. In 1954 he moved to Hollywood, where he soon found himself specializing in near-psychotic types. His versatility made him the perfect candidate to replace Douglas as the succession of masked characters throughout *Adrian Messenger*—rigging an elevator for a fatal plunge, planting a bomb aboard a passenger plane, pushing a wheelchair-bound man to his drowning death and other diabolical deeds.

In recent years, Merlin has done more writing than acting, scripting for TV (he received two Emmy nominations, and won once, for the daytime drama *Another World*) and penning a series of novels; one of them, *Shooting Montezuma: A Hollywood Monster Story*, is a much-fictionalized Hollywood yarn fancifully based on his *Adrian Messenger* experiences. But here in this interview, Merlin recalls the actual year-long ordeal, from months of trial and error in the Bud Westmore–John Chambers makeup lab at Universal, to London and Dublin production and beyond. After four decades, he rips the mask off *Adrian Messenger*.

How did Universal happen to come to you to handle this unusual job?

I worked at Universal many, many times after I came out to Hollywood. I worked there far more than at any other studio, so Universal was more familiar with my work than any studio in town would have been, although everybody else also knew me. They knew me as an actor who did all kinds of roles. I didn't play young leading men, I did all the nut parts then—played bad guys and people with accents and psychos and Nazis and all those nasty types. Universal was grooming young leading men and they didn't want *them* touching those kinds of roles.

While I was on the Universal lot one day, doing one of the *Laramie*s, I got a call from my agent asking whether I'd be interested in doing something rather *weird* and *strange*. It would also involve working with John Huston, and the agent was very encouraging about that. He told me, "John Huston has a kind of a stock company. Almost all the time, the same people show up in his pictures." My God, to work for John Huston was, to *me*, a very exciting proposition, but I was curious about what my agent meant by "a strange film." He said, "*If* you're interested, I'll contact Universal and say, 'Yes, you can talk to Jan about it.'" Well, things progressed, and I was asked to go to the makeup lab at Universal to talk to Bud Westmore—it appears that Bud was the man who would make the decision. And I went up there—

Still not knowing what this was all about.

Not at *all*. Well, the whole project was very hush-hush. When I got to the makeup lab, I saw plaster casts hanging on the wall of the faces of various actors that I'd seen in films like, oh, Charles Laughton, Lon Chaney, Jr., Boris Karloff, Bela Lugosi—they all looked like death masks. That was really fascinating to me. And I saw a lot of the stuff they used in pictures—for instance, the Creature from the Black Lagoon's head and hands were up there, parts of the foam rubber costume. And there was Bud. Bud was very pleasant and quite charming and affable, and he showed me some work that he was doing. He and his helpers were using clay to make character faces on plaster heads of Kirk Douglas. Bud said he wanted to talk to me about a project that was … kind of a secret. He told me it would involve my playing a number of different roles. I was nodding my head and being vastly interested, and then he said the peculiar thing that [*laughs*]—that I really should have taken note of more than I did: He said, "But you won't get any credit for it." I said, "Well … uh … are you gonna tell me about it, or is it gonna stay such a secret that I'm gonna do something I don't know nothin' about?"

Bud then began to explain to me that this would be a film based on a book [Philip MacDonald's 1959 mystery novel *The List of Adrian Messenger*] and that Kirk Douglas was to play a guy who was a murderer *and* a master of disguises. The studio was so carried away with the idea that they were also going to use *other* stars in disguises in the film. I still didn't quite *get* it, but … okay. I asked, "If you're gonna *do* that, how come the great man [Douglas] isn't gonna do the stuff under the masks himself?" Bud said it would take an enormous amount of time to create the masks and that Douglas couldn't possibly always be available [to take part in the process]. "We want to hire a good actor who *knows* what he's doing and take you to England and Ireland and you'll do those roles *there*. And Kirk Douglas will do *his* roles *here*." I thought, "Well … sounds good to me. I'll be workin' with John Huston and he'll get to know *me*, I'll get to know *him*"—I thought it was a wonderful deal. So I agreed to do it.

What was the first step?

Bud said, "You have to go to work right away. We'll make a plaster cast of your head now, and starting tomorrow, we'll start working on creating masks on *your* face." Then he showed me one of the Kirk Douglas heads that they were already using and he said, "We'll make two sets of masks of each we need, one for you and one for him. If he's able to do any of those roles, he'll have those masks available. If he's *not*, you'll be doing the part." I thought that was fascinating, and I got really involved in this whole creative process of making these characters look *real*.

Who else was involved makeup-wise?

The main one was John Chambers, who made the actual masks in his oven. He was at his experimentation best, inventing new rubber-based full-face pieces and working hard at creat-

Jan Merlin as he appeared in 1962, the year *Adrian Messenger* was shot.

ing a latex substance that could move *with* your face instead of just being a stiff kind of mask. I was involved in a very fabulous kind of project, I thought. It was totally, totally *different* to me, it was an aspect of the business I had never even conceived of before. I learned a lot there. I was practically an apprentice.

Did you ever happen to learn whether there had been other contenders for the job?
I did wonder whether Bud had seen anybody else for this, and he said, "No. *We* know you, *we* know your work. What's the point? There's enough of a resemblance between the two of you [Douglas and Merlin] so that it'll work." He added that at some point I would be taken down to be introduced to Douglas, and get *his* approval.

First they made a head of me out of plaster and then turned that into several *more* heads that they were able to work on. They then used clay to create a mask directly on the plaster head of me, molding it into whatever face they wanted. That was duplicated on Kirk's plaster head and then John Chambers would turn *those* into masks which they could glue onto either of us with spirit gum. I would have to go through various movements and exercises with it, to test how much wear and tear it would take when I was speaking or moving or even just plain *wearing* it all day or most of the day.

What else was made for you or used on you?
They had bald caps which were put on over my hair and glued in place. A dozen wigs were made along with mustaches and beards. If they needed ear pieces or neck pieces or hand pieces or teeth, they had those made too. I also spent a lot of time getting different colored glass eye lenses to put on my eyes. They were bigger than contacts because they had not only the pupil of the eye and the iris, they also had the whites with bloody-looking veins running through them and whatnot.

Were you sworn to secrecy about your participation?
At no time was I asked to keep it a secret, but it was implied, and I understood that I wasn't to say any*thing* to any*body*. There were only four people altogether, up in the lab, who were in on the secret [Westmore, Chambers, Nick Marcellino, sculptor Chris Mueller]. Well, I *thought* it was a secret, until after I had sat in the chair for some weeks and discovered how little the secret meant to Bud. He kept inviting people in to see what he was doing—he invited Rock Hudson in at one point. I felt, "Jesus, everyone who comes *in* here has a mouth, and they'll talk about it." So Bud himself had lots to do with *not* keeping the secret, because he couldn't contain himself. He wanted everybody to see what wonderful things he was doing.

Did Westmore do much hands-on work?
Yes, Bud sculpted faces too. For a gag, he made one into a mask which resembled one of his brothers, Perc Westmore. It would have been a *very* inside gag for people in the business, because it was just so *much* like Perc. Bud and Perc didn't get along—well, Bud didn't get along with his brothers, he was not a very nice person. Which I didn't know at the time. I thought he was a *won-der-ful* guy with *bril-li-ant* talent who was allowing me to be part of this incredible project.

Were there screen tests to see how each of these faces would look on film?

No, there was no need for screen tests—why waste film? Once I was made up, they took still pictures of me in each mask, while wearing appropriate wardrobe.

At what point did you first meet Kirk Douglas?

After we'd been working ... oh, a couple of days had passed, I guess. Bud said, "Before we put another mask on, I'll take you down to Kirk Douglas' dressing room bungalow"—Douglas had a bungalow on the lot which was a real cottage. I was looking forward to it: I was a fan, I'd seen him in quite a number of pictures and was interested in finding what the guy was like and I wanted to talk to him about these characters. By now I'd seen the script and, knowing which characters I was going to be doing for him over in England and Ireland, I thought he'd tell me how he'd like each of them played. Or tell me what he would be doing with those characters when *he* was in those masks. At that time, I still thought that surely he was going to be playing those parts, and that I would just be doing long shots, stuff that was really not important enough for him to do himself.

As an inside joke, Bud Westmore made up one of Merlin's masks to resemble his (Bud's) own brother Perc, another prominent makeup man. The "Perc" mask was not accepted for use in the film.

Bud and I walked down to the bungalow and we sat and waited in an anteroom for a while. I saw African carvings on the walls and I was fascinated immediately because I'd *been* to Africa more than once and I knew a helluva lot about Africa. I examined the things and began to chuckle over them, because I recognized 'em as being items you could buy in a Los Angeles store called Akron, which was selling cheap-o wooden African-style souvenirs. They're turned out by the *zillions* [*laughs*]. I'd been told that Mr. Douglas had recently gone off on a safari—and that's *not* the kind of stuff you bring back from a safari. I knew, because I'd *been* on safaris. Bud was a little bit annoyed because I was picking these objects off the walls or off the shelves to look at them. Bud didn't think I should touch them, so I put them back and then we were asked by David Grayson, Mr. Douglas' personal makeup man, to enter the dressing room to see Mr. Douglas.

It was a very, very brief meeting. The walls of the dressing room were lined with floor-to-ceiling mirrors and he was in a barber chair, in his jockey shorts—I assumed he was going to be made up for whatever film he was doing on the lot. Sitting there staring at himself in the mirrors, on this great throne of a chair, he eyed me only in the mirrors, he didn't look directly *at* me. Which was a little uncomfortable for me, but I thought, "Okay..." He and Westmore talked about ... well, nothing, really. Westmore was very obsequious and he showed Mr. Douglas what he had—*me*. Douglas looked at my image in the mirror, looked at me from head to toe, I suppose gauging whether I was the right size, or whatever, to match him. I knew I was taller than he was, but he didn't stand up to see. I fully expected that he'd say *some*thing, *any*thing about getting together to talk about the roles. But—not a word. Not a single word. He just looked at me and he finally just nodded and said, "All right." As I recall, he never spoke to me directly. I felt I was not supposed to talk either. And then we were *dismissed*.

So [*laughs*], I went off without knowing whether I was to see him again or not. I asked Bud if I was going to see him, to discuss the roles, and Bud said, "Oh, *sure* you will, *sure* you will. But that's not what we're interested in right now. Right now we're interested in getting all these masks made…" There were about six disguised characters that Douglas was to play. Then there were five [other masks] which were for other stars [Tony Curtis, Elizabeth Taylor, Burt Lancaster, Robert Mitchum, Frank Sinatra], all of which were also going to be created on me. I assumed I was going to do some kind of work in 'em. Also, creating these masks on me would give John Huston a chance to see what these characters would look like. I didn't get to meet Mr. Huston for quite a while, because we were first tied up with making all these masks.

Incidentally, the plaster head of Kirk Douglas that the guys were working with was redone after we had begun. The first ones had been made before the Douglas-publicized "safari." I was present when they brought in the new plaster head, which we used after breaking and discarding the old ones. The new one lacked the wrinkles and age of the other. I may have been wrong, but suspected that *some*one went to a plastic surgeon instead of to Africa … which may explain Bud's nervousness about me examining the African objects in the Douglas bungalow. Bud knew I had been on a real safari a few years earlier.

And he knew you might smell a rat.
   That's right.

At what time each morning would the makeup work begin on you?
   We started usually at eight o'clock in the morning. I'd sit in the chair and they'd attach a latex mask to me which John Chambers had baked in his ovens. It was a pink, ugly thing made of his special material. During the next four hours, they'd glue it on and make it up and try to make it look real. Sometimes they'd also have me put on clothing similar to what the character would be wearing in the film and then took photographs to see if it looked any good. We generally did two masks a day, sometimes even three, finishing quite late. But in the beginning it was only two masks a day. It was a very slow, long process. It always took at least four hours to put on a mask, and took almost as long to take the damn things *off*, because they were glued on with spirit gum. My face was rapidly turned raw. It was so painful, because I couldn't simply pull it off, it would tear my skin. In desperation they often used liquid called carbon tetrachloride [to help dissolve the glue]. I knew nothing about those chemicals, and *still* don't know much more today. But it would take 'til sometimes six, seven, seven-thirty or eight-thirty at night before I'd leave the stu-

Lab technicians Don Cash (left) and Elmer Lernd (right) flank makeup apprentice Michael Westmore and sculptor Chris Mueller in the Universal makeup lab with some of the foam rubber castings made for Merlin and Kirk Douglas.

dio. Practically nobody knew that I was there. The guards at the gate knew that I came in early and that I left each night, but they had no idea what I was doing. The industry didn't know what had happened to me; I'd more or less vanished. At that time I'd *been* working almost every week in *some* TV show or some film or whatever, I was almost never without any work—and all of a sudden I was just *not around*. I was doing *this* thing.

For weeks? Months?

Months ... almost a year! I started, I think, in February of '62 and we just kept at it daily throughout the entire spring and summer. There were lots of difficulties involved. We had wardrobe and hair experts helping us in the studio, but most often I'd be left alone in the lab with John Chambers and Nick Marcellino. (Our talented sculptor, Chris Mueller, was finished with his tasks.) When we had decided which mask to use, Bud would leave and John and Nick applied the makeup on the mask, after it was glued on. The two of them were constantly working on me, and I saw more of them than I did of Bud.

One day my face was *so* painful, I could scarcely bear it, and Nick felt so sorry for me, and wondered how the hell we could protect my face. I asked, "Would it help any if we put a pancake makeup on as a base for it?" He said, "The glue won't stick to that." He thought about it some, then reached into his box and brought out a stick of Red Indian Stein's Makeup and smeared my face with it. He wiped it so that it was only lightly coating my face, and then he glued on the mask. And, oh!, it felt so much better, because I wasn't getting that instant agony from the spirit gum. Later that day, after we finished with the makeup, we started to take the mask off. Nick's hand slipped as he was tugging at the top of it—and the thing fell right down. We gaped at each other and we just couldn't believe it: We had stumbled on a way to be able to take the masks off instantly.

Of course we told Bud, and Bud didn't believe it. So we had to do it all over again for *him*. Then after he'd seen it for himself, he got excited and said, "We have to go to the producer and show him," because that was the main thing [producer] Edward Lewis worried about: For the stars' bows at the end of the picture, the masks had to come off easily, with just one pull, and not injure any of them. Bud had promised Mr. Lewis that he'd solve the problem.

So we did it all over *again*, we put that Stein's Makeup on me and then the mask and then Bud, Nick and I went to the producer's office. Nick and I stepped into the room but Bud hung back at the doorway warily; he looked as if he was gonna run like a son of a bitch if the mask didn't come off easily. He was sort of pushing Nick and myself into the room [*laughs*], and stammered nervously at Mr. Lewis, "We're able to take the mask off now without any trouble." The producer said, "Oh? Let me see." I reached up and just peeled it right off. Whereupon Bud brushed past Nick and myself and approached the desk to tell the producer how *he'd* worked it all out.

Did you and Nick leave Westmore there, or did you wait for him?
Well, after an expectant pause, not being noticed any more, Nick and I left quietly to go back to the lab and work again ... miserably ever after [*laughs*].

What did you do about lunch every day?
One of the problems with the masks was that, although I could speak in them, I could not *eat* well in them. The mask would give way at my mouth. I could drink soup or coffee through a straw. Whenever they had a lunch break between masks, they ordered food brought up, and then I could eat a sandwich. The lunch breaks were as long as it took to eat. Eating with a mask on was a problem never solved. We were unable to have the mask stick in place if eating. So I was instructed that if, during actual shooting production, I ever found I was wearing a mask when they were going to break for lunch, I would then ask for something like soup and *that* would be my lunch. I lost weight on that job.

Had you ever worn this much makeup in any previous movie or play or TV show?

No, never wore anything like those makeups ever before. Doing plays in New York and other theaters on the East Coast, I used greasepaint at first—we all used it in summer stock. It cleaned off readily with cold cream. When I finally got into films, they used pancake, a water-based makeup, and *that* washes off with water. But now I was in this jam where I was doing a painful, ghastly thing all the time. My face became overly tender and remained so. I was to keep to my hotel rooms on location after work because I looked so bad.

You were without eyebrows for months?

I did get to keep my eyebrows. Many people are unaware of little tiny hairs all over their faces—not just beard and mustache, there are hairs all over. When a mask is taken *off*, those little hairs will come *with* it. And if you keep *on* doing it often enough, you're gonna end up with a raw face. I had to live with it, but it was crazy—I was living a peculiar existence. I was getting up before the crack of dawn and going to the studio and sitting in that chair for eight to nine hours sometimes. I began to lose *track* of the world outside.

*What about your hair—did you get a crewcut, or do any*thing*, to make things easier?*

I did get my hair trimmed, but not into a crewcut. When I first began this project, I had every expectation of working in *other* shows during this period. I had no idea how much of my time it would take. To my horror, I discovered I was *trapped*, I was working eight- and nine-hour days. Because Bud was running things, I *had* no contract—I wasn't given a Screen Actors Guild contract to do this lab work. So I had to keep track of my hours, and give the list to Bud at the end of each week, and Bud would turn those in. After about a month or so, Bud came charging in one day during our lunch break, having a hissy fit, saying, "You're asking for too many hours. You've got to ask for less hours." I replied firmly, "*No* I don't. I worked that many hours, and I've given you my lists of exactly what I worked." He said, "The production manager, Dick McWhorter, is complaining it's too much for my budget, you've got to report less hours." I said, "I'm *not* gonna report less hours because I've *worked* those hours. You have an accurate record." He said, "Well, we're gonna put you on the clock," and I retorted that'd be fine with me. After he stormed out, I got sulky and told Nick and John I was going to quit. John warned me I could be blackballed in Hollywood if I did, and I [would be losing] the chance to work with Huston. I grumbled, but agreed he was right. After that, every day when I came in, I punched in on a studio time clock in the lab, and every evening when I went out, I punched *out* on that clock. An amazing thing happened. Prior to that, I hadn't been putting down the half-hours when I was on breaks, so I got even *more* hours on the time clock—which made Bud angrier! But there was nothing he could do, because the machine couldn't tell a lie! He was no longer Mr. Nice Guy with me.

On rare occasions when Bud felt he could risk it, he'd put me in a studio car at lunchtime, wearing a full makeup and wardrobe, and he and Nick and I, sometimes John Chambers, too, would be driven to a quiet Italian restaurant in the Valley. They'd have lunch, and I'd sit with them to have soup and coffee. If the waiter gave me any peculiar looks, the makeup was a failure. But when he did *not*, we were very pleased and left in high spirits because nobody realized that this odd old man sitting there was *not* a little old man at all. *That* was kind of fun. It also gave me a taste of what it was going to be like when doing something where I was not the person that *I* thought I was, I was the *thing* that everybody saw. It was strange—it was *really* strange.

Adrian Messenger production manager Richard McWhorter and a masked Merlin.

When did you finally meet John Huston?

When it came time for me to meet John Huston, I was taken to him in full makeup and full costume. I was escorted down to his office on the lot, and I was looked at by this tall, gaunt, wiry man, with a great charm about him. He was surrounded by all these little clay artifacts from the Incas and Aztecs, small statues and objects all over his desk and throughout his office. I was fascinated with the objects—they were the kinds of things I try to collect myself. (Though I collect mostly African artifacts.) I gathered he had a big interest in doing a picture about Montezuma, and I was given to understand by Bud that Huston was directing *The List of Adrian Messenger* because Universal was also going to let him make his Montezuma picture.

That became a routine, we'd go over to Huston's office, in full makeup, so that he could approve each character when it was completed. He'd look me over and make his criticisms, whether he wanted a change in the kind of clothing or whether he wanted a change in the type of character. Sometimes we had to throw the mask away—not there in his office, but we'd be told to create a totally different mask for the character. So, slowly, over the months, he assembled and chose the characters, 11 in all. For Douglas, the Whistling Man, a Clergyman, a Tourist (not seen in the movie because I looked too much like myself), a Civil Servant, a Workman and a Shepherd, plus for other stars a Hurdy-Gurdy Man, a Merchant Seaman [also not in the movie], Slattery, a Gypsy and a Hunt Protester Woman. The only mask eventually performed in by Douglas was that of Mr. Pythian the Civil Servant—which was done in Hollywood, with Dana Wynter, after the company returned from foreign location.

But you still had no way of knowing how Kirk Douglas might want you to play each of these characters.

That's correct. I also had no way of knowing what Mr. Huston would want, because we hadn't really *talked* to each other. When I was brought to his office, I was just a movable prop [*laughs*]. I didn't understand when I accepted the job that I was going to be treated as such—I thought I was going to be a character actor doing a number of roles, guided by the director. It wasn't quite so. He gave me a minimum of direction, evidently satisfied with whatever I did. But, in a curious way, being regarded as a prop became a kind of wonderful opportunity for me. I was *there* and thus was an observer of what everybody was doing, and they were totally unconscious of the fact that I was watching them and listening to them and they behaved as they would as if I were *not* there. This later—*very*, very much later—was of help to me when I wrote the book [*Shooting Montezuma*] about my experiences on *Adrian Messenger*.

Where did you shoot first, England or Ireland?
We first went to London, England. We were to be sent to England three weeks before the rest of the company arrived, and John Chambers and Nick Marcellino were saying, "Gee, we'll get to spend some free time there before we start the picture. We can see London and enjoy the sights and maybe go the theater," and I was just delighted, looking forward to it. That's the reason that I brought my wife, actress Patricia Merlin, with me. We needed a vacation. The two of us had a jolt upon arrival at Customs, because when I answered I was there to work in a film, I had no work permit to show. We were held at the airport a couple of hours until someone from Universal somehow straightened it out for us, and we were permitted into the country. But when we got to London and wanted to see the sights, we were prevented when Bud Westmore declared, "*No*, I want you to practice the makeups. Every day until the picture starts. Things have to be perfect." Bud kept John and Nick and me working at the makeup studio at Shepperton from the crack of dawn until evening, every day of those three weeks. My unhappy wife was left to her own devices while all of the British studio's makeup people were invited in by Bud to see what we were doing. They'd hang around for a while watching, and they were astonished.

At the end of each day, Bud always had John and Nick clean the room up—lots of stuff would fall on the floor, all the makeup stuff that was discarded. They were cleaning it up one night when the head of the British studio makeup department came in and asked, "What are you *doing*?" They said, "We're cleaning up." He said, "We've got night people that do that. You don't have to do any of it." John looked at Nick and Nick looked at John and they both looked at *me*, and then Nick looked up at the fellow and he said, "No, we *have* to do it," and they continued to clean up. And I began to realize fully that the sly rumors and hints I'd been getting from people about Bud were actually quite true. He *wasn't* the charming, sweet little guy that you met with the big smile and the laugh like the bray of a donkey. He was really quite ... nasty. But I let that go, I didn't get totally angry at him until another time, at the hotel.

They were afraid not to clean up the floor themselves because they knew they'd get in trouble with Westmore if they didn't.
Of course. And *he* wasn't there, he was out seeing London—

[Laughs] And enjoying the sights and maybe going to the theater!
Yeah, he was having a great time. I'll get to *that*!

What did you shoot first?
The first scene done for the film was at night, on a city street in London, where I [playing the Whistling Man] was to go into a building and rig an elevator to fall. I arrived at the location all made up in the Whistling Man's outfit, which looked like a pleasant businessman with a gray mustache. Very dapper. When I got there, John Huston looked at me and he stared and he stared and, consulting his book of photographs of the masks, he asked, "Is *this* the makeup I approved?" I didn't answer—I thought it wasn't my place to answer. But I knew that John and Nick had run out of the supply of Whistling Man masks with all their practicing and so, under Bud's order, they had put another mask on me and put the makeup of the Whistling Man on it. Huston said, "It doesn't look right, it's not what I approved. Where's Bud? *Bud*! Where's Bud?!" And nobody answered—Bud wasn't on the set. Finally somebody spoke up and said that Bud was off … oh, I don't remember what he said, but that Bud was off sightseeing or something. Mr. Huston said, "All right, we'll *wait* for him," and he sent people out to look for Mr. Westmore.

We waited, oh, I suppose about an hour and a half, and Bud showed up finally, quite desperately unhappy, and Huston said—without any preamble—"Is *this* the mask that I approved?" Bud said [*talking quickly*], "Oh, yes, yes it is!" And John said, "No it's *not*. It's not what I approved. I have a picture here and it does *not* look like the picture." Bud lied, "Yes, but this *is* the mask." Huston stared at him for a long time and then he said, "Well … we'll go with what we've got, kid." And we shot the scenes, we shot my walking on the street and all the interior rest of it. But Bud had been thoroughly put down. *That* was when working in this picture *stopped* being fun for me.

[Laughs] Oh, great—the very first night!
I'd been thinking, "Gee, I'm gonna be working with John Huston, I'm gonna be doing all these parts. Even though there'll be no credit on the picture, people will know about it…" But it wasn't like that at all. It had become a dreadful experience. I'd get up at four o'clock and we'd start, because I had to be on the set at eight. We had rooms in the Dorchester Hotel and we had a makeup room there too. A chair

Merlin wore the Whistling Man mask the first night of London production—and realized that working on the picture had already stopped being fun.

had been placed on a low platform where we did the work. Bud would come in about halfway through, about six or six-thirty. Often he'd have a little lady with him, sometimes he didn't. He brought in a young woman with him one particular morning, and they sat at a little side table to share some breakfast. It arrived promptly and they began to eat while he regaled her with what was taking place on the improvised stage in that room. He was talking to her about me as if I wasn't there. About how they made up his *dummy*. I really got hot, and I started to pile out of the chair in a fury. John Chambers, who was a huge man, just grabbed and pushed me back gently, saying softly, "…It's not worth it. It's not worth it." And I kept my mouth shut. I returned that favor on another similar occasion, when John got into an argument with Bud and wanted to belt him—I stopped *him* [Chambers]. It stemmed from some remarks Bud kept making about his "assistants" carrying out "his" creations. (Generally, Universal pictures listed Bud Westmore as *the* makeup man, though it was usually his subordinates who had done *all* the work. Yet he was credited for it on the films.) From then on, we just did our own jobs and Bud did *his* own thing. To us, it was as if *he* wasn't there.

The picture progressed with what we had to do in England, and then we moved to Ireland. The only time I really had a sense of pleasure was when we got to Ireland and we were shooting the fox hunting scenes. It was so beautiful out on those rich green fields. I had my camera and got some grand shots of the hunt and of Huston and his kid [Tony Huston]. How they loved and enjoyed those wild chases! I even got a good picture of the stunt man going over the stone wall as his horse got hung up on it. That was the moment Kirk's supposed character in the film got his just deserts near the ending.

Before we get to Ireland, what more did you do in England?

I did the Clergyman at Heathrow Airport, the character who brings a suitcase to the counter and checks it in as though he's going to take the plane—there's a bomb in it, which is how the plane is destroyed. It was the only scene in which I had dialogue, speaking to the woman behind the counter [Delphi Lawrence] and to John Merivale [playing Adrian Messenger]. I then went into an airport men's room but the scene that takes place inside the men's room was shot in Hollywood, with Kirk Douglas removing the Clergyman's mask.

Which is the first time we see him in the movie.

It was a very brief moment but enough so that you see that it's Douglas as a master of disguise. It was in the script for him to do. But I was certain that to let the audience of the *film* see him removing a mask at the very outset destroyed the mystery of "Who is the murderer?"

Is that your voice we hear when the Clergyman speaks at the airport? I know it's not Kirk Douglas' voice.

Yes. As I was doing the Clergyman, I fully expected that they would dub Kirk's voice into it. But they didn't. When the film came out and Hedda Hopper wrote about it in her column, she praised Kirk Douglas for how wonderfully he was able to change his appearance and his voice, too [*laughs*]. I thought that was amusing ... but considered it sloppy to have happened.

Once Westmore got on Huston's bad side for not being around the first night of shooting, was he on-hand more often, or did he continue to go off and do his own thing?
 Bud made himself more available but didn't do any of the work on me—that was John and Nick's job. I don't know what Bud did with his time, besides avoid more of Huston's scorn.

What was your wife doing in England all the time you were working?
 She'd go off to see London by herself, or see a play, but she was having a terrible time because she was doing everything alone. She saw the musical *Oliver!* and told me all about it. I felt like an orphan! It got so bad that, before the company moved to Dublin, I suggested she go home. And she *did*, she went home.

In your fictionalized Shooting Montezuma, *the makeup men give their boss, the Bud Westmore counterpart, the "middle-finger salute" after he'd leave a room.*
 John Chambers was the guy who did the finger bit. Well, there was John creating masks that could show reactions and Bud was busy taking the credit for it all. John simmered even though he was furious. Because, hell, it was due to *John's* work, those were *John's* latex masks that were impressing everyone. Bud was just somebody who appeared once in a while, or dragged in strangers to see what "he" was creating. God, in England he couldn't wait to haul in all of those English makeup people and his female friends to admire what "he" was doing. And *we* [Merlin and the other makeup men] were treated like some kind of funny creatures in a cage. Bud finally got John's goat and John almost hit him. After I stopped him, John said he didn't care—he was planning to leave Universal anyway, he wasn't gonna have any more to do with Bud after the picture.

And Nick Marcellino?
 Poor Nick, he was always quiet and did whatever he had to and didn't make any waves at all. I don't know *how* he held it in. And Bud was forever crowing, "Oh, I'm gonna get the Academy Award for this! I'm gonna get the Academy Award for this!" "Best Makeup" wasn't yet a category for the Oscars then, but they were thinking about *making* it one, and Bud was certain that he was going to get the first Best Makeup Oscar, he was *positive* of that. Of course, he didn't. And I was so delighted when, in 1969, an Honorary Academy Award for Makeup *was* presented—and it went to John Chambers, for *Planet of the Apes* [*laughs*]! It was poetic justice. And of course Nick Marcellino became the head makeup man at Universal. I think everybody eventually had their own little moment of glee. It may have been *rueful* glee [*laughs*], but it was still glee!

What were some of the things you shot in Ireland?
 The waterfront scenes were all shot on the Dublin waterfront—that's beside the River Liffey. We shot in a pub there and I was a Workman in the pub, the guy who later knocks out Robert Mitchum and dumps him into the river. Mitchum was also wearing a mask playing his character, Slattery, a man with a blind eye. We did

that at night. He was a little disgruntled with the whole thing [*laughs*], but he did it, and he was glad to finally reach the end of it. But he still had to do the bow for the end of the picture, and at his insistence they took care of that right then and there.

The same day he shot all his other scenes.

Well, he wasn't gonna go through the makeup ordeal all over again [*laughs*]! It's sheer hell when you wear those things—you sweat like a pig under masks like those. When you finally take the bald cap off, your hair is sopping wet. It was a constant problem to try to figure out how to keep the sweat from loosening the mask and all, but it never did get past the spirit gum that much.

We were supposed to have in that Dublin pub scene a character called the Merchant Seaman. It was *another* role I was to play, for which Elizabeth Taylor was going to take a bow at the end. But in order for her to take the bow, she'd have to have the mask put on her. When I arrived in England, she was there too—Elizabeth had a suite up at the top of the Dorchester Hotel. Her friend Roddy McDowall was also there. Roddy ran into me in the Dorchester lobby one Sunday afternoon when I wasn't working and he said, "I've been wanting to see you. I want to ask you something. Elizabeth wants to know what it feels like to put the mask on and to take it off." I had him sit down in a corner with me and I explained to him what the process was like. "First of all," I said, "they're going to shave her face." His jaw dropped [*laughs*], and he said, "She'll *never* go for that." I said, "Well, if they don't, every hair on her face will stick to the mask when it comes off." I told him how painful the whole thing had been for me—my face certainly showed the damage from wearing the masks. He thanked me and went off to see Elizabeth. The next thing I knew was that when the day came to *do* the scene in that pub in Dublin, the Merchant Seaman role was crossed off the list of characters working on that day's call sheet!

It was originally planned that Merlin as a Tourist would spy on the Bruttenholm estate in an early scene, but the mask ended up looking too much like Merlin and was rejected. He became the Clergyman for the scene instead.

The mask for Slattery, the wheelchair-bound pensioner, was made on Merlin (seen here) but worn by Robert Mitchum in the film itself.

So your horror stories must have been passed along to her, and she bowed out.

I was sorry she did. I'd been looking forward to doing the role—it was the best mask of all. And I thought it'd be a kick to do something Elizabeth Taylor would take a bow for! Tony Curtis was the Hurdy-Gurdy Man on the River Liffey waterfront—like Mitchum, Tony Curtis did wear the mask and he did actually play the scene himself. Burt Lancaster was supposed to play the role of a woman protesting the fox hunt, but he did *not* do it. The part was played by an Irish actress named Marie Conmee, and evidently she didn't understand what the score was. They cut her hair and put her in a mask and she played her part. And when she learned what she had done [played a role for which someone else would get the credit], she contacted Michael Knight, a tabloid columnist for I *think The Mirror* in England, who produced a column in which he featured a head shot of her in the mask, and his column was titled "Unmasked—Four Famous Men Whose Gimmick Is Taking the British Public for a Ride." Marie Conmee blew the whistle on everything; she told him all about the guys who *were* doing the roles and the famous stars who were *not* doing the roles [*laughs*]. I have no idea if it was ever circulated or was picked up by any other publication. An English friend sent it to me. Nothing was in our American papers at all.

Oh, and there was the Gypsy character supposedly played by Frank Sinatra. Actually, that was the same mask as the Hurdy-Gurdy Man, but with different makeup and different clothing. I understand an actor named Dave Willock, who I didn't know, played the Gypsy in the scene. Sinatra only did the bow. The guest stars were all cute as hell with their bows. I particularly relished Burt Lancaster winking at the audience so coyly. Incidentally, that Hunt Protester mask that Lancaster supposedly used was modeled after my mother! When my mother once visited the Universal lab during a spring [1962] afternoon to see what I was up to, the sculptor, Chris Mueller, modeled *her* face on one of my heads, and they planned to use it as the mask for the Hunt Protester. Which they *did*, but they changed the clothing and the makeup so much from the original version that it no more resembled my mother than…

Than Burt Lancaster!

[*Laughs*] Right, no more than Lancaster!

Why was part of the movie shot in Ireland when no part of the story is set in Ireland?

Because John Huston was the real Master of the Hounds at Galway, where he and his family lived, and he wanted to have hunt

Early plans called for Merlin to also play a Merchant Seaman (for which Elizabeth Taylor would take the climactic bow).

scenes and saw to it that they were shot in Ireland. So [*laughs*], he had his hunt scenes, and he had a wonderful time riding in the hunt—he even played a minor role in the picture during the final hunt scene. He and his son had a wonderful time racing along after those hounds and jumping those horses. It was a pleasure to see them work together.

I wasn't much impressed with George C. Scott as an Englishman in the picture.

George C. Scott, a brilliant actor, was ill-at-ease with accents. His British accent for the film wasn't up to snuff. When I worked in *The Hindenburg* [1975] 13 years later, I was amazed to be instructed by the director, Robert Wise, that none of us were to use German accents since George didn't wish to assume one. As a result, we had a supposed German Zeppelin crew speaking with an assortment of American accents which were totally out of place!

On *Adrian Messenger*, the only time George blew up was after getting an early call to be on the set, and he sat around all morning without being used. He left the set in a huff for the hotel, informing John Huston that thereafter he was to be called when actually needed. During the fox hunts, George rode all the chases himself, jumping fences and stone walls despite the peril—and we had a number of skilled Irish riders fall off their horses during those scenes. George had enormous courage, I admired him for it, but a stunt double would have been safer to use. The production could have ended had he suffered an accident.

While working in Adrian Messenger, *you never once talked with the star, Kirk Douglas, and you talked with the director ... how many times?*

I hardly had any discussion with John Huston at all, and I've always wished I could have. At the end of the film, on the last day of shooting, they had a wrap party after the day's work was done—it was held at the Shelbourne, where most of us had rooms while in Dublin. I even got

The Hurdy-Gurdy man in *Adrian Messenger* was played by Tony Curtis, but in this pre-production shot, Merlin sports the mask.

Merlin models the mask and makeup of the Woman Protester in the fox hunting scenes. Radically changed, it was worn in the movie by Irish actress Marie Conmee and in the "bows" by Burt Lancaster.

my official invitation—"The Gleneyre Hunt Society—Cocktails and Buffet—7:30 P.M.—pre-supper cocktails in the Shelbourne Rooms, followed by Buffet Drinks and Dancing in the Adam Suite. Monday 17th, September, 1962." And then I couldn't attend! I thought I was finally going to encounter John Huston with my own face. But I couldn't get there; I was removing a makeup. By the time I was finished, as usual everyone else had dispersed and gone off to whatever *they* did at night, and I never did get to see John with my own face. I had done a major portion of a film with him and, when it was over, he still wouldn't have known me if he fell across me, and… [*Pause*] It doesn't matter. That's in the past.

Incidentally, the result of all the makeups didn't really hit me until I was done with the film and I'd gotten back to the States, and I was again driving my own car along Laurel Canyon and discovered to my horror that I'd lost my sense of balance. It was extremely difficult to maneuver the many curves of the twisting roads that went up and down from my house. I felt dreadful for a long, long, long time. It took me, oh, I imagine about six months or more before I finally felt comfortable in the car again. No, I didn't see a doctor about it. I was too miserable as it was, without being turned into a patient who would always have a "next appointment."

And what do you think brought this on?
 I think it was the carbon tet. Some friends have expressed horror at the remarks I made about having it used on me. But it was something that finally wore off and went away and I was back doing the same ol' stuff I'd *been* doing, killing and being killed in pictures and operating in my own little field. But then in early January [1963], I was called by a Universal secretary who asked in a *very* pleasant, lovely voice, and lovely manner, if I would *please* come in and do the bow sequence for them [wear the Shepherd, Workman and Clergyman masks-makeups in the post–THE END sequence]. Kirk's stuntman would be under the Civil Servant mask, because there wasn't time for me to be made up for *all* the masks involved. They wanted all these guys to parade across the screen one at a time, and the last one would be Mr. Douglas [disguised as the Whistling Man], who would then take off his mask. I was almost going to say no, because I had no contract with 'em to do it. I thought, "Why the fuck *should* I?"—I didn't want any part of that film any more. Then I thought, "What the hell, I'd better, because if I don't, they can blackball me." One seldom says "no" to a studio. So I went in and did my job.

How many days did it take to shoot that bow sequence?
 Just the one day, at Universal. There was at least an hour between each face change, maybe an hour and a half, depending upon how much they had to do with it. They didn't have to be as tightly laid on me, but they still had to look good. And then I stayed to watch Mr. Douglas. Since he preferred using his own personal makeup man, it must have been Dave Grayson who put the mask on him, because Kirk's wasn't done the way it was for me. Perhaps no one told Dave anything about putting a greasepaint base under it [to make removal easy and painless], so it stuck to his face like crazy when Kirk tried to take it off. When you watch the movie, you can *see* his anger as it happens. He pulled it off as best he could and plucked and

plucked at the shreds [*laughs*], and still gave us a half-hearted "*Wasn't I wonderful?*" bared-teeth grin. I was sitting in the apse of the vast stage to watch, and I thought it was a howl ... imagining what Douglas would have to say to Bud about it. When everyone left, none gave me so much as a glance as they went out the huge open doors. Camera crew, director, producer, star ... I'd worked for them nearly a year in length, and none recognized me for their "movable prop."

You didn't bother to see Adrian Messenger *when it came out.*

No. I didn't see the movie 'til a long time after it was released—I saw it for the first time on television. I didn't go to see it in a movie theater because I just wanted to put it in the past altogether as a professional mistake I had made. And I didn't speak to anybody about what I had done. I felt, "A secret's a secret." I got a letter from England from some friends I had there, from my safari days, who wrote that they'd just seen the most peculiar film [*Adrian Messenger*] and had decided that I was in it, and they wanted to know, *was* I in it? I didn't admit it then, but I did later.

You got that letter when the movie was in theaters?

Yes. And, incidentally, the movie wasn't particularly successful. In Kirk Douglas' autobiography *The Ragman's Son*, he wrote that he was disappointed in the film's income, only $1.5 million, which I guess was considered chicken feed.

How much of Bud Westmore had you seen in the years before Adrian Messenger, *and much did you see of him after?*

I worked at that studio so much—I started there in 1954 and *Adrian Messenger* wasn't done until 1962. During that eight-year period, I was working at Universal so often, I ran into him *many* times. But I didn't see him after *Adrian Messenger*. We avoided each other to such an extent, I was not to lay eyes on him again. We had parted with very antagonistic attitudes towards one another. But I always knew when he was on the lot because I often passed the red Thunderbird he'd gotten as a present for his work in *Adrian Messenger*, parked in front of the Makeup Building.

What prompted you to write a fictionalized novel about your Adrian Messenger *experiences?*

I wrote *Shooting Montezuma* because I was annoyed with a *New York Sunday Daily News* magazine column [December 30, 1984] titled "Ask Mr. Entertainment" which was forwarded to me. In it, Kirk Douglas responded to a question about my having played the clergyman in the film by saying that, to the best of his knowledge, he played *all* the parts. Then there was a suggestion that I may have "tried on" his assorted disguises for John Chambers. I was kind of p.o.'ed about that! I was stewing about it for a long time, and everybody kept telling me, "Hey, you really oughta write a book about what happened!," but I said, "No, I don't want to write about Hollywood." Then I saw the [1996] Academy Awards show where they gave Mr. Douglas his Honorary Oscar, and behind him they showed clips from many of the pictures he did. And they showed the ending of *List of Adrian Messenger*, where the various older men [almost all Merlin] came out and finally Douglas strode in, masked, and took off his mask. I looked at that and thought, "Jeez, isn't that nice? *I got an Oscar too!*" [*Laughs*] And now that I'd finally gotten to be amused by it instead of sullen about what a rotten experience it had been, I finally thought, "You know ... that *would* make an interesting novel. I could take essences of these characters and put 'em together..."

You changed things around quite a bit in the novel.

I remembered Huston's desire to do a picture about Montezuma, so in my novel I made *that* the movie with the gimmick of stars in disguises. I'd been writing books about Africa, Japan, the Philippines, and everyone was begging for a Hollywood story ... so they got one. I put John Huston in the book and he's very amusing in there, it's very much like him. Of course I don't call him John Huston, I call him Hugh Johnston [*laughs*]. Roddy McDowall's in it, but I used the name "Roddy" for Roddy, I used "Elizabeth" for Elizabeth Taylor. Those were the only people whose real names I used. Much of what I've told you today is *in* the fictional story, but in different versions, and much more is there that I've *not* told you [*laughs*]. I made a monster out of the character [Sunny Moreland] I modeled from Bud Westmore. That was just my own childish kind of revenge [*laughs*], for all the torture he gave us! The book is listed on both Amazon.com and on the Barnes & Noble site, or may be obtained directly through Xlibris.com/bookstore. It's listed under my own author name along with other books of mine.

Merlin, seen here as the Shepherd in the climactic scene, was anxious after the close of production to "put [*Adrian Messenger*] in the past altogether as a professional mistake I had made."

Are you still acting these days?

I'd act if somebody wanted me to do something I like, but without an agent, nobody's apt to ask. So now I just write novels—I've done seven so far. The newest one is called *The Paid Companion of J. Wilkes Booth*, which concerns the unfortunate Confederate boy, Lewis Paine, who was eventually hung as a conspirator in the Lincoln tragedy. It's done from the point of view of the boy, about whom very little is known. He was painted at the time as being a monster and evil, but I saw his photograph and he was a perfectly handsome young man. My coauthor, Dr. William Russo of Curry College, Massachusetts, had done enormous research. We reconstructed that boy and his whole involvement from *Paine's* point of view, so that whatever he didn't know about is *not* in the book. We've gotten some fine reviews on it, and I've also had calls from readers who told me they wept at the end of this book. Because the boy was *not* a monster, they had cried when they got to the chapter in which he was hung. I was pleased with that, because I feel that we made him *live* again. It's a book I'm quite content with. Next to be published is a two-story book titled *Crackpots*, about characters I've run into in filmland here and abroad, a pair of fictions I hope amuses readers.

The List of Adrian Messenger
(Universal-International, 1963)

Presented by Joel Productions; 98 minutes; Produced by Edward Lewis; Directed by John Huston; Screenplay: Anthony Veiller; Based on the Novel by Philip MacDonald; Photography: Joe MacDonald; Music: Jerry Goldsmith; Editor: Terry O. Morse; Art Directors: Alexander Golitzen, Stephen Grimes & George Webb; Set Decorator: Oliver Emert; Makeup Created by Bud Westmore; Makeup Artists: John Chambers, Nick Marcellino & David Grayson; Makeup Dept. Sculptor: Chris Mueller; Hair Stylist: Larry Germain; Unit Production Manager: Richard McWhorter; Assistant Director: Tom Shaw; Sound: Waldon O. Watson & Frank H. Wilkinson; Music Supervisor: Joseph Gershenson; Associate to Mr. Huston: Gladys Hill; Photographer, European Unit: Ted Scaife

Tony Curtis (*Cameo*), Kirk Douglas (*George Brougham*), Burt Lancaster, Robert Mitchum, Frank Sinatra (*Cameos*), George C. Scott (*Anthony Gethryn*), Dana Wynter (*Lady Jocelyn Bruttenholm*), Clive Brook (*Marquis of Gleneyre*), Gladys Cooper (*Mrs. Karoudjian*), Herbert Marshall (*Sir Wilfred Lucas*), Jacques Roux (*Raoul LeBorg*), John Merivale (*Adrian Messenger*), Marcel Dalio (*Anton Karoudjian*), Bernard Archard (*Inspector Pike*), Walter Anthony Huston [Tony Huston] (*Derek Bruttenholm*), Roland Long [Ronald Long] (*Carstairs*), Bernard Fox (*Lynch*), Barbara Morrison (*Nurse*), Jennifer Raine (*Student Nurse*), Nelson Welch (*White*), Alan Caillou (*Insp. Seymour*), Constance Cavendish (*Maid*), Eric Heath (*Orderly*), Richard Peel (*Sgt. Flood*), Tim Durant (*Hunt Secretary*), Anne Van Der Heide (*Stewardess*), Stacy Morgan (*Whip Man*), Patty Elder, George Steele, Arthur Tovey (*Ad Libs*), Anita Sharp-Bolster (*Mrs. Slattery*), Delphi Lawrence (*Airport Stewardess*), Noel Purcell (*Ugly Countryman*), Joe Lynch (*Cyclist*), Mona Lilian (*Proprietress*), John Huston (*Lord Aston*), Paul Frees (*Various Voices*), Jan Merlin (*Disguised Double for Kirk Douglas*), Dave Willock (*Disguised Double for Frank Sinatra*), Marie Conmee (*Disguised Double for Burt Lancaster*)

Mary Mitchel

> *It's weird how films seem to "change."*
> *Some of the good ones get better, some of the*
> *good ones get worse—and some of the*
> *bad ones get better ... because they're so funky!*

Mary Mitchel's genre career began with a bang—an atomic blast that wiped out Los Angeles in the opening minutes of *Panic in Year Zero!* Playing the teenage daughter of Ray Milland in the 1962 SF melodrama, Mitchel joins her family (parents Milland and Jean Hagen, brother Frankie Avalon) in fleeing the scene of devastation, only to find that other survivors have also retreated to the surrounding countryside—and, as promised on the movie's posters, have embarked on "An Orgy of Looting and Lust!" That right there ought to be enough hardship for any beginner actress, but Mitchel was soon facing further perils in two other cult titles, Jack Hill's off-the-wall horror comedy *Spider Baby* (1964) with Lon Chaney, Jr., and the gory Irish-made shocker *Dementia 13* (1963), written with Mitchel and her actor-husband Bart Patton in mind by a former UCLA classmate, 23-year-old Francis Ford Coppola.

A native of the movie capital, Mitchel began acting on stage and quickly moved into movies and TV (*Perry Mason*, *The Munsters*, *Hogan's Heroes*). Several years later, when her acting career stalled, she moved behind the scenes, working in different capacities on a variety of motion pictures, many of them Coppola productions (*The Godfather*, *Apocalypse Now*, *Bram Stoker's Dracula*, more). Her career recently came full circle—dizzyingly!—when Mitchel, now a script supervisor, returned to acting to play a script supervisor in director Joe Dante's *Looney Tunes: Back in Action* [2003].

[No opening question.]

I was born in L.A. and I got into acting because, when I was at UCLA, I worked in theater. Then I did a small play at a professional theater in Hollywood, *Send Me No Flowers* with Phyllis Coates. It was a silly kind of a comedy that was making the circuits at the time. I had two small parts in it—[the actor playing Coates' husband] has two dreams, and I played two different characters, sort of bimbo types, *in* his dreams. While I was doing that, I decided to look for an agent. Fred Roos, who was then just beginning as an agent, came to see that show and he took me on, into his agency. He's now a producer for Francis Coppola, he produced *The Godfather Part II* [1974] and *III* [1990] and a bunch of other films.

Once you did get into movies and TV, what were some of your first credits?
Some of the very first things I did were one of the *Leave It to Beaver*s and a TV show for Disney, *Sammy, the Way-Out Seal*.

How did you get such a great part in Twist Around the Clock *[1961]?*
I next signed with Jack Gilardi at Creative Artists, and they started submitting me for things. I just went in and read for it, and I got it.

That's quite a jump, from being a beginning actress playing small parts right into a co-starring role in a movie. Were you ready for the experience?
Well ... yeah. See, it was all the *same* to me, because I didn't know very much [*laughs*]! I just showed up! On one of these early things, they asked me to do some looping, and so I called home and spoke to my husband Bart Patton and I said, "I'm not going to be home 'til later, I have to do some looping." He said okay. Then I asked, "What's looping?" [*Laughs*] At UCLA, he was in the motion picture department and I was in the painting-sculpture-graphic arts division of the art department, so I was really not knowledgeable about the mechanics of film!

Your real name was Mary Dingman; where did Mitchel come from?
It was my grandmother's name. She left me a hundred dollars in her will, and when it came time to join the Screen Actors Guild, my mother wasn't quite sure she approved. My mother was from Kansas, right? So I took the hundred dollars that my grandmother gave me and joined the Screen Actors Guild. And Jack Gilardi said, "Mary Dingman? I don't *think* so." [*Laughs*] So I went with Mary Mitchel. I couldn't be Mary Patton 'cause there already was one.

Your first—and only—science fiction credit was AIP's Panic in Year Zero!, *starring, and directed by, Ray Milland.*
I thought it was sort of ... a foolish part I had [*laughs*]. The world blows up, the end of the world has occurred, and *my* line is, "What a drag!" [*Laughs*]

I was going to bring that up. You do play a very annoying character in that movie. Someone who just doesn't get it!
I called up Jack Gilardi and I said, "I thought you told me this was *well-written*!" [*Laughs*] Snippy, wasn't I?

Did you have to audition for that?
Yeah, I guess I read. When we were making that movie, the title was *Survival*.

What was the experience like?
The three guys they hired to play thugs, one was an actor and the other two

Young and eager-to-please, beginning actress Mary Mitchel did whatever she was told, whether it was to loop, to play a love scene or to *Twist Around the Clock*.

were thugs. So the scene where they rape me was ... interesting, shall we say. And there was one very long day when I went to sleep in the trailer. [In the movie, Milland and his family travel around in a car and trailer.] The trailer started moving and I just thought they were moving it to another location. I was sorta half-asleep and it sure was bumpy, but I didn't bother to wake up. Then when it stopped, I thought, "I'm gonna get out, we're there," wherever "there" was. I opened the door and came out, and everyone had this ashen look on their face! I said, "W-w-what...?"

It turned out that they'd just used the trailer for a stunt scene [*laughs*]! Immediately it became "Whose fault was it?," was it the first a.d.'s fault, the stunt people's? Why didn't anyone look inside? I didn't see why it was a big deal, but of course I hadn't seen what they had been doing! I thought it was funny that everyone was so upset, I couldn't figure out what was the big deal. 'Cause I was young and foolish!

What was Ray Milland like as a director?
He was *annoyed*. Maybe he wasn't sure he wanted to do the movie. Maybe they weren't paying him enough. Maybe he didn't have any support. I don't know. But I got the feeling that he was just a little bit ... *nervous* as a director. He was really an *actor*, primarily, and not every actor *has* those other skills [directing skills]. I don't think it was because he didn't *know* what to do as a director, but I think ... maybe he wasn't the kind of person who liked *dealing* with a lot of people. *You* must know how stressful it is to be the director. So just a lot of times, he seemed unhappy and impatient.

With everybody?
Well, with him*self*. Like somebody in a bad mood. He didn't *yell* at anyone, he didn't do anything like that, but he ... he just wasn't a fun person.

Milland did complain that AIP rushed him—probably that's what he was grumpy about.
Exactly. I mean, think of the big pictures he worked on as an actor and the way they used to work at the major studios, how meticulous and all. Think of all the big directors he worked with. And now, to make *Panic in Year Zero!*, suddenly he's got, I don't know, 20 days or whatever he had—not a long time, I'm sure.

So, did you get much direction from Milland?
I think he would simply say, "Okay, that's good, let's move on" or have us do it over. One or the other. The more I think about it, I believe he was under some time constraints. I don't think there was a lot of money for this movie—which you can probably tell just by looking at it! It doesn't have a lot of production value. You could tell by the way it was written that it was written to *not* be too extravagant.

Jean Hagen?
Jean Hagen said she had been so depressed over a recent loss. She told me the only reason that she took this film was that she was sooo lost without this person— she said she would do anything to get her mind off of it. She had been sort of semi-retired for a long time and then [co-starred in *Panic*], I think partly as a favor to Ray Milland and partly just because ... well, you know how when you're so distraught, you think, "Maybe if I work, it'll make me feel better"? Evidently this person who had died was her true love and she was just totally *lost*. She was also very professional, but obviously not in a happy mood, particularly.

Between a grumpy director and a woman who's just there to take her mind off a dead loved one—did that make the experience a bit of a downer?

It just made it serious. But Frankie Avalon was very, very nice. I wasn't one of his biggest fans, I was "older than his fans" if you know what I mean—teenagers liked him, and I was in my twenties. But he could not have been nicer, could not have been more professional. Of all of us at that moment, he had the most going for him in terms of being a current hero. Everybody knew Frankie Avalon, whereas most people under a certain age who weren't film buffs probably were not familiar with either Ray Milland or Jean Hagen. So Frankie was the guy with the little entourage, he was the guy who was, at that moment, The Star, the big moneymaker. And he in fact was probably the draw for the movie. He could not have been more cordial and friendly, to everyone.

Where was Panic *shot?*

Out in the Santa Monica Mountains, at some movie ranch—that's where we shot a lot of the exteriors. A scene at, say, a gas station would have just been some … funky place [a real-life gas station]. The interior of the cave was a set.

Milland's character—once he realizes it's now a dog-eat-dog world, he becomes kind of ruthless in order to protect his family. As I watch the movie, I say to myself, "He's turning into an s.o.b. … but, you know what? If this really happened, this is the kind of s.o.b. I'd want to be with."

And probably everybody would get that way, too [after an atomic attack]. Because you obviously have to look after yourself. There are a lot of people who, when the ship is sinking, would become [ruthless]. It probably would be scary.

One of the best things about Panic, *I think, is that it's the kind of movie where, every step of the way, you the viewer plays along. Each time the family faces a tough choice, you ask yourself what you would do.*

Yeah, that's true. And like a lot of those early [science fiction] films, too, it uses not so much blood and gore and effects as imagination. Like *The Twilight Zone* or something. It was based on a good idea.

Getting back to the rape scene—you remember Dick Bakalyan as an actor, but the other two guys [Rex Holman and Neil Nephew] as not?

They were just punks.

The girl we'd most like to be stuck in a bomb shelter with: Mitchel as she appeared in the duck-and-cover era *Panic in Year Zero!*

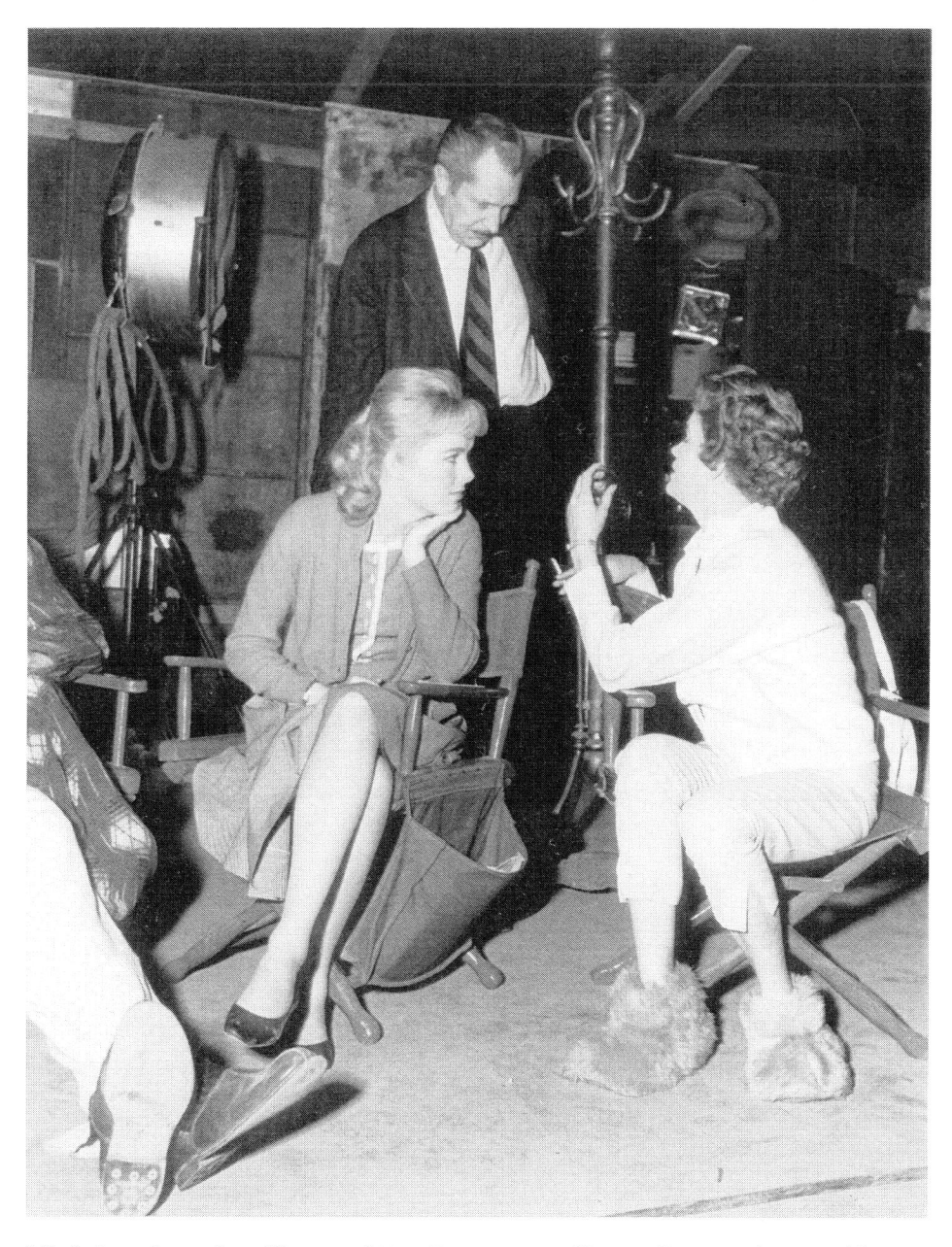

Mitchel watches as Jean Hagen and *Year Zero* set visitor Vincent Price catch up on old times.

In real life?

Yeah! I don't know if they were actors, or if they were actors *and* punks. But they were ... like ... weird. Dick Bakalyan was a professional actor, but the other two were like just ... I don't know. I got a very weird vibe! When you're doing that kind of scene, you're supposed to choreograph the action and do only what's choreographed. But they were very rough with me.

A couple times in that scene, as they're shoving you around, it does look like you were lucky not to lose your footing, they get so rough.

Yeah. And their banter was like … it was like they *dug* it.

In the days building up to the filming of the rape scene, did you see it as a good dramatic opportunity, or as something that you weren't looking forward to?

It was *all* an opportunity. I didn't think *any*thing would be something I would *not* look forward to. It was just … interesting.

With all the talk these days of terrorists on U.S. soil and "dirty bombs," a picture like Panic in Year Zero! *would be very timely today.*

Exactly, because people are more scared than they have *ever* been. In the '50s, I was one of those school kids who was supposed to drop and get under their desk, and I remember it sort of entering into my childhood mind, "Gee, maybe the atom bomb *will* come and maybe I *could* die." But only as a sort of boogie man, not a *real* thing. At the same time, I also remember that anybody who built a bomb shelter and who talked about "When the A-bomb comes…" was considered a nut! I think

The young actors (Rex Holman and Neil Nephew) who assaulted Mitchel in *Year Zero* played too rough and behaved as though they really "dug it," the actress recalls.

I took that cue from my parents, who just thought, "Oh, for God's sakes…" [*Laughs*] They were from Kansas and they were like, "Oh, get your act together. That's nothing to be worrying about—what the heck you gonna do about *that*?" It's exactly like people today who say that you'd better go arm yourself and build a bunker, because the U.S. government's going to let loose robots, or take away our civil rights, or … well, what*ever* alarmists are alarmed about *now*, there were those same people after World War II who were sure that the Commies were gonna bomb us and that we were all going to die. People who liked to scare themselves. That was my "take" on it, at least. Educated, civilized people didn't bother thinking that an A-bomb was going to annihilate us, because after all, in a way, what can you do about it [*laughs*]? Even then, everybody knew that getting under your desk was not gonna prevent you from being blown up! Even as a child, I thought, "Getting under my desk? Flying glass? If there's radiation, we're all going to be dead anyway—why get under your desk?" [*Laughs*]

In the final analysis, is Panic *a good picture?*
   I couldn't tell you 'cause I haven't watched it for a long time. At the time I did it, it was a step up. Afterwards, though, I seemed to remember its flaws. It's weird how films seem to "change." Some of the good ones get better, some of the good ones get worse—and some of the bad ones get better [*laughs*], because they're so funky, or so *some*thing. I'd imagine it would be an "okay" film. I don't think it would *ever* be considered a *great* film!

Your next picture was Francis Ford Coppola's Dementia 13, *produced by Roger Corman and shot in Ireland. How did you get that part?*
   It was just through my friendship with Francis and his wife Ellie.

Who were not *yet man and wife.*
   Correct. I could tell when I read the script that it was going to be a good horror film. I *still* think that. It just had more going for it. And I remember when I was doing it, I was happy to be there, and thought it would be good. Again, I didn't think it'd be a *great* film—we didn't have a lot of money. But I think that Francis was able to give it some production value.

So Coppola offered you the part?
   Francis knew that Bart and I were planning to go to Europe anyway, so he called and said, "Would you come be in the film?" Francis wrote *Dementia 13* while he was working as a sound man for Roger Corman in France, on *The Young Racers* [1963]. He wrote it thinking of us. And then he told Roger that if Roger would give him the equipment, he could run over to Ireland and make this movie.

How did you get to know Coppola in the first place?
   He was a friend of Bart's 'cause they were in the UCLA film department together. Bart was very experienced and efficient as an a.d.—he was one of those people who knew how to put things together, and people *liked* him. Francis at that

time was a funny guy, but he did *not* have some of the qualities that Bart had, of working with people, getting them to do things and just making a set a very comfortable and happy place. At that time, Francis was a little more shy, and was kind of like "that weird guy from New York." [*Laughs*]

At UCLA, Francis had done a film called *Eamonn the Terrible*, which was shot in L.A., very cheap. It was about a crazy sculptor. They used a character actor, a wonderful, older character actor with a really craggy face, Richard Hale—he was fabulous. *Eamonn the Terrible* was for Francis' Master's thesis, and his claim to fame in the theater department at that time was, he was the first person in like ten years to finish a film [*laughs*]. Nobody else in the film department ever finished a film, they just stayed *on* and on and on at the campus and worked on their films, they didn't have any concept of the "business" part of "show business." So Francis and Bart just kind of locked together, because Bart knew how to get it done and Francis *wanted* to get it done. They went to the studios and they got a Chapman crane from some studio, to shoot at Forest Lawn, and they got all these concessions from the studios because they were the first kids who thought, "Well, we live in Hollywood—let's go *ask* 'em!"

At that time, the studios had *no* interest at all in young filmmakers. Nobody came out of the universities, nobody was considered to be knowledgeable or be of any value at *all*. In fact, [young filmmakers] were totally barred from any kind of jobs whatsoever, couldn't get near a studio *or* a set. They was no mentoring, there was no *nothin'*, 'cause there was nothing in it for the old guard. There was only one person who offered young actors and filmmakers an opportunity, and that was Roger Corman. His was the only company where you could maaaybe get a foothold. Because … [his pictures] were *cheap* [*laughs*]! Not only is Roger a discriminating filmmaker, but he's a businessman. He was and he *is*. He always used to offer actors the lowest possible amount you could imagine. But he *paid* it. Which can't be said for *some* companies, where they would, like, flake out. Whatever Roger said he would do, he would do. So in that way, he was quite fair. He got everybody real cheap and he made inexpensive films, and he was quite a marketer.

Anyway, to get back to your question, I met Francis through Bart, who was then my boyfriend. And, because I was in the theater department a lot doing plays and stuff, Francis stopped me one day and asked if I would be in a film that he was making. I said I couldn't because I was failing French IV. Francis *still* throws it in my face, he *loves* to say, especially when there are a lot of people around, "Oh, Maaary … just think where you could be *now* if you hadn't been failing French IV…" [*Laughs*]

He wanted you to be in one of his UCLA films.

Well, actually, he told me later he just wanted to meet me, he didn't really have a film!

So Coppola called from overseas and offered you parts in Dementia 13, *you and your husband. Had you ever been overseas before?*

No.

Where did you stay in Ireland?

We rented a house from an English colonel and his daughter Bridget. The colonel lived in sort of like a neo-classical home ... think of a Southern plantation, kinda ... in Wicklow County, south of Dublin. The colonel looked like ... who's the man on the can of peanuts?

Mr. Peanut? With the monocle and the top hat?

He was like from Central Casting, it was hysterical! The colonel's daughter Bridget considered herself a decorator and she'd taken a little caretaker's cottage on her father's estate and turned it into the *most* charming, corny, English-style, chintz curtains, stuffed sofas—I guess what was considered cute at the time in England. It was like a guest house for perhaps a young family with two children or something. She had knocked herself out, she had worked really hard, and everything was provided down to the last little teacup, just finished off very, very cute. So who comes along but Francis and Ellie, wanting to rent this guest house. But they sent Bart and me as sort of "front people," 'cause I guess we looked the straightest and the most respectable—they sent us to tell the colonel and his daughter that we would like to rent it. And then to tell them that, actually, we had several people on a film crew shooting nearby who would like to stay there too. They looked askance at that because, to the old guard English, a film crew of Americans was probably a bunch of hooligans. But somehow we charmed them into thinking that it was going to be *just* lovely. And like ten people moved into the house. Then, because we didn't have any money, [Coppola and the gang] ended up stripping the house completely and taking everything in it, the rugs, the furniture, everything, over to Ardmore Studios, to dress the sets for *Dementia 13* [*laughs*]! And who do you think opened the door the day that Bridget came over to see how things were?

Uhhh ... you?

I said, "...Oh... Hello..." She said [*cheerfully*], "I just thought I'd come by and I ... I ... I..." She looked around, and there was nothing there [*laughs*]! What could I say?? It was funny.

How upset was she?

She was in shock. She'd obviously led a sheltered life, the sheltered, land-owning, English rich of Ireland. This cottage was her baby, it was very cute inside, it was like a dollhouse—and now she comes to the door, and she sees that the place is stripped [*laughs*]! I still remember the look on her face, as she looked past me!

How did ten people fit into this dollhouse?

It was a house with three stories. Up in the attic were two little beds. Then down on the second floor were two bedrooms, and down on the bottom floor was a dining room and a living room with two couches. There were people everywhere!

Another thing: The colonel and his daughter invited us to tea or something, before we had moved in, and they said, "*Don't* trust the Irish, they'll steal from you." Their way of discussing and speaking about the Irish people who were on their

Dementia 13 writer-director Francis Ford Coppola wrote two of the cult classic's leading parts with his former UCLA classmates Mitchel and Bart Patton in mind.

estate and in whose country they were living, was like a bigoted Southerner would speak about black people. That they were a subspecies, that they were just worth nothing. *Meanwhile*, the guy who worked for the colonel, his right hand man Willie Vines, was a guy who lived in abject poverty on the estate—Willie and his family lived next to the pig sty, in what would be considered a hut. And Willie was like a *brilliant* guy! He probably never went to school beyond the fourth grade, but he knew hydroelectricity, he knew plumbing, he knew construction, he knew agriculture—in other words, he could do *anything* they wanted. He was just one of those really smart guys, and a wonderful, wonderful guy.

The colonel was English and Willie was Irish.
 Indeed.

Whenever William Campbell, the star of Dementia 13, *talks about the movie, he mentions shooting in the castle. But the credits say—and you just told me—it was shot at a place called Ardmore Studio. Who's right?*
 We shot on the grounds of a castle but we didn't shoot *in* the castle that I remember. Well, maybe there *were* scenes shot in the castle on a day I wasn't working, but *I* really don't remember myself shooting in the castle. I remember them

shooting an exterior of the castle at night, a scene where Ethne Dunn came stumbling out and found a ring or *some* little something, I forget what, on the ground. She was supposed to come out the front door and run down the tall flight of stairs *to* the camera (the camera was on the ground, in the gravel) and reach down and pick up this little item. They had to light with arcs and it was a big part of the budget to shoot the exterior of the castle at night, but it was to give the picture production value, right? So they took *hours* and hours to set up the shot while the rest of us were all *in*side the castle and it was very cold and it was like three in the morning and everybody was bored and cold. And there was a little rum or something, a little Irish whiskey to keep the people feeling okay. Francis used a double to set the shot up, then he called, "All right, Miss Dunn, we're ready," and he showed her what was to be done.

So now the door opened and Ethne Dunn ran down the stairs and she ran up to where the camera was, to pick up this little thing ... and she reached for it and she *missed* it [*laughs*]! Because she was [*loudly*] *drrrunk*! They had to do it until she [got it right], and then of course they realized that she was *running* like a drunken person! And they were afraid she'd fall down the stairs! It was just so ludicrous. Of course, Francis was really mad, 'cause he expected her to be a professional!

What kind of place was Ardmore, compared to a Hollywood studio?
About the same as one of the smaller studios around town. In other words, it wasn't like Warner Bros. with 31 huge stages. Maybe Ardmore *was* larger than I'm remembering, but I just remember a small sound stage.

What did you do nights, you swingin' young people thousands of miles from home?
Actually, we were kind of stuck out on this little location, maybe a half an hour or an hour from Dublin. And I myself didn't have a car to cruise around. At some point, Bart and I did have a car, and looked around a little bit. But actually, he was quite busy, because he was also working on the picture as like the first a.d.

In addition to co-starring in the picture.
Right. So he was working with Francis a lot.

What was Coppola like on this movie director-wise?
He was like he *always* is. He hasn't changed. He was thinking, and saying what he needed to say, and trying to make it good, and frustrated when there were things that he couldn't have but he wanted. But he was always very good and gentle with the actors—he's always had an understanding of that whole "world."

Reportedly his sister Talia was also there.
She *was* there for part of the time, right. She was still in school, I think, at the time.

Remember the scene where you arrive at the castle and kiss Campbell, and Bart Patton is standing there? Campbell told me that he felt awkward kissing you right in front of your husband—and that he thought Bart felt awkward too!

I think it was more likely the love scene in the hay where he felt that way. Seems to me that scene was supposed to be ... erotic, or whatever [*laughs*]!

Yeah, he mentioned that one too. So Campbell *feels awkward, he thinks* Bart *feels awkward. How do you feel?*

Awww, just *do* it, y'know? [*Laughs*] But nobody should have *really* felt awkward—it's just what you *do* [when you're an actor]. Incidentally, Roger sent a famous telegram at that time, and I reminded him of it recently. We [the *Dementia 13* moviemakers] didn't get to see the dailies, they were shipped back home and only Roger got to see them. And he sent Francis a telegram, a "famous" telegram in *my* mind, which said, DEAR FRANCIS, DAILIES LOOK GREAT. MORE SEX AND VIOLENCE. LOVE, ROGER.

[Laughs] That sounds very much like a telegram he would send!
What can I say? It was the perfect telegram!

Jack Hill tells me that Corman always called you "the perfect victim."
[*Softly*] It's true. I don't know why. I just remember thinking, "I hope he means not in my *real* life!"

Karl Schanzer, who plays the poacher in Dementia 13, *and who later appeared in* Spider Baby—*was he there in Ireland with you?*
No, we shot that when we came back to Los Angeles. They either needed more scenes ... maybe it wasn't long enough ... or maybe they needed more "suspense."

Schanzer does get killed in the picture—decapitated with an axe.
Maybe that was the MORE VIOLENCE. I'm sure they shot that in a vacant lot in the dead of night for a nickel [*laughs*]. A bit of the picture was photographed at our house in the Hollywood Hills, in the middle of the night. This stuff was all added later, and it was really kind of ... funky, fly-by-night kind of footage.

Did you work long hours on Dementia 13?
I wasn't in some of it, so I never had a sense that I was working long, long, long. And the truth is, you *always* work long hours. People who aren't in the industry forget that for *us*, a 16- or 17-hour day is fairly normal. What it means is that you start to understand just how far you can push yourself! If you're on a big feature and you work those long hours, especially a six-day week, for a couple of months, you start being *not*-normal. And at the end, it's two weeks before you're normal again! You're so exhausted.

I can see working 16-hour days for maybe a week ... but not again the next *week!*
Maybe for two weeks you can do it. But when you start getting into, like, the second month, you start waking up feeling like somebody beat you up. Your whole body is saying, "Don't get out of bed." And then on your days off, too, you're a vegetable. All you can do is do your laundry and get depressed, because you have no

energy to get up. And it's extra-depressing on location, because if you're working in an interesting place, you want to take those days off to at least *be* there. When I worked on location on films like *The Mask of Zorro* [1998], or when we were on *Bram Stoker's Dracula* [1992], the days were just sooo long that you become a shadow of your former self. And all of your papers and bills, they build up like a big sandwich, 'cause you never get to tend to anything! So, in addition to everything else, at the end of a feature, your life is a complete shambles [*laughs*]!

You ride a horse in Dementia 13.

Yeah, Champ. We rented a horse from this young guy whose name escapes me, but he was the son of one of the cooks who came in to cook for us. The deal was, for £200, Bart and I could keep the horse the whole time we were there, feed him and then give him back. We gave him £200 and we were supposed to get 100 back. Francis put the horse in the movie, because—why not? Use *every*thing! The horse is in the movie because … we had a horse [*laughs*]!

Well, our deal to rent the horse turned into one of those classical scams where, when it came time for us to get our £100 back, the guy put it off and put it off. Bart and I were getting ready to leave, we were going to take the boat across the Channel to England, and still no money. The final schlemiel-schlimazel part was, he said, "I'll meet you at the boat and return your money"—isn't that the classic sucker thing? Okay, okay, so we got all ready to leave Ireland, we showed up ready to take the boat, and he just didn't come and didn't come. And so we didn't take the boat, 'cause … we were stubborn. We went to his mother's house in Newtown Mount Kennedy, a *very*, very small little town, knocked on the door and said, "*Where* is X with our money?" And she was so ashamed, and she said, "He lost it all on a dog race." [*Laughs*] Well, we *needed* that money. We wanted to do some touring but we didn't have a lot of money. £100 was like … I don't know, a couple hundred dollars.

A heck of a lot of money in 1962.

Maybe if it had been *ten* pounds, we would have said, "Oh, the heck with it." That's what *he* was hoping, that we would just get on the boat. Well, we didn't. We were stubborn and hung around, and finally everybody scraped up some money for us. And *that* was the story of Champ the horse!

At the end of the picture, of course, Patton turns out to be the axe murderer.

That scene at night, that exterior, where I'm in the wedding dress and he's attacking me with the axe—that was shot on our first wedding anniversary. I thought that was sort of ironic. I said, "I hope this doesn't portend our marriage!" [*Laughs*]

On a laserdisc audio commentary for Dementia 13, *William Campbell said that you and Bart Patton were "very, very passionate" about being in the picture business.*

Well, Bill was kind of a jaded guy at the time—he was kind of like "the old experienced guy" who'd been in a hundred movies and done it all. That was just his air, he was "the man of the world," a very grand guy. After we finished the picture, Bill, because he had been (in *his* mind) suffering, decided he would go to a very fancy English hotel—one of the old guard, fancy hotels where all the movie stars stayed. But before he left [Ireland], he told Bart and me, "Oh, you must call me when you get to London, and I'll take you to Rules," which was a famous English actors' restaurant. So when Bart and I got to London, we called him and he said, "Come on up to my suite and we'll have a drink and then we'll go to Rules." So we went up and a *butler* answered the door! The butler was hysterical, he had, like, this smile at the corner of his mouth because here was this completely uncivilized American chap [Campbell] who didn't know *what* to do with him! Here was Bill, the "high roller," ensconced in a suite of this *very* grand English hotel, with a cocktail in his hand, and this butler waiting on him hand and foot, hanging around and putting Bill's slippers on his feet and serving him whatever he wanted to drink, liquor, at any hour of the day or night. And Bill was trying to show off for us, he was telling the butler [*grandly*], "All right, bring us all a *drink!*" And then he was saying things like, "He'll even put on my *socks* if I ask him to!" [*Laughs*] "Won't you?" And the butler was going [*with an English accent*], "Yes sir, yes sir..." Clearly, the butler thought that Bill was a very funny American who had no idea what to do, and the guy was obviously just humoring Bill!

Incidentally, when we were in Ireland the first time, it was a very poor country—people with no teeth, no nice cars, nothing nice. If children had problems, medical problems, nobody had any money to fix anything. *Very*, very poor. Then the second time Bart and I went, around 1966, the place had changed immensely. It was such a delight to see that it was beginning to prosper. Then I went back to Ireland about ten years ago, and it was amazing—now it's like Silicon Valley. New cars, healthy people, they're buying back their own palaces and so on. There are a lot of wealthy Irish people, and it's really wonderful to see. Because the first time I was there ... anybody who had *any*thing, it was an English person living there.

A little earlier, you mentioned the colonel's right hand man Willie Vines. I see in the credits of Dementia 13, Best Boy: Michael Vines.

Michael Vines was one of Willie's seven children.

And they all lived in that little hut near the pig sty?

Yeah, the pigs were right outside the door. Picture this muddy, whitewashed two-room place that you walk through the pigpen to get to the front door. And, it was so sad, something was wrong with all the Vines' children. One boy had a severe limp. One girl was cross-eyed. One child was mentally ... not there. Every child had some small or great deformity, and one of the *greatest* ones was, one of their sons was like a dwarf, he was physically quite grotesque, stunted, whatever. Years later, Bart and I went back to visit them—we called to tell them that we were there and asked, "Could we come by?" We had our first child Jeffrey with us, who was a baby, he was two at the time.

This is the second visit to Ireland that you were telling me about before.

Right. And the Vines said, oh, they'd *love* to have us come by, would we like to come to tea? Now, these people were the age of, like, your grandparents, because they probably started young having children and *continued* to have children—they were Catholic, right? Willie was probably in his fifties or sixties, and of course they looked older than they were because they had hard lives. We arrived and we went to their little house beyond the pig sty, we went in the front door, and here was an immaculate, perfectly set table with beautiful white Irish linen, serving this most beauuutiful tea in this beauuutiful tea set. It was so moving. And they'd had another baby, this darling little baby, and Mrs. Vines said [*beaming*], "…We've finally got a *perfect* one." It was sooo … [*cry of anguish*]! It was very sweet to see.

If you'd had your druthers, what roles would you have played? Did you want to be the next Katharine Hepburn, the next Sandra Dee, the next…?

I didn't entertain that thought. I just sort of wanted to make *more* films, and *good* films. Even at the time, I didn't feel quite comfortable being cast as what I *was*, which was a young, cute, pert blonde. It wasn't that I longed to be taken as a complete, serious, dramatic actress, but I *did* have illusions of doing some films that … [*laughs*] that I would like to see! Films that had interesting parts. Good parts. I wanted to be a part of good movies.

As an actress, did you ever do a good movie?

That's for *you* to say, my friend!

Next up, Spider Baby—*or, as it was titled when they were initially starting out,* Cannibal Orgy.

Yes! Bart was going to be working on it as a first a.d., helping [writer-director] Jack Hill out. That was *his* gig, and then they wanted me to play a part because Jack liked me, or because it was convenient, or because we could get some money [*laughs*], or … *all* those things! So I did.

It was made very, very quickly.

And it was fun. Jack, like Francis, just liked making the film. He was tremendously excited and enjoying the experience. Everybody was kind of young and everybody kind of had fun. Jack was interested in the weirdness of the Spider Baby girls, and he had cast these two girls who he thought were quite good and interesting. Beverly Washburn was [in real life] like a regular, happy, nice person, but playing this twisted part. But Jill Banner, the other girl—she was quite a strange girl. She really was. She was young and strange. Which was kind of interesting, because she was *supposed* to be strange, but she really *was* just very … strange.

Anything you could put your finger on or, like the two guys in Panic in Year Zero!, *just funky vibes?*

She was just a very bizarre girl. I mean, she didn't *do* anything, she just had a funny way *about* her.

Jack Hill had been the second unit director on Dementia 13. *Did you initially meet him on that?*

Maybe. I don't remember.

Ankles away! Jill Banner (with saw), Sid Haig and Beverly Washburn give Mitchel a taste of Spider Baby-*style hospitality.*

Lon Chaney — did you see enough of him to come away with any strong impressions?
  Yeah, he was just a great ol' guy. You knew that he had had this long career — even *I*, who knew nothing, knew that he was like somebody special. Everyone made a great effort to make him feel comfortable, because at that time he was quite old, and he was a little ... overwhelmed by the craziness of everything. But he was happy to be working, you got the impression. And it was a hot afternoon when he had to do that scene in the car. It was hard for him. Everybody did everything they could to make him feel comfortable, but I'm sure it was always much faster and more confusing than he was used to.

Jack Hill says that Chaney liked the movie enough that he cut way back on his drinking in order to do the best possible job.
  He was just shaky ... fragile. But I wouldn't say that he was drunk or didn't know what he was doing. Even while being confused, I remember it was very important to him to do things correctly. He was a professional.

And another oldtimer in the movie, Mantan Moreland — did you encounter him?
  Mantan Moreland — a darling guy. Happy to be working. But I felt completely embarrassed at the stereotype that was written, and that he played. But *that* was what he *did*, and he was *still* playing, "Oh, boss! Oooh, no!!" It was a little late for that — it was the '60s, you know what I'm saying? Here's this guy co-existing with the Black Panthers [*laughs*]? So that was pretty weird!

Some of your other co-stars, Sid Haig and Quinn Redeker?
Sid was a serious actor at that time, and so professional and such a wonderful guy. We remained friends afterwards. I haven't gone to a lot of the [*Spider Baby*] reunion-type things, but I went to one and saw him and he was just as nice as ever. Quinn Redeker was and is a very nice guy, a funny, funny person trapped in a normal, "straight" leading guy's body.

According to Jack Hill, Spider Baby *was financed by a couple of real estate guys.*
It was the beginning of the days of, say, doctors financing films and things like that. I remember that they were just sort of ... bogus [*laughs*]. You meet really weird people in these fringe areas of films. guys like you would meet in Vegas [*laughs*]. Slick, slick! They all had the same attitude; whether they were selling cars or selling movies, it was the same attitude. "Let's get this show on the *road*, come *on*, come *on*, let's make some mmmoney, heeeey!"

The first time I saw Spider Baby, *I didn't have much use for it—but it's kind of grown on me.*
They get better. The more you watch 'em, the better they get! The first time I saw it, I thought it was ridiculous. I thought it was the silliest thing I ever saw. I thought it was funny, like a takeoff.

So you enjoyed it—but in a "ridiculous" way.
I don't even know if I enjoyed it. I just thought it was really silly. I mean, I liked Jack, and I knew what it was and what it was for. But I just thought it was completely silly. What a silly plot—the spiders, and *all* of that! I thought I was pretty funny in it, because I was the only "straight man." I was the foil, to play off of.

What prompted you to give up on the acting career?
During that time, I felt that I was just sort of "faking it" as an actress, and that there was more *to* it. I felt *I* was going on instinct and I knew that there were actors who were *trained*, and my fear was that something would come along, a really difficult and good part, and that I would be unprepared, and that I would waste a good opportunity. So, I studied acting.

This is after *your movies?*
Yeah. I went to New York and studied with Stella Adler and Uta Hagen, both renowned teachers. Afterwards, I came back to Los Angeles, I was maybe 30—and I couldn't get arrested! Because I was no longer 20. I did some live theater in Los Angeles, I worked with several local theater companies, the Provisional Theater and so on, but mainly I did commercials. I did *very* well doing commercials. But there came a moment ... there came a moment, Tom ... when I was on the set with Mr. Whipple and I squeezed the Charmin ... and I thought, "For *this*, I studied??" I just went, like, "This is *it*. This is the end. I'm outta here!" I just said I wasn't gonna do that any more.

Then I started doing my own projects, I started writing and directing and doing theater and multimedia performance art, conceptual art—it was *that* time, the avant garde art scene. Bart was of great help during that time, and helped me to mount a lot of productions. I found myself working as an artist again, because I wanted to do something I could *do*. If you start waiting for someone to call you and you're not doing the work you want to do, well, then, do it your*self*!

Then I became affiliated with Francis Coppola again. I was in New York, he knew I needed a job, and he asked me if I wanted to work with his production designer Dean Tavoularis. So I became a researcher for Dean on *The Godfather* [1972], and my job was to get all the period magazines for a scene at a newsstand where the Godfather [Marlon Brando] is shot. I was dealing with this guy, this old guy who had a warehouse out in Brooklyn where he had every magazine in the world. But he wasn't sure if he wanted to give them to me! *Months* passed in pre-production and I would *romance* him and he would give me *one*, he would give me *two*, but he would tell me he had a *warehouse* full of 'em. Fiiiinally I went out in my VW van and he let me into the stacks and I chose about 50 of them. I literally drove up to the set with them the day they were shooting. It was *quite* dramatic [*laughs*]!

How come my memory is that the Godfather got shot at a fruit stand, not a newsstand?

Because he *did* get shot in a fruit stand. At the time I was getting the magazines, it was at a newsstand, but later it was *changed* to a fruit stand!

[Laughs] All that work went to waste??

After months and months and months and months...! But they used the magazines in other places. When you're dressing a set, like the Corleones' house, or what*ever*, you always want to have those period magazines around. Then Francis sent me down to Little Italy to get some scrapbooks and do some research on the Mafia. All these young punks came running out of all the doorways in Little Italy saying, "*I'm* in the Mafia! *I'm* in the Mafia!" [*Laughs*] If they *were* the Mafia, would they have come running to *say* they were in the Mafia? It was all very ... surreal.

Francis and Ellie ... our kids were all the same age and I was friends with Francis and Ellie, so I saw them a lot during that time. They had a little apartment down in Greenwich Village. Francis was a hireling—Paramount didn't have any respect for him particularly, he was just "that kid." One time he got so frustrated that he kicked a door down at Paramount. And he said to me, "Y'know, it's no fun kicking a door down around here, because they send a carpenter and he just puts it *up* again..." But then, somewhere about halfway through the film, Paramount decided they had *some*thing. *Then* the money started coming. *Not* when Francis needed it, but practically too late. So that's why it was so sweet, on *Godfather Part II*, when *he* was the Big Guy. But on the first *Godfather* they did not have much respect for him and did not cooperate—he had to fight for everything.

I worked with Francis at American Zoetrope on many different films, *Hammett* and *One from the Heart* [both 1982] and a lot of films that were shot there. I was the art department coordinator for several years on and off. I even had a small

Top: Director Joe Dante, a Mitchel fan right from the start of her career, put her (and Roger Corman) *Back in Action* acting-wise in his 2003 *Looney Tunes*. *Bottom:* Roger Corman is flanked on the *Looney Tunes* set by Mitchel (who plays a script supervisor) and the movie's *real* script supervisor, P.R. Tooke.

part in *Peggy Sue Got Married* [1986], I played the teacher of Peggy Sue [Kathleen Turner]. I was working as an assistant to the art director on that, *and* I had a nice part ... but it's on the cutting room floor! Then at some point, I said, "Well, this is all cute and everything, but there are no benefits, I am not in a union, I get no overtime ... I better get in a union." That's when I became a script supervisor.

You recently acted in a film for the first time in almost 40 years, Joe Dante's Looney Tunes: Back in Action.

My son Tyler, who's a prop man, was on the set with Joe Dante, and Joe said, "I want Roger Corman to come and do a scene," and Tyler said, "Oh, my mom knows Roger Corman." Joe asked, "Who's your mother?" When Tyler said, "Mary Mitchel," Joe went, "*Mary Mitchel*? I'm her fan, I know all *about* her!" Tyler was totally taken aback and went, "Whhhhat??" Then Joe asked, "Do you think she'd come and be with Roger in this little funny bit I'm doing?" So Tyler called me and said, "Joe *knows* you!" [*Laughs*] I couldn't believe it! It was so much fun to meet him, he's so darling, he's so cute. Roger was there, too, and it was really so much fun.

Now and then over a period of years, Joe Dante has been sending me e-mails asking when I was going to try and find and interview you.

Isn't that hysterical? I had no idea...

What do you think these days when you see yourself in your 1960s movies?

It's sort of funny: It's like when you see pictures of yourself as you were at certain times in your life. You don't particularly recognize that person, but you remember immediately the sensation of having been in that place. Does that make sense to you? It's like looking at old photographs. And you're still criticizing yourself, you're still saying, like, "Boy, did my hair look dumb!" Or, "I did pretty well ... that was pretty good..." Or, "Oh my God, was I horrible!" [*Laughs*]

I have to tell you, I am so surprised that anyone today has any knowledge of some of my movies—like, say, *Spider Baby*. I can't fathom why you, or Joe Dante, or anyone, would even know about this movie! You have to remember that when these films were made, they weren't, like, the biggest films coming out, they were B films. Made to be seen, and to disappear. No one ever thought that they would be seen again on tape or DVD. It's come as a surprise to many of the people who worked in those old horror films— a surprise of varying degrees of embarrassment—to realize that they are still around and that there are people watching them!

Mitchel in the clutches of murderous Sid Haig in the black-comic *Spider Baby*.

Elliott Reid

> *[The Absent Minded Professor's Shelby Ashton]*
> *was an awful,* awful *creature! But he was fun to play—*
> *I loved,* loved *playing the part.*

It might be difficult for movie fans to name a supporting character more smug and insufferable than Shelby Ashton, the high-handed college English department doyen who, in two classic comedies of the early 1960s (*The Absent Minded Professor* and *Son of Flubber*), is the constant thorn in the side of his romantic rival, science prof Ned Brainard. But then, unfortunately for Shelby, the worm turns: Prof. Brainard invents "Flubber" (flying rubber), a substance possessing powerful anti-gravitational energy. Brainard uses it to help the school's basketball team spring to victory; to help the school bounce back from the brink of bankruptcy ... and, best of all, to give Shelby his well-deserved comeuppance.

Perhaps it's the situations and dialogue that make Shelby such a memorably maddening character, but more likely most of the credit should go to Elliott Reid, the veteran comic actor who was at his best in arrogant and condescending roles—and who was never better than as Prof. Brainard's (Fred MacMurray) needling nemesis. Born in New York, Reid broke into show business via radio as a kid, began acting in *March of Time* broadcasts as a teenager and became a member of Orson Welles' fabled Mercury Theatre at 17. Movie and TV roles followed, some (but not enough) taking advantage of the talent for mimicry that he honed in a succession of stage productions (Reid often wrote his own material). He even battled foreign agents attempting to wage germ warfare in the U.S. in the SF-tinged suspenser *The Whip Hand* (1951)—although Reid's rendition of a two-fisted hero in this Howard Hughes production remains one of his least-favorite performances.

The master of on-stage arrogance proved to be the exact opposite in real life as he recently settled down to recount some highlights of his nearly lifelong career.

At what point did you decide you wanted to be in show biz?

When I was ten years old, in Siwanoy School in Pelham Manor, New York, where I grew up. They did a play at the school of Dickens' *A Christmas Carol*, and they gave me the part of Scrooge. In all modesty, I did very well with that part, and got some very good laughs. I had never *heard* laughs from an audience before, really. The whole experience, the lights, the warm laughs, an audience that was appreciative … that's when I decided I wanted to be an actor. And my parents offered no objection whatever. Of course, I wasn't able to go and *be* an actor at the age of ten!

A few years later, my mother, who was a fashion artist, and knew some people in the theater and so on, heard of a new play that was currently being cast, called *Little Ol' Boy*, a play set in a boys' reformatory. Burgess Meredith made his first big success in that play. Somehow or other an appointment was made for me to meet the director and, on a very rainy day, my mother and I took the train from Pelham and went to the office of Chamberlain Brown, a well-known theatrical agent of that time. My hopes were soaring, but quickly dashed. The director was very nice indeed, but told me immediately that unfortunately I was too young to play any of the characters in that play—they were looking for boys 15 or 16 years old. I was about 12 then. So that was that. As my mother and I walked back to Grand Central, in the pouring rain, I matched the downpour with my own tears. When you're that young, you think that's the only chance you're ever going to have, to get a job. Once settled on the train, my mother, in the kindest possible way, said she thought it would be best that I stay in school for a few years and not worry about getting work in the professional theater since, at the moment, not being chosen for a part was so upsetting to me. I agreed, and did stay in school, and did get older, but never abandoning the main goal: to become a professional actor.

And how did that come about?

Actually, it was only a couple of years later. My mother wrote some very good material for me, I auditioned for the Horn and Hardart *Children's Hour* [a radio series] and was hired by its emcee Paul Douglas, and I was on that show for quite a number of weeks. But it was rather tiring for my mother to write new comedy material every week, and Horn and Hardart didn't reward their young performers with so much as a penny. Soon I began to meet other kids my age who were acting on various radio shows, and being *paid*. This appealed to me as—clearly—a better arrangement than the one I had with the Horn and Hardart Company. By now I had been accepted as a student in the Professional Children's School—indispensable to children who worked in theater or radio, as the student could leave the school (at 1860 Broadway) at any time, if he had a meeting, or audition, or rehearsals, or even a tour. They taught the same curriculum as other schools, grammar school through high school. The daily schedule and homework for each of the classes was printed out on what we called "Correspondence" and if a child was on the road, the lessons and homework assignments were mailed out to him. Still indispensable to this day, the school continues, but at a different address.

I was 14 when I entered P.C.S. and my daily ritual after school—well, almost daily—was to make the rounds of the offices of theatrical producers and also advertising agencies such as BBD&O who had various radio shows. Visits to theatrical producers' offices never yielded anything, but radio was far more promising, and I

When not appearing in films, Elliott Reid (seen here outside the New York Public Library in the 1950s) was often capitalizing on his talent for mimickry on stage and television.

began to get work. My mother had been helpful in our getting a very good audition together, and I had confidence in the characters and material I was presenting. By far the most important audition was for Homer Fickett at BBD&O, who produced *The March of Time*, a radio show which dramatized events of the day. *The March of Time* was the top of the line, perhaps the most prestigious of all the radio shows of that time. That's what made a big change in my career—a very, very drastic change for the better.

Working on The March of Time *did.*

Yes! I got an audition together with help from my mother, who was English originally. She said, "Why can't we find a little segment of something English and put it in? You can do an English accent so well." I said sure, and I did, I inserted it into the material I had. So I went into a studio on Madison Avenue and this plump gentleman came in, Homer Fickett. He said [*sternly*], "Okay, are you ready?"—he was not brimming with good fellowship. I said I was, and I launched into it, including the English part of it. He said, "Thank you very much," I said, "Well, thank *you*, sir," and I went back down to Madison Avenue. And the *next week* they phoned me and said, "This is *The March of Time* and we need you for this week's show." I could hardly believe it! Lots of times after an audition, you *never* hear from them! So here I am the *very* next week, and it was because, within a few days of my audition, Edward VIII had abdicated. The guys at *March of Time* of course prepared a sketch about Edward with several different scenes in it, including his early childhood, then his adolescence when he was 16. And I *was* 16 years old, and I had just done an English piece for Homer Fickett the director. So obviously they wanted a young actor who would sound young and who would sound English, and that was how I got hired. I walked into that studio, and that was the beginning of lifelong friendships for me. And also a big [step up] in my career—I began to get called for all kinds of shows because I was on *The March of Time*. So Homer Fickett, and his liking my work, and *giving* me work, was tremendously important to me, and I cherish his memory. He was a very amusing and very fine man.

What was your first job on stage?

It was the Mercury Theatre with Orson Welles. I was 17 years old and Orson Welles and I were actors every week on *The March of Time*. Orson was then an actor doing a *lot* of radio work. He came to me at one of the *March of Time* rehearsals and he said, "I'm going to start a repertory company and call it the Mercury Theatre, and we're going to do plays. Would you be interested in being in it?" I said, "Oh, God, *would* I." He said, "Okay, come down to the Empire Theater on Tuesday and get together a little Shakespeare, because the first thing we're going to do is *Julius Caesar*." I was no real expert with Shakespeare, I wasn't very experienced in it, but I went down and staggered through some Shakespeare. John Houseman was there, Orson's partner in the Mercury, and they said, "That's fine, that's fine," and I was hired. *Finally.* I'd been trying to get on the stage in New York for the last four years, but [without success because] I was very tall.

After having lost out on the first *role you tried out for, on account of being too small!*

That's right! By 17, I'd shot up—I was then six-one or six-two and I couldn't get a job playing The Son [of the star of a play], which was the kind of role I would be right for, if the star was a man of medium height. You'd go in to try for a part and you'd read well, they'd like you and you'd go from one room to another until finally you were in the inner sanctum, and there was the star, whoever he may have been. Now, when the star gets up to shake hands with you, and you're there about playing his *son* on stage, you are not going to get the part if you're six-foot-one. And so *radio* was a kind of savior for me, because obviously in radio it didn't matter *how* tall you were, you could be *eight* feet tall ... though you'd need a special mike! So I concentrated on radio, and finally became really very successful in radio.

Anyway, Orson invited me to be part of the Mercury Theatre and I jumped at it. After four years of my going in and out of all these producers' offices and getting *nowhere*, Orson suddenly *gave* me this. It was just practically handed to me. I began in this modern-dress version of *Julius Caesar* playing one of the conspirators, Cinna by name. And the show was the hit of all time. We had an opening night that was historic. What great notices! It "made" Orson—that's what *began* the great career of Orson Welles, the Mercury Theatre. Through the years I did *many*, many of his radio shows [*The Mercury Theatre on the Air*] and we played that season of repertory with the Mercury—I was in *Julius Caesar* and also Thomas Dekker's play *The Shoemaker's Holiday*, a bawdy Elizabethan comedy. So that's how I began in the theater.

There are a couple Mercury Theatre people I want to ask you about because of their connection with horror and science fiction movies. Did you get to know Vincent Price?

Oh, yes, of course, Vincent was in *Shoemaker's Holiday*. In fact, the entire company went to his wedding, at St. Thomas' Cathedral in New York, at 53rd and Fifth Avenue—he married a lovely actress who was also in *Shoemaker's Holiday*, Edith Barrett. Down through the years, I would meet him here and there. We weren't *close* personal friends, but he was always very warm and friendly to me, and wrote me a lovely letter about a year before he died.

What prompted him to write to you?

It was Easter time and I found some very fine hand-painted cards. Of course, Vincent was a great art expert, very well-known as such, and I thought, "I'm going to send Vincent this," because I'd heard from a good friend of mine, Norman Lloyd, another ex–Mercury actor, that Vincent was not very well. I mailed Vincent a card, and a letter with it, and I got back a lovely letter in which he made an ironic reference to "these so-called 'golden years.'" Vincent was a very fine and delightful person.

The other Mercury Player I wanted to hear about—William Alland?

Oh, of course! He later became a producer and did *Creature from the Black Lagoon* [1954] and all sorts of horror pictures. Orson picked Bill Alland to be his go-for, and he renamed him Vakhtangov. Vakhtangov, as it happens, *was* a real person, there was a very famous Moscow art director named Vakhtangov; the name appealed to Orson for some reason, and [*laughs*] he decided to call William Alland, in those days a rather small, frail-looking guy with a lot of black hair, Vakhtangov. And Orson was just terrible to him! But in a way that was half in fun. He would call out, "Vakhtangov!"—I can still hear his voice. "Vakhtangov, where *are* you? Will you get out here!"—just after he'd sent him off on some *other* errand! Poor Vakhtangov! He was also in *Caesar*, he was an extra, really. He was on stage with us, and he was very patient and resilient. And he was in *Citizen Kane* [1941]—he was the

In the Orson Welles–Mercury Theatre production *The Shoemaker's Holiday*, **Reid (center) shared the stage with Hiram Sherman, Edith Barrett (later Mrs. Vincent Price), Joseph Cotten and Norman Lloyd.**

reporter who talks mostly off-screen. Orson gave him a key role, actually, although he's seldom seen in the film.

I saw Bill in his later years, up at [actress] Peggy Webber's house on Whitley Terrace, a social get-together. In later years, you would not have recognized him, he was a *totally* different-looking person. He was bearded, heavier, somewhat lame.

We had a very cordial reunion, and some interesting talk. At one point, he said of Orson, just in passing, "Of course, he tried to destroy me ... but I survived." It was an arresting thing to say, and what he meant by that, I will never be able to tell you, because I [didn't ask follow-up questions]. I wish I *had*.

But as Bill Alland said, he did indeed survive, building a solid career as producer at Universal. I'm so glad we met again at that get-together. He always tried his damnedest, even in those distant days when he had to play the serf to Orson's czar. He well deserved the success he had, when he freed himself and went out on his own. I liked him, *always*, even back in the early days, and my heart went out to him, too, because he *was* sort of appointed as Orson's ... body-servant, almost. And it involved, in Orson's case, as you can imagine, an awful lot of assignments!

And he put up with this because he was so anxious to be a part of the Mercury Theatre?

I think so. And Orson had suddenly become an *idol*—Orson got notices that were unbelievable. So Bill Alland was associating *with* and working *for* Orson in a way that, really, nobody else *was*.

You co-starred in a horror spoof during your summer stock days: The Gorilla *with Buster Keaton, in 1941.*

It was a wonderful week. I reverenced Buster Keaton even *then*—I was 21 years old. I got hired by the Ridgeway Theater in White Plains, New York, and I was in a play ... not *every* week, but *almost* every week for the entire summer. And it was wonderful news when I heard Buster Keaton was coming, especially as I'd had a *miserable* week doing a play called *The Male Animal* with Conrad Nagel, who conceived the idea that I was trying to upstage his daughter. In *no way* was I interested in upstaging *any*body, let alone his daughter. *You* know what "upstaging" is—an actor moves to the rear of the stage [so that the other performers will be forced to turn their backs to the audience in order to talk to him]. That's all gone and dead, it's all ancient history—I haven't heard the word in 40 years!

Anyway, I spent most of my time on stage in front of a couch, so how *could* I have upstaged her? But Nagel would come to me and he was *not* pleasant, and he'd say, "You're upstaging my daughter." I said, "Mr. Nagel, I'm standing where the director *told* me to stand. And I'm front of a couch. If I *wanted* to upstage your daughter, I couldn't. Why don't you ask the director to come and talk to us? He'll tell you that I'm where I'm supposed to be." Nagel never responded to that, he said, "Well, you just [watch yourself]."

Incidentally, on the last day, Nagel came to my dressing room and he apologized and said, "I don't know why I was the way I was..." And I said [*coldly*], "Thank you." When you're 21, you're more judgmental. Nowadays I'd say "Forget it!," but in 1941 I think I gave him a somewhat frosty "thank you." He *had* made life miserable for me, the whole week he was on about this. Anyway, Keaton arrived, and it was like salvation. He was so charming and so nice. We really liked each other. Keaton brought with him an oldtime movie comedian named Harry Gribbon. Harry Gribbon was *very* well-known, he was a star in *his* way, but not in the way that Keaton was—he was an international celebrity, Keaton.

Gribbon was in the show, too?

Oh, absolutely. Keaton brought him along as his pal, an Irishman with the real "bay window" (that's what we used to call stomachs). Delightful! Sitting around with these guys was such a treat.

So you enjoyed the whole experience?

The experience was very enjoyable, except I had to memorize a part longer than Hamlet! I had a huge part, which was really to no effect: It was the straight man, really. I was the detective, and I had to ask all the questions. I *learned* it all, arduously—it was very difficult, because it was all questions. And when you've got a part where you have to ask all the questions, *you* don't get any help from the other actors because they're waiting for the questions. If you "go up," you're in deep, deep trouble.

At rehearsals, Keaton was delightful. He did his famous backward fall which he breaks only *inches* before he hits the floor. It was terrifying to watch! I asked, "How can you dare *do* it?," and he said, "I've been doing this since I was a kid"—he was in vaudeville with his parents. He had a little picture of the three of them, he and his mother and father, in their vaudeville makeup. In the picture, he as a little boy was wearing a sort of bald wig—he was supposed to be an old man or something. He had it on his dressing table in the dressing room, in a little frame.

What part did Keaton play?

I don't remember the story too well, all I remember about the character Keaton played is that it was *some* kind of a schnook. A "Buster Keaton kind of part" where he really didn't know *what* was going on, but had gotten involved in the thing anyway. What I was going on and on about as the detective, I don't remember either. There must have been a killing or something. It was all in fun, it was just a ridiculous thing that was not meant to be taken seriously.

A poor, unfortunate apprentice had to wear the gorilla suit. The gorilla suit had to be worn by the person that *fit* in it—it was not going to be altered. And it was rather big. We had one apprentice who was a six-footer, a big blonde kid, and he fit. He said, "Oh, Jesus ... *I'm* the only one that fits it." I said, "Well, you'll survive. You're young and you'll survive it." But it *was* a hot summer, and this kid had to get into this *heavy* suit. You can imagine what a gorilla suit is like, *you've* seen them. It's not easy. It was all covered with hair, it had the phony leather breast thing, and the head had to go over *his* head. And this poor guy had to do a lot of running about. He almost fainted during one matinee performance—afterwards, he said, "I almost fainted today." The theater supposedly was "air cooled"—but in those days, an electric fan blowing on big cubes of ice, *that* was the air conditioner. It was far from adequate. And of course the cool air didn't reach the *stage*, so you were bathed in perspiration on matinees. I told the kid who played the gorilla, "Thank God you *didn't* faint. It would be very hard to ad lib around a fallen gorilla!" [*Laughs*] Imagine trying to ad lib around a thing that's just lying there when it's supposed to be menacing everybody!

Anyway, Keaton and I became friends. The week after *The Gorilla* was the one week I was off, and Keaton and I had gotten along so well that I went over to some

The Gorilla, a horror-comic-whodunit stageplay, teamed Reid with an actor he long revered, funnyman Buster Keaton.

other theater, a theater that wasn't *all* that far from ours, and saw him *again* do *The Gorilla*, this time of course with another guy playing the role of the detective. *Now* I could relax and enjoy it! And we also went and we had dinner. He had just been married recently to a lovely woman named Eleanor. Incidentally, when I went to see him at the other theater, of course I went backstage and I was in his dressing room—and there once again was the picture of Buster and his parents. He treasured and cherished that.

I never really pursued a friendship with him out here [Hollywood]. Out here, I got in with a group of people, very fine, interesting, good people in the business, and I really didn't think about Buster, the fact that *he* was here. I never saw Buster again. But he was a lovely, lovely man, and I'm so glad I touched some great people like him through the years. I really cherish that, that I had that week with him. It made up for Conrad Nagel!

Once you got out to Hollywood, you made a number of appearances on the classic radio series Suspense.

That was when radio was radio! A man named Bill Spier was the producer of *Suspense*, and very often the director. I knew him from the early *March of Time* days—he was a young director then, I'd say in his early twenties. He liked my work—on a show like *The March of Time*, you have an opportunity to do many, many different kinds of parts and accents and *every*thing. Later on, there was another show that Bill directed and that I was on, *Sam Spade* with Howard Duff. It was a show that was half-comedy, it didn't take itself too seriously, and Bill cast me every single Sunday in *some* implausible role. I once said that Bill Spier had to have the kind of actor who feared nothing, and would stoop to *any*thing. He also did *Suspense*, and he must have had a good opinion of me, I guess, because he put me on quite a few *Suspense* shows too! I even did a two-character *Suspense* with Bette Davis. I have tapes of most of those *Suspense* shows, through the kindness of an organization called SPERDVAC—that's an acronym for a long, drawn-out thing [the Society to Preserve and Encourage Radio Drama, Variety and Comedy]. I did *many* *Suspense* shows, with Bette Davis, with Agnes Moorehead, with all *kinds* of people. Bill knew us all from New York, and so it was a completely relaxed situation to walk into the studio—even with Bette Davis. Bill Spier was there, and he was the most charming, witty man, and he put you, and *every*body, so completely at ease. And, incidentally, he was a wonderful musician—he could play the piano (it seemed like) concert level. He would sit down and go straight through a whole movement of a Beethoven sonata. He was *very* gifted musically.

Now the fun is over ... let's talk about The Whip Hand.

I think there's enough sadness in everyday life without discussing *The Whip Hand* [*laughs*]!

How did you end up at RKO and in contention for the part?

The Whip Hand began life as *The Man He Found*, a B movie that had real quality and a great denouement—until it was traduced, trampled upon and totally destroyed by Howard Hughes. I was sent over to RKO to see about this part, I read for it, and I *did* read well. Now, [writer-producer] Stanley Rubin claimed in his interview with you that he later realized that the reason I gave the best reading was because I was a very proficient radio actor, and "give good readings" is what radio actors *do*. Stanley accepts that as the reason I read well. It *may* be partially that, because in radio you can't dawdle around, you've got to come up with a performance in an hour, generally. So I don't discount [his opinion], but I think he somewhat overstresses the radio thing. I was sent over to RKO and I read a scene where I tell off the villains, or I've seen through their plotting—an important scene. I read it, and Stanley looked at me and he said, "That's extremely good." He was plainly impressed with my reading. Then he said, "I must confess to you, I'm really not familiar with you, I just don't know your work." I said there was no need to apologize; the reason he didn't know me, I told him, was because I spent most of my time in the East. He asked, "Is there anyone you can think of that knows you and your work, that I could talk to?" I said, "Well … John Houseman is a producer on this lot. Houseman was Orson Welles' partner in the Mercury Theatre and I'm sure he would be able to tell you about me to some extent." "Oh!," he said, "very good!," and he wrote that down. There's no question in my mind that Houseman got me the part.

By putting in a good word for you?

Oh, undoubtedly! I never asked Jack Houseman, it didn't seem a world-shaking matter, but I would bet my last dollar that Stanley called Houseman—why *wouldn't* he? It's just logical. And I'm sure Houseman, who liked me, and liked my work, said, "Oh, he's a good actor" and so on, and that was enough for Stanley. A day or two later, I was hired.

Did you come out from New York to try out for The Whip Hand?

No, I happened to be here [Hollywood]. I was still living in New York but I was out here for some other reason, which escapes me at the moment. Probably some job.

Did you feel you were right for this heroic "tough guy" part?

Yes, because I was only 30 years old, and I was used to doing any part that was thrown at me, as with summer stock. I didn't look at it and feel, "Oh, this is not for me"—I felt perfectly capable of doing it. It was only when we were actually filming it that *some* of it made me feel uncomfortable. But I didn't let it surface and become a conscious thing because, when you're acting, you have to try and believe the scene; you're not going to approach it saying, "I don't like this." Down *deep* you have that feeling, that you wish someone else was doing it, but it was only once or twice in that picture. Stanley told me that it wasn't 'til he was putting the picture together that he realized I wasn't really "tough." And that's right—I'm *not* a "tough guy," I'm a comedian, really, and a character actor. A "Robert Mitchum toughness," I think, is the quality Stanley would have liked, but that's not my persona, I don't have that quality. I think I'm okay in this, and people who see me in the picture don't say, "Why in hell is that man playing that part?"—at least, I don't *think* so!

Lines like "Okay, tough boy," delivered to germ warfare minion Robert Foulk, make Reid want to avoid *The Whip Hand* like ... well, the plague.

But you don't care for it.

Well, I like comedy, and it's what I do best. But if you're an actor, you take the part, whatever it may be, and you do the best you can with it. Especially when you're young and you need the work. You're not going to say, "Gee, I don't know if I'm completely comfortable in this"—I mean, come *on*! This is a tough world when you're 30 and you've got family responsibilities and bills to pay, you're not going to say, "Oh, I'm not sure I'm right for this." In *some* ways, I was not. My character was really, basically, "the serious Rover Boy." Do you know who the Rover Boys were? That was a series of books aimed at teenage boys—there were three Rover Boys, Tom, Dick and Sam. "The serious Rover Boy" is sort of a catchphrase if a part is gung ho and no laughs and very, very serious, very dedicated. *That* was "Dick, the serious Rover Boy"—Dick was 200 percent irreproachable in his behavior and his ideals and everything. Audiences rarely warm to that sort of character. So I referred to that part as being "the serious Rover Boy," but I meant it in a sort of joking way.

The Whip Hand had some *good* things in it, starting with a very good script by Stanley Rubin, and the great black-and-white photography of Nick Musuraca. It's really beautifully photographed thanks to [director] William Cameron Menzies and Musuraca. But Menzies never directed me, *ever*. He was very involved with the setups, with the look of it. I think his focus was more on the visual aspect of a film. And of course Menzies was really an icon in early Hollywood...

When he was a production designer—not a director.
That's right. He did the sets for Douglas Fairbanks movies—he designed *The Thief of Bagdad* [1924], for example. He was a very, very gifted man, and quite successful in early Hollywood. I was delighted to meet him and work with him, and we got along fine. Menzies was fascinating. He talked about London in the '20s, he talked about Fairbanks and *his* oddities ... we were riveted. I think we all felt this film might turn out to be something really good—unaware of course that Howard Hughes would do what he did. Even so, I've had quite a few people say that they really like *The Whip Hand*. Bob Osborne, the host on Turner Classic Movies, is a friend of mine, and he said to me, "I think this movie is a better movie than *you* think it is. And I like *you* in this movie."

I feel the same way. On both counts.
Of course, I so *deplore* what happened to the movie, when Howard Hughes *ruined* it. *Destroyed* the movie with a disgusting new ending.

The movie was originally titled The Man He Found *and the villains were Nazis.*
Correct. It was a modest, very nice B movie that was directed by a distinguished man, Menzies. The Nazis were hiding out in this little Minnesota town, and in the big finish, Matt and Janet [Reid and leading lady Carla Balenda] are in a canoe out on a lake at night and suddenly—it was Wagnerian, almost—suddenly this madman comes out onto the little balcony of a mansion on an island in this lake. And it's *Hitler*! Out comes Hitler, raving mad and screaming and half his face has been burned away by the fire in the bunker. *That* was the original ending.

I didn't know his face was burned.
Oh, yes, he had the rubber appliance put on, and it was a wonderful makeup. It was frightening! Hitler was played by Bobby Watson the vaudevillian, who played Hitler in many, many movies. He *did* look like Hitler, and he had a good living out of Hitler! Anyway, that was the denouement, and then it was just killed by Howard Hughes, who had bought RKO and I guess ran all the movies. He ran this movie and he said, "The Nazis aren't villains any more." The war was over. He said, "Make the villains Commies. Rewrite the picture." So they rewrote and changed the villains from Nazis to Communists. They were able to keep a whole lot of what we'd shot; of course, unexplained are all these blonde Aryan-looking guys in black uniforms around the town, who were meant to be the Hitler group.

After The Man He Found *had wrapped, you returned to New York. You had to come out to Hollywood a second time to do the picture over, Hughes' way.*
That's right. And an actor named Otto Waldis was brought in for the second round of shooting, to play a Commie mad scientist. He was a German actor, a very sensitive, nice man. In these new scenes, he was playing, like, the head honcho of

the Communists, and [in his island laboratory] he rode herd on a roomful of crazed, broken human beings whom he had maimed and tortured and disfigured and injected with God knows what, and they were hobbling around in bandages and crutches. It was preposterous, it was contemptible, it was so bad. So embarrassing and so disgraceful! And Otto Waldis felt terrible guilt doing this, because this was when the anti–Communist furor was starting, and the McCarthy era. Hollywood was making anti–Communist pictures, *I Was a Communist for the F.B.I.* [1951] and all those things, all this *junk*, in this dark period in our history. This was all coming along right at that time. So it's perhaps not that surprising that [Howard Hughes and RKO] did what they did to *The Man He Found*. Stanley Rubin had his name taken off the picture, and rightly so, and he had nothing further to do with it. That was the sad ending for Stanley, his "baby" had been [taken away from him]. It was an unpretentious but really very well-done B movie, as it was originally.

Memories of Carla Balenda, your leading lady, and villains Edgar Barrier and Raymond Burr?
My memory of Carla Balenda is that in the first round of shooting, her name was Sally Bliss. And by the time I came back for the retakes, she had the new and rather exotic name of Carla Balenda. Never to be seen again—I've never seen her again, and I don't know if she was in other movies! We were all in deep trouble doing these retakes. She didn't like them, *I* didn't like them, *no*body liked them. But Howard Hughes was like an oldtime potentate, and what he wanted was what had to *be*. And of course he had the money to back it up.

Did you ever set eyes on him?
Never. I don't know how long it took us to do those retakes—it must have taken a week or two, or maybe *more*. At the time I said, "I'm making my salary all *over* again," but my salary was nothing to write home about. It was just okay for a B movie. Edgar Barrier was an actor I knew from the Mercury Theatre. Edgar was a very fine actor with a delightful sense of humor. Raymond Burr I had never met before, and he was nice. He had a kind of ironic sense of humor, a little bit ... well, there was a bit of needling to it. But in fun, not for real. I saw him after the movie, he invited me to lunch at a place called La Rue, which was very famous and rather elegant, and he had an idea about starting a theater—that's what the luncheon was hung on. He wanted to do the Greek classic drama *Oedipus* and we were all going to be in tunics, and he wanted it performed at a Mexican restaurant out here called the Chili Bowl! It was a chain of restaurants and I guess he knew of one that had maybe gone out of business and was available. All of them were totally round, to look like a bowl, and there were niches in the walls where they had big jars and things. This was going to be theater in the round—well, naturally, because the whole *building* was round—and Ray was going to be on the floor in the center and then the other actors were going to stand in niches in the wall! I thought, "Well ... what if you need to go to the john or something, and you're in the niche?" [*Laughs*] He described it all as he wanted to do it, and I guess I responded courteously but maybe not with enormous enthusiasm—I thought it was the bleakest outlook for a

supporting actor I had ever heard! What are you going to get, standing in a niche, behind the audience, in a Greek tragedy? I don't think too much! It sounded, frankly, crazy to me. I decided then that *he* was one of our better eccentrics, if he was really seriously considering this! The whole thing, to me, was just bizarre.

We also had a guy in *The Whip Hand* named Peter Brocco—a *very* good villain. He was nice ... a very quiet man. And there was a guy in it named Michael Steele, a handsome juvenile, very blonde. I've never seen him from that day to this—or *heard* of him. *Whip Hand* really was a "mystery picture," a lot of people vanished! I guess I'm lucky to *be* here! A lot of 'em vanished into thin air, like Carla Balenda and Michael Steele! That was a strange, misbegotten movie, really and truly. Stanley Rubin deserved better.

Reid and Carla Balenda react to studio head Howard Hughes' edict that *The Whip Hand* needs a new denouement.

And Otto Waldis, you said, was a sensitive, nice guy.

Oh, a *lovely* man! He said, "I haff played in Berleen, I haff played Shakespeare—and look vhat I haff to do now." I said, "Otto, listen: Do you think *I* like to come back and do this, when we had a nice little movie? I *have* to do it, I can't *not* do it—I mean, they've got two-thirds of the movie already with me *in* it, and they're not going to shoot it again!" So I came back and I did it, and *almost* missed a great, great event for me back in New York. Thank God I *didn't* miss it.

What was that?

Thanks to my good friends Betty Comden and Adolph Green, I was hired for a musical revue called *Two on the Aisle* with Bert Lahr, to work in sketches—and Abe Burrows, our director, decided I should also perform a sketch of my own, my one-man impression of the Kefauver Crime Committee hearing. I was quite a good mimic, and I did the whole Kefauver Crime Committee hearings. Well, I didn't do *all* the characters, I couldn't have, but I did a number of them, including the interrogator Rudolph Halley, who had a very distinctive voice with a lisp. A wonderful voice to mimic. So after doing *The Whip Hand*, I was doing what I really *should* [comedy], and that turned my career around. And I *almost* missed being in that show because I was in Hollywood doing *The Whip Hand* retakes. Coming out here for *The Whip Hand* the second time almost lost me *Two on the Aisle*, the most important professional engagement I've ever had.

In the Kefauver thing of yours, you mimicked Halley and other Crime Committee characters?

Well, sure. Including Frank Costello, who was the quarry—he was the biggest guy in the mob at that time. And I did him very "bad," I made him sound almost animal-like. Really low-down and gravelly. I did the senators, I did Kefauver himself, who had a very gentle manner—I did all of them, just sitting behind a table. They'd close the main curtain behind me and there I was. It really was quite a success. And most all of them [the people he was imitating] all came to the show. Even Kefauver came.

Even Frank Costello?

Yes! He took the front row center, maybe 14 seats [for himself and his entourage]. This is true! I had an understanding with the cast of this show that nobody would tell me who was out front. Well, first of all, I don't like to know. Some actors love to know if someone's there. I don't have good concentration, I guess, because it bothers me a lot, and so I don't like to know. So after I finished my routine one matinee, when I was now off in the wings, one of the chorus kids said to me, "Look out at the front row." I looked out and I said, "Well ... what is it?" She said, "It's Frank Costello...!" He was right there in the center. And I had just done him [*Reid again talks in a snarling, animal-like way*]! Then the other chorus kids started coming around saying things like, "Uhhh ... when we leave the theater, please don't walk with me!" And when I came out for the bow at the end, at the curtain call, I bowed straight at him, and smiled. He was clapping, and then he raised his hands to me, clapping. Very gracious. Very, very gracious. I think he liked the celebrity of it—although, God knows, he didn't need it, he was the most famous Mafia figure we had.

You were in a Wild Wild West *TV episode ["The Night of the Sudden Plague"] about a villain out to kill hundreds of thousands of Americans with deadly bacillus. I wonder if the person who cast you remembered you in* The Whip Hand.

I remember that particularly because I liked the character, the condescending territorial governor. I enjoyed that experience very much. Bob Conrad was a bit short, a rather short guy, and he seemed a bit sullen at the beginning, in the early morning; he was polite, but distant. The producer Michael Garrison had a slightly mean tongue and he said, "Our star doesn't seem very *happy* this morning..."—a little bit bitchy, to tell you the truth. Bob denied it, of course. We began work; and the atmosphere was not exactly festive. But later, after I fluffed a line very badly, I made Bob laugh, I said something that was kind of self-deprecating. Bob said, "No, no, you're doing great." I think that he liked that I put my*self* down, and then he relaxed. Then when I left, he came over and we shook hands and he was very gracious. And I've never seen him since [*laughs*], but that's how show business is!

In 1962, Time *magazine called you a guy who "has endured 25 years of being faintly praised as the one saving grace of uniformly bad productions."*

I had just done an impression of JFK, *for* JFK present there, in Washington. The piece tells about it.

Was that a fair summation of your career?

Well, I think it was *generous*! I've been in quite a few shows, and some of them were good and some of them were not. I wish I'd been in lots more, but I kept coming out here [Hollywood] if there was a dollar to be grabbed. That *Time* piece, I thought, was very generous and very nice. It's hard to believe I was only 42 years old. Now I'm double that, *plus* a year!

A lot of fans of a certain age probably remember you best as the insufferable Prof. Shelby Ashton in the Disney movies The Absent Minded Professor *[1961] and* Son of Flubber *[1963].*

Oh! Well, there again, terrific timing: I was in another New York revue, called *From A to Z* with Hermione Gingold. I did three pieces of material of my own, and was very lucky with the notices. Hermione was not so fortunate, and we only did two weeks at the Plymouth Theater. *Now,* if we had done *longer,* I would have missed *Absent Minded Professor* because, with unbelievable timing, my agent Sid Gold called at a time when the notice was already up and I knew we were closing. Sid called me from [Hollywood] and he said, "Listen, I've got something for you at Disney. They *want* you. What's with the show?" I said, "It's *closing*." He said, "Oh, thank God!" [*Laughs*]

I asked what it was, and he said, "It's a picture called *The Absent Minded Professor.* They saw a *Loretta Young Show* that you were in, and the director [of *Absent Minded Professor*] *liked* you in that, for what he wants you to play." Which actually was a terrible, condescending, *awful* guy! Really, Shelby was the villain—the Disney villain. So Sid said, "They *want* you, but ... I told them you're in a show." I said, "Well, I won't be in it as of Saturday." Again he said, "Oh, thank God!," 'cause *Absent Minded Professor* was a good job! To close in a New York show on a Saturday and get right on a plane on Tuesday to go out to Walt Disney ... I mean, once in a while the timing just works out beyond belief. I came out and went to this *wonderful* studio. Working at Disney was like a paid vacation! It was such a pleasant, friendly atmosphere, all due to Walt Disney of course.

About the second or third day, I had a big, big scene, the scene where Fred MacMurray's flying car is bumping *my* car from up above, and I think there's some alien force above me. Then I crash into the cops' car and I come out screaming and yelling because I'm really freaked out. The cops think I'm drunk. And Shelby is outraged, *outraged* by this treatment—this guy's very, very egomaniacal, and he says, "How *dare* you!" and "I'm a professor!" and so on. You had to play that just right, and I felt I knew what to do with it. The next day, the director Robert Stevenson said to me, "Elliott, at lunchtime, you have a booking in the projection room. Walt has ordered that the projection room show *you* the scene you did with the cops yesterday. He *loves* it, and he wants *you* to enjoy it, too. It's set up for 12 o'clock, you can still get your lunch, it won't take that long. But he *insists* that you see it." That was *so* nice—can you imagine any other studio doing *that*? So I went there, to what-

Road rage (with a touch of Reid rage): *The Absent Minded Professor* **Fred MacMurray turns on his tormentor.**

ever the room number was, and the projectionist in the back behind the glass waved and he asked, "You're Mr. Reid?" I said yes, he said, "Okay, take a chair, and if you're ready, we'll start right away." I sat down in a nice big leather chair, and on came this scene. And I *do* have to say I liked it.

I was going to tell you that that was your best scene in the picture, by far.
    I think so. Because *that* demanded something. And Walt, when I talked to him later, said, "Oh, God, that scene, the way your eyes were bugging out … the whole

thing was just so wonderful!" I said, "Well, I'm so glad you liked it and I appreciate your showing it to me." "Oh!," he said, "you *had* to see it!" He was *so* nice, he really was. Well, that *was* a showy scene—that was an attention grabber! And, I'll tell you, it was *very* tiring—physically tiring. But fortunately I had prepared for it and I knew it, and the two cops [James Westerfield and Forrest Lewis] were wonderful. It *is* a very funny scene—beautifully written. So that was a happy beginning at Disney, and I did several more pictures there.

Did you like working with Fred MacMurray?

I had already worked with Fred in one other movie over at Fox, called *Woman's World* [1954]. It was not a successful movie, because of being boring. But I was in it and Fred was in it, so Fred and I had this acquaintance. But we didn't really *know* each other. Fred was a very reticent man, he was not one to lope up and start a conversation. He was of Scottish background. (My father was a Canadian with a lot of Scottish blood, and I understand Scottish people.) So Fred and I met again, because here I am in this picture. And, because I ended up working at Disney three, four times with him, we got to be *really* good friends, finally.

What did you like about him?

Oh, *every*thing. I remember this situation: There are people who will draw up a chair, if there's a star, and sit down and, really, start *interviewing* them. It's *not* a conversation, they say, "Mr. MacMurray, what do you think about this?," "What do you think about that?" Once or twice I saw that happening to him. He was such a nice, polite man, but you could see him *squirming* and you could tell he was thinking to himself, "How can I get this guy to go away?" Finally he would find some way, like he suddenly "had" to go to his dressing room.

Because Fred and I worked so much at Disney together, we gradually, easily [became friendly]. I never drew the chair over to him, I never bothered him with that kind of conversation. And I think Fred appreciated that I was good in that part—I did know how to play that part, and we had fun doing those scenes. I did what he *needed* me to do, for *his* part, for *his* reactions, and he respected me as an actor. *Then* we began to like each other. We had a couple of night shoots out on the back lot at Disney, and there was coffee, and [under those conditions] you *do* kind of chat a little bit—especially when you're the only two actors who are being used. So we got to like each other, and he could see I wasn't hustling him or trying to interview him. So we gradually built up this friendship. I knew he really liked me when, maybe on the second picture, he invited me to come to his dressing room because he had made these trout flies, these things that fishermen fling out into a river and they're very bright and gaily decorated with red and yellow. And of course the hook! He showed them to me in his dressing room and he talked about 'em, and I said, "Oh, Fred, these are works of art, my God, these are wonderful…" *Then* I realized, well, he accepts me, because I don't think he invited many people to his dressing room.

So I was greatly, greatly fond of Fred, and I think he was of me. We did another movie that wasn't a Flubber movie, we did one called *Follow Me, Boys!* [1966] which

Even at a masquerade party, Reid (as King Neptune) tries to make waves in the Fred Mac-Murray–Nancy Olson marriage (from *Son of Flubber*).

was a kind of a big Boy Scout movie. Fred played an older man who is the scout leader, and of course I played the town bastard, the *mean* guy. It was the same part as Shelby, except that it was not named Shelby, it was the vice-president of the bank. And Lillian Gish no less played my aunt! I was so impressed—that really rocked me, to walk onto a set and Lillian Gish is playing my aunt, my God! It was thrilling. So Fred and I, as I say, we had a history of working together, and after he passed away I wrote a letter to his wife, to June Haver—I wrote her about Fred and how I felt about him, how deeply I was fond of him and admired him and all of that. And I got back the *loveliest* letter saying, "Fred loved working with you and he said so many times." So I have nothing but fond memories of Fred MacMurray, I admired him, and he was so good. I think, in a way, that he had no conception of how *good* he was. His timing was impeccable, he was a *good* actor, a *wonderful* actor. I think that one he did with [Barbara] Stanwyck shows that [*Double Indemnity*, 1944]. Anyway, he was top drawer as an actor *and* as a person, he was exactly the same person as he was before he ever walked on a movie set. There was absolutely no movie star nonsense. He was the person he was, just terrific. He just wanted to do his job and then have his time off and go fishing—obviously, he loved all that. He would rather be out in hip boots in a stream than on a movie set! I greatly, greatly admired him.

And Nancy Olson as Fred MacMurray's fiancée, the gal Shelby had his eye on?

Nancy was so beautiful and a very fine actress. I remember her as being on the phone quite a bit. She was "a busy cup of tea," as my English mother used to say! She had many people she had to speak to, and a very full life, I guess. But she was very nice, very sweet to work with, never complained.

Did you see any of the Flubber effects done in person?

The basketball players wearing the Flubber shoes were on wires—obviously. There was one guy who was extremely skillful, a short, kinda blonde guy. Nancy and I were watching from the stands, with Fred sitting behind us. My character was so arrogant and awful, he made it so that Fred couldn't sit next to his own girl. Oh, he was an awful, *awful* creature! But he was fun to play—I loved, *loved* playing the part, because those parts are so much more fun than just a straight guy going to a lake in Minnesota [*The Whip Hand*]. Not to raise *that* subject again!

Reid pays the price for trying to rain on inventor Fred MacMurray's love life in *Son of Flubber*.

Robert Stevenson, the director?

A very nice, very soft-spoken Englishman. Stevenson said to me once, about his hiring me for the original *Absent Minded* [*with an English accent*], "You know, I liked you in that *Loretta Young Show* that they sent over." It was a two-character thing, Loretta Young and me in an empty apartment, no furniture in it. I thought that was interesting, that Stevenson saw *some*thing [in that *Loretta Young* performance] that made him feel I might be right for Shelby.

Your best scene in Son of Flubber *is a variation on your best scene in* Absent Minded Professor—*this time, Fred MacMurray creates within your car storm clouds, lightning and rain.*

I should have demanded a stunt check! It was no picnic. But they had an hatch in the roof of that car mock-up that would open in case something went wrong and the level of the water didn't stop rising when it was supposed to. Otherwise I would have been [at risk] of drowning because I couldn't open the car doors, the doors were buttressed closed with all kinds of junk and paraphernalia. Anyway, I had that escape hatch, but I never had to use it.

I was tucked into this fearsome thing and the water started—and it wasn't warmed either, it was cold! I will say, I had a moment of real fear, hearing that bubbling sound of the water as it began to fill the car, and knowing that it was going to go up, up, up, up, up. I couldn't hear anybody once I was in there, with the water going on and all, so everything had to be done with lights for me: Different lights let me know when to talk, when to start yelling, when to do *this*, when to do *that*, even when to turn the wheel in certain ways they wanted. It was extraordinary, and quite an ordeal. And afterwards—imagine this on a Disney set!—one of the crew brought me a nice little pony of brandy and said, "Listen, you've *earned* this." I said, "And I'll *take* it!" I was freezing!

Reid in a more recent pose.

Did you see the recent [1988 and 1997] remakes of the Flubber movies?

I wouldn't go to the Robin Williams [*Flubber*, 1997]. Everyone said it was no good, and I thought, "Well, if it's no good, why should I bother with it?" If I *had* gone, it would just have been out of curiosity, to see who played *my* part. But I thought, no, I'm not going to bother with this.

Have you got a favorite movie part?

I would say *Absent Minded Professor*. Those Flubber pictures were such a complete pleasure to work in, far and away the most enjoyable times I ever had working in pictures. And in particular working with Fred MacMurray and getting to know him—those are memories I cherish. Also, I felt I knew what I was doing. In some movies, I *didn't* feel ever quite ready or rehearsed enough, but in those Flubber pictures, I felt I knew what to do with that part. I walked into a great, great thing with those Flubber movies at Walt Disney.

Stanley Rubin on The Whip Hand

> *The anti–Communist hysterics in Hollywood,*
> *as led by John Wayne, Ward Bond, Hedda Hopper,*
> *etc., were extreme. I didn't want to add to that hysteria.*

Stanley Rubin's first movie as a producer was the surprise hit *The Narrow Margin* (RKO, 1952); a suspenseful cops-and-crooks drama almost entirely set aboard a moving train, it was a model of B-movie efficiency that drew well-deserved industry attention to the first-time producer. After this strong start, however, it was Rubin's misfortune to follow up with a production that suffered severely at the tampering hands of RKO's enigmatic jillionaire owner Howard Hughes: *The Man He Found*, a noirish, pseudo-science fiction story of a journalist (Elliott Reid) who, on a fishing vacation in the wilds of Minnesota, stumbles upon a tiny town populated by (what would today be called) a "sleeper cell" of foreign agents preparing to wage germ warfare on the U.S. of A. Their leader, the titular Man He (Reid) Found, was revealed in the film's closing minutes to be a burn-faced, raving Adolf Hitler, the report of whose death at the close of World War II was, apparently, greatly exaggerated.

No movie audience ever saw Rubin's offbeat melodrama: After viewing the finished film, the unpredictable Hughes suddenly ordered rewrites and reshoots, prompting Rubin to quit the production and ask for his name to be removed from it. At Hughes' behest, *The Man He Found* became *The Whip Hand*, a more conventional drama, with Hitler excised and replaced in the plot by Commie agents—a crass attempt by Hughes to capitalize on fervent anti–Communist sentiment then loose in the land.

Rubin, of course, easily survived this delirious debacle, going on to produce TV series and many movies (including *River of No Return* with Robert Mitchum and Marilyn Monroe, *Promise Her Anything* with Warren Beatty and Leslie Caron and *Revenge* with Kevin Costner). And yet he still recalls with annoyance the saga of the sabotaged *The Man He Found*, a movie which in its intended and no doubt superior form has never been seen outside RKO screening rooms and almost certainly no longer exists.

[No opening question.]

My first RKO assignment was writing a screenplay for Bob Mitchum and Jane Russell, *Macao* [1952]. The deal that my agent made for me was that *if* the screenplay I wrote was made, then RKO would let me produce it. Well, Robert Mitchum and Jane Russell accepted it and they went on to shoot it, but RKO *didn't* let me produce it. But they did give me the right to buy a low-budget property and make a low-budget film. So I bought a story that was making the rounds of the studios, a story which I liked. It was called *Target*, but we changed the title to *The Narrow Margin*, and that became my producing assignment at RKO, my first job as a producer.

When we finished shooting *Narrow Margin* and we were just completing the editing of it, they told me I could go ahead and find another property and produce another low-budget picture. I found a story. I have no recollection of the name of the author, but the screen credits say Roy Hamilton and I will accept that. I *believe* it was called *The Man He Found*—I *know* that was the title when I was working on it. I wrote the screenplay, and it was going to be my first picture as both writer and producer. I hired William Cameron Menzies to direct because I was an enormous admirer of his work as a production designer, and we shot the entire picture. The budget was low—I'm pretty sure that it was under 250,000. About the same budget as *Narrow Margin*.

In an offbeat bit of casting, writer-producer Stanley Rubin hired New York–based character actor Elliott Reid to handle *The Whip Hand*'s heroics.

You say you produced it, but one of my books says Man He Found *was produced by Lewis Rachmil.*

Lew Rachmil was a very good friend of mine. He did *not* produce *The Man He Found*. I wrote the screenplay *and* produced it. But several things happened, that I'm about to tell you about.

We finished shooting *Man He Found*, and we presented for Howard Hughes' approval a kind of a semi-final, penultimate cut. By the way, I never met Howard Hughes. Never. I got memos relayed to me from Mr. Hughes, *or* personal notes from Mr. Hughes relayed to me by the senior producer on the lot, whose name was Robert Sparks. Sparks was the only guy who *I* knew of on the lot, certainly the only *producer* on the lot, who met with Hughes in person. I never met Mr. Hughes.

The picture was run by Hughes, probably at midnight in some screening room. Mr. Hughes said he thought it was a nice little picture *except* ... he didn't want to do an anti–Nazi picture, he wanted to do an anti–Communist picture. Now I have to explain something: The structure of *The Man He Found* was such that you could change the villain in it by just redoing the last five minutes of the film. Because up to that point, you didn't know what the heavies were up to—[Hitler and the other Nazis] didn't come into play until the last few minutes. So I got the message that what Mr. Hughes wanted to do was to take out the anti–Nazi end, the Hitler thing, which was the essence of what I bought and what I wrote, and then he wanted to change it to make Communists the heavies.

Okay, that was presented to me—and I turned it down. And the reason I turned it down was very simple. This was about 1951, and there was a lot of anti–Communist hysteria going on around the country and particularly in Hollywood at that time. The anti–Communist hysterics in Hollywood, as led by John Wayne, Ward Bond, Hedda Hopper, etc., were extreme. *I* didn't want to add to that hysteria. I had bought an anti–Nazi story and that's what I wanted to make. When I was asked to change this into an anti–Communist story, I did not want to do that. So I sent word that I would *not* make the changes that Mr. Hughes requested, and I also said I wanted my name removed as writer and producer of the film.

And that's when Lewis Rachmil came into the picture?

At that time, there were only three or four producers on the lot. As I said, Bob Sparks was the senior producer, Lew Rachmil I guess had next seniority, and then came *me* as the young punk on the lot. The picture was turned over to Lew Rachmil and it was Lew who hired [screenwriters] George Bricker and Frank L. Moss to write the changes on the ending. I didn't know Bricker, but Frank Moss was an old friend of mine.

We're getting ahead of ourselves. Were you the one who cast Man He Found?

Yes, I cast the picture. I read a lot of young actors for the role of the young male lead in it, and the guy who gave me the best reading was Elliott Reid. By *far* the best reading. I found out later that one of the reasons he gave me the best reading was that he was a *very* proficient radio actor—and radio actors are *used* to giving good readings 'cause that's what they *do* [*laughs*]! I was a very young and inexperienced producer, this was my second picture, and so because he gave me the best reading, I thought he'd be the best actor. I've learned a lot since then and I know now that you don't necessarily cast the one who gives you the best reading, 'cause he's not always the best actor.

Or maybe not the best "type."
Right. Also, he was clean-cut, he looked like a good young leading man. I've seen him recently, he still looks great, he's still a very nice guy, and I'm not unhappy that I cast him. However—in looking back on the picture, I didn't think it was the smartest casting I'd ever done. He did lack a certain "toughness," a toughness in his character, that I think would have made him more believable as the story went on.

About when did you begin to have your reservations about casting him?
When I cast him, I had no reservations. As I was editing the picture, I began to have reservations [*laughs*]! *None* of that should reflect on Elliott Reid. If Elliott Reid was in any way wrong in that picture, it was my fault, not his. It was my fault for perhaps a slight miscasting. I *don't* think that miscasting was terminal [*laughs*].

Do you remember who else was up for the part?
No, I don't. I would say conservatively that I read at least 20 young would-be leading men around town.

And you said that you selected Menzies as director because you were impressed with him as a production designer.
I thought he was absolutely the best production designer in the business. *And*, I liked him very much personally. But by the time he finished shooting the picture, I had decided in my mind that he was a better production designer than he was a director. The reason for that feeling in me was that he was more interested in his set-ups, in the angles, the design, the look of the scenes, than he was in the performances. As a result, the performances (*I* felt) tended to be "restricted," to be narrowed-down instead of opened-up. Because he was always interested in the "look" of where the people stood or moved.

One of my past interviewees, director Lee Sholem, told me that Menzies drank. Any memory of that?
I'm very bad on that. I have worked with people who I was told later were on cocaine—I never knew it! I hired George C. Scott to direct a movie for television [*The Story of Leroy "Satchel" Paige*, 1981], and I didn't realize that he was an alcoholic until he *told* me, and I had to fire him. Three days into the shooting of this film, I had to fire George C. Scott. That was a very tough night, believe me. Tough for *me*. Not so tough for him, because he had begun to suspect that this might happen.

I assume the Man He Found *interiors were shot at RKO—yes?*
That is true.

Whip Hand director–production designer William Cameron Menzies concerned himself more with the look of the movie than the players' performances, Rubin charges. Left to right: Commie rats Edgar Barrier, Lewis Martin and Raymond Burr and leading man Elliott Reid.

What about some of the exteriors, the "ghost town" and the lake—where were they photographed?

I won't swear to this at all—remember, now, that this is over 50 years ago—but my distant memory is that we were at Big Bear Lake. But I would not put on a bond on that [*laughs*]!

Bobby Watson reportedly played Hitler in Man He Found.

I don't remember whom I hired. It certainly could have been Bobby Watson, 'cause I remember that he *did* do Hitler both comedically *and* seriously.

Putting an actor who played Hitler in comedies into the Hitler role in a serious picture seems like another strange choice—kinda like putting whoever used to play Ronald Reagan in comedy skits on Saturday Night Live *into the Reagan role in a dramatic movie!*

You saw very little of Hitler in my complete version of *The Man He Found*. It was always at a distance.

Did he speak in the picture?

I wish I had a copy of my screenplay, but I don't, and I don't recall. I was *so* upset with Hughes. After all, that was my very first job as writer *and* producer, and I was really kind of proud of that, and very happy to be *doing* that. I wanted to go *on* doing that. Then Hughes, in a sense, pulled the carpet out from under me by wanting to make a change that I simply couldn't countenance.

Was there interference from Hughes all along?

There's a double answer on that. He never interfered *while* you were making the picture. His interference came *after* you made the picture. For example, Hughes got into the act on *Narrow Margin*. Dick Fleischer, Earl Felton and I were the team on *Narrow Margin*: I had bought a story with money from the studio, a story called *Target*, I was the producer and I hired Earl Felton to do the screenplay and I hired Dick Fleischer to direct it. *Narrow Margin* was my very first production, and it went very, very well. In many ways, strongly due to Dick Fleischer's efficiency. Dick Fleischer was, first of all, a very good director, and second of all, a very efficient, well-organized person. He had directed previously; I was producing for the first time. I learned a *lot* from Dick Fleischer. Anyway, the picture went well, we had an excellent cast [Charles McGraw, Marie Windsor, Jacqueline White et al.], everything went swimmingly. We finished the picture and the initial reaction to it was very, very good. *Excellent* reactions. Then it went to Howard Hughes. And we got word back that Hughes thought it was a very, very good picture, he liked it a lot—but he was just unhappy that this had to go out as what was then called a B picture, a program picture. The word we got was that he would hold it for a while and see if he couldn't think of a way to make it an A picture. So *Narrow Margin* went under Hughes' arm, and quite some time passed. Now, meanwhile, I was working on *Man He Found*. Then, subsequently, [the 1951 comedy] *Behave Yourself!*

Hughes finally decided that the only way to make *Narrow Margin* into an A picture was to re-cast it and re-shoot it. (I could have told him that in five minutes if I'd ever met with him!) There *was* no other way. Because he didn't want to do *that*, he decided to tamper with it, he fiddled a little with the editing and he introduced one more heavy to it. And, oh, he did a terrible thing—in re-editing certain sections of *Narrow Margin* to add this other heavy, Hughes forgot one thing: At the very end of the Hughes-edited version of the picture, Charles McGraw and Jacqueline White go off into the sunset—without checking on Marie Windsor [a self-sacrificing undercover policewoman who, unbeknownst to them, has been killed in the line of duty]. In *our* complete, finished version of the picture, both in the script and what we had on film, they of course found Marie Windsor's body and there was this moment of regret and silence and understanding of what she did, of the sacrifice she made. And *then* they go off into the sunset. Hughes forgot about this, and in his re-editing just skipped that scene. People ask me, "How could they *not* check on Marie Windsor?" I say, "Ask Mr. Hughes!"

How soon after Man He Found *wrapped did you get the Hughes edict about changing Nazis to Commies?*

A scene *un*seen: Unidentified player, Reid, Carla Balenda and Frank Wilcox in a sequence not found in the final cut of *The Whip Hand*.

I would say within a week or two. When I said I would not make Mr. Hughes' changes, and that I wanted my name removed as both writer and producer, very shortly afterwards I heard that it had been turned over to Lew Rachmil.

How soon afterwards did the shooting of all the new footage begin?
It began, I would say, probably within a few months.

Did Menzies and cinematographer Nicholas Musuraca work on both versions?
I don't know whether Bill Menzies directed the added scenes. [Author's note: Research done subsequent to this interview shows that he did.] But I would think that Nick Musuraca did the added scenes, because it would be very important to keep the same cameraman, to match the lighting and so on.

According to "the books," The Enemy Within *was briefly the title of the "new-and-improved" Commie version—does this ring a bell with you?*
Yes, vaguely it does. And, obviously, that's a much better title for the picture Hughes wanted than *The Whip Hand*. I don't know where *The Whip Hand* comes from.

I think it's an awful title!
I totally agree.

Refusing to do the "new version"—did that affect your relationship with Hughes and RKO?

Well, *Narrow Margin* had achieved some reputation in town, even before Hughes allowed it to go out into release. Studios were requesting it and running it. Darryl Zanuck ran it at Fox, and I had an offer to go to Fox almost immediately thereafter. I went. And that led to the three pictures I did at Fox—*My Pal Gus* [1952] was the first one, with Dick Widmark; *Destination Gobi* [1953]; and then I developed literally from scratch the picture *River of No Return* [1954]. The funniest part about *River of No Return* was that we were totally finished, and I had to run an answer print to check the color. I took a date with me to see that answer print—that was in early 1954. My date was a young actress named Kathleen Hughes [who became, and still *is*, Mrs. Rubin].

You just recently re-watched The Whip Hand. *How much of it is stuff that you did? Half? Three-quarters? More??*

I would say probably 75 to 85 percent.

Rewatching the movie in 2002—what did you like/dislike about it? Do you think your version might have been a bit better?

Yes, I think my version was better. My version had a "wholeness," a "oneness" about it, because that was the way the story was designed.

One of the problems with the redone version of The Whip Hand *is that most of the movie plays like a mystery—but the opening scene of the Russian officer ranting and raving in the Kremlin gives the game away in the first three minutes!*

That scene, of course, was added—that was Bricker and Moss and Lew Rachmil and Howard Hughes. That was *not The Man He Found*. *The Man He Found* kept its mystery right up to the last five minutes of the film.

I'll give you the final irony. The final irony is that *The Whip Hand* paid residuals to the producer Lew Rachmil. It would have been the only residuals I would ever have *gotten* for that picture if I'd kept my name on it. So that taught me a lesson, too: Never take your name off *anything*!

Rubin, who began screenwriting in his early twenties, is still (60-plus years later) visible on the Hollywood scene.

The Whip Hand
(RKO, 1951)

82 minutes; Produced by Lewis J. Rachmil & (uncredited) Stanley Rubin; Directed by William Cameron Menzies; Screenplay: George Bricker, Frank L. Moss & (uncredited) Stanley Rubin; Story: Roy Hamilton; Photography: Nicholas Musuraca; Production Designer: William Cameron Menzies; Art Directors: Albert S. D'Agostino & Carroll Clark; Music: Paul Sawtell; Music Director: C. Bakaleinikoff; Set Decorators: Darrell Silvera & James Altwies; Editor: Robert Golden; Sound: Earl Wolcott & Clem Portman

Carla Balenda (*Janet Keller*), Elliott Reid (*Matt Corbin*), Edgar Barrier (*Dr. Edward Keller*), Raymond Burr (*Steve Loomis*), Otto Waldis (*Dr. Wilhelm Bucholtz*), Michael Steele (*Chick*), Lurene Tuttle (*Molly Loomis*), Peter Brocco (*Nate Garr*), Lewis Martin (*Mr. Peterson*), Frank Darien (*Luther Adams*), Olive Carey (*Mabel Turner*), Jameson Shade (*Sheriff*), Art Dupuis (*Speed Boat Pilot*), Robert Foulk, William Challee (*Guards*), G. Pat Collins (*Nelson, Gate Guard*), George Chandler (*Jed*), Douglas Evans (*Carstairs*), Gregory Gaye (*Scientist*), Milton Kibbee (*Grocery Service Manager*), Billy Nelson (*Ed, Delivery Man*), Frank Wilcox (*Bradford*), Leonid Snegoff (*Russian General*), Mary Baer (*Miss Price*), Don Dillaway (*McIntyre*), Roy Darmour (*Harry Jones*); **Scene deleted:** Bobby Watson (*Adolf Hitler*)

Frankie Thomas *on* Tom Corbett, Space Cadet

> *I made my first personal appearance
> [as Tom Corbett, Space Cadet]
> on a Saturday in Philadelphia, some large department store.
> There was a line all the way out the door—
> there were 10,000 people there!*

Actor Frankie Thomas feels that he's had "the best of several lives," appearing on stage, in motion pictures during what he calls "their golden days," on radio and finally on live television right at the dawn of the medium in New York. His claim to TV fame is an impressive one: Thomas was the title character in network TV's first-ever outer space series, the pioneering *Tom Corbett, Space Cadet* (1950–55).

Beginning as a 15-minute, three-times-a-week CBS series, the kid-oriented show focused on three cadets enrolled at Space Academy in the mid–2300s: future space aces Tom Corbett, brave, resourceful, and a born leader; Roger Manning (Jan Merlin), equally courageous but also cocky and belligerent; and Astro (Al Markim), a hard-working and sensitive young man from the planet Venus. *Tom Corbett* was light on monsters and other outlandish elements, emphasizing instead comparatively "believable" stories involving deep space rescue missions, stranded rocketships, meteor storms and, most memorably, relationships between the characters as they patrolled the solar system in their ship the *Polaris*. The series jumped networks the way the boys planet-hopped: It ran on all four major networks (CBS, ABC, NBC and Dumont), always live, and always in the catch-as-catch-can style of early TV—rehearsing in hotel rooms or a church, broadcasting out of a converted gymnasium, etc.

None of this was any great challenge for Frankie Thomas, who was born in the proverbial trunk (he was the son of actors Frank M. Thomas and

Mona Bruns) and who had been performing on stage and in films since his boyhood in the mid-1930s. Return now with Thomas to the era of early TV and that medium's first depiction of the age of the conquest of space...

How did you get the Corbett role? Were you a New Yorker at the time?

Yes, I was in New York. I came to New York after the War because my parents were there, running in a hit Broadway show called *Chicken Every Sunday*. I'm an only child and I've been very close to my family all my life. When I got to New York, I started to work in radio, and there was no reason to leave.

So I was living in New York and I got a call about meeting with the producers of *Tom Corbett*, which *then* they were intending to call *Cris Colby, Space Cadet*. It was a call put in to my service—I had a telephone service, every actor did, and it was probably Mort Abrahams, the show's first producer, who phoned. Now we get to the spot that's hard to believe: I met them at the Rockhill Radio office on 54th Street, between Madison and Fifth. Rockhill was a radio production outfit that had a show called *Mark Trail* on radio, two half-hours a week. I walked into this room and here was George Gould, our first director, and Mort Abrahams, and Jan Merlin and Al Markim—I'd never met any of them before. They asked Jan and Al and me to stand together, they lined the three of us up ... and it just clicked. There was no doubt. I didn't have to read a line. It was kind of weird! I know it sounds unbelievable, but that's the way it happened.

Did they hire you then and there?

No, but they obviously went into a huddle as soon as I left. I had no sooner arrived at the Lambs Club on West 44th Street and there was a call, and I found out we were in business.

Had you done any television at that point?

I did a lot of early television—*Studio One*, *Philco TV Playhouse*, *Celanese Theatre*. And the first soap opera on television, *A Woman to Remember* [1949], on which I played one of the leads. *Woman to Remember* was the first five-a-week, 15-minute television soap opera. The show wasn't particularly successful, it only went 26 weeks.

Did you ever find out why Rockhill Radio branched out into the production of a sci-fi TV series?

How they got into this, I imagine, was because Kellogg's was the sponsor of Rockhill's *Mark Trail* [radio show], and Kellogg's was looking now for a television series. They took the name *Space Cadet* from a Robert Heinlein novel, but the show had absolutely no connection with the book. The only character in *Tom Corbett* that was in Heinlein's book was Commander Arkwright—that's all there was. The story in the book was nowhere near what *we* did.

You say they saw and cast Jan Merlin and Al Markim before you.

Oh, yes, they had Jan and Al set, and now they were just looking for a Tom Corbett—well, at *that* point, a Cris Colby. As I recall it, the original idea was to

Network television's first men in space, Frankie Thomas (center), Jan Merlin and Al Markim, at the helm of their rocketship *Polaris* in the pioneering *Tom Corbett, Space Cadet*. Thomas, playing a youngster, was 28 when the series premiered, 33 when it was cancelled.

have Cris Colby kind of a junior cadet, the youngest of the three, and following the other two, more experienced cadets around. [The producers] wanted what they assumed would be the show's largest TV audience, which would be children, oh, maybe from 10, 11, 12, up to 17 or 18, to identify with Cris Colby. Well, when I got on the scene, they decided to switch the format around. They changed the name to Tom Corbett—I can't remember why—and now they wanted him to be the dominant leader. Tom was the same class as the other two, but he wasn't going to be asking *them* questions, he was going to be more the take-charge type.

Do you know if any other actors were considered for the part?
They said they'd gone through everybody in New York [*laughs*]. Jack Lemmon was up for it, and Dickie Moore, and a chap who was quite active in New York, a nice young fella, Peter Fernandez, who played a lot of juveniles. But ultimately I was selected. Well, I'd had a lot of experience that was valuable for television. I was doing a lot of television shows at the time, and I'd had the motion picture experience, which was important.

And stage experience.
And the stage. Now, that was a big problem at this time [the dawn of East Coast TV history]: The advertising agencies only knew radio actors. Radio actors, many of them, could not memorize lines, they'd never done it. But somebody with stage experience, *they* could memorize the lines. Jan had some stage experience, and Al had worked in a stock company somewhere. So ... that was it, we became "the Three Musketeers."

Who were the key behind-the-scenes people involved with the show at the very beginning?
Well, I mentioned two of them. George Gould had worked for Marc Daniels, a big television director at that time; George was the guy in the control room handling the dials for Daniels. And now George was going to be our director on *Corbett*. He was a very quiet type of chap and he never bothered me *or*, I think, the other people with a lot of "Do this," "Do that." If we had some line that we thought was a little better than what was in the script, George was not averse to a change. He just let us go our way. Which was very fortunate. So there was George, and there was Mort Abrahams. For Mort, *Tom Corbett* was his absolute beginning on television and, according to Mort, he said this to me years later, he didn't know what he was doing [*laughs*]! But he did pretty well, I'll tell you that! So those were the two principals. Then there was Albert Aley, our story editor. He was a key man in the operation—he'd had a lot of experience and he wrote a lot of scripts which were very good. We also had a wonderful little gal called Muriel Maron, who was sort of let's-fix-everything.

I'm getting ahead of myself but give me, very briefly, the broadcast history of Tom Corbett, *and then I'll ask you about working for each of the networks.*
It started on CBS, 15 minutes, three times a week [October–December 1950]. Our stories on the 15-minute format ran for nine episodes—we did a complete adventure in three weeks, in nine parts. From there it moved to ABC [January 1951–September 1952], still 15 minutes, three times a week, nine parts to each story. But when we were at ABC, I also did a half-hour on Saturday nights on NBC. For that NBC version of *Tom* [July–September 1951], Rockhill cut old kinescopes of our nine-episode stories into *half-hour* stories—which was no easy job [*laughs*]. And to explain

Thomas (Tom Corbett) and Merlin (Roger Manning) first met in the New York offices of Rockhill Radio, *Tom Corbett*'s production company. Fifty-five years and 2500 miles later, they're close neighbors in the Hollywood area, and even closer friends.

the unavoidable holes in the plots and make the stories understandable to the audience, I would be there in person at NBC, 30 Rockefeller Plaza, doing live narration in a number of spots. They needed a "bridge," and I was the bridge—I had to be there live to look into the camera and say, "After we repaired the ship, we continued on to Venus," or whatever the heck it was, before the story could resume again.

At that point I *think Tom Corbett* was the only show to ever run on two networks at the same time.

Next was Dumont [August 1953–May 1954]. For Dumont, we shifted from three a week to one half-hour every other Saturday. Then we came back to NBC, a half-hour once a week, Saturday morning [December 1954–June 1955].

Where were some of the places that you shot Tom Corbett? *Starting with when it was on CBS.*

In those days, we're talking 1950, there were no television studios around. What they were using were the largest radio studios, or just simply large places—for example, they took over a theater on occasion. When we were doing *Corbett* and it was on CBS, we were in a studio somewhere around Grand Central Station. After three months, we switched to ABC because ABC offered us more outlets. Outlets at that time were very important. I think, after about three, four months, Milton Berle's show had the greatest number of outlets, and Fulton Sheen, who was an almost hypnotic man of the cloth, was number two. And *Tom Corbett* was number three.

Oh, wow.

Yes, we were up there! At first ABC had us in a studio in a new building that they had uptown, around the 60s, off Central Park West. Then they secured a floor of what had been a gymnasium on West 57th Street, and *that* became our studio. No other show was in there, so now we had the benefit of having our big sets remain permanent. The control room, the exterior of the spaceship, the cadets' room at Space Academy, etc.—those didn't have to be put up and taken down any more. They all remained standing, which was a lot of help for the crew.

At CBS, you never had permanent sets, but once you got to ABC, you did.

Uh-huh. After ABC we were on Dumont, and we worked at the Dumont Studios, around 56th Street. Then, at the end, for NBC, back at the NBC Studios, 30 Rockefeller. There was a large studio on the seventh or eighth floor, and that worked out fine.

Was it live the whole run of the series?

Always live. In those days, everything was done live.

And Tom Corbett *was kinescoped.*

Yes. We were kinescoped because there was a very popular show in Philadelphia, I think it was an interview-type local show with a man who was playing an Indian. We didn't want to go up against him, he had a big rating. So in Philly, they showed the kines [kinescopes]. Our kines came out remarkably well. To this day you can see all sorts of *Tom Corbett* shows, and they're in very good shape.

If you did a Tom Corbett *in New York at, say, six o'clock, would it play at three o'clock on the West Coast?*

Mm-hmm. We didn't do a re-broadcast.

So you only did each episode once, as opposed to some of the live shows where they did it a couple of times for different parts of the country.

That's right, other shows did what they used to call "the Coast re-broadcast." Most of our run was Monday, Wednesday and Friday, in prime time. Then we also took on a *Tom Corbett* radio show, two half-hour shows a week, Tuesday and Thursday.

After the day when you first met everybody and found out you were hired, how long before you were on the air, live, in the first Tom Corbett *episode?*

I met everybody and was hired on a Friday. The following Monday, we started rehearsals, and we rehearsed almost a week. Then we went on after that. Boy, it was instantaneous. Those things don't happen too often!

Would you walk me through the making of an episode of Tom Corbett?

We'd finish an episode, let's say a Monday show. Then we would take a little break. And then we'd go into rehearsal for the next episode. First we'd do a reading for time.

Scripts in hand.

Yes. You *had* to do that because you wanted to mark where you moved. And George Gould could figure out his camera angles. Then we'd go home; Tuesday we'd do the radio show; and we'd come back on Wednesday, I guess mid-morning or late morning, and we'd do another run-through. Now the crew was involved, and that would take quite a bit of time. We'd rehearse it maybe two or three times, and the final rehearsal would be the dress rehearsal, right before the show.

How long was it before you and the rest of the cast and crew realized it was becoming a popular show?

Now, here's another one that's hard to believe: Almost by the second week. The disc jockeys all picked up our lingo: "Blast your jets," "Don't fuse your tubes," "Spaceman's luck!" We were hearing all of this and we said, "Hey, if they're saying it, they're *watching* it." *Tom* really caught on very fast. When I say "the second week," I know *I* had a feeling that it was going great guns. Then, later, when Bert Lahr was on Broadway in a show called *Two on the Aisle*, I saw pictures of him in a space costume in one of the New York papers. That was another indication of how well the show was going, 'cause when you've got a star the caliber of Bert Lahr [spoofing a TV show], people have *got* to know about it! Oh, I was delighted to see that!

Very quickly, we got into the secondary rights stuff [the *Tom Corbett*–related merchandise]. The *Hopalong Cassidy* TV show was making a ton of money with secondary rights, and that's what Rockhill was shooting for—they hoped to follow in his [William "Hopalong Cassidy" Boyd's] footsteps. I think there were 135 products bearing the name of Tom Corbett. Fortunately or *un*fortunately, that took care of my weekends. I was flying to Boston … going down to Philly … I even went to the Coast … making appearances all over the country in stores where they were selling the suits and all the rest of the paraphernalia.

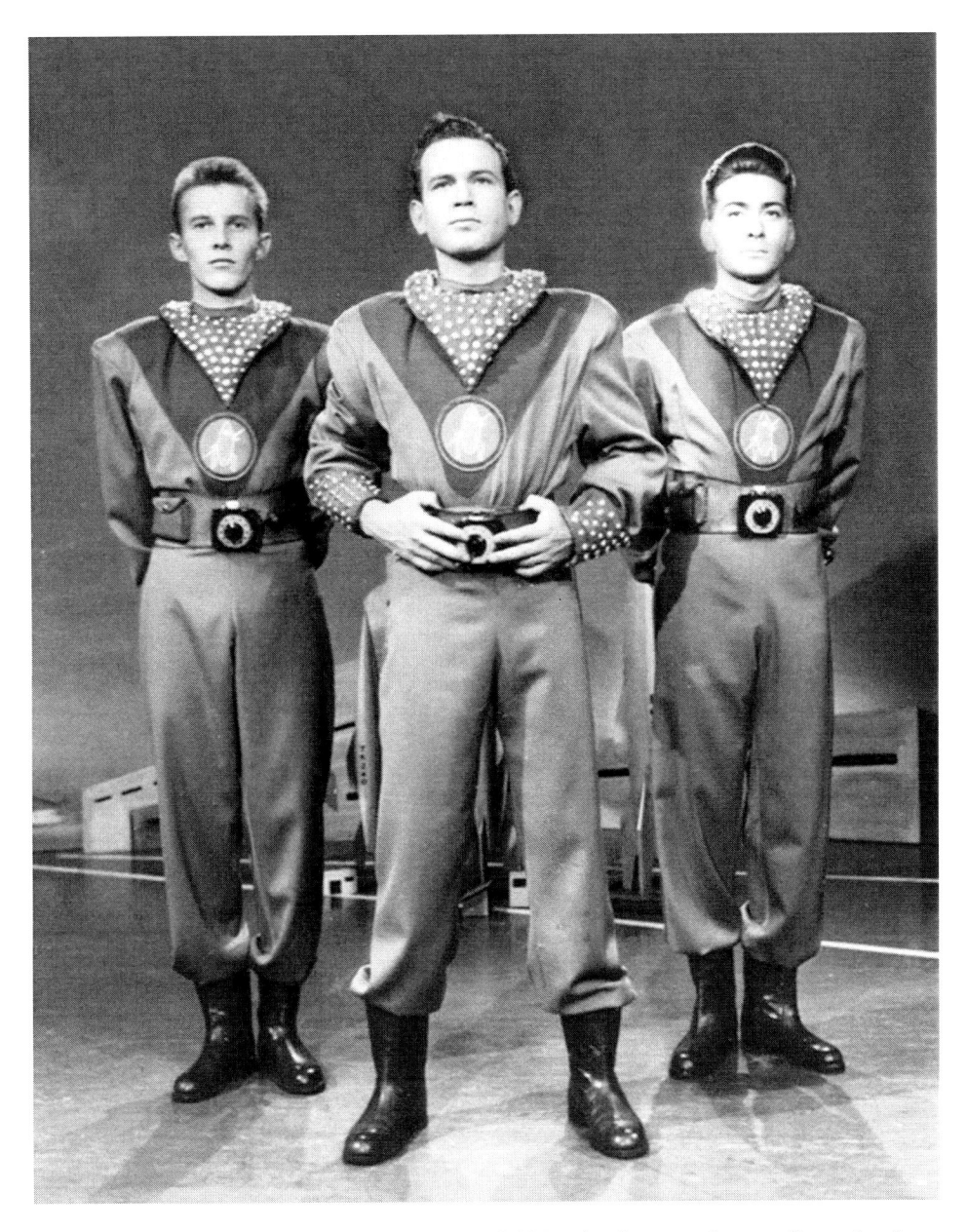

Roger, Tom and Astro (Jan Merlin, Thomas and Al Markim), intrepid young Space Academy cadets, "came of age" in an age of marvels.

Were you paid extra to make those personal appearances?
    Getting paid extra by Rockhill Radio was *very* difficult [*laughs*]! We sort of had a little arrangement: They would give me the time to go out and do some [non–*Corbett*] radio shows. See, if I was supposed to do a rehearsal for *Tom*, I couldn't do a radio show at that same time. So they'd say, "Frank, you can skip the first half-hour of rehearsal and do the radio show, and then get over here." I'd pick up some extra

money that way. They were very good about that—because they didn't want me to ask for more money [for playing Tom Corbett]!

So you don't think you were paid for making personal appearances.
I do *not* think I got paid for that. But we were trying to put the show over. It was rather interesting: I made my first personal appearance on a Saturday in Philadelphia, some large department store. There was a line all the way out the door—there were 10,000 people there! I was shaking hands and saying "Spaceman's luck!" and all of that. I remember, I saw this frail little lady in line, she was quite a ways back, and she was carrying her son. The son was *not* that young, and he was obviously crippled in some way. So I waved her up and got her up there right by me and sat her down, and now the poor mother could rest a little bit. And I talked to the boy in between.

In between signing autographs.
Actually, there wasn't *time* to sign autographs. What I was doing was shaking hands with the children and thanking their parents for bringing them. I had the store people get me a chair and I got her seated. The boy sat too, either in another chair or on his mother's lap, and I talked to him in between talking to the people in the line. Well, years later, I got a letter from him, telling me how much he appreciated it and how much he remembered of that day.

Would you enter the stores already in costume?
Oh, yeah. And when I make an appearance now, I still wear it. I've still got the original.

And it still fits?
Yep!

Between doing Tom Corbett *Monday-Wednesday-Friday, and on the radio, and with p.a.s on the weekend ... was* Tom Corbett *your whole life?*
Yes. I saw more of the cast than I did of my family. But, look—from your own experience, see if I'm not right about this: Actors have one phobia and that is, when a job is finished, they are convinced that they'll never work again.

I have heard that from my interviewees!
Well, I never had to worry about *that*. When *Tom* was going, there wasn't time for much of anything else [*laughs*]! But it was a very pleasant time.

Really? So you had no objection to Tom Corbett *taking over your life?*
Not really, no. I liked the character, and the public liked the character. And I knew I wasn't going to be out of a job for quite a while!

You were born in Manhattan, correct?
That's right, I was born in Manhattan and [as a kid] I went out to the Coast

after RKO bought the rights to a quite-successful play that I was in, *Wednesday's Child* [1934]. RKO bought it to make it into a film [also 1934], and I went out and starred in the film. After that, I went back and forth from Broadway to Hollywood. I did *The First Legion* [1934] which was a successful play, and right after that I did *A Dog of Flanders* [1935] at RKO; then I did the play *Remember the Day* [1935] in New York and had the extreme pleasure of playing with my father. Then I did a play called *Seen But Not Heard* [1936] and it was successful, and it was the first job for a little girl called Anne Baxter. After that, things got so busy on the Coast [movie-wise] that I remained out there until the War. After the War, as I told you, I came to New York because Mother and Dad were there, and that's how I got into radio and television and *Tom Corbett*.

So you were still living with your mother and father when Tom Corbett *began?*
   Mm-hmm. We had an apartment in the London Terrace Towers on 23rd and Ninth, and we had a farm in New Jersey. They spent a lot of time there and I did, too, whenever I got the chance.

Where was the farm?
   [*Laughs*] If you blink, you missed it: Berkeley Heights. It was about five miles out of Summit, which is a fairly large city.

Did you have any interest in science fiction when you were a kid?
   Yes. As a matter of fact, I was a fan of Robert Heinlein—I thought his *The Puppet Masters* was one of the greatest political satires of all time and that he was a heckuva writer. And naturally, like all kids my age, I was brought up on the *Buck Rogers* comic strip and the radio show—mostly the radio show. Did you know that Kellogg's [*Tom Corbett*'s first sponsor] was a sponsor of *Buck Rogers* on radio?

And Buck Rogers *was also a serial.*
   Oh, yes. Buster Crabbe did three *Flash Gordon* serials, and he also did *Buck Rogers*.

Did you see those as a kid?
   At Universal I did a serial called *Tim Tyler's Luck* [1937], taken from a very popular comic strip. We finished shooting the same night that one of the *Flash Gordons* with Buster Crabbe finished shooting. So I wasn't just watching *Flash Gordon*, I was working opposite him [*laughs*]!

Did you make a good living playing Tom Corbett?
   Very.

Really? A lot of my interviewees tell me that early TV acting jobs paid about enough for them to brush their teeth.
   Oh, yes, that was true. I saw Ed Kemmer, who played the lead in *Space Patrol*, and he told me that they were making eight dollars a show—hard to believe! That

The son of actors Frank M. Thomas and Mona Bruns, Thomas made his first movies as a boy. His 1934 debut *Wednesday's Child* also featured his parents in smaller parts; it was followed a year later by *A Dog of Flanders*.

was not the situation with *Tom*. In *some* respects, *Tom* was the end of my acting career. It was the beginning, more or less, for Jan and Al, but it was my finish, and I had quite a few credits. So, no, *Tom* did very well by me.

You must have a favorite "war story" or two about doing Tom Corbett *live.*

Actually, one favorite "live TV" story concerns the soap opera *Woman to Remember* which I mentioned previously, the five-a-weeker. We did it in a radio studio at Dumont Television and there were three rows of seats, and tours going through Dumont would take people into the studio to watch things. One hot day when the air conditioner blew, I was doing the last scene of a *Woman to Remember* along with Patricia Wheel, who played the female lead, and I was seeing out of the corner of my eye the speed-up signal. I picked up steam. Pat, who was *very* efficient, caught it from me, so *she* picked up steam. We *raced* through that scene like mad. The music came up for the finale and we went to a commercial, and the director rushed out and said, "My God, Frank, what did you *do*? We're three minutes early!" I turned around, and here was this audience sitting there, these little ladies ... all *fanning* themselves in this hot studio. That's what I'd been seeing out of the corner of my eye [*laughs*], thinking it was the speed-up signal. That was early television!

Any incidents on Tom Corbett?
   Well, I'm reminded of an incident we had with an actor (who shall remain nameless) who was playing a warlord. He was a little weak on learning the lines, so he had his script planted on the floor near the microphone that he would be speaking into, in a scene where he was broadcasting to another rocket ship or to ... whoever. He wanted to just stand there and *read*. Well, our technical crew had become very protective about the show—this was *their show*. So one of them was sweeping up the set before the scene, and he swept up the script too! The actor made his entrance and he picked up the microphone and he said, "All right, now..." and he looked down to read ... and there was nothing there [*laughs*]! Ohhh boy! He fought his way through it, though!

The sweeper swept it up on purpose, you're saying?
   Sure he did! The [sweeper's] attitude was, "You're not gonna do that with our boys [the *Tom Corbett* regulars]! They have to learn *their* lines!" They were very protective!

For a kid's show out of New York, you had a surprising number of soon-to-be "name" actors show up in guest roles.
   The show acted as a launch pad for a lot of young actors who went on to do very well. Some of them, it was their first jobs. Jack Lord was on *Corbett* and once he had some very nice things to say about the show in *Saturday Morning TV*, a very large book on television. Tommy Poston started out with us ... we had Woody Parfrey ... Frank Sutton. Jack Klugman was just the guest of honor at a Pacific Pioneer Broadcasters luncheon and, talking about his credits, he said, "It was a looong way from *Tom Corbett, Space Cadet* to my own show, *Quincy*!" [*Laughs*]
   Jack Warden has had quite an illustrious career, a lot of very good parts. He came out of Newark, and I'm sure that *Tom* was the first job that he did. He played "Joe Yakker, Chief Construction Engineer of the Venusian Mud Lake Tunnel Project." I had to memorize that line, and *say* it, and I worked on that one so hard I never forgot it! His first scene was with me, and I know what he did: He wanted to be good, this was his first job, and he memorized the whole scene. He memorized his part and mine as well—he was gonna be darn sure that he got the right cues. He

made his entrance and he walked over to me, as was called for ... and then he said my line. I had written that show and so I was kinda familiar with it, so ... I said *his*. And he said *mine*. And I said *his*. We went through the whole thing, reversing our characters. We came into the commercial, and the producer rushed over—by this time, that was Allen Ducovny. He said, "Gee, Frank, that was a great scene!" He didn't even *know* it had all been reversed [*laughs*]!

When we were in our heyday, when we were doing three a week, I got the scripts a week in advance—I wanted to be ahead because, over the weekend, my time was frequently wrapped up with personal appearances. So I was "up" on the lines when we'd do our first run-through. Jan was too. I remember one run-through where we read the show, everyone in the cast holding the scripts and reading them. And then, after this first run-through, Jan and I threw our scripts in a corner. There was a fellow there [a member of the guest cast] who saw this and was panic-stricken! He said, "Oh my God, these guys have photographic memories. They read through the script once and they *know* it!" We had to quiet him down a little [*laughs*]—I don't think he wanted to work with us!

Did you or Jan or Al ever use cue cards or anything along those lines on Tom Corbett*?*
No.

The first actor to play Capt. Strong played the part only briefly, a guy named Michael Harvey. What memories of him?
Awfully nice fellow. Physically perfect for the part. But he had a problem with the lines. Bless his dear heart, he just couldn't get it. If you ever get a chance to see [episode] number one—

He does stammer a lot.
Remember his long speech? Well, he was up higher than a kite! He was very nervous about his lines. Some people are that way, they just don't memorize easily. I was very fortunate, I *did* memorize easily—thank God! Of course, my memory *now* is not all that great. Nowadays I'm always asking Jan, "Jeez, what was the name of..." I hope you haven't reached that period yet, Tom!

Anyway, Michael Harvey was an awfully nice guy but, after the first two weeks, [the producers] realized he wasn't going to work, so they got Ed Bryce to replace him. I don't know what happened to Michael. I got a phone call from him, oh, about two or three months after the show was on, and he wanted to congratulate me about how well it was doing. It was very nice of him. Then I lost track of him.

And what was Edward Bryce like?
Eddie was very dependable, always knew his lines, and he was very *real*. He was a pleasure to work with. Of course, we *all* had to have a sense of humor. If a show isn't fun, it's not going to look good. If you're a little "light," it makes the day easier.

Carter Blake [Commander Arkwright]? Margaret Garland [Dr. Joan Dale]?
Carter Blake had been the stage manager of *Remember the Day*, the play that I spoke of before.

So he was not primarily an actor?

Yes, he had been, but then he'd gone into stage managing. I don't know how he happened to be on the show; I suppose he was a friend of Mort Abrahams. Margaret Garland was the dear girl who played Dr. Dale. Margaret was very pleasant. We knew nothing, actually, about her, and she wasn't in any particular hurry to tell us—why *should* she? Sometimes, *after* doing the show, and after doing our run-through [of the next show], Jan and I and maybe Muriel Maron, the production assistant, we'd go to Cherio's, a classy restaurant-bar in the East 50s, and sit around and yak for a while. Maggie never did that. But that was perfectly all right. Everybody was nice to work with.

John Fiedler [Cadet Alfie Higgins]?

Johnny played a character who came in right in the beginning, a small, frail egghead named Alfie Higgins, and of course he was ideal for the part. He looked *so* perfect as this little "brain trust"! He later moved out to the Coast. I'll never forget seeing him in *True Grit* [1969]—he played the part of a lawyer in that and it was hysterical, he was so funny. He's since moved back to Brooklyn, where he came from.

Was Tom Corbett *the first show of its type? Did all the other space shows of the early '50s follow?*

Captain Video was on before us, but that was not at that time a space show. Captain Video [Richard Coogan] would be in his secret headquarters, high in the mountains somewhere, contacting his "agents in the field"—who were Buck Jones and Tom Tyler. In other words, he was running old B-Westerns! *Space Patrol* was produced out on the West Coast, and it was local. We were the first real space show *nationally*. But after *Tom Corbett* "made it," *Captain Video* changed its formula quickly, and then *Space Patrol* went national. A CBS program called *Rod Brown of the Rocket Rangers*, starring Cliff Robertson, came on—there was a big fuss about that, a lawsuit brought by Stanley Wolfe, the president of Rockhill, against CBS. CBS had gotten a-hold of George Gould, our director, and lured him with money, along with two of our best writers, Jack Weinstock and Willie Gilbert. *Rod Brown* looked like a carbon copy of *Tom Corbett*—it had a unit of three as the principals, it was all laid in space, *every*thing. But that didn't slow *us* down, and we knocked *Rod Brown* off in 26 weeks [*laughs*]! We knocked off all the rest of those shows too, *except Space Patrol*—that stayed.

Did you ever see a Space Patrol?

I never saw *Space Patrol* until after we were off the air—I saw a kine at a friend's home. They were a totally different show. They had sinister villains and all sorts of weirdos, whereas we stuck close to what was scientifically possible. Willy Ley was our technical director—he had been the president of the German Rocket Society, he was Wernher Von Braun's closest friend, and he checked over every [*Tom Corbett*] script. When I was writing some of the *Corbett* shows with my writing partner Ray Morse—Ray and I were in the service together—I would have a conference with Willy, and it was amazing, the things that he said we *could do*, things which he said *were* in the realm of scientific possibility. There was only one thing that he said would never work, and that was the Paralo-Ray, which froze victims into immobility with non-fatal results. However, we had the Paralo-Ray and kept it [*laughs*]!

What prompted you to also write for Tom Corbett?

My father had done quite a bit of writing in his day, he wrote with a man called Albert Payson Terhune. Terhune was very well-known, he made the collie dog famous in America by writing *Lad: A Dog*, a tremendous best-seller; *Buff: A Collie*; *Bruce*; these were all collies. Terhune was a guy who could send in a story to *The Saturday Evening Post*, and before they *looked* at it, they bought it. He had a big reputation. Anyway, I wanted to write, and I knew the Corbett character. So I wrote! And I continued on [with the writing]. It's a far cry from Tom Corbett to Sherlock Holmes*, but … what the heck?

Did you just see Ley on the set, or also socially?

When you as a writer were envisioning a *Tom Corbett* adventure, and they were going to have you write it, you checked it with *him*. Maybe over dinner together. (By the way, he could drink Manhattan cocktails faster than anybody I ever saw. It didn't bother him a bit!) He would check your story's "scientific possibility"—those were the words that he used—and if it was scientifically possible, okay, go ahead with the story! I had very few problems with him, everything I came up with, he okayed.

What was he like personally?

He was very interesting. After we'd finish our business about what was possible for the show or not, he had many a story to tell. I remember one time I asked, "Willy, what about these smalltime wars?" [like the Korean War], and he said, with his broad German accent, "Vell, vee are going to develop a small, miniature A-bomb. And vhen a var starts, vee just drop the A-bomb and dat *stops* it!" Say, it wasn't a bad idea now that I think about it!

[Laughs] I'd have no objection to it nowadays, that's for sure!

Willy was a stout, broad-shouldered, sort of roly-poly, jovial German fellow. Very nice, very pleasant to work with. I'm sooo glad I can say this: I felt that way about everybody on the show.

Did you ever have monsters or anything outlandish on Tom Corbett, *or was it always "scientifically possible"?*

Always. Although we did have one show with dinosaurs. I should mention that the show developed something that revolutionized television in one respect, and that was the matting amplifier. That was developed by George Gould and two technical men at ABC. Before they came up with the matting amplifier, you could have

---

*In more recent years, Thomas has written a series of books featuring a bridge-playing Sherlock Holmes.

on TV a superimposition, one image superimposed over another, but when you looked at it you *knew* that it was one image on top of another. But the matting amplifier created a void in one image and fitted another image *into* it. In that one show I mentioned, we landed on a planet of dinosaurs, and the dinosaur actually was a baby alligator. But, boy, on the screen, combined with a small image of *us*, it looked very large and very real! With the matting amplifier, in scenes where we were supposedly on the outside of the *Polaris*, we would be shot in miniature and the *Polaris* model would be shot in magnification, and it looked like we were walking on the deck of the *Saratoga*!

Other than that, though, no, we didn't go in for horror stuff. We tried to stick with "the scientifically possible." We were totally different from *Space Patrol*. They had monster shows and Dracula-like characters. We had man-against-man a *little*, man-against-nature and man-against-himself. As I mentioned, all of our stories were run by Willy Ley, and he would make sure that the stories involved things that were scientifically possible. They didn't have to exist, but they *could* exist.

Kids obviously watched Tom Corbett *but did you have older viewers also?*
Twenty-five percent. And we actually got a lot of fan mail from them, too. *Dorothy and Dick* was very big at that time—that was a radio interview show in New York. Dorothy Kilgallen and Richard Kollmar. Their son was a big *Corbett* fan so they had me as a guest, and I found out they watched the show too [*laughs*]! There were a lot of those interview shows at that time, and I hit most of 'em.

What do you think attracted adults to the show?
Probably the scientific accuracy. Because what we did made sense, it was feasible. On that momentous day when we landed on the Moon and the fellows came out of the hatch, "Boy," I said to myself, "They look just like our space costumes!" And they *did*. With the bulbous head piece and everything! Man, those were tough to get in and out of, too!

What was it like under the TV studio lights in those spacesuits?
Hot! The lights in those days were a lot hotter than they are now, and you could really burn off a few pounds.

It also looks to me like the helmets fogged up on you pretty regularly.
They didn't fog up *too* much, although there *were* a few situations where that happened. The trouble was keeping the durned things together—the helmet was split into two parts, and it wasn't too well secured. Of course the helmets had the hole in the front [a big opening, even in scenes set in airless space] and *that* was not too realistic [*laughs*], but we did the best we could!

We've actually segued into what was going to be my next question: What difficulties did you run into on Tom Corbett *that might not occur to the average, casual viewer?*
You know [Jack] Warden played with us, [Jack] Lord played with us, [Tom] Poston started out with us, [Jack] Klugman. These were all young actors around

New York. Now, in what I'm about to say, I'm not referring to *these* chaps. But sometimes we'd have a guest actor who rehearsed just fine ... and then, when the red light came on and it was now or never, he suddenly was playing Hamlet, and everything got slowed down. See, with live television, that's your big problem—time. You had to finish on time.

And you'd cope with this situation by speeding up yourself?
That's right. Tom Corbett was always looking through the porthole, to see where the *Polaris* was going. Well, looking out through the porthole, I would get the speed-up from the floor manager. Now, here's the funny thing: When I would turn away from the porthole, the boys [Merlin and Markim] *knew* that I had gotten the speed-up. Before I opened my mouth. How they sensed that, I don't know, but we played an awful lot of those last scenes *very* quickly!

Tom Corbett *being a live show, did you ever get to see any of them?*
Actually, not too many.

You probably didn't see most of the Corbetts *'til the home video age, correct?*
Right.

Being the star of a kid's TV show, and perhaps even a role model, did you feel you needed to keep your nose extra-clean in your off-camera life as well?
Well, I felt that way about all my business. I sometimes wonder about this *illusion* that people have about the "wild life of Hollywood." Listen, I worked in 35 pictures and ... you didn't have any *time* to misbehave. You had to be in the makeup room by eight o'clock, probably earlier, and you worked all day and you had lines to learn, and you didn't have any time for [hijinks]. And if you *were* fiddling around, it would begin to show.

Were you and Jan and Al free to develop your own characters over the years a little bit, or did the Rockhill Radio brass and the writers have all the say in that?
We were *completely* free. Rockhill, the producer, the director—they never got into it. We were at ease

What better way to advertise *Tom Corbett* and its stars to kids than on the boxes of popular cereals?

with the characters and we developed them as we went along. Rockhill wasn't particularly interested in *that*. The show was going good, so they were interested in secondary rights—and I don't blame them. As a result, they left *us* alone.

What persons connected with Tom Corbett *don't get enough credit, or get no credit, when the show is talked and written about?*

Eddie Taliaferro, who was our costume designer. He did something else he never got credit for: He was a quick-change artist! I again want to mention Muriel Maron, who was just wonderful. She was a production assistant and she really took care of things. And Ralph Ward, who was the second director we had. Prior to that, Ralph ran the dials in the control room for George Gould. As I mentioned, George left the show in our second year to go over to CBS to do *Rod Brown*—CBS wooed him away from us, along with Jack Weinstock and Willie Gilbert, two of our lead writers. When George left, Ralph came up, he took over as director and he was just great. Ralph stayed with us right until the finish.

When you mention the costume designer being a quick-change artist, you mean he helped you guys *change quickly between scenes.*

That's right. And we were doing a *lot* of quick changes! For instance, we'd have to get out of our cadet uniforms and into the spacesuits, and sometimes I didn't think we were going to be able to *do* it in time, but we did! Eddie never seemed to be in a hurry, but he got things done awfully fast. Oh, and I remember another time, Jan, Al and myself were playing our regular parts, but the show also had scenes with Mercurians, and we all got into the Mercurian costumes and masks [*laughs*]. In addition to playing Tom, Roger and Astro, we were also running around as Mercurians! If you want me to tell you how we made the change from our uniforms into those other outfits as quickly as we did, *I don't know* [*laughs*]. It was a strain, but we did it!

George Gould and the two writers, the guys who jumped ship for Rod Brown—*how did you feel about that?*

Well ... we weren't averse to it. After all, they were in the entertainment profession, they had to do the best they could. I didn't think it was such a good idea ... and I was right, actually [because *Rod Brown* was short-lived]. After we lost George, our other lad Ralph Ward took over so nicely and easily. Well, he was familiar with the show. I never saw George again until Jan and I went to Newark, New Jersey, in 1993 to appear at a convention put on by the Friends of Old-Time Radio, where we did a re-creation of a *Corbett* radio show. George came ... Al Markim came ... Ed Bryce, who's dead now alas, came. It was a thrill. And a funny thing happened—at least, it surprised *me*. I had a recording of that same radio show as we had done it originally, back in the '50s, and some time after the convention a friend sent me a recording of the re-creation that we did in Newark. They sounded *just the same*. I mean, come *on*—a half a century had gone by! But they sounded *identical*. I've had other people listen to both and they've confirmed it, so ... I guess we didn't change too much!

But you asked originally about the boys jumping ship. Well, what the heck. We were sorry to see 'em go, but ... onward and upward.

Any idea what the budget of each episode was?
No, but it was pretty low, I'll tell you that—as low as Rockhill could make it. If we had had the budgets that they've got now, we'd still be running! I know that they allocated $50 for special business like an additional gun or something like that—it was crazy. I don't mean to speak adversely of Rockhill but they really, in some respects, missed the boat. If they had laid into it and kept the show up, I think probably we'd have run even longer. But, my God, we *had* a long enough run.

You mentioned earlier that you got fan mail.
Rockhill made darn sure we never saw it. Ohhhhhh yeah! I heard something like 10,000 letters. And—I know this is true, because a fellow who worked in the office told me—I got three proposals of marriage [*laughs*]! Rockhill suppressed all the fan mail. They were worried that we were going to start to ask for more money, so they kept that quiet. I didn't find out about that until after the show was over.

How did you feel having your mail kept from you? Technically, isn't that a crime?
Well ... yes it is. Of course they were doing it because they were in deathly fear that I'd ask for more money. That was *always* their problem. I did not actually know, until the end of the show, that we were getting that much. Ten *thousand* letters! I'll never understand it because my mind doesn't run that way, but Rockhill had a big winning thing [the *Corbett* show] and they should have kept doing things to keep it going, they should have kept *promoting* it. But they were very chintzy about salaries—I had to fight like mad. As I mentioned earlier, one thing they would do was allow me to do other work in radio at times when I would otherwise have been at rehearsals. I was doing [the radio shows] *Mr. Keen, Tracer of Lost Persons* and *Mr. Chameleon* and *Stella Dallas* and picking up extra money on the side.

Did it ever start to "get old"? Five years of Tom Corbett, *did you ever begin to get a little bored with it?*
No. Nope, nope, nope. There was always something new, something different, and I never got tired of it. Now *Jan*, at the end of the fourth year, he decided to go to the [West] Coast. I said to him, "God, Jan, if you stay with the show, we'll be playing this thing forever." Well, I was wrong and he was right, it *was* a good move. He felt that he'd be typecast if he'd stuck with *Corbett* and ... that might have happened.

Someone named Jack Grimes, with whom I'm not familiar, came in as the new cadet, "T.J. Thistle."
Jackie Grimes was a very proficient actor who had been around a long time. Before *Tom Corbett* he did a CBS morning radio show called *Let's Pretend* for 20 years—our story editor Al Aley had played the lead in it! But with Jack Grimes in the part of the third cadet, it was not the same character, it wasn't like [Merlin's

character] Roger Manning, the troublemaker and lovable rogue. We had good shows with Jack, but it wasn't quite the same.

The episodes I've seen from the last season, the season with Jack Grimes, have a lot of comedy—for instance, one featured the Today Show *monkey J. Fred Muggs! Was that a good direction for the show?*

Well, it wasn't bad. We didn't have it [the comedy] before, but now we had Jackie, who was a comic character. By the way, in the J. Fred Muggs thing, we didn't have the *vaguest* idea what that monkey was gonna do next. *And*, Jack was deathly afraid of monkeys—and *he* was the one who had to work with this thing [*laughs*]! Oh, boy! Let's say it was a little confusing! You saw it?

Just last night!

Well, maybe you remember the last scene, where Ed Bryce is dressing us down, and the monkey is running around. You can *see* if you're "onto" it that, in that scene, Ed is saying to himself, "What is this monkey gonna do next??" The monkey was running around the set, it started up a ladder—needless to say, this is all impromptu!

It didn't seem to me to be a good idea, to have a monkey on a live show. It seems like askin' for trouble.

[*Laughs*] I guess they figured that, after all the other stuff we'd done, we could handle that.

Why did Tom Corbett *finally go off the air?*

I guess we ran out of sponsors! At the end, Kraft Caramels was sponsoring *Corbett*, and we couldn't sell enough of those. I mean, if we sold a ton of them, it didn't make much difference—do you know what I mean? You've got a small-priced item, and—how many caramels can you sell [*laughs*]? Now look, there's nothing wrong with Kraft Caramels *except* that we couldn't sell enough of 'em to warrant the expenditure of the show. Kellogg's, our first sponsor, had a variety of things—Kellogg's Corn Flakes, Kellogg's Rice Krispies, Kellogg's Raisin Bran, and they had our pictures on the boxes and everything. That was *big*.

A 2001 *Tom Corbett* "mini-reunion": Thomas, Merlin (with wife Barbara) and the series' technical director Ib J. Melchior (seated with wife Cleo).

Did you eat Kellogg's cereal?

Yes [*laughs*]! I liked 'em! I liked Kellogg's Pep, too—that became the Solar Cereal! Anyway, after the cancellation, there *was* talk about bringing the show back, but by that time I'd sort of lost interest. You ask "Why did *Tom Corbett* go off the air?" ... well, we'd been *on* a long time! There weren't many shows that ran as long. Very few shows had the run of *Ed Sullivan*—that was on for about 20 years, I think.

Your reaction to the cancellation? Were you disappointed?

Yeah, I was sorry to see it go but ... what the heck, you can last just so long.

Did you do much acting after Tom Corbett?

I didn't do *any*. After the show, I wrote for a while for television, for a show called *My True Story*, which was on Saturdays, 12 noon to 12:30. Then I was the lead writer on a radio show at ABC called *Theater Five*, when they tried to bring back daytime radio—it was not successful. So I went on to bridge. I had been familiar with contract bridge since I was eight years old, Mother and Dad taught it to me. I had a friend in New York, an actor who did a lot of work, called Stephen Chase. He was a Life Master—you have to win any number of bridge tournaments to get *that* rating. He and I started going to tournaments together as a team; I was particularly lucky and Steve was particularly good, so I began to win a lot of cups. Later, on the West Coast, Steve and I started something that nobody had done before, teaching in department stores. They went over very well, those bridge lessons. You didn't have to charge very much because you had large classes. We worked in the cafeterias or restaurants of the department stores. Pretty soon I was teaching 130 people just in one class. It just grew and grew.

The American Bridge Teachers Association had a publication called *The Bridge Teachers Quarterly*. Well, I took over the editorship of that, I became the editor and publisher. It went very well. While I was still doing that, there was a very well-endowed magazine called *Popular Bridge* and *they* signed me on as associate editor.

So two magazines at once!

And the lessons! So I found myself working almost as hard as I had with *Tom Corbett*. Steve, alas, left us a number of years ago, and then eventually I started cutting down because I was doing *so* much traveling. Pomona, Long Beach, Marina Del Rey—I was burning up the highways. Anyway, I decided that I'd about had it. Steve was gone, I wasn't playing as much as I had, and so I resigned. I resigned from the magazine—*Popular Bridge* went out of business, actually. I hope I didn't *put* them out of business [*laughs*]. I left the classes and everything. And devoted myself to what is now my business, investing.

But you still write books in which Sherlock Holmes is a bridge player.

When I was a very small boy, a friend of my father's was A. Romaine Callender, who had been with [legendary stage star] William Gillette when Gillette toured in *Sherlock Holmes*. He got me an Annie Oakley (that's what they used to call a free ticket) and I saw Gillette play Sherlock Holmes—his last performance on Broadway. I was knee-high to a grasshopper, but I was *intrigued* by this character. And, years later, I decided to write a book called *Sherlock Holmes, Bridge Detective* [1973]. Now of course, Sherlock Holmes never played bridge, it wasn't even *around*, but his character, his observation, his intuition, all the things that Arthur Conan Doyle had given this character were admirably suited for bridge! Well, little ol' *Sherlock Holmes, Bridge Detective* was quite successful—Pinnacle Books printed it, and then they printed the sequel, *Sherlock Holmes, Bridge Detective Returns*. Then my editor Andrew Ettinger at Pinnacle came to me and he said, "Frankie, you can write just so many bridge books. How about a novel?" So I did. And I did and I did... [*Laughs*] My tenth and eleventh Sherlock Holmes books are on Amazon.com now, *The Secret Files of Sherlock Holmes* and *Sherlock Holmes and the Sacred Sword*. I just kept writing 'em—and they are *fun*. In a month, *Sherlock Holmes and the Panamanian Girls* and *Sherlock Holmes and the Bizarre Alibi* will be out.

Starting in the late '50s, America had its own thriving space program—which must have looked like old news to you. What Tom Corbett–*related thoughts crossed your mind?*
   Well, as I told you, when I saw the astronauts get out of that spaceship on the Moon, I swear I thought to myself, "They look *just like us!*" [*Laughs*] When *Corbett* was on the air, there was talk about going to the Moon, and I asked Willy Ley if we were ever going to get there. In those days, we didn't know. He said, "Oh, yes. In ten years." And he was not far off.

Do you still follow space-related news today?
   No more than the normal.

Who from the show have you kept in touch with over the years?
   Jan, for sure. Al Markim lives in New York State and comes out to California, La Jolla, but I haven't seen him in seven years, not since Newark. Ed Bryce of course has left us. I don't know about Maggie Garland, I don't know where she is or what she's done.

How have you enjoyed meeting Tom Corbett *fans at conventions in recent years?*
   Oh, they're a lot of fun. Look, it's always nice, we all have a little bit of ego. You see fellows who remember what you did and like it and ... it's great. *Tom* is all over the Internet now. There's a site, Solar Guard [www.solarguard.com], and two or three others, and they've got the history of *Tom Corbett* and interviews and everything. Actually... [*Pause*] Actually, I'd better admit I'm surprised that after half a century, the show could be so well-remembered.

Do you have in your collection a lot of the episodes?
   Yes, quite a few. I'm amazed that so many are available and in good shape. And I recently got sent to me, by some dear fans in Virginia, 24 of the radio shows. So [*laughs*], I'm surrounded by memorabilia, if I ever get a chance to sit down and look at it!

Did you save a lot of the memorabilia from the old days?
Oh, dear heavens. Oh, if I had just *done* it!

You didn't?
[*Groans*] Noooo! We didn't know at that time that they'd be selling *Tom Corbett* lunchboxes for $1500. I mean, come on! Even the cereal boxes with our pictures on them command quite a bit of money. I never realized, and neither did any of the other boys, how valuable those things would become.

You and I will never know the answer to this question, we'll both be dead, but—will there ever be space cadets and a Space Academy, or anything even remotely like what we saw on Tom Corbett?

I don't know why not *except* ... you're going to have an awful lot of trouble fusing the world into one nation. In theory, Space Academy was a training ground for spacemen who were working for *every*body. I think there *could* be a Space Academy someday. There might even be, eventually, two or three planets involved, if we find life on any of them. But now we're goin' waaaay out!

What was the best thing about the Tom Corbett *experience and what, if anything, was the worst?*
The best thing? The best thing was the people that I was privileged enough to work with. I cannot say *any*thing about them except to laud them. And that's kind of the way it *had* to be—the show would never have been as successful as it was if it hadn't been for a rapport. We were all gung ho.

And the worst thing was when it went off.

Thomas—still in Space Academy uniform (his actual one from the show)—and Merlin at a 2002 film festival.

Burt Topper on The Strangler

> *The fact that [Victor Buono] would walk off the set, that tells you something. That's an ego trip.*

It was summer in Boston and yet the city was in the cold grip of fear: On September 8, 1963, the Boston Strangler, the first modern serial killer, claimed his newest victim, a 58-year-old divorcee, garroted in her Salem, Massachusetts, apartment with two of her own nylon stockings. The shock waves emanating from the scene of his eleventh murder spread across the nation—including Hollywood, where producers Samuel Bischoff and David Diamond were within days of starting production on a movie capitalizing on the ongoing killing spree: *The Strangler* with Victor Buono.

Chosen to helm the Allied Artists production, 35-year-old Burt Topper was a construction worker-turned-actor-director whose résumé then consisted mainly of low-budget war movies like *Hell Squad* (1958) and *Tank Commandos* (1959). According to early plans, the psycho-sexual thriller would be titled *The Boston Strangler* and shot on location in Boston, but these plans were scrapped and the locale changed to an unspecified major city. No audience failed, however, to make the connection to real-life events as the blubbery Buono (playing hospital chemist-schizophrenic mama's boy Leo Kroll) begins the movie with his eighth strangulation murder and, in the course of the next 89 minutes, raises the number to 11—the actual current body count. There were other un-subtle reminders too, like making two of Buono's victims nurses (real-life Victim #6 was a nurse) and giving him, at his workplace, a young black female assistant (reminiscent of Victim #7).

On the fortieth anniversary of the Boston Strangler's final murder, Topper reminisces about the making of his torn-from-the-headlines horror flick, and speculates about the identity of the real Boston Strangler.

How did the job of directing The Strangler *come your way, do you recall?*

I did a picture called *War Is Hell* [1963] and Allied Artists bought the U.S. rights. I did *War Is Hell* on my own, I financed it myself and made this picture and sold the rights to Allied Artists, and there I got acquainted with [producers] Dave Diamond and Sam Bischoff. Sam Bischoff had been at Warner Bros. years before, he was a producer on Errol Flynn's *The Charge of the Light Brigade* [1936]. Diamond and Bischoff saw *War Is Hell* and from that they wanted to hire me to direct *The Strangler*. They asked me if I would be willing and I said, "Yeah, sure!" So they put me with the writer, Bill Ballinger, and that's how it all started.

According to the Hollywood trade papers, the original plan was to call it The Boston Strangler *and film it in Boston.*
That's true, we *were* gonna go to Boston. I don't know why they changed that. We actually shot that at the Paramount lot, and it was shot like in ten days.

The initial plan even called for shooting on the very same sites where the real-life killings were committed.
Well, the problem with [making the movie in Boston and calling it *The Boston Strangler*] is, you don't know how the real-life story will end. The way we ended the picture, Victor Buono falls out of a window and he dies on the pavement. The Boston Strangler was still on the loose, and if they would have caught him and we had a different ending, it'd be ridiculous.

Diamond and Bischoff also made a movie called The Phenix City Story *[1955], another true story of a terrorized community, right in Phenix City, Alabama.*
That was before *The Strangler*.

So to read that they were thinking of shooting The Strangler *in Boston, on the crime scenes—that fits in.*
Yeah, they liked the locations. But there was the risk of the real Strangler being caught and [being nothing like Buono's character]—a hell of a gamble.

So they made Buono a strangler, not the Boston Strangler.
Right. Also, maybe they didn't want to spend that much money [to go cross-country]. That's one of the reasons I guess I came into the picture: They knew I was very aware of budgets. On a stage, I'd go in and lay everything out. All of my shots are diagrammed, they're laid out so that the crews can be ahead of me. The crews can pre-light, they can do all

At the height of the Boston Strangler's real-life reign of terror, Victor Buono starred as a split (literally here) personality in Burt Topper's *The Strangler.*

of this stuff before I even get there, 'cause they know where my people are going to be and where my movement is going to be. Anyway, I'm sure that's one of the reasons they hired me. And they liked my war story, *War Is Hell*. I was also *in War Is Hell*, as an actor, but I killed myself off. I was the lead in the first 20 minutes of it.

And then your character gets killed?

Yeah, he gets shot in the back. Thank *God*! That's a tough job, producing, directing *and* starring.

This is an awful question, but I'll ask it anyway: When moviemakers are doing a picture like The Strangler, *about a real-life killer, and timeliness is everything ... do they find themselves having to worry that he will be caught?*

No, I wouldn't say that. You're talking about people bein' killed. You've got to *live* in this world, y'know!

What were Bischoff and Diamond like? Hands-on producers?

They left me alone pretty well. They were nice, seasoned guys who knew the ins and outs of the financing and how to put it through the studios and what they were doing. They were on the set and I used to have conferences with 'em. They were good people.

Bill Ballinger—did you work with him on the script at all?

He did the script, but we used to talk about it. He was a pretty bright guy. I forget how many weeks he had to do it, but he did it quite quickly.

Was he around when you were shooting?

Yeah, Bill would come on the set a couple of times. He was interested, of course, in what was going on, as the writer. Incidentally, you'll notice in the picture, [actor] Jim Sikking had a one-day bit as a police sketch artist. He wound up on that TV series *Hill Street Blues*—he's done quite a lot of work.

And in addition to Sikking, you had several members of "the Burt Topper Stock Company" in there, Wally Campo and—

That's right, Wally *was* there. And Baynes Barron and Russ Bender [other Topper regulars].

You must have done some of the casting.

Oh, sure! The main leads, we passed 'em by Allied Artists, they had to make the final decision because they were the ones who were going to put the picture out. The lead, David McLean, had been on a Western TV series called *Tate* [1960], as a one-armed gunfighter. Victor Buono had been around for a few years doing TV and that picture *What Ever Happened to Baby Jane?* [1962], which I didn't look at 'til years later, long after *The Strangler*. But I knew *of* him and his reputation.

When you were offered the picture, was Buono already aboard?

I didn't come up with him. I can't remember whether they already had him

Buono as the Oedipal wreck Leon Kroll adds a doll to his collection after each killing.

pegged, or if we all sat around and we suggested this and that and he came in and they made a deal with him. I was not involved in the casting of him.

What was Buono like?
 I'll tell you an incident I had with him. There was one time he left the set—in fact, it was written up by one of the gossip guys, maybe Army Archerd. In the scene in the hospital where Buono visits his invalid mother Ellen Corby, I set a shot up where the camera goes around him as he walks, and all the while I was holding him in the foreground and holding her in the *back*. When you're crabbing with a camera that close, you gotta keep your people in focus, especially if they're split—the mother was in bed about 10, maybe 12 feet behind him. I moved the camera wanting to keep his face and her face together all the time, because she was belittling him and I wanted to see the anger in his face as she was talking. For a moving camera shot like that, your measurements are critical, you have to stay within certain confines, and there were certain marks that he had to hit.

And he didn't hit his marks.
 That's right. We went over and over this thing, we tried it again and again, and finally I started to talk to him, I said, "Listen, Victor, *I* have been an actor and *you're* an actor. But part of this whole thing is *discipline*…" When I mentioned "discipline,"

he came un*glued* [*laughs*]! "Don't talk to me about discipline!," and he walked off the damn set. I had to shoot around him all the rest of that day. Finally he *did* come back the next day.

Did he raise his voice?

No, he just was very abrupt. It wasn't a screaming match, he just said [*in a snappish, angry voice*], "Don't talk to me about discipline!," and then just walked off. But he came back, I give him credit for that. He came back and he offered a "sideways" apology [*laughs*]. I accepted that. Hey, when you're handling actors, part of their bearing is that egotistical thing that comes in. That's what makes 'em what they *are*, I guess. He was like a Method actor, supposedly…

I was just about to ask you, "Was he one of those Method actors, 'I have to walk where I want to walk' and all that crap?"

Yeah, well, so much for the Method [*laughs*]! There's another scene where he comes out of an arcade and he's got tears on his face. We're setting up for the scene, and the assistant calls for Victor. He doesn't show up. So I go and I walk behind the set, and there he is taking a smoke and puffing it and putting it in his eyes. To make the tears.

Blowing smoke into his own eyes.

That's right. Normally we use glycerin and all that sort of stuff [for tears], but he supposedly could come up with that kind of emotion. And I'm sure he *has* at some time, I'm not gonna doubt it. When I saw him doing that, I just came out, came right out from behind the set. I think he did see me, but I'm not sure. Then *he* came out and he had the tears and we took the shot.

Except for Victor Buono, who'd recently been Oscar-nominated for Baby Jane, *the cast had a lot of unknowns in it. Was that a conscious decision, or were unknowns all you could afford?*

Truthfully, the film was made as a low-budget film—they didn't want to spend a lot of money. You can tell from the cast. Davey Davison was the female lead and Diane Sayer was her friend in the arcade. Diane was the daughter of a good friend of mine who ran a gym—she was an actress, so I gave her a break. The point is, we didn't have a lot of money to spend on above-the-line, which is the cast. When you're makin' a picture on a budget, you're not lookin' for big-name people because you're not gonna *get* 'em [*laughs*]. So your actors are mostly people who have done some work but they're not well-known. You *try* to get the best you can for the money you've got to spend. We found McLean, and he had a face we liked. He had a lined face, a real masculine face.

As I was watching it last night, I said to myself, "In any other movie, David McLean and Baynes Barron would be bad guys with those lined, mean faces!"

Sure! Baynes was in my *War Is Hell* film, and then *Space Monster* [1965] and a picture called *The Devil's 8* [1969] and so on. Ellen Corby was a great old lady—she was a character, she really was! And she did a good job.

In the big picture, did you end up liking Buono?

Oh, absolutely. I understand actors—I mean, they're a pain in the ass most of the time. I *was* an actor, I started out as an actor. I didn't like it particularly. I was actually a carpenter and [in the early 1950s] I was working construction out in Beverly Hills on a roof. I came down to have a drink. I was in good shape, and along came a guy named Frank Melford, a producer. He started talking to me, "Did you ever think about being an actor?" and so on, and he gave me his card. Well, most of it's bullshit when people do things like that. But one day I just went up and saw him anyway, and (because I hadn't had any experience) he gave me a letter to the Actors Lab. I was gonna go there, and then of course it closed [because of the flap over its Communist ties]. Instead I went to Ben Bard's Dramatic School, and that's how I started acting. Stu Whitman was there, [John] Beradino, there were a few people there. But I also kept on in construction. Years later I decided to make my own film. The first picture I made was *Hell Squad*.

For the most part, Victor was a very competent guy. He was a good technical actor who wanted everybody to think it was coming from the depths and the *this* and the *that*. Like you say, "the Method." But he was a good technician. He did a great job and it was easy to work with him except for that one time.

In the scene where he kills Jeanne Bates the nurse, Buono is trying to give the impression he's getting a sexual charge out of killing her.

Well, that was the point, yeah. The whole point was that he was coming while he was choking her. Also when he was handling the dolls he kept in his desk drawer [dolls representing his victims]. When he handled them he'd turn his face up to the heavens, look up at the heavens.

Were you keeping the censors in mind as you were shooting?

We *had* to, sure. They were pretty strict at that time. In those days, I remember we used to have to shoot scenes for Europe which were really risqué. And it's completely reversed nowadays. Europe has *less* sexual connotations in pictures than we do.

Did you do European scenes for The Strangler?

No.

According to the written foreword at the beginning of the movie, the screenwriters and producers examined police station files and had the guidance of psychiatrists.

I don't know if Bill Ballinger the writer got into that. *He* would be the guy. At some point all these pictures wind up being discussed [publicity-wise], everybody sits around and decides they're gonna do this and that. And out comes all this bullshit! I did a picture for Joe Barbera and AIP, it was a co-production called *C.H.O.M.P.S.* [1979], about an electronic watchdog. One of the things that I was embarrassed about was the fact that we had an interview for dogs—we were supposedly looking for dogs and gonna give 'em parts in the picture. All these people came with their dogs and I was sitting there like a dummy and I had to "interview"

By helping to save the life of Kroll's nagging mother (Ellen Corby, seated), nurse Clara (Jeanne Bates) places herself on Kroll's hit list.

them and act like their dogs had a chance ... and I knew damn well that we already *had* our dogs in the picture. We already had the dogs cast and everything else. These people would come up with such hope in their eyes and they'd have their puppies stand on their back paws and bark and do all these things, and I felt like *such* an idiot. It was allll publicity. But that's what happens in this business.

So The Strangler's *written foreword about getting the advice of police and psychiatrists— you think that falls into the bullshit category?*

Bill *may* have had some interviews with a few people, I can't say he didn't. But there was nobody on the set saying to me I should do this or do that, "That's not the way it is" and so on. Incidentally, when I was shooting *The Strangler*, Jerry Lewis was also shooting something at Paramount. We were shooting on a street in front of some building—and he came out of the building when I was right in the middle of a shot! I was shooting the front entrance and I said, "Action!," and *he* comes out of the door. He started clowning and doing all this shit, and I yelled, "*Cut!* What the hell's goin' *on* here? I'm shooting a picture!" "Ohhhhh!," he said, and he kinda just waltzed away...

Was he trying to screw you up?

I don't think he did it deliberately. He just came out of the door and he saw we were shooting, and he just started to perform his crazy antics. I don't think he'd deliberately come out to ruin a shot—he's a professional. But he did then start to clown around. On a big-budget picture, you wouldn't care, you'd laugh with him. On a little budget ... I really got pissed.

What were your hopes for the picture? The Boston Strangler being an ongoing, in-the-news thing, I bet you thought The Strangler *had good box office potential.*

Yeah, sure. I was not hired on a percentage deal; my deal was, when I finished the picture, finished the editing, turned over the answer print, that was the end of my participation. But I thought the picture would do pretty good for 'em. As I think it did. In fact, I'm sure it did.

Were you a fan of horror pictures?

Not really. I did a lot of action pictures.

Not even a fan of horror pictures as a kid growing up?

No, as a matter of fact not. I loved Westerns.

How does a director who hasn't even seen many, or any, horror movies walk onto a set and direct one?

I was still dealing with *people*. People are people. There's only a few emotions you're dealing with—you're dealing with fright, you're dealing with anger and so on. When Victor's getting his jollies off, well, okay ... that's an emotion that I'm aware of. And you *deal* with it. In today's market, when a horror movie director has to deal with so many *effects, then* it becomes a specialty. He has to go into sessions with all the special effects people. In our day, we did [the special effects] on camera, most of 'em.

It had *to be more fun making movies then than now.*

I was recently on the set of a picture that Donna Roth is producing with Jennifer Garner, *13 Going On 30* [2004]. I went on the set and ... I have to tell ya something, it's *so* technical now. The director of photography is sitting in front of a screen instead of on the set. The camera operator has a screen and two handles and he's 25 feet away from the camera. Everything is done remotely! And then they have a separate lens that's shooting the scene on videotape, and the director watches it on video after he shoots the scene. They shoot a scene, then they go back and they *watch* the scene, and then they go try it again—so it takes twice as much time, right? Meanwhile, they've got all these crews sittin' around. But obviously, today, they don't give a damn.

Was all of The Strangler *shot at Paramount?*

Yes. We even built the arcade. You know, at a major studio, they can really sock it to you. They charge all they can charge off on people who rent stages there. They rigged me with lights and all that stuff, and they tried to charge me for all this stuff. I got a-hold of [cinematographer] Jack Marquette and we went over all these bills, even for the sets and stuff, and we called for a meeting with Paramount's head of production and we just started knockin' off all this stuff we never even used. But in most cases, producers think, "Hey, it's not my money," and when they see a bill come in, they sign it, get it out of there. Today it's probably worse because it's really a money-moving industry, when you talk about stars getting 20 million bucks. God almighty. It's unbelievable.

I haven't been on that many sets, but when I am, and I see soooo many people, most of them doing soooo little work, I almost get—
You almost get sick.

I was gonna say "depressed."
Well, God, it can make you sick It's the unions. But I'll tell you something about my own pictures: I always used the same crews. They—even the Teamsters, who usually just sit around and play Hearts if they're not driving—*they* used to work with me, they'd help. They were nice guys, good guys. It depends on how you treat 'em.

Who was the Boston Strangler? Do you have an opinion?
I don't think they ever caught him, did they? Well, they caught somebody who *said* he was the Strangler, Albert DeSalvo, but that guy was nuts, a guy who wanted that "star in the sky"! I think that poor soul DeSalvo wanted recognition *so* badly that he put himself into that position. I don't think he was the killer, I really don't. His own brother disputes it. But what do I know?, I don't know anything about the forensics, I haven't studied the entire case. They recently exhumed DeSalvo's body and now, with DNA, they're going to try and find out if he really was the Strangler.

A lot of the people who do know all the ins and outs of the case don't think he did it.
The family of one of the victims, they didn't believe he did it either. We may never know the real story now—Jesus, it's been 40 years now, the real killer could be dead. DeSalvo was killed in jail years ago, stabbed to death. I wonder why he was killed. Not normally would they [fellow prisoners] kill him because he was a killer—they live in there with killers every day, what the hell's a killer? DeSalvo must have been so obnoxious that somebody got in his face and did it, and it probably had nothing to do with the fact that DeSalvo told everybody he was the Strangler, 'cause they don't give a damn I don't think. If he was a child killer or a child molester or something like that, then, yeah, maybe. But a killer—what do they care? Most of those guys have raped and murdered anyway. They're not that particular [*laughs*]!

The Strangler is half horror scenes with Victor Buono, half police procedural scenes. Do you think it could have used more of one or the other, or do you still like the balance you struck?
If I would have used more of the police scenes, I think that would have been

"Bueno for Buono," *Variety*'s man on the aisle wrote of the actor's smashing *Strangler* performance. "There's always a place on the screen for a fat man who can act."

boring as hell. The character of the strangler, we're following the intrigue of this guy and his problem. That's where the meat of the picture was. Maybe it could have used more horror, maybe there might have been a little more room for it. What do you say, maybe another killing [*laughs*]? A little extra gore? You'll notice, when he strangled these women, you didn't *see* much.

What did you think of the picture then and now?
    I kinda wish it was in color—I'm wondering what it would look like in color. But, for the money we spent and for the time we had to shoot it, especially at a major studio, I thought it came off pretty well. And Victor Buono did fine—I think he did a good job. I don't know what happened to him after that [movie-wise]; he did TV, but I didn't see him in too many features after that. He was still a young man when he died. His weight made him [right for the role]; he was just the kind of a guy that no girl would ever talk to. He looked the part of this character that the girls thought of as a geek. To tell you the truth, I don't know how far he could have gone in his career if he *wasn't* heavy. He was used [when he looked the part], like the suitor in *What Ever Happened to Baby Jane?*, like in *The Strangler*—

he was that kind of a character. If he'd been skinny, he would have been nothin' [*laughs*]!

Back then, reviewers liked to call him "the next Laird Cregar."

I think *every*body in the business at that time thought he was gonna be the next Laird Cregar.

Did he *think so?*

He probably didn't think Laird Cregar was the kind of actor that *he* was [*laughs*]! The fact that he would walk off the set, *that* tells you something. That's an ego trip. When I said what I said to him—and I said it very nicely, I never got mad, I don't scream or yell. I remember what I said to him, I said, "Look, I've been an actor, Victor. Part of our deal here is *discipline*." And when I got to "discipline," he blew up. He did a good job … but he had a pretty good ego. You don't just walk off a set if you don't have any ego, you know! Because you can get your ass sued. I as a director have the right to tell him anything I want, provided it's not abusive—I can't call him an asshole or something like that. There *are* directors who *do* that [*laughs*], but I wouldn't put myself in that position. My approach was always a very workmanlike, nice approach. But his ego just couldn't handle that word "discipline." He was "The Method," you know…

That's funny.

It *is* funny. I did a picture with John Cassavetes [*Devil's Angels*, 1967], and Cassavetes has always been "the Method type." I went to a screening of one of his pictures, he invited me, and I couldn't sit through the whole thing, I was embarrassed as hell. It was so way-out. It's as though ["Method" actors] make pictures for them*selves* and then they sit in a screening room and they laugh at this and laugh at that. Is it funny?, hell, no, but they particularly like the picture because of what they created. They're not aware of audiences. When you're makin' a picture, you've got to be aware that somebody's gonna have to pay for a ticket and *look* at this picture! So, yeah, there's always a part of the actor that has to conform, I don't give a damn how much "Method," how much this and how much that. I was a writer too, I've done a lot of my own screenplays, and I always used to tell an actor, "Look, that's *my* dialogue. If you want to say it different, if you feel you can say the same thing in different words and be more comfortable, you go right ahead. *But …* the purpose of that line better be the same at the end." They can change the dialogue—it makes the whole thing a better working atmosphere. Whereas if my ego got in the way, there'd be trouble. Some writers, you vary from their script and they're *screamin'*.

A minute ago, were you leading up to saying that Victor Buono thought he was even better *than Laird Cregar?*

Yes. The industry thought that he would be the next Laird Cregar, but as far as *he* was concerned, I think he thought he was a much better actor than Laird Cregar. [*Pause*] And he may well have *been*.

The Strangler
(Allied Artists, 1964)

89 minutes; Began production in mid–September 1963; Released in April 1964; Produced by Samuel Bischoff & David Diamond; Directed by Burt Topper; Screenplay: Bill S. Ballinger; Photography: Jacques Marquette; Music: Marlin Skiles; Production Manager: Edward Morey, Jr.; Editor: Robert S. Eisen; Art Directors: Hal Pereira & Eugene Lourie; Assistant Director: Clark Paylow; Sound Recording: Hugo Grenzbach & Charles Grenzbach; Set Decorators: Sam Comer & Jim Payne; Makeup Supervisor: Wally Westmore; Hair Styles Supervisor: Nellie Manley; Script Supervisor: Robert Gary; Construction Coordinator: James West

Victor Buono (*Leo Kroll*), David McLean (*Lt. Frank Benson*), Diane Sayer (*Barbara Wells*), Davey Davison ("*Tally" Raymond*), Baynes Barron (*Sgt. Mack Clyde*), Ellen Corby (*Mrs. Kroll*), Michael M. Ryan (*Detective Mel Posner*), Russ Bender (*Dr. Clarence Sanford*), Jeanne Bates (*Clara Thomas*), Wally Campo (*Eggerton*), Mimi Dillard (*Thelma*), Byron Morrow (*Dr. Morton*), John Yates (*Intern*), James Sikking (*Artist*), Robert Cranford (*Jack Rosten*), Sellette Cole (*Helen Lawson*), Victor Masi (*Attendant*)

Index

Numbers in *italics* represent pages with photographs.

Abrahams, Mort 345, 347, 357
The Absent Minded Professor (1961) 313, 329–*30*, 331–33, 334
The Absent-Minded Professor (1988) 334
Ackerman, Forry *127*
Adamson, Al 76, 78–79, 80–83
Adler, Stella 309
Adventures of Smilin' Jack (1943) 167
Aijala, Eric vii, 87
The Alamo (1960) 67
Alden, Richard 188, 193, 194, 197, *198*
Alexander, Ruth 129
Aley, Albert 347, 362
Alfred Hitchcock and the Making of Psycho (book) 230
Alfred Hitchcock Presents (TV) 223, 229–30, 235
Alland, William 317–19
Allen, Irwin 31
The Alligator People (1959) 270
Alone (book) 248
The Amazing Colossal Man (1957) 122–23
Ames, Heather *15*
Anderson, Maxwell 226
Ankers, Evelyn 120–*22*
Ankrum, Morris 145
Another World (TV) 272
Antosiewicz, John vii
Apache Woman (1955) 117, 118, 120, 124, 130
Apocalypse Now (1979) 292
Apsara Jet (book) 209–11

Arkoff, Samuel Z. 115, 116, 117, 118, 121, 126, 128–29, 131
Arness, James 133, 146
Arnold, Jack 120
Art of the Vineyard (book) 31
Ashley, John 74
Ashton, Tara *see* Lucht, Darlene
Assignment Redhead (1956) 120
Astaire, Fred 46, 72
Athena (1954) 71
The Atomic City (1952) 3, 6
The Atomic Submarine (1959) 114
Atwill, Lionel 96
Autry, Gene 114, 115, 117, 118, 161
Avalon, Frankie 292, 296
Averback, Hy 212, 213, 214, 217, 219

B.J. and the Bear (TV) 258
Baa Baa Black Sheep (TV) 74
Badlands of Dakota (1941) 66, 67, 74
Bainter, Fay 99
Bakalyan, Richard 296, 297
Balenda, Carla 325, 326, 327, *327*, *341*
Ballinger, Bill S. 368, 369, 372, 373
Bambi (1942) 87, 100, 101, *102*, 103, 109, 112
Bandit Island (1953) 260–65
Banner, Jill 307, *308*
Barbera, Joseph 372
Barnett, Buddy vii
Barnett, Jim 213

Barrett, Edith 317, *318*
Barrie, Elaine 4
Barrier, Edgar 326, *339*
Barron, Baynes 369, 371
Barry, Gene 3, 4, 5, *6*, 7, 8, *9*, 10, *11*, 12
Barrymore, John 3, 4
Bat Masterson (TV) 3, 10
Bates, Jeanne 372, *373*
Bates, "Peg Leg" 88
Batman (TV) 212–13
Battleground (1949) 133
Baumann, Marty vii
Baxter, Anne 353
Beatty, Warren 335
Beck, Billy 234
Beery, Noah, Jr. 123
Beery, Wallace 123
Beginning of the End (1957) 133, 145
Behave Yourself! (1951) 340
Behlmer, Rudy vii
Ben Casey (TV) 233, 238
Bender, Russ 369
Bendix, William 235
Benny, Jack 151
Beradino, John 372
Berghof, Herbert 135
Berle, Milton 349
The Best of Cinerama (1963) 48, 49
Beyond the Blue Horizon (1942) 121
The Big Chase (1954) 260, *264*, 265
Biography (TV) 134, 137, 140, 146–47, 148
Birch, Paul 118

Bischoff, Samuel 367, 368, 369
Bissell, Whit 31, *36*, *39*, 41
Black Beauty (1946) 122
Black Cloak (1965 TV pilot) 215
The Black Pirates (1954) 260, 265–68, 269–70
Blaisdell, Jackie *119*, 128
Blaisdell, Paul *119*, 125–28
Blake, Carter 356–57
Bliss, Sally *see* Balenda, Carla
Blood of Dracula's Castle (1969) 76–78
Bloom, Harold Jack 224, 226, 228–29, 230
Bohus, Ted vii
Bonanza (TV) 17, 230
Bond, Ward 337
Boone, Richard 239, 252
Bowman, Isaiah 57
Boyd, William 350
Bradley, David 17
Brady, Scott 79
Brainard, Karl 129
Bram Stoker's Dracula (1992) 292, 305
Brando, Marlon 310
Bricker, George 337, 342
Bride of the Monster (1956) 25
Bridges, Lloyd 117, 120
Brinegar, Paul 19, 44
Bring On the Empty Horses (book) 75
Brinkley, David 129
Brocco, Peter 327
Broder, Jack 116
Bronson, Lillian 154, *158*
Brooks, Mel 27, 28
Brown, Chamberlain 314
Brown, Gilmor 226
Brown, Johnny Mack 121, 123
Brown, Tom 167
Browne, Kathie 256
Bruce (book) 358
Brunas, John vii
Brunas, Mike vii
Bruns, Mona 345, 353, 364
Bryce, Ed 356, 361, 363, 365
Buck Rogers (1939) 353
Buff: A Collie (book) 358
Buono, Victor 367, *368*, 369–70, 371, 372, *373*, 374, 375, 376–77
Burke's Law (TV) 3, 31, 37
Burns, Bob vii, 45
Burns, Ronnie 227
Burr, Raymond 326–27, *339*
Buzzi, Ruth 227
Bwana Devil (1952) 156, 260
Byrd, Richard E. 248

Cabot, Bruce 53
Cabot, Susan 33
La Cage aux Folles (stage) 3
Cagney, James 123
Cahn, Sammy 9
Calhoun, Rory 134
Call to Danger (1966 TV pilot) 146
Callender, A. Romaine 364
Campbell, William 302, 303–04, 305–06
Campo, Wally 369
Candoli, Pete 130
Canutt, Yakima 115, 162
Captain Video and His Video Rangers (TV) 357
The Captains and the Kings (play) 141
Caron, Leslie 335
Carpenter, Johnny 115, 123
Carradine, John 77
Carré, Bartlett A. 118, 120, 129
Carrol, Regina 83
Carroll, Joan 98, *100*
Carroll, Leo G. 228
Case History of a Movie (book) 159
Cash, Don 277
Cassavetes, John 377
Castle, Peggie 145
Catherine Was Great (play) 9
Celanese Theatre (TV) 345
Chamber of Horrors (1966) 212–13, *214*, *215*, 216–27, *218*, 219, *220*, 222
Chambers, John 272, 273–74, 276, 277, 278, 279, 281, 282, 283, 284, 289
Chaney, Lon 261
Chaney, Lon, Jr. 116, 260, 261, 262, 263, 265, 267–68, 269–70, 292, 308
Chang (1927) 56, 57–58
The Charge of the Light Brigade (1936) 368
Chase, Stephen 364
Chennault, Claire 207
Chicken Every Sunday (stage) 345
C.H.O.M.P.S. (1979) 372–73
The Choppers (1962) 161, 164–69, 170, 178, 201
Christie, Joel 176, 199, 211
Cimarron (1931) 61, 66
Citizen Kane (1941) 317
Claman, Julian 249
Clarke, Frank 54
Clarke, Gary 13, 14, *15*, 16–18, *19*, *20*, *21*, 22, *23*, 24, *25*, *26*, *27*, 28, *29*, 30, *43*, 44
Clarke, Robert 265, 267, *268*
Clatterbaugh, Jim vii
Clement, Kevin vii
Close Encounters of the Third Kind (1977) 197
Coates, Phyllis 292
Cobb, Lee J. 13, 28–30
Cocchi, John vii
Cohen, Herman 17, 18, 22, 31, 35–*36*, 38–*39*, 42, 120
College Capers (1953) 260–61
Collins, Stephen 143
Colton, David vii
Combat! (TV) 185
Comden, Betty 327
Conan Doyle, Arthur 365
Conklin, Chester 124
Conmee, Marie 286
Connors, Mike 124, 144
Conrad, Robert 33–34, 74, 238, 252, 253, 254, 256, 328
Conway, Gary 13, 18, 20, *21*, 31, *32*, 33–34, *35*, *36*, 37, *38*, *39*, 40–42, *43*, 44
Coogan, Jackie 100
Coogan, Richard 357
Cook, Tommy 24, 25–26
Coon, Gene L. 251–52
Cooper, Gladys 228
Cooper, Merian C. vii, 45–46, *47*, 48–50, *51*, 52–59, 60
Coppola, Eleanor 299, 301, 310
Coppola, Francis Ford 292, 293, 299–300, 301, 303, 304, 305, 307, 310
Corby, Ellen 370, 371, *373*
Corman, Roger 31, 32, 33, 34, 117, 118, *119*, 120, 124, 129, 142, 144, 299, 300, 304, *311*, 312
Corrigan, Ray "Crash" 163
Costello, Frank 328
Costner, Kevin 335
Cotten, Joseph *318*
The Couch Trip (book) 238
The Court-Martial of Billy Mitchell (1955) 145
The Court of Last Resort (TV) 250, 251
Cowan, Will 224, 225
Crabbe, Buster 353
Crackpots (book) 291
Crawford, Joan 149
Crazy Horse 170
Creature from the Black Lagoon (1954) 120, 317
Creelman, James 59
Cregar, Laird 377
Crosby, Bing 246
Cruise, Tom 3
La Cucaracha (1934) 47
Cunha, Richard E. 61, 74
Curtis, Tony 137, 220, 271, 276, 286
Czar, Nancy 183, *183*

Dalton, Abby 33
Damato, Glenn vii

INDEX

Damn Citizen (1958) 226, 227, 228
Dangerous Holiday (1937) 129
Daniels, Marc 347
The Danny Thomas Show (TV) 154
Danova, Cesare 212, 214, *220*
Dante, Joe vii, 184, 292, *311*, 312
D'Arcy, Alex 77
Darro, Frankie 72, 115
Date Bait (1960) 22
Davis, Bette 37–38, 322
Davis, Bob 175
Davis, Jim 79, 260, 262, 263, 265
Davis, Nancy 149, *150*, 151–*52*, 153–*54*, 155, *156–57*, *158*, 159
Davison, Davey 371
Day the World Ended (1956) 114, 115, 118–*19*, 120–*22*, *123*, 124, *125*, 126, *127*, *128*, 129–30
Day the World Ended (2001) 131–32
Deadwood '76 (1965) 75–76, 80, 202, *203*, 206
The Dean Martin Show (TV) 147
The Deer Hunter (1978) 197
Dekker, Thomas 317
de Maupassant, Guy 253
Dementia 13 (1963) 292, 299–*302*, 303–7
DeMille, Cecil B. 123, 124
Denning, Richard 13, 115, 120, 121, 122, 124, 131, 144
DeSalvo, Albert 375
Desilu Playhouse (TV) 235
Desperate Journey (1942) 129–30
Destination Gobi (1953) 342
Devil's Angels (1967) 377
The Devil's 8 (1969) 371
Dexter, Anthony 260, 265, 268
Diamond, Bobby 166–67
Diamond, David 367, 368, 369
Discover: The World of Science (TV) 148
Disney, Walt 100, 101, 329, 330–31
Dix, Richard 61–63, 64–*65*, *67*, 68, 69, 70, 75–76, 83
Dix, Robert 61, *62*, *67*, *73*, *75*, *78*, *81*, *82*, *84*, 85
Dixon, Denver 80
Dr. Kildare (TV) 230
Dr. Voodoo (unmade movie) 116
A Dog of Flanders (1935) 353, *354*
Donovan's Brain (book) 175
Doolittle, James H. 52
Double Indemnity (1944) 332
Douglas, Kirk 271, 272, 273, 274, 275–76, 280, 283, 287, 288–90
Douglas, Paul 314
Downs, Cathy 130
Dracula (1931) 116
Dragnet (TV) 228, 238, 250, 251
Dragstrip Riot (1958) 16–17, 22, 23–24
Drake, Oliver 76
Drivas, Robert 253
Drury, James 13, 29, 72, *73*, *73*
Dubov, Paul 118, *128*
Ducovny, Allen 356
Duff, Howard 322
Dukesbery, Jack vii
Dumbrille, Douglass 115
Dunagan, Donnie 1, 86, *87*, 88, *89*, *90*, 91–92, *93*, 94, *95*, 96, *97*, 98, *99*, *100*, 101, *102*, 103–5, *106*, *107*, 108–10, *111*, *112*
Duncan, Kenne 115
Dunn, Emma 96
Dunn, Ethne 303
Dutko, Edward 270

Ebeier, Jacqueline 20
Edward VIII 316
Edwards, Vince 233
Eegah (1962) 161, 162, 168, 169, 170, *171*, 172–*73*, 174–77, *178*, 179–80, 181, 184, 187, 188, 198, 199, 201, 204, 207
Ellison, James 122
Ellsberg, Daniel 105
Elvira 184
Erwin, Stuart 226, 228

The Face of Terror see *The Sadist*
Fairbanks, Douglas 325
The Farmer's Daughter (1947) 133
The Fast and the Furious (1954) 117, 118
Father Is a Bachelor (1950) 154
Feindel, Jock 129
Felton, Earl 340
Fenady, Andrew J. 26–27
Fernandez, Peter 347
Fickett, Homer 316
Fiedler, John 357
The First Legion (stage) 353
Fitzgerald, Michael vii, 157
Five Bloody Graves (1969) 61, 79–81
Five Guns West (1955) 117
Fleischer, Richard 340
Flesh and the Spur (1957) 124
Florey, Robert 233, 234, 235
Flubber (1997) 334

Flying Down to Rio (1933) 46–47, 55
Flynn, Errol 130, 368
Follow Me, Boys! (1966) 331–32
For the Service (1936) 123
Forbes, Bob 45, 46, 47–48, 49–50, 51, 52, 55, 56, 59, 60
Forbidden Planet (1956) 72–73
Ford, John 48, 55, 58, 144
The Forgotten Woman (1939) 97
Fort Apache (1948) 48
Forty Guns (1957) 73
Foster, Preston 62
Foulk, Robert *324*
The Four Feathers (1929) 46, 56
Foy, Bryan 244
Francis, Anne 72
Franco, Francisco 245
Frankenstein (1931) 116, 233
Frankenstein's Daughter (1958) 74, *75*
Frederic, Fred vii
Frederic, Mark 27
Freiberger, Fred 265, 268–69
Frith, Christopher vii
From A to Z (stage) 329
The Fugitive (1947) 48
Fuller, Samuel 73
Fury (TV) 134, 145, 166

"G" *Men* (1935) 123
Gammill, Kerry vii
Garland, Beverly 142–44
Garland, Judy 129
Garland, Margaret 356–57, 365
Garner, Jennifer 374
Garrison, Michael 238, 251, 252, 255–57, 328
Gautier, Dick 26
Geller, Bruce 146
General Electric Theater (TV) 253
The George Burns and Gracie Allen Show (TV) 227
Get Smart (TV) 13, 26–28
Getting Straight (book) 238
The Ghost Ship (1943) 61
Gilardi, Jack 293
Gilbert, Willie 357, 361
Gillette, William 364–65
Gingold, Hermione 329
Gingold, Mike vii
The Girl from Jones Beach (1949) 157
Girls in Prison (1956) 118, 121, 122, 124
Gish, Lillian 332
The Glass Slipper (1955) 71
The Godfather (1972) 292, 310
The Godfather Part II (1974) 293, 310
The Godfather Part III (1990) 293

Gordon, Alex 114–16, 117–25, 126–32
Gordon, Bert I. 122–23, 145
Gordon, Richard vii, 114, 115, *116*, 120
Gordy, Berry, Jr. 176
The Gorilla (stage) 319–21, 322
Gould, George 345, 347, 350, 357, 358, 361
Grant, Kathryn 246, *247*
Grass (book) 46
Grass (1925) 46, 56, 57
Graves, Peter 1, 133–35, 136–*38*, *139*, 140, *141*, 142, *143*, 144–46, *147*, 148
Gray, Dobie 176, 211
Gray, Gary 149–*50*, 151, *152*, 153, *154*, 155, *156*, 157, *158*, *159*, 160
Grayson, David 275, 288
Green, Adolph 327
Greene, Graham 228
Gregory, Paul 141
Gribbon, Harry 319
Grimes, Jack 362–63
Gun Smugglers (1948) 157
Gunsmoke (TV) 133, 146
Gurrola, Ernesto 176, 199, 211
Gusse, Millie 141

Hackman, Gene 226
Hagen, Jean 292, 294–95, *297*
Hagen, Uta 309
Haig, Sid *308*, 309, *312*
Hale, Richard 234, 300
Hall, Arch, Jr. 1, 76, 80, 161–62, *163*, 164–68, *169*, 170, *171*, 172, *173*, 174–77, *178*, 179–81, *182*, *183*, 184–85, 186–*89*, 190–*94*, *198*, 199–202, *203*, 204–6, 207–*10*, 211
Hall, Arch, Sr. 61, 75, 76, 80, 161, 162–66, *163*, *164*, *165*, *166*, 167–72, 173, 174, 175, 176, 177–78, 179, 180–81, *182*, 183, 184, 185, 186, 187, 188, 190, 191–92, 193, 197, 199, *200*, 201, 202, *203*–5, *206*, 208–9, 210, 211
Halley, Rudolph 327, 328
Hamilton, Guy 83
Hamilton, Patrick 272
Hamilton, Roy 336
Hammett (1982) 310
Hanawalt, Chuck 129
Hardin, Ty 224
Harris, Robert H. 13, 18, 19, *25*, *43*, 44
Harry O (TV) 217
Harryhausen, Ray 243–44, 246, 249
Hart, Susan vii
Harvey, Michael 356

Haskin, Byron 7–8
Hatton, Raymond 121, 123–24
Have Gun—Will Travel (TV) 238, 249, 250, 251
Haver, June 332
Hawaii Five-O (TV) 238
Hawaiian Eye (TV) 33–34, 74
Hayward, Jim 154–55
Hayworth, Vinton 217
Haze, Jonathan 118
Head, Edith 225
Heinlein, Robert A. 345, 353
Hell Squad (1958) 367, 372
Henry, Buck 27, 28
Henry, Thomas Browne 145
Hepburn, Katharine 55
Herrmann, Bernard 246
High Noon (1952) 260
Hill, Jack vii, 292, 304, 307, 308, 309
Hill Street Blues (TV) 369
Hilton, Nicky 151
The Hindenburg (1975) 287
Hit the Deck (1955) 71
Hitchcock, Alfred 190, 229–30, 235
Hoffman, Dustin 226
Hogan's Heroes (TV) 292
Hold Back the Night (1956) 139
Holliman, Earl 72
Holman, Rex 296–97, *298*
Holt, Tim 157
Hondo (TV) 13, 26–27
Honey West (TV) 238
Hopalong Cassidy (TV) 350
Hopper, Hedda 129, 283, 337
Horner, Harry 136
Horror of the Blood Monsters (1970) 80, *82*, 83
Horton, Edward Everett 226, 228
Hot Rod Girl (1956) 227
Hould, Ra *see* Sinclair, Ronald
House of Wax (1953) 213, 214, 216, 260
House of Wax (1966 TV pilot) *see* *Chamber of Horrors*
Houseman, John 316, 323
Hovey, Helen 188, *189*, 190, 191, 192, *198*
How to Make a Monster (1958) 13, *15*, 17–*19*, 20, 21, 22, *23*, *25*, 31, 37, 42, *43*–44
Howard, Joan 191, 193, 194, *195*, *198*
Howes, Basil 234
Hudson, Rock 137, 274
Hughes, Howard 313, 323, 325, 326, 335, 337, 340–41, 342
Hughes, Kathleen 342
Hughes, Robin 224, 225
Huntley, Chet 129
Huston, John 271, 272, 273,
276, 279, 280–81, 282, 283, 284, 286–87, 288, 290
Huston, Tony 283, 287
Hutchinson, Josephine 86, 96
Hutton, Betty 130
Hyatt, Bobby 150
Hyde, Donald 135, 136–37
Hyde, Johnny 135
Hyde-White, Wilfrid 212, 216

I Spy (TV) 214
I Was a Communist for the F.B.I. (1951) 326
I Was a Teenage Frankenstein (1957) 13, 17, 31, 34–*35*, *36*, 37, *38*, *39*, 40–42, 43, 44
I Was a Teenage Werewolf (1957) 13, 17, 18, 31, 36–37, 40, 42
Ihnat, Steve 17, 20–22, 26, 28
The Incredibly Strange Creatures Who Stopped Living and Became Mixed-up Zombies (1964) 199–200
Indusi, Jeff vii
Indusi, Joe vii
Ireland, John 117
Ireland, O'Dale 17
Iron Horse (TV) 213, 217
It Came from Beneath the Sea (1955) 241
It Conquered the World (1956) 133, 142–*43*, 144

Jackson, Brad 33
Jackson, Janet 141, 144–45
Jackson, Sherry 154
The Jackson Five 176
Jensen, Paul vii
Jergens, Adele 120, 121, 122, *123*, 128, 130
Joan the Woman (1917) 123
Jones, Buck 123
Jones-Moreland, Betsy 33
Jordan, Dorothy 45, 49, 54, 55
Julius Caesar (stage) 316, 317, 318

Kandel, Stephen 212–*21*, 222
Karatnytsky, Christine vii
Karloff, Boris 28, 43, 86, 90–*93*, 94, 96, 97, 98, *99*, 223, 230, 231–*32*, 233, 234, 235
Kay, Roger 234, 235
Kearney, Carolyn 223–*25*, *226*, 227–28, *229*, 230–31, *232*, 233–35, *236*, 237
Keaton, Buster 319–*21*, 322
Keel, Howard 72
Kellaway, Cecil 228
Kelly, Jack 72
Kemmer, Ed vii, 353
Kennedy, Douglas 155
Kennedy, John F. 329

INDEX

Kiel, Richard vii, 161, 172–73, 174, 175, 176, 177, 178, 179, 203, 206
Kilgallen, Dorothy 359
Killers from Space (1954) 133, 137–39, 140, *141*
King, Andrea 135
King, Bob vii
King Kong (1933) vii, 45, 46, *47*, 48–*50*, 51–2, *53*, *54*, 55, 56, 58–*59*, 60
The King's Thief (1955) 71
Kirby, Joe 252
Kiss of Death (1947) 190
Klugman, Jack 355, 359
Kneubuhl, John 244, 248, 251
Kolb, Ken 238–39, *240*, 241–59
Kollmar, Richard 359
Kovacs, Laszlo 166

Lad: A Dog (book) 358
The Lady and the Monster (1944) 175
Lahr, Bert 327, 350
L'Amoreaux, Clarke F. *see* Clarke, Gary
Lancaster, Burt 271, 276, 286
Land of the Giants (TV) 31
Landis, James 184, 185–87, 188, 190, 191, 192, 193, 195–96, 197, *198*, 199, 200
Landon, Michael 13, 17, 22, 42, 43, 44
Langan, Glenn 122–23, 262, 265
Lansbury, Angela 257
Lansbury, Bruce 257
Lanza, Anthony M. 199
Laramie (TV) 272
Larrinaga, Mario 52
Las Vegas Strangler (1969) 76
Lasky, Jesse L. 57, 62
Lassie (dog) 157
Lassie (TV) 223
The Last Days of Pompeii (1935) 48
Laughton, Charles 140, 141, 142
The Lawless Rider (1954) 114, 115, *116*, 118
Lawrence, Delphi 283
Lawrence, Jay 262, 263
Leave It to Beaver (TV) 293
Lee, Gypsy Rose 49
Lee, Rowland V. 93, 94, 95, *95*, 96, 97
Lemmon, Jack 347
Leno, Jay 144–45
Leonard, Sheldon 214
Lernd, Elmer 277
Let's Pretend (radio) 362
Levinson, Richard 37
Lewis, Edward 278
Lewis, Forrest 331

Lewis, Jerry 373–74
Lewton, Val 61
Ley, Willy 357–58, 359, 365
Lights, Camera, Action (TV) 134
Lime, Yvonne 17
Link, William 37
Lippert, Robert L. 73, 260–61, 264–65, 270
Lippert, Robert L., Jr. 260–61, *262*, 263–70
The List of Adrian Messenger (book) 273
The List of Adrian Messenger (1962) 271–75, 276, *277*, 278–79, *280*, 281, *282*, 283–84, *285*, *286*, *287*, 288–89, *290*–91
Little Ol' Boy (stage) 314
The Little Prince vii
Little Women (1933) 48, 55, 58
Live and Let Die (1973) 83, 84
Lloyd, Harold 74
Lloyd, Harold, Jr. 74
Lloyd, Norman 230, 317, *318*
The Long Gray Line (1955) 144, 145
Looney Tunes: Back in Action (2003) 292, *311*, 312
Lord, Jack 355, 359
The Loretta Young Show (TV) 329, 333
The Lost Patrol (1934) 48
Lucas, Donna vii
Lucas, Tim vii
Lucht, Darlene 61, 71, *81*, *84*, 85
The Lucky Devil (1925) 68
Lugosi, Bela 25, 114, 116
Lund, John 117
Lupino, Ida 252
Lussier, Dane 175
Lussier, Deke 175

Macao (1952) 336
MacDonald, Philip 273
MacMurray, Fred 313, 329, *330*, 331–*32*, 333, 334
MacQueen, Scott vii, 87, 110
Magers, Boyd vii
Mahoney, Jock 78
The Male Animal (stage) 319
Malone, Dorothy 117
Man from Atlantis (TV) 215
The Man He Found see *The Whip Hand*
Man Made Monster (1941) 116
Man of Conquest (1939) 66–67
Manning, Marilyn 173–74, 175, 176, 177, *185*, *189*, *198*, 199
Mantz, Paul 54
Marcellino, Nick 274, 277, 278, 279, 281, 282, 284

The March of Time (radio) 313, 315–16, 322
Mark Trail (radio) 345
Markim, Al 344, 345, *346*, 347, *351*, 354, 356, 360–61, 365
Marlowe, Scott 229
Maron, Muriel 347, 357, 361
Marquette, Jacques 375
Marr, Eddie 18, *19*
Martin, Andra 224, 225
Martin, Jeffrey vii
Martin, Lewis *339*
Martin, Ross 238, 252, 253, 254, *255*
Martucci, Mark vii
The Mask of Zorro (1998) 305
Mathieu, Paula vii, 87
Matinee Theater (TV) 229
Maverick (TV) 72
Mayo, Virginia 157
McClure, Doug 29, 37
McCrea, Joel 49
McDonnell, Dave vii
McDowall, Roddy 285, 290
McGraw, Charles 340
McKnight, Marian 31
McLean, David 369, 371
McWhorter, Richard 279, *280*
Means, Bobby 202
Means, Russell 202
Medic (TV) 238, 239–41, 252
Medved, Harry 184
Medved, Michael 184
Melchior, Ib *363*
Melford, Frank 134, 372
Menzies, William Cameron 324–25, 336, 338, 341
The Mercury Theatre on the Air (radio) 317
Meredith, Burgess 314
Merivale, John 283
Merlin, Jan 271–72, *273*, 274, *275*, 276–79, *280*, 281, *282*, 283–84, *285*, *286*, *287*, 288–89, *290*, 291, 344, 345, *346*, 347, *348*, *351*, 354, 356, 357, 360–61, *362*–*63*, 365, *366*
Merlin, Patricia 281, 284
Merriweather, Nicolas (novelist) *see* Hall, Arch, Jr.
Merriwether, Nicholas (director) *see* Hall, Arch, Sr.
Michael Shayne (TV) 13, 23
Middleton, Burr vii, 167, 168
Middleton, Charles 168
Mighty Joe Young (1949) 45, 48, 50, *51*
Miles, Vera 230
Milland, Ray 292, 293, 294, 295
Miller, Dick 124
Million Dollar Manhunt see *Assignment Redhead*

Miner, Allen 267
Missile to the Moon (195) 13, 24–26, *27*
Mission: Impossible (TV) 133, 134, 146–47, 148, 213
Mr. Chameleon (radio) 362
Mr. Keen, Tracer of Lost Persons (radio) 362
Mister Roberts (stage) 271
Mitchel, Mary 292–*94*, 295, *296*, *297*, *298*, 299–301, *302*, 303–7, *308*, 309–10, *311*, *312*
Mitchum, Robert 141, 271, 276, 284–85, 286 335, 336
Monroe, Marilyn 335
Monster from the Ocean Floor (1954) 118
Moore, Dickie 347
Moore, Roger 83, 84
Moorehead, Agnes 322
Moreland, Mantan 308
Morrow, Vic 185
Morse, Ray 357
Moser, James E. 239–40, 252
Moss, Frank L. 337, 342
Moss, Rod *182*, *198*
Mother Carey's Chickens (1938) 89, 90, 94, 99
Mueller, Chris 274, *277*, *278*, 286
Muggs, J. Fred (monkey) 363
The Munsters (TV) 292
Murder in the Family (1938) 120
Murphy, Barry vii
Musuraca, Nicholas 324, 341
My Hollywood Diary (book) 48
My Pal Gus (1952) 342
My True Story (TV) 364
Mystery Science Theater (TV) 184

Nagel, Conrad 319, 322
The Naked Spur (1953) 228
The Name of the Game (TV) 3
The Narrow Margin (1952) 335, 336, 340
The Nasty Rabbit (1964) 172, 200–2
Nazimova 129
Needham, Hal 78
Nelson, Lori 115, *119*, 120, 121, 126, *127*, 129
Nelson, Rick 182
Nephew, Neil 296–97, *298*
"The New Accelerator" (story) 253, 254
The Next Voice You Hear... (1950) 149–*50*, 151, *152*, 153, *154*, 155, *156*, 157, *158*, *159*, 160
Nicholson, James H. 41, 116, 117, 118, 121, 124, 125, 126, 128–29, 131

Nicholson, Sylvia 117, 118, 129
Nielsen, Leslie *73*, 215
Nielsen, Ray vii, 72, 153
The Night of the Hunter (1955) 140–42
Niven, David 75
Novak, Kim 227
Nugent, Frank 45, 48, 49, 50, 51, 54, 55, 57, 58

Oboler, Arch 260
O'Brien, Willis H. 49, *56*
O'Connor, Carroll 256
O'Day, Alan 176, 177–78, 181, *182*, 183, *198*, 199, 211
Odlum, Floyd 55
Of Mice and Men (1939) 270
O'Hara, Maureen 144
The Oklahoma Woman (1956) 124
Olson, Nancy *332*, 333
One from the Heart (1982) 310
O'Neal, Patrick 212, *214*, 215–16, 217, *218*, 219
Osborne, Bob 325
Osborne, Bud 115
Other People, Other Places (TV) 148
Over the Top (1987) 44
Overland Stage Raiders (1939) 166

The Paid Companion of J. Wilkes Booth (book) 290–91
The Painted Hills (1951) 151, 157
Pal, George 3, 7
Panic in Year Zero! (1962) 292, 293–95, *296*, *297*, *298*, 299
Parfrey, Woodrow 355
Parker, Suzy 219
Parrish, Leslie 24, *27*
Pascaretti, Erin Ray vii
Pascaretti, Nicholas *see* The Little Prince
Passion Street, U.S.A. (1964) 22
Patri, Dan vii
Patton, Bart 292, 293, 299–300, 301, *302*, 303, 304, 305, 306–7, 310
Paul, Louis vii
Payne, John 139
Peggy Sue Got Married (1986) 312
Pendleton, Steve *141*
Perry Mason (TV) 292
The Phantom from 10,000 Leagues (1956) 130
The Phenix City Story (1955) 368
Philco TV Playhouse (TV) 345
Pierson, Carl 261, 262–63
Planet of the Apes (1968) 284

Playhouse 90 (TV) 223, 229, 230
Porter, Zoe *54*
Poston, Tom 355, 359
Powell, Jane 71, 72, 151
Power, Tyrone 144
Powers, Mala 252
Prange, Gary vii
Presenting Lily Mars (1943)
Price, Frank 248
Price, Vincent 216, *297*, 317
Prince, William Wood 145
Promise Her Anything (1966) 335
Provost, Jeanne vii
Provost, Oconee vii
Psycho (1960) 190, 230
The Puppet Masters (book) 353

Queen of Burlesque (1946) 122
The Quiet Man (1952) 48, 55

Rachel and the Stranger (1948) 149, 157
Rachmil, Lewis J. 337, 341, 342
The Ragman's Son (book) 289
Rappaport, Fred vii
Rathbone, Basil 86, 93, 94, 95–96, *97*, 98, *99*
Rawhide (TV) 44
Rawlins, John 134
Raymond, Gene 80
Raymond, Paula 77
Reagan, Nancy Davis *see* Davis, Nancy
Reagan, Ronald 17, 156–57, 253
Rebello, Stephen 230
Red Garters (1954) 10
Red Planet Mars (1952) 133, 134–35, 136–37, 145
Red Planet Mars (stage) 135, 136
Redeker, Quinn 309
Reid, Elliott 313–*15*, 316–*18*, 319–*21*, 322–24, 325–27, 328–*30*, 331, *332*, *333*, *334*, 335, *336*, 337–38, *339*, *341*
Reif, Harry 129
Reinhardt, Max 9
Remember the Day (stage) 353, 356
Return of the Bad Men (1948) 149, 150
Revenge (1990) 335
Revenge of the Creature (1955) 120
Reynolds, Debbie 71
Reynolds, William 224
Richards, Deke *see* Lussier, Deke
The Rifleman (TV) 251
Rio Grande (1950) 48
The River (1984) 197

River of No Return (1954) 335, 342
Roberson, Chuck 263
Roberson, Lou 263
Roberts, Clete 206
Robertson, Cliff 357
Robinson, Ann vii, *5, 6, 7, 8*
Rod Brown of the Rocket Rangers (TV) 357, 361
Rogers, Ginger 46
Rogers, Jean 123
Rogers, Wayne 219, *220*
Rogue River (1950) 133, 134–35, 138
Rooney, Mickey 129
Roos, Fred 293
Rope (stage) 272
Rosalinda (stage) 3, 9
Rose, Ruth 48, 49
Ross, Diana 176
Roth, Donna 374
Roth, Martha 266, 267
Rubin, Stanley 323, 324, 326, 327, 335–42, 343
"Rufus" vii
Runaway Daughters (1956) 121, 122
Runser, Mary vii
Rusoff, Lou 118, *125*
Russell, Don 188, 191, 192, 193, *198*, 205
Russell, Jane 336
Russell, Ray 213, 214

The Sadist (1963) 161, 184–85, 186–*89*, 190–*94, 195, 196–98*, 199–201, 204, 205
The Saga of the Viking Women and Their Voyage to the Waters of the Great Sea Serpent (1957) 31, 32–34, 35
Salome (1923) 129
Sande, Walter 145
Sarnoff, David 55
Sayer, Diane 371
Scapperotti, Dan vii
Schanzer, Karl 304
Schary, Dore 150, *154*, 156, 159
Scheer, Philip *20, 38, 39*
Schneer, Charles H. 238, 241, 242, 243, 244, 245, 246, 247, 248
Schneider, Don 175
Schoedsack, Ernest B. 46, 48, 56, 57, 58
Scott, Al 174, *182*
Scott, George C. 287, 338
Scrivani, Rich vii
The Sea Gypsy (book) 46
Sea Hunt (TV) 212
The Searchers (1956) 48
Seay, James 145

The Secret Files of Sherlock Holmes (book) 365
Seen But Not Heard (stage) 353
Selznick, David O. 59
Send Me No Flowers (stage) 292–93
Serling, Rod 235
7th Heaven (TV) 143
The 7th Voyage of Sinbad (1958) 238, 241–*42*, 243–*45*, 246–*47, 249, 250*
The She-Creature (1956) 114, 126
She Wore a Yellow Ribbon (1949) 48
Sheen, Fulton 349
Sherlock Holmes and the Bizarre Alibi (book) 365
Sherlock Holmes and the Panamanian Girls (book) 365
Sherlock Holmes and the Sacred Sword (book) 365
Sherlock Holmes, Bridge Detective (book) 365
Sherlock Holmes, Bridge Detective Returns (book) 365
Sherman, George 169
Sherman, Hiram *318*
Sherman, Sam 61, 67, 76, 80
Shire, Talia 303
The Shoemaker's Holiday (stage) 317, *318*
Shofner, Rob vii
Sholem, Lee 338
Shooting Montezuma: A Hollywood Monster Story (book) 272, 281, 284, 289–90
Sikking, James 369
Sinatra, Frank 71, 271, 276, 286
Sinbad on Mars (unmade movie) 248
Sinclair, Ronald 129–30
Sitting Bull 170
Skotak, Bob vii
Skotak, Denny vii
Smith, Art 154
Snyder, L. Steven 190–91
Son of Flubber (1963) 313, 329, *332, 333*–34
Son of Frankenstein (1939) 86–87, 89–*90*, 91–*93*, 94–*95*, 96–*97*, 98, *99, 106*, 109–10, 112
Space Mission to the Lost Planet see *Horror of the Blood Monsters*
Space Monster (1965) 371
Space Patrol (TV) 353, 357, 359
Sparks, Robert 337
Spider Baby (1964) 292, 304, 307, *308*–9, *312*
Spier, William 322
The Spirit of St. Louis (1957) 248

Stalag 17 (1953) 133–34, 137, 140, 146
Stalag 17 (stage) 140
Stanwyck, Barbara 332
Star Trek (TV) 213, 252
Starkweather, Charles 186
Steckler, Ray Dennis 161, 181, *182*, 199–200, 211
Steele, Bob 121
Steele, Michael 327
Stein, Ronald 130
Steiner, Max 45, 58
Stella Dallas (radio) 362
Stern, Leonard 27
Stevens, Connie 16, 17
Stevens, K.T. 24–25
Stevenson, Robert 329, 333
Stewart, James 248
Stormy (1935) 123
The Story of Leroy "Satchel" Paige (1981) 338
The Strangler (1964) 367–*68*, 369–*70*, 371–*73*, 374–*76*, 377–78
Stratton, Gil 140
Streets of San Francisco (1949) 157
Striganza (unmade movie) 172, 181
Strike Me Deadly (1963) 22
Strock, Herbert L. 18, 22, *36*, 37, *39*, 40
Studio One (TV) 345
Styne, Jule 9
Sullivan, Dave 183, *198*, 199
The Sun Shines Bright (1953) 48
Suspense (radio) 322
Sutherland, Donald 76
Sutherland, Kiefer 76
Sutliff, Larry vii
Sutton, Frank 355
Swanson, Gloria 37

Taeger, Ralph 13
Taliaferro, Eddie 361
Tank Commandos (1959) 367
Tarantino, Quentin 210
Target Earth (1954) 120
Tate (TV) 369
Tavoularis, Dean 310
Taylor, Elizabeth 151, 276, 285–86, 290
Taylor, Joan 117
Taylor, Kent 130
Temple, Shirley 14
Terhune, Albert Payson 358
Terr, Mischa 200
Terry and the Pirates (TV) 118
The Texan Meets Calamity Jane (1950) 122
Thatcher, Torin 244
The Thief of Bagdad (1924) 325

Index

The Thing That Couldn't Die (1958) 223–25, *226*, *227*
Things Men Die For (book) 46
13 Going On 30 (2004) 374
This Is Cinerama (1952) 47, 48, 52, 54, 55, 56
Thomas, Frank M. 344, 353, 358, 364
Thomas, Frankie 344–46, 347–*48*, 349–*51*, 352–*54*, 355–60, 361–*63*, 364–66
Thomas, Harry 139
Thomas, Lowell 47, 48
Thoroughbreds Don't Cry (1937) 129
3 Godfathers (1949) 48
Three Wise Fools (1946) 151
Thriller (TV) 28, 223, 229, 230–*32*, 233–34, 235, 236
Thundering Jets (1958) 74
Tim Tyler's Luck (1937) 353
Timpone, Tony vii
The Tingler (1959) 220
The Today Show (TV) 363
Todd, Michael 9, 10
Tom Corbett, Space Cadet (TV) 272, 344–*46*, 347–*48*, 349–*51*, 352–*60*, 361–63, *364*–66
Tombstone, the Town Too Tough to Die (1942) 66
The Tonight Show (TV) 144–45, 168
Topper, Burt 367–78
Tower of London (1939) 94, 98, *100*
Travis, Richard 24, *27*
Travolta, John 210
True Grit (1969) 357
The True Story of Lynn Stuart (1958) 244
Turner, Kathleen 312
Tuttle, William 151
24 (TV) 76
The Twilight Zone (TV) 223, 234–35
Twist Around the Clock (1961) 293, *294*
Two on the Aisle (stage) 327–28, 350
Two Weeks with Love (1950) 151, 154

The Underwater City (1962) 114
Universal Pictures (book) 157

Valentino (1951) 265
The Vampire's Tomb (unmade movie) 116
Van Cleef, Lee 142
Van de Kamp, Walter 68–69
Veiller, Anthony 135, 136–37
The Virginian (TV) 13, 17, 19, 26, 28–30, 72
Vogel, Virgil 29
Volante, Vicki 80–81, 83
Von Berblinger, Gregory vii, 191
Von Braun, Wernher 357
Voodoo Woman (1957) 114, 126

Wagon Master (1950) 133
Wagon Train (TV) 251
Waldis, Otto 325–26, 327
Wallace, Edgar 48, 59
War Is Hell (1963) 367–68, 369, 371
The War of the Worlds (book) 3, 8
The War of the Worlds (1953) 3, 5, *6*, 7, 8, *9*, 12
War of the Worlds (2005) 3, 12
Ward, Ralph 361
Warden, Jack 355–56, 359
Warner, Jack L. 216, 217, 220
Warrenton, Gilbert 261, 263, 264, 266, 267
Washburn, Beverly 307, *308*
Watson, Bobby 325, 339–40
Watters, William *see* Hall, Arch, Sr.
Wayne, John 63, 67, 163, *166*, 263, 337
Webb, Jack 256
Webber, Peggy 318
Wednesday's Child (1934) 353, 354
Wednesday's Child (stage) 353
Weinstock, Jack 357, 361
Welles, Orson 313, 316, 317, 318, 319, 323
Wellman, William A. 149, 150, 153, *154*, 155, *156*, 159
Wells, H.G. 3, 8, 253
West, Mae 9
Westerfield, James 331
Westmore, Bud 272–73, 274, 275–76, 278, 279, 280, 281–82, 283, 284, 289, 290
Westmore, Michael *277*
Westmore, Perc 274
Whalen, Michael 24
What Ever Happened to Baby Jane? (1962) 369, 371, 376
What's Up Front! (1964) 199
Wheel, Patricia 355
Wheeler, Bert 151
The Whip Hand (1951) 313, 322–28, *324*, *327*, 333, 335–43, *336*, *339*, *341*
The Whispering Chorus (1918) 123
White, Jacqueline 340
White, Jesse 235
The White Sheep of the Family (stage) 226
Whitman, Stuart 372
Whitmore, James 149, *150*, 151–52, *153*, *154*, 155, *156*, *158*, *159*
Widmark, Richard 190, 342
Wilcox, Frank *341*
Wild Guitar (1962) 161, 174, 181–8*3*, 184, 204
The Wild Wild West (TV) 74, 212, 238, 251–*55*, 256–57, 328
Wilde, Cornel 71
Wilder, Billy 133, 137–38, 140, 146
Wilder, Myles 138
Wilder, W. Lee 137–38, *141*
Williams, Elmo 260, 261
Williams, Lucy Chase vii
Williams, Robin 334
Willock, Dave 286
Willson, Henry 134
Wilson, Harry 75
Windsor, Marie 340
Winterset (stage) 226
Wise, Robert 287
Witchcraft (1964) 270
The Wolf Man (1941) 270
Wolfe, Stanley 357
A Woman to Remember (TV) 345, 354–55
A Woman's Face (1941) 149
A Woman's Story (2004) 31, 44
Woman's World (1954) 331
Wood, Edward D., Jr. 114, 116
Wood, Natalie 202
Wray, Fay 17, *47*, 49, 52–53
Wymore, Patrice 219
Wynn, Ed 234–35
Wynn, Keenan 235
Wynter, Dana 280

York, Dick 223, 229, 230, 231
Young, Loretta 333
Young and Wild (1958) 229
The Young Racers (1963) 299

Zanuck, Darryl F. 342
Zsigmond, Vilmos 161, 166, 186, 191, 192, 193, 196–97, *198*, 200, 211
Zukor, Adolph 58